*Understanding and Teaching*
*U.S. Lesbian, Gay, Bisexual, and Transgender*
*History*

# The Harvey Goldberg Series
# for Understanding and Teaching History

The Harvey Goldberg Series for Understanding and Teaching History gives college and secondary history instructors a deeper understanding of the past as well as the tools to help them teach it creatively and effectively. Each volume focuses on a specific historical topic and offers a wealth of content and resources, providing concrete examples of how teachers can approach the subject in the classroom. Named for Harvey Goldberg, a professor renowned for his history teaching at Oberlin College, Ohio State University, and the University of Wisconsin from the 1960s to the 1980s, the series reflects Goldberg's commitment to helping students think critically about the past with the goal of creating a better future. For more information, please visit www.GoldbergSeries.org.

### Series Editors

**John Day Tully** is an associate professor of history at Central Connecticut State University and was the founding director of the Harvey Goldberg Center for Excellence in Teaching at Ohio State University.

**Matthew Masur** is an associate professor of history at Saint Anselm College, where he is codirector of the Father Guerin Center for Teaching Excellence. He is a member of the Teaching Committee of the Society for Historians of American Foreign Relations and writes on American-Vietnamese relations.

**Brad Austin** is a professor of history at Salem State University. He has served as chair of the American Historical Association's Teaching Prize Committee and has worked with hundreds of secondary school teachers as the academic coordinator of many Teaching American History grants.

### Advisory Board

**Kevin Boyle**  Northwestern University
**Ross Dunn**  Professor Emeritus, San Diego State University
**Leon Fink**  UIC Distinguished Professor of History, University of Illinois at Chicago
**Kimberly Ibach**  Meeker High School, Meeker, Colorado
**Alfred W. McCoy**  J.R.W. Smail Professor of History, Director, Harvey Goldberg Center for the Study of Contemporary History, University of Wisconsin–Madison
**David J. Staley**  Director, Harvey Goldberg Center for Excellence in Teaching, Ohio State University
**Maggie Tran**  McLean High School, McLean, Virginia
**Sam Wineburg**  Margaret Jacks Professor of Education and (by courtesy) of History, Director, Stanford History Education Group, Stanford University

# Understanding and Teaching U.S. Lesbian, Gay, Bisexual, and Transgender History

Edited by

LEILA J. RUPP

SUSAN K. FREEMAN

The University of Wisconsin Press

The University of Wisconsin Press
1930 Monroe Street, 3rd Floor
Madison, Wisconsin 53711-2059
uwpress.wisc.edu

3 Henrietta Street, Covent Garden
London WC2E 8LU, United Kingdom
eurospanbookstore.com

Printed in the United States of America


Library of Congress Cataloging-in-Publication Data

Understanding and teaching U.S. lesbian, gay, bisexual, and transgender history /
edited by Leila J. Rupp and Susan K. Freeman.
pages     cm — (The Harvey Goldberg series for understanding and teaching history)
Includes bibliographical references and index.
ISBN 978-0-299-30244-3 (pbk.: alk. paper)
ISBN 978-0-299-30243-6 (e-book)
1. Gay and lesbian studies—Study and teaching—United States.
2. Sexual minorities—History—Study and teaching—United States.
I. Rupp, Leila J., 1950-, editor of compilation.
II. Freeman, Susan Kathleen, editor of compilation.
III. Series: Harvey Goldberg series for understanding and teaching history.
HQ75.16.U6U53          2015
306.76071—dc23
2014009612

# Contents

# Contents

## Part Three: Discovery and Interpretation of Lesbian, Gay, Bisexual, and Transgender History

CONTENTS

# Preface

As the title of this book announces, it is designed for those who teach U.S. history at the secondary or university level and want to integrate lesbian, gay, bisexual, and transgender history into the U.S. history curriculum. But we also hope it will reach anyone who simply wants to understand what queer history has to add to the traditional historical narrative. We offer here inspiring stories of teachers in the trenches, short essays on topical and chronological slices of history that sum up what we know, and reflections on a variety of means of accessing queer history for use in the classroom and beyond.

The enthusiasm with which the twenty-seven authors featured in these pages responded to our request to contribute to this volume is a sign of how committed scholars and teachers of queer history are to making a difference. Digesting the scholarship on a particular topic and thinking through the ways that it can be incorporated in a U.S. history survey, reflecting on the experience of teaching in a way that speaks to others, and laying out different resources that engage students are all exercises very different from engaging in historical research and presenting it in article or book form. They are also, sad to say, less rewarded kinds of contributions in many academic institutions. We are grateful to all the scholars and teachers who took time from their busy schedules to craft these essays. That our contributors continue to express their belief in the importance of this project means more to us than they can know.

We would also like to thank the series editors, John Tully, Matthew Masur, and Brad Austin, all former colleagues in the Department of History at Ohio State University. Their commitment to this book, only the second in the Harvey Goldberg series, gives us confidence that those of us who are lesbian, gay, bisexual, or transgender are not the only ones who care about this history. We are also grateful to the terrific team at the University of Wisconsin Press, especially Matthew Cosby, Carla Marolt, Adam Mehring, Rose Rittenhouse, and Gwen Walker, and to the anonymous reviewers of the proposal and final manuscript for their careful readings and helpful suggestions.

Leila would also like to thank Jeffrey Stewart, Anissa Stewart, and Jacqueline Reid of Teachers for the Study of Educational Institutions, which is, among other things, working to implement the FAIR Education Act in the Santa Barbara area, and the teachers who attended a conference sponsored by the group, all of whom are committed to making a diverse educational experience a reality. Hearing from middle and high school teachers on the ground was an inspiration. Leila is also grateful to Tony Mastres, who performed his usual magic on many of the illustrations, and Flower Conroy, who brainstormed on the cover concept on a lovely Key West afternoon. Susan extends gratitude to Patty DeLoach for her generous and competent administrative support. Finally, we are both fortunate in having partners—Verta Taylor and Cathryn Bailey—who are also colleagues. We thank them, as always, for all they do to keep us smiling.

# Introduction

# The Ins and Outs
of U.S. History

*Introducing Students to a Queer Past*

SUSAN K. FREEMAN and LEILA J. RUPP

When the editors of the Harvey Goldberg Series for Understanding and Teaching History first approached us about editing a volume on lesbian, gay, bisexual, and transgender (LGBT) history, our immediate response was that only researchers in the field teach courses on this topic so no one would need such a book. Leila recalled that one of her former colleagues, when some years earlier she proposed to write a module on lesbian and gay history for the customized U.S. history reader *Retrieving the American Past*, commented that it was "silly, but, well, I guess it's okay if she wants to do it." In response to our hesitation about creating this book, John Tully, one of the series editors, pointed out that younger teachers are likely open to teaching the subject even if it is not their primary field of research and that older faculty members who might be interested would be unlikely to have encountered much of this history when they earned their degrees. And, of course, the move to expand what is taught in high school history classes in at least some states means that teachers could find such a resource a lifesaver. It was not a hard sell, given our missionary zeal for the topic. Voilà, *Understanding and Teaching U.S. Lesbian, Gay, Bisexual, and Transgender History* was born.

Harvey Goldberg's excellence as a teacher and scholar in a much different intellectual, social, and political climate offered a vital source of inspiration too. We share a motivation with the editors and authors of other books in the Goldberg series as we seek to explore a "usable past." Our goal is to provide both content and approaches for those committed to integrating queer history into the U.S. history curriculum.

## Queer Is In

Tune into any number of media outlets today and you are rarely more than a few clicks away from a feature about same-sex sexuality or gender nonconformity. Young people grow up in the twenty-first century in a media-saturated environment where queer life is remarkably visible. Whether delivered through journalism, politics, entertainment, or social media, a focus on queer individuals and the LGBT community has become a prominent fixture of public discourse. In such a context, students enter high schools and colleges with a sense of the current status of lesbian, gay, bisexual, and transgender communities, or at least some familiarity with the hot-button issues and stereotypical portrayals. Yet most students have little grasp of the historical precedents to today's coming out and gay pride spectacles, and few are critical of the narratives that locate queer liberation as beginning in the present-day United States. Although October is sometimes recognized as LGBT History Month, activities tend to center on National Coming Out Day, which is more likely to celebrate the present than the past.

Educators have a crucial role to play in contextualizing the flood of information made possible by the Internet and the heightened recognition of queer people in the news and beyond. As the number of books, films, television shows, and websites proliferates, generating a flurry of facts, perspectives, and fantasies about LGBT lives, the need for students to understand the queer past intensifies. Yet not all students at colleges or universities, and hardly any in high school, have the opportunity to take classes on the history of same-sex sexuality and gender nonconformity. They almost all are, however, required to study U.S. history. This opens up the potential to incorporate these topics in the same way that the best courses have integrated the history of race, ethnicity, and gender into the survey curriculum.

This book offers a manageable entry into the best historical scholarship on same-sex sexuality and gender nonconformity in the United States. It is designed for teachers of U.S. history, who have a tremendous opportunity to provide context and nuance about the changing realities and perceptions of queer people over time. *Understanding and Teaching U.S. Lesbian, Gay, Bisexual, and Transgender History* brings together personal narratives of educators, topical chapters about significant historical moments and themes, and pedagogical essays about sources and interpretive strategies well suited to the history classroom. It is our hope that the volume will help instructors in a range of institutions, from high schools to universities, to find ways to integrate queer history into their U.S. history surveys without having to read and digest the burgeoning scholarship on the topic.

## Why This, and Why Now?

The relevance of same-sex sexuality to history is best captured by the unexpected development in California discussed in Emily K. Hobson and Felicia T. Perez's essay in this volume. In 2011 the state Senate passed, and the governor signed, the Fair, Accurate, Inclusive, and Responsible (FAIR) Education Act, the nation's first legislation requiring public schools to teach about the contributions of LGBT Americans alongside those marginalized by gender, ethnicity, race, and disability.[1] The law amended the language of the state's education code, adding "lesbian, gay, bisexual, and transgender Americans" and "persons with disabilities" to the list of those, including "men and women, Native Americans, African Americans, Mexican Americans, Asian Americans, Pacific Islanders, European Americans . . . and members of other ethnic and cultural groups" whose contributions must be included in classroom instruction and materials.[2] Passage of the FAIR Education Act marks the long distance California had traveled from the 1978 vote on the Briggs Initiative, which, had it passed, would have blocked gay men and lesbians, and potentially anyone supporting gay rights, from teaching in the public schools. Whether or not high school and college teachers elsewhere across the nation are compelled—or even allowed—to adopt LGBT-inclusive curricula, growing evidence suggests a voluntary interest in and enthusiasm for doing so.

Yet the world of publishing often lags behind the demand for resources. Despite the voluminous scholarship on queer history, in the form of books and articles, and a number of texts available for courses focused on queer history or the history of sexuality more generally, there is little available for the teacher short on time to read up on a new topic.[3] History textbooks offer some encouragement to instructors who want to incorporate queer content into their classes, and the inclusion of same-sex sexuality in college textbooks has expanded somewhat in keeping with the growing body of historical scholarship. The breadth and depth of information is necessarily limited in textbooks, with the greatest attention paid to the gay movement and AIDS, and infrequent, if any, references to the pre–Second World War era.[4] Similar to racial and ethnic minorities, women, people with disabilities, and other marginalized groups, queer lives first appear as "sidebar" stories, which are important to introducing, say, prominent individuals or significant acts of protest.

This is, of course, a start. So, too, are the growing number of workshops, conferences, seminars, and online resources providing guidance to interested teachers. The Gay-Straight Alliance Network has supported a project to propose revision of the California Department of Education K-12 History–Social Science Framework to incorporate queer history. From expanding textbook coverage to changing the required curriculum in California to providing resources for teachers at all levels across the country, change is under way. We offer this book as a modest point of departure for those open to the challenge of making their history classes more inclusive.

There is another reason, an urgent one for many students, who feel that now is the time to act, and that is the widespread phenomenon of bullying of queer and gender-nonconforming young people. At the university level, the case of Tyler Clementi, the Rutgers University student who jumped off the George Washington Bridge after his roommate secretly videotaped him in a same-sex encounter, attracted national attention. At the secondary school level, the National Center for Lesbian Rights and the Southern Poverty Law Center, supported by the Justice Department, filed a lawsuit against the Anoka-Hennepin, Minnesota, school district after a gag order kept staff from discussing queer issues in the aftermath of eight suicides, four by gay or bisexual students.[5] The suit cited a California school climate study that showed that *any* mention of queer people or issues increased student safety and improved the climate for queer students.[6] As this case makes clear, educators recognize that even as popular acceptance of same-sex sexuality and transgender identity has expanded, both remain contentious issues in schools and the broader society. Administrative, political, and logistical constraints, as well as a climate of uncertainty and for some fear, shape the environment in which many teachers—particularly in high schools—enter this territory.

Brave queer students and their allies have altered school climates in the past few decades, forming gay-straight alliances and building queer resource centers on campuses across the country. Comparatively speaking, academic classes have lagged behind in terms of addressing school climate. Class assignments, such as ones that Susan uses with her college students, might make use of students' inquisitiveness to address barriers to learning about LGBT lives. In one homework assignment, for example, students visit a public or school library to use the catalog, explore available material, and seek help from a librarian. They report back to their peers what they learned (e.g., "The librarian had to ask me what LGBT meant!," "They didn't have any young adult books about growing up with gay parents," or "I felt self-conscious when researching this topic in public"). Students consider what action library patrons might take to ensure that queer material is visible and available, and they discuss why shame persists for some people seeking information. For another homework assignment, students assess the LGBT friendliness of a high school—everything from nondiscrimination policies and gender-neutral bathrooms to student clubs and queer-inclusive curricula. Here they discover that a school that is "not all that bad" in terms of bullying or outright discrimination could nevertheless make progress toward meaningful inclusion, especially in health, literature, and social studies classes. Or they learn that schools seem comparatively better equipped to deal with gay students than transgender kids.

As the contributors to this book show, incorporating LGBT history into traditional history courses does not necessitate throwing out existing lectures or sacrificing the important work already being done. And the value is greater than simply engaging students with a "current" topic, as Emily Hobson and Felicia Perez propose in their essay in part one: LGBT history "pushes them to ask creative, critical questions about the past—the kinds of questions we want them to use in approaching all aspects of history." Accordingly, this book provides classroom-tested, meaningful ways to integrate the queer past into U.S. history classes, in the service of enlightening students about the value of history and the significance of difference in the twenty-first-century world.

## How We Got to This Place

The focus, and some might say fixation, on LGBT lives is a culmination of social movements seeking greater rights for marginalized people. The same impetus that led to the FAIR Education Act and the 2013 partial repeal of the federal Defense of Marriage Act has also fostered significant scholarly output. Since the 1970s, scholars have created and delved into archives, generating countless books and articles, a number of which have earned the historical profession's top prizes.[7] Historians are integral to the interdisciplinary field of queer studies, which supports numerous academic journals and book series, conferences, research institutes, and degree programs.[8] The acclaim for scholarship about same-sex sexuality owes much to historians, who were among the earliest to establish stand-alone college courses in gay studies. They created and joined short-lived Gay Academic Union chapters and worked with alternative (Gay/Lesbian) Lavender Universities, queer bookstores and archives, and community-based gay history projects to produce and extend knowledge beyond the academy in the 1970s. The examination of identities, communities, and social movements pioneered by this new generation of scholars displaced older frameworks of "abnormal psychology" and "sociology of deviance" that had informed nearly all scholarship prior to the 1970s.

Although a generation of high school and college students now find gay and lesbian studies described as a possible college major when accessing Princeton Review's college admissions and test preparation services, institutional recognition was, and remains in a number of locations, contested. It also took decades for academic LGBT studies to emerge. Similar to women's and ethnic studies courses, gay studies classes arose on college campuses in the wake of the various social movements of the 1960s, yet they were less warmly received in most locations. Thanks to grassroots support from students and activists, and the growing reputations of a number of courageous and diligent gay, lesbian, and queer scholars, recognition of the field improved. By the end of the 1980s, the first LGBT academic department existed at City College of San Francisco, and the Center for Lesbian and Gay Studies was established in New York City. At the same time, faculty and graduate students were routinely discouraged from associating with the field. Caution diminished by the end of the twentieth century, as a growing community of professors and graduate students wholeheartedly embraced queer scholarship.[9] We have come a long way since the early days when "there was little sense in the profession that what we today call LGBT history had any depth or substance to it, or that it was anything more than a curiosity on the margins of what really counts as history," as John D'Emilio describes in his essay in this volume.

## What's in a Name

The naming of the field of scholarship, like the naming of the larger movement from which it grew, has emphatically rejected the overly medicalized and pathologized term *homosexuality*. Conveying a similar meaning without its historically specific and homophobic baggage, *same-sex sexuality* appears as an alternative in the writing of many authors, particularly appropriate in times before conceptualization of homosexuality as a characteristic of certain people. Yet *gay*, *queer*, and *LGBT* (and other, longer lists of letters, including *LGBTQIA*, which adds *Q* for *queer* or *questioning*; *I* for *intersex*; and *A* for *ally* or *asexual*) are perhaps the most common terms that historians use when describing their work.

In step with the gay liberation movement of the early 1970s, the earliest historical scholarship bore the title "gay history." This was soon extended to acknowledge lesbians by name, recognizing that women's experiences are shaped by gender in ways different from those of gay men. In the 1980s, inclusion of bisexual and transgender people within the movement, and within the scope of history about marginalized sexualities and genders, led to the adoption of the acronyms LGBT and GLBT. Nearly simultaneous with this development was the growing popularity of the term *queer*, a reclaimed epithet that has been mainstreamed by its use in television programming and other media. Both a politicized assertion of difference and a concept uniting a coalition based on sexual dissent and gender variance, *queer* remains a provocative and preferred designation for many activists, writers, scholars, and teachers.

In this volume, we use *queer* and *LGBT* interchangeably in this way, and other, more specific terms where relevant and historically accurate. In the period before the invention of the term *homosexuality*, we use *same-sex sexuality*. Before the development of the concept of transgender, we use *gender nonconforming* or *gender-crossing*. As terms came into use by both observers and people with same-sex desires, we follow their lead, using *homosexual*, *gay*, *lesbian*, *bisexual*, *queer*, and *transgender*. Students, who today embrace a wider variety of identities, including "pansexual," "fluid," "heteroflexible," "trans," and "genderqueer," can learn from the changing ways people in the past have been named and named themselves.[10]

## What Queer History Adds

While the relevance of historical scholarship to the larger field of gay and lesbian studies is easily apparent, the reverse is usually less evident. Yet queer studies adds remarkable, and often underappreciated, value to the study and practice of history. The changing conceptions of gender and sexuality in U.S. history and the development of queer identities, communities, and social movements—and opposition to them—contribute important elements to the story of the American past and present. Attitudes toward same-sex sexuality and gender transformation tell us a great deal about the sexual and gender systems of Native Americans, European colonists, and the new "Americans." Same-sex sexuality is part of the story of the evolution of regional differences and the growth of cities. Questions about civil liberties and the role of government in individuals' lives are central to LGBT history, and the collective resistance of sexual minorities is as much a part of U.S. history as are the struggles of other marginalized groups, whose histories intersect with queer history.

In the midst of abundant discussion about queerness, students nevertheless arrive in our history classes with a deficit of historical understanding. "Despite greater cultural and social visibility and a huge expansion of historical writing," notes John D'Emilio in this volume, "with very few exceptions undergraduates [have] no knowledge of a queer past." A steady diet of social media and celebrity gossip primes students to be curious about private lives and relationships of famous people, leading them to wonder about which figures in U.S. history had same-sex lovers. At the same time, as Will Grant points out in his conversation with Daniel Hurewitz about teaching queer history in high school, "there's a lot of concern among teachers about teaching [this material to] younger students." A middle-school teacher worried aloud at a conference on the FAIR Education Act whether identifying a historical figure's nonnormative sexuality or gender would simply shut down the conversation.[11] Grant talks about the difference between teaching about sexual identity and discussing sex: "And the example I give is Queen Victoria and Albert—how their children became the ruling family of Europe, and World War I in many ways was a family feud between all these cousins who were all related. So their sexuality, their normative heterosexuality, was clearly a part of that history, but we never stop and talk about sex. You don't need to." Of course, as Leila's essay "Outing the Past" reminds us, sometimes we do need to talk about sex acts and body parts. Emily Hobson and Felicia Perez, too, are insistent that we must not "allow LGBT history to be taught without speaking of the connections between sexual desire and love . . . not simply romantic love but a love of the marginalized, a love of resistance, a love of justice."

One of the biggest challenges we face is helping students to understand the concept of the social construction of sexuality, since so many students of all sexual identities embrace Lady Gaga's message that we are all "Born This Way." The near consensus among queer historians is that societies shape the way sexual desires are understood, the sexual practices in which people engage, the meanings people attach to their sexual desires and behaviors, and the identities that people embrace. Queer scholarship is almost entirely and unapologetically social constructionist, while the LGBT movement, if sometimes only for strategic reasons, emphasizes an inner essence that determines our sexual and gender identities. We both find that students, even after reading about all the different ways societies have shaped sexuality in the past, remain firmly convinced that they were born straight or lesbian or gay or bisexual or transgender. The challenge is to help them see that their desires and behaviors could have quite different meanings and consequences in other times and places.

Another challenge is attending to the intersections or variability of multiple identities shaped simultaneously by not only gender and sexuality but also race, ethnicity, class, nationality, age, disability, and more. As Kevin Mumford writes in his essay, "an intersectional approach moves beyond an older diversity project of bringing 'forward the lives of the formerly silenced,'" an important starting place for queer history but one with limited utility. In a similar vein, Felicia T. Perez's framework for her survey U.S. history course—one that focuses on social justice, perspective, and context—yields a fresh approach. Mumford urges us to interrogate absence, identify ambiguities, and attend to the "connections across difference and sites of repression," and he discusses the fraught ways in which the complex identities of students and teachers alike come into play in the classroom. It is essential that, as we integrate queer history along with attention to gender, race, ethnicity, class, and disability in the U.S. survey, we attend to the multiple identities of all people—Franklin Roosevelt as a white, heterosexual, upper-class disabled man, as well as, say, a hypothetical transgender, queer, working-class, able-bodied Asian American woman.

The FAIR Education Act in California illustrates the challenges of integrating LGBT history into the curriculum at every level. Note that the language calls for the inclusion of the contributions of LGBT individuals to U.S. history. This is what, in the field of women's history, Gerda Lerner long ago critiqued as "contribution history."[12] If all we do is insert into the existing narrative of U.S. history the contributions of a few individuals who might (or might not) have desired, loved, or had sex with others with biologically alike bodies, or who might (or might not) have thought of themselves as a gender not associated with their sex, we add little to our understanding of sexuality and gender in the past. Those who worked to implement the FAIR Education Act in California did so in the spirit, rather than letter, of the law. That is, we set ourselves the task, as we have in this volume, of not just adding "another other," as Catherine J. Kudlick has described the need for the history of disability.[13] Rather, we ask, how do we understand history differently when we recognize it not as the single story of a dominant group but as the convergence of several histories?[14] If we consider gender-crossing among some Native American peoples; the homosocial worlds of sex-segregated factory work, education, and settlement houses, where romantic friendships flourished; urban working-class culture, immigration, and the emergence of new sexual systems; the emergence of the concept of homosexuality as a mental illness; sexual experimentation in artistic communities, including the Harlem Renaissance; the ways in which the Second World War both mobilized and contained gay and lesbian communities; the Red Scare's cousin, the Lavender Scare, in the aftermath of the war; the homophile and gay liberation movements as part of the story of civil rights; and changing conceptions of citizenship—if we consider all this, we confront a history enriched by an understanding of how concepts of sexuality and gender, in conjunction with race, ethnicity, class, disability, age, and other categories of difference, have changed over time.

Such context fuels new ways of thinking about contemporary debates, including same-sex marriage, gays in the military, immigration and citizenship, AIDS, and discrimination on the basis of gender and sexual identity. What a historical perspective brings is a deeper understanding of why change has happened, and why some things have not changed. Legal, social, political, urban, and cultural history lend multiple dimensions to thinking about the queer past and present, and, in turn, the history of same-sex sexuality and gender queerness expands our understanding of all these facets of history. Our aim is to show how the central narratives of U.S. history speak to queer lives and, just as important, vice versa.

## What This Book Offers

Following this introduction is an essay by Leila, "Outing the Past: U.S. Queer History in Global Perspective," that places U.S. queer history into a global context. Although our focus is on integrating LGBT history in U.S. survey courses, a global perspective sheds light on changing conceptions of what it means to desire, love, or have sex with someone of the same sex, and on changing conceptions of what it means to cross or mix genders. A global perspective helps us to understand that sexual and gender transgression are not modern western phenomena, and that queer history is not the story of unrelenting progress. Incidentally, this essay provides some information for teachers interested in incorporating queer history into non-U.S. courses.

The body of the book is organized in three sections, which provide tastes of the great variety of approaches one might take in refining U.S. history courses to be more LGBT inclusive. Part one, "The Challenge of Teaching Lesbian, Gay, Bisexual, and Transgender History," offers four reflective essays on teaching queer history, both as an independent course and as part of general U.S. history courses at the survey or advanced level. We are grateful for the contributions of leading scholars and outstanding teachers, whose essays address developments in the field along with their personal observations and concerns. The collective wisdom of these essays reflects the field's multiplicity, as well as the variability that necessarily results from teaching in different contexts. College and high school teachers employed in public and private schools, and working in various regions of the country, offer different perspectives on how to present knowledge about queerness to students effectively. The authors convey imaginative strategies and hard-won insights about fitting queer history into the central narratives and practices of U.S. history.

Part two, "Topics in Lesbian, Gay, Bisexual, and Transgender History," offers seventeen essays on specific topics that relate to those generally covered in introductory U.S. history courses. Contributed by teachers and scholars who have, in many cases, literally written the book on their topics, these essays distill the content of monographs and articles, making it easy for teachers to integrate this material without having to engage in a massive amount of reading. They describe and analyze specific events, individuals, and issues in LGBT history and explain how they contribute to our understanding of U.S. history and how they might best be integrated into a survey or upper-level course. The authors of these topical essays have taken a variety of approaches, but all concentrate on what queer history can add to the general U.S. history curriculum.

Building on the coverage of various topics in part two, the five essays in part three, "Discovery and Interpretation of Lesbian, Gay, Bisexual, and Transgender History," supply inspiration about the practice of teaching and supervising students' research on same-sex sexuality and gender nonconformity. The essays serve as a guide to the world of print, film, and online resources, showcasing, for example, how digital media make possible access to primary documents and the circulation of historical knowledge that might otherwise remain inaccessible. Each author considers critical approaches, class activities, and projects that grow out of the available sources. Significant emphasis is placed on working with students to interpret primary documents in the context of historical scholarship. As in the other sections, authors draw from their secondary and postsecondary teaching experience as well as their involvement in historical research.

Between the covers of this book are ideas and resources for teachers at all levels intended to aid in educating students about the complexities of LGBT history. If students acquire an understanding that in the past same-sex sexual desire did not always mark one as a homosexual, that women and men did not always have to hide their same-sex love and desire, that changing gender and changing sex are not just recent phenomena, that in a variety of contexts same-sex sexuality was accepted, and that same-sex sexuality is an important part of history—if they understand all this, it might make an impact in the classroom, on the streets, online, and in public policy.

We believe fervently that knowledge can make a difference. Many years ago, when Leila was teaching the second half of a U.S. survey in a large lecture format, she ran into a student waiting tables at a gay restaurant in town. He told her that he had never heard of Stonewall until she discussed it in a lecture on social movements of the 1960s, that he had gone home and talked to his roommate about it, and that then he and his roommate, who had never discussed their sexual identities, came out to each other. He described the moment as life changing. Robert King, a high school teacher whose story appears in Daniel Hurewitz's contribution to this volume, tells a similar story about Jack Davis, a student in his class. If the mere mention of an event in queer history can make a difference in a student's life, just think what a transformed curriculum might do. In a society in which bullying, hate crimes, homelessness, and suicides are all too common, instruction about queer history, we believe, will inspire young minds to imagine and work for a more open and accepting future society. That is what Harvey Goldberg meant by a usable past. It is our hope that *Understanding and Teaching Lesbian, Gay, Bisexual, and Transgender History* provides such a past and moves us toward a better future.

#### NOTES

1. The Our Family Coalition maintains a website devoted to the FAIR Education Act and its implementation. See http://www.faireducationact.com, accessed July 15, 2013.

2. See "Frequently Asked Questions: Senate Bill 48," http://www.cde.ca.gov/ci/cr/cr/senatebill48faq.asp, accessed July 15, 2013.

3. See John D'Emilio and Estelle B. Freedman, *Intimate Matters: A History of Sexuality in America* (New York: Harper and Row, 1988); Leila J. Rupp, *A Desired Past: A Short History of Same-Sex Love in America* (Chicago: University of Chicago Press, 1999); Allida M. Black, ed., *Modern American Queer History* (Philadelphia: Temple University Press, 2001); Vicki L. Eaklor, *Queer America: A People's GLBT History of the United States* (New York: New Press, 2008); Michael Bronski, *A Queer History of the United States* (Boston: Beacon Press, 2011).

4. According to an assessment conducted in 2003, the majority of the twenty-three U.S. textbooks reviewed contained coverage; by contrast, in a similar assessment in 1991, only three texts had a paragraph or more on the

topic. Vicki Eaklor, "How Queer-Friendly Are US History Textbooks?," History News Network, 2004, http://hnn.us/articles/3200.html, accessed July 27, 2013.

5. See National Center for Lesbian Rights, http://www.nclrights.org/site /PageServer, accessed July 27, 2013. We are grateful to Arcelia Hurtado for information about the case.

6. See the report "Implementing Lessons That Matter: The Impact of LGBTQ-Inclusive Curriculum on Student Safety, Well-Being, and Achievement," GSA Network, http://www.gsanetwork.org/files/aboutus/ImplementingLessons _fullreport.pdf, accessed July 15, 2013.

7. For example, Margot Canaday's *The Straight State: Sexuality and Citizenship in Twentieth-Century America* (Princeton, NJ: Princeton University Press, 2009) won the Organization of American Historians Ellis Hawley Prize for the best book-length historical study of the political economy, politics, or institutions of the United States and the American Society for Legal History's Cromwell Book Prize, among others. George Chauncey's *Gay New York: Gender, Urban Culture, and the Making of the Gay Male World, 1890–1940* (New York: Basic Books, 1994) won the Organization of American Historians Merle Curti Prize for the best book in social history and the Frederick Jackson Turner Prize for the best first book in history.

8. See Michael A. Warner, "Queer and Then?," *Chronicle of Higher Education*, January 1, 2012, http://chronicle.com/article/QueerThen-/130161, accessed July 21, 2013.

9. Toni A. MacNaron, *Poisoned Ivy: Lesbian and Gay Academics Confronting Homophobia* (Philadelphia: Temple University Press, 1996); Marc Stein, "Crossing Borders: Memories, Dreams, Fantasies, and Nightmares of the History Job Market," *Left History* 9 (Spring–Summer 2004): 119–39.

10. See Leila J. Rupp and Verta Taylor, "Queer Girls on Campus: New Intimacies and Sexual Identities," in *Intimacies: A New World of Relational Life*, ed. Alan Frank, Patricia Clough, and Steven Seidman, 82–97 (New York: Routledge, 2013).

11. Discussion at Beyond Diversity: What Is a FAIR Education?, a miniconference organized by Jeffrey Stewart, Jacqueline Reid, and Anissa Stewart, University of California, Santa Barbara, April 18–19, 2013.

12. Gerda Lerner, *The Majority Finds Its Past: Placing Women in History* (New York: Oxford University Press, 1979), 146.

13. Catherine J. Kudlick, "Disability History: Why We Need Another 'Other,'" *American Historical Review* 108 (June 2003): 763–93.

14. This reflects the conversation at the Beyond Diversity: What Is a FAIR Education? conference.

# Outing the Past

## U.S. Queer History in Global Perspective

LEILA J. RUPP

When the Supreme Court in 2013 invalidated a crucial part of the federal Defense of Marriage Act, opening the door to federal benefits for same-sex couples legally married under state law, public opinion polls emphasized both how swiftly attitudes toward same-sex marriage had changed and the generational divide on issues of sexuality. Given the younger generation's greater acceptance of gay, lesbian, bisexual, and transgender people—despite the persistence of bullying in the schools—and the increasing media presence of LGBT people and issues, it should come as no surprise that students tend to hold a whiggish view of queer history, assuming that it is a story of progress from the bad old days to the much better present. U.S. queer history can begin to undermine this notion, showing, for example, that the Puritans were not so puritanical about sexuality, that the Victorians allowed a lot of latitude for same-sex intimacy and physical affection, and that queer- and gender-nonconforming people built communities and resisted oppressive practices before the mid–twentieth century. But a longer and cross-cultural view of same-sex sexuality is useful in making clear what we mean by the social construction of sexuality and what more we can do to put what is, in the end, the relatively short and recent history of the United States in perspective.

The not so shocking news is that, throughout time and around the world, people engaged in same-sex sexual acts long before the invention of the term *homosexuality* in the late nineteenth century. They did so in many different contexts, some of which make the term *same-sex sexuality* problematic.[1] Sometimes acts that, from a modern western perspective, would be considered sexual would not have been seen that way by the people involved. Sometimes such acts would not have been considered "same-sex," since what was defining for those involved was not their genitally alike bodies but their difference in terms of age, gender, or other factors.[2] Exploring the different manifestations of what, for lack of a better term, we still call *same-sex sexuality* shows that there are many different ways to view sexual acts and many different ways to think about their meanings for the people engaging in them. That people are defined by the sexual acts they desire and participate in and that the most important characteristic of a sexual interaction is the nature of the bodies of the people involved are not givens throughout time and place. A global perspective provides context for understanding queer U.S. history.

### It's about Age

In some cultures, same-sex interactions are structured by age difference between individuals. That was the case in ancient Athens, perhaps the most familiar example of same-sex sexuality in the past. One has only to look at the art of ancient Athens to see that young men's bodies represented the pinnacle of beauty. Vase paintings of male youths engaged in sexual interactions with older men tell a story of transgenerational same-sex relationships in which age difference was as important as the fact that men and boys belonged to the same sex. Such relationships reveal how differently societies can organize sexuality. Adult male citizens of Athens had the power to penetrate social inferiors, including women, foreigners, slaves, and boys. Although John Boswell, a pioneering scholar of same-sex sexuality in the ancient world, called men who preferred sex with boys "homosexual," and even "gay," other scholars argue that not only were elite men having sex with boys not homosexual, but what they were doing was not sexual in the way we understand it. Rather, an adult man with power wielding his penis was performing an act on the body of another, not engaging in a sexual relationship. As long as a man was penetrating another, not being penetrated, the act had no consequence for his status, as continues to be true in many cultures and subcultures around the world.[3] What was deviant was for a man to be penetrated or to engage in a sexual act with a social equal.

Age difference was also crucial in seventeenth-century Japan, where men expected to desire both women and boys. As long as they also married and fathered heirs, elite men had the privilege of taking young male lovers. Youths and men dressed and wore their hair differently, creating visible categories based on age and emphasizing their difference. Boys marked their advent into manhood by donning adult dress and shaving their distinctive boyish forelocks, at which point they were no longer available for penetration by men but, rather, could assume the role of the penetrating man in a new relationship. It was not impossible for men to hold onto the youth role into adulthood, using dress and hairstyle to belie their age, but what was crucial was the appearance of age difference, which marked a relationship as appropriate.[4]

Another much-discussed example of transgenerational male same-sex sexual interaction goes beyond showing that age difference might be more important than sex sameness by raising the question of what acts count as sex. Gilbert Herdt has shown that among the Sambia in New Guinea boys must incorporate the semen of older men into their bodies through fellatio in order to grow into adulthood. All boys participate in such ritual acts, and once they become men, either by marrying or by fathering a child, they may take on the adult role with a younger male.[5] As in the above examples, age difference is what is critical. But the central question here is whether engaging in ritualistic oral sex for the purpose of attaining adulthood can be considered a sexual act. Carole S. Vance, in a classic essay on the social construction of sexuality, quotes a student who was not willing to classify it as nonsexual by pointing out that "you don't see them eating it with a bowl and a spoon."[6] Recognizing that cultures in a variety of times and places can imbue acts we would consider sexual with very different meanings is an important perspective to bring to the history of same-sex sexuality.

As these examples suggest, we know the most about age-differentiated relations among men. In a few cultures, sex between older and younger women may have served the purpose of initiation into marriage. In ancient Sparta, a ritual called for girls to have sex with adult women before marriage. In what might be comparable to the Sambia case, lactating mothers among the Baruya in Melanesia nourish girls other than their daughters with breast milk, which they consider to be produced from men's semen and as a result essential to becoming an adult woman.[7] As with the boys in New Guinea, the question is whether a girl's mouth on a woman's breast has sexual connotations.

Perhaps the best examples of female transgenerational relationships come from southern Africa, where slightly younger schoolgirls take on the role of "babies" to older girls' "mummies." Such relationships have roots in traditional cultural forms, including initiation ceremonies for girls, and they provide socialization into the adult roles of domesticity, intimacy, and sexuality. Mummies and babies kiss, embrace, lie in bed together, and sometimes engage in genital activity. Because long labias are considered desirable, girls in small groups may engage in the practice of stretching their own or others' labias, providing an opportunity for autoerotic or mutual stimulation. Yet none of this is considered sex, simply because sex, in these cultures, requires the involvement of a penis.[8] Once again, we need to take seriously the question of what counts as sex.

In all these cases, the age difference between individuals in interactions is at least as salient, if not more so, than the fact that participants are of the same sex. In addition, what might look to us to be sexual acts have other or additional meanings. Although we do not find examples of these kinds of ritualized transgenerational interactions in U.S. history, age difference was important in some male same-sex relationships. Peter Boag, for example, has shown that in the world of transient labor in the mining and timber industries in the Pacific Northwest in the nineteenth century, transgenerational relationships between "wolves" or "jockers" (older men) and their "punks" or "lambs" (youths) combined sexual and domestic functions.[9] Recognizing the existence of age-differentiated relationships at different times and in different places emphasizes the important perspective that our contemporary way of thinking about same-sex sexuality is just one among many. It also emphasizes that age itself is socially constructed. What we may think of as children vulnerable to sexual abuse might, in other times and places, have been considered, and functioned, as sexual beings with their own desires and subjectivities.

## It's about Gender

In other societies, same-sex interactions are structured by gender differences between partners, with one taking on a feminine and the other a masculine gender. This is how the sexologists who first developed the concept of homosexuality explained people with same-sex desires: they were feminine men attracted to masculine men and masculine women attracted to feminine women. Globally and across time, attractions between individuals differentiated in some way on the basis of gender are probably the most common form of same-sex interactions and relationships for both men and women. Sometimes this means that an individual with same-sex desires adopts a gender different from the one assumed to match his or her sex, either crossing the line of gender or adopting a third or fourth gender, what we would now call being transgender. Sometimes it means simply that one partner in a relationship or interaction is more feminine and the other more masculine, whether they are both women or both men. In other words, neither is transgender in a contemporary sense; both are what is sometimes now called "cisgender," referring to people whose gender identity matches the sex assignment they were given at birth.[10]

Gender differentiation takes two different forms, one institutionalized and the other not. Some societies make room for gender-crossing and recognize men who take on the dress, roles, and activities of women and, less frequently, make room for women who present as men. In such cases, individuals who cross genders or inhabit a third or fourth gender category may engage in sexual relations with individuals with genitally alike bodies but a different gender. Where gender-crossing is not institutionalized, people sometimes secretly take on a gender different from the one assigned to them at birth. In these cases, we know little about people's motivations and subjectivities, and only if the act of gender-crossing is discovered do such stories come to light.

In U.S. history, institutionalized transgender relationships are confined to a number of Native American cultures. The early European explorers expressed horror at the existence of male-bodied individuals who adopted the dress, occupations, and characteristics of women, dubbing them *berdache*, a derogatory French term adopted from an Arabic word for a boy slave used for sexual purposes. Evidence of gender-crossing by Native women comes primarily from the nineteenth century, at a time when the disapproving attitudes of white settlers made Native people more reluctant to discuss gender-crossing in the past or present. Although gender-crossing did not necessarily have consequences for sexuality, cross-gender individuals in Native American cultures could have sex with and marry non-cross-gender partners.[11] As the essay by Thomas A. Foster points out, scholars disagree about the degree of acceptance of gender-crossing by indigenous cultures in the Americas. The contemporary term *Two-Spirit* recognizes the spiritual, rather than sexual, nature of the cross-gender role.

Knowing that other societies, too, make room for more than two discrete genders is an important perspective to bring to a consideration of Native American gender-crossing. In India the category *hijra* exists for men who consider themselves neither male nor female because they are impotent with women but cannot bear children. They have their male genitals surgically removed, dress and wear their hair like women, and seek out men for sex. They have religious and ceremonial functions in traditional Indian society, performing at marriages and the births of male children, although they are much despised. They live in *hijra* communities and are recognized as a distinct gender category.[12]

Contemporary Brazilian society, too, has a category for individuals born as men who take on some of the physical manifestations and social roles of women, although they do not consider themselves women. *Travestís* are males who, prompted by desire for men, take on female names; wear women's clothes; ingest female hormones; inject silicone to enlarge their buttocks, thighs, and breasts; and support themselves through sex work. They take as clients and boyfriends men who define themselves as resolutely heterosexual. The *travestí* sexual system divides the world into those who penetrate and are never penetrated (men) and those who are penetrated (women, homosexuals).[13] Like *hijras*, they are a recognized category in their society, although they are feared and subjected to violence and discrimination.

Other than among Native American cultures, there is little evidence of institutionalized cross-gender roles for women that include same-sex sexual activity. Some scholars point to "sworn virgins" in the Balkans and "female husbands" in some African cultures as transgender individuals who take on male dress and occupations and, in the latter case, marry women to carry on the family name by claiming children born to their wives through heterosexual sex. But the evidence about sexuality within these relationships is minimal and controversial, with African scholars in particular denying that female husbands engage in sex with their wives.[14]

It is secret gender-crossing that was more common for women in the past, including, as Emily K. Hobson and Felicia T. Perez point out in their essay, during the U.S. Civil War. Throughout early modern Europe, numerous cases have come to light of women who dressed and worked as men, often joining the military. Some of them married women and, when discovered, faced punishment, including execution, especially if they were found to have had sex with their wives by means of what the sources called "material instruments." Such was the outcome for Catharina Margaretha Linck, who fought as a soldier in eighteenth-century Germany, went to work as a dyer, and met and married her wife. When her mother-in-law suspected that something was amiss and tore off Linck's trousers, finding equipment made of leather and a pig's bladder, Linck was tried and beheaded for her "hideous and nasty" outrages.[15]

What we cannot know is whether women in these contexts crossed the gender line in the interests of mobility or occupation rather than out of sexual desire for women or what today would be called transgender subjectivity.[16] There are also cases of men in various places around the world who secretly changed gender. Since they had nothing to gain and everything to lose in terms of status and mobility by becoming women, we assume that sexual desire and/or transgender subjectivity was the motivation.

A public but noninstitutionalized form of gender-differentiated same-sex relationship pairs a traditionally gendered (cisgender) person with one who takes on some characteristics associated with the other/ another gender but does not alter the body or cross the gender line. Such feminine men and masculine women can be found in many different cultures and time periods. In this volume, we encounter "fairies" in early-twentieth-century New York who dressed in distinctive and recognizable ways, wore makeup, and sought out "real men" for sexual encounters, along with butch women and their fem lovers who frequented working-class lesbian bars in cities such as Buffalo, New York, in the mid–twentieth century.

Gender-differentiated attraction can be found in many contemporary cultures as well. The Tagalog term *bakla*, in the Philippines, refers to a person with a male body and female heart. Effeminate *bakla*, like *travestís*, seek masculine men as sexual partners.[17] In a number of contemporary Asian cultures, including those of Thailand, Hong Kong, Taiwan, the Philippines, and Indonesia, masculine/feminine difference is central to female same-sex sexuality. A variety of terms make clear the importance of gender difference: *toms* and *dees* (from the English words *tomboy* and *lady*) in Thailand, *TBs* and *TBGs* (tomboys and tomboys' girls) in Hong Kong, *Ts* and *Pos* (the *T* standing for *tomboy* and *Po* from the Chinese word for *wife*) in Taiwan, and *tomboys* or *lesbis* and their girlfriends in Indonesia.[18] Masculine women in these cultures do not consider themselves men, but they also distinguish themselves from feminine women, and their girlfriends mostly consider themselves heterosexual or "real" women. The category "lesbian" is generally known in these cultures and embraced by some women, but indigenous gendered identities are the dominant way of organizing same-sex sexuality.

As we can see, some cultures make a place for people who cross the lines of gender or adopt a gender outside a binary gender system. Others do not, yet individuals sometimes secretly cross gender for a variety of reasons. In yet other societies, gender difference between partners structures interactions and relationships even though there is no recognized cross-gender or third-gender role. As with age difference, gender difference may be as or more important than the fact that two people have the same kinds of genitals. A global and historical perspective provides important context for the past and present phenomena of gender-differentiated relationships in U.S. society. The ubiquity of these relationships even raises the question John D'Emilio asks in another context: "Is it possible, I wonder, that fifty years from now, the reigning wisdom will argue that gay and lesbian proved to be relatively short blips on the historical screen and that transgender—or what I am referring to as gender crossing—provides the more robust framework for historical understanding?"[19] For contemporary students who identify as transgender or genderqueer, knowing this history can go a long way toward fostering self-acceptance and, we hope, creating a more accepting environment.

## Love and Desire between Social Equals

More familiar historical and global patterns of same-sex relationships, from a contemporary U.S. perspective, are those in which differences of age and gender do not come into play in any systematic way. That is not to say that there are no cases of older men with younger men or masculine women with feminine women. What distinguishes such pairings from transgenerational and transgenderal relationships is that differences do not structure them.

Nondifferentiated intimacies among women are especially common in different times and places, although we also know about passionate male friendships between social equals in the past, as David D. Doyle

Jr.'s essay points out. Women's lack of access to public space throughout most of time and space has meant that they were less likely than men to have contact with those in different social categories, with the exception of mistresses and their servants or slaves. In a number of different spaces, including brothels, prisons, and various kinds of households, women had the opportunity to form intimate relations with others of the same status. A nineteenth-century form of Urdu poetry known as *rekhti* portrays erotic and sexual relationships between elite secluded women in India, at the very least showing that such relationships could be imagined.[20] Same-sex passionate and romantic relationships between schoolgirls existed around much of the world in the nineteenth and twentieth centuries, including in Europe, the United States (as Dáša Frančíková's essay points out), Latin America, China, and Japan. Sexologists who wrote about such schoolgirl friendships could not agree about their nature, some condemning them as perverse and others seeing only harmless emotional attachments. Sex-segregated spaces such as girls' schools continue to provide a context in which same-sex love and desire might flourish.

Another form of eroticized sameness can be found in love and desire between wives married to the same man. In China, India, and the Middle East, such relationships could make for more harmonious households, and as long as men still had sexual access to their wives, they might have no objection to such bonds. Chinese literature, from the late sixteenth century to the early twentieth, includes tales of cowife lovers happily married to the same man. Some even feature two women in love working to engineer marriages to the same man so they might live together. Although such tales are fictional, they lend credence to the reality of love between cowives.[21]

That in different contexts, intense, loving, physically affectionate relationships between women friends and cowives have met with social approval sheds light on the different ways societies view and have viewed sexuality and intimacy. When women and men lived in different social worlds and compulsory heterosexuality ensured that almost all women would marry men and bear children, sometimes it mattered little what women did with their hearts and bodies. Sometimes same-sex love and intimacy fit neatly with heterosexual marriage. Recognizing this history complicates our understanding of what was possible in the past and shows that people with same-sex desires have come together in many different social contexts. Students can see that what we would call bisexuality existed in many different cultures long before it came to be named.

## Beyond Lesbian, Gay, Bisexual, Transgender

The creation of the category "homosexual" in the late nineteenth century, originating with sexologists in Europe and spreading around the world, went hand in hand with the development of an identity based on sexual object choice and, eventually, the formation of movements organized around same-sex sexuality as a fundamental characteristic of individuals rather than simply a behavior in which people might engage. Homosexuality as a concept and identity was the product of a complex interplay between the writings of the sexologists, who distinguished homosexuality from heterosexuality, which they then deemed "normal," and the behaviors and communities of people with same-sex desires, whom the sexologists studied. The concept of homosexuality held important consequences for both public thinking about same-sex sexuality and the self-understandings of at least some people with same-sex desires. For one thing, homosexuality was a category that encompassed both men and women, while throughout much of time and in many places male and female same-sex sexualities were considered separate and discrete phenomena. For another, homosexuality took on an association with the West, fostering the notion that same-sex sexual behavior was not indigenous in many places but had been imported from abroad. Authorities in various parts of the world, especially in Africa and parts of Asia, have denounced homosexuality as a western perversion, ignoring the forms of same-sex sexuality that have long existed in their own cultures. Yet, as the recent case of the influence in Uganda of U.S. evangelical Christians on the proposed bill to make homosexuality punishable by death makes clear, it is in reality antihomosexual sentiment, rather than homosexuality, that has often been imported.

Finally, the category of homosexuality, despite the fact that it was labeled deviant, helped to construct an identity that people might choose to embrace. In the Euro-American world, the identities of homosexual and later gay, lesbian, bisexual, and transgender served as the basis for community formation. In other places around the world, where people had their own ways of thinking about their sexual desires and gender identities, the concept of homosexuality imposed assumptions that individuals might embrace, adapt, or reject.

There is no question but that the sexological concept of homosexuality and the identities of lesbian, gay, bisexual, and transgender have had global impact. Tom Boellstorff, studying Indonesia, uses the metaphor of dubbing to analyze the ways that western concepts of gay and lesbian interact with Indonesian subject positions of *gay* and *lesbi*, terms obviously derived from English but with their own meanings. As with dubbed films, there is never an exact fit between the voice and the movement of lips. *Gay* and *lesbi* Indonesians, for example, expect to marry heterosexually out of choice and love as a way to belong to the nation. They see no contradiction between their same-sex loves and desires and the need to marry and produce heirs.[22]

A global history of same-sex sexuality, then, provides a larger and wider frame for the project of integrating queer history into U.S. survey courses. Understanding the complexity involved in ritualized same-sex sexual acts in times and places such as ancient Athens and twentieth-century New Guinea allows us to see that such acts may have very different purposes. Knowing that sex between early modern Japanese men and boys was fully compatible with heterosexual marriage shows us that acceptance of same-sex sexuality is not simply a modern development. Knowing about the ways in which different societies have created space for gender-crossing or third- or fourth-gender categories puts such Native American practices in perspective, and learning about secret gender-crossing in early modern Europe helps us to understand the cases of individuals who followed a similar path in the United States, including, as Genny Beemyn points out in hir essay, the twentieth-century case of jazz musician Billy Tipton. Understanding that, for a variety of reasons at different points of time, same-sex relationships were not only tolerated but accepted undermines the notion that history moves inexorably forward to a better and more progressive future. And knowing that Indonesians have adapted the terms *gay* and *lesbian* to their own uses makes clear that our contemporary way of viewing sexual identities is only one way of thinking about what it means to love and desire someone of the same sex.

Like a map of the world with, say, Asia rather than North America in the center, a global history of same-sex sexuality decenters what is familiar. This, in turn, helps us to see what we know with different eyes. A global perspective on the history of same-sex sexuality is a powerful tool for showing that societies have the potential to shape sexuality in many different ways and that there is nothing new about the varieties of desires, behaviors, and identities that students experience in the twenty-first-century world.

## NOTES

1. Leila J. Rupp, "Toward a Global History of Same-Sex Sexuality," *Journal of the History of Sexuality* 10 (2001): 287–302.

2. Synthetic scholarship on the history of same-sex sexuality offers classification schemes that differentiate between relations structured around difference and sameness. David F. Greenberg, in *The Construction of Homosexuality* (Chicago: University of Chicago Press, 1988), identifies transgenerational, transgenderal, transclass, and egalitarian forms of homosexual relations. Stephen O. Murray, in *Homosexualities* (Chicago: University of Chicago Press, 2000), organizes his synthesis around age-structured, gender-stratified, and egalitarian homosexuality.

3. John Boswell, *Christianity, Social Tolerance, and Homosexuality: Gay People in Western Europe from the Beginning of the Christian Era to the Fourteenth Century* (Chicago: University of Chicago Press, 1980); David M. Halperin, *How to Do the History of Homosexuality* (Chicago: University of Chicago Press, 2002); Robert Padgug, "Sexual Matters: Rethinking Sexuality in History," in *Hidden from History: Reclaiming the Gay and Lesbian Past*, ed. Martin Bauml Duberman, Martha Vicinus, and George Chauncey Jr., 54–64 (New York: New American Library, 1989); Leila J. Rupp, "Sexual Fluidity 'before Sex,'" *Signs: Journal of Women in Culture and Society* 37, no. 1 (2012): 849–56.

4. Paul Gordon Schalow, "Male Love in Early Modern Japan: A Literary Depiction of the 'Youth,'" in *Hidden from History: Reclaiming the Gay and Lesbian Past*, ed. Martin Bauml Duberman, Martha Vicinus, and George Chauncey Jr., 118–28 (New York: New American Library, 1989).

5. Gilbert Herdt, *Guardians of the Flutes,* vol. 1: *Idioms of Masculinity* (Chicago: University of Chicago Press, 1981).

6. Carole S. Vance, "Social Construction Theory: Problems in the History of Sexuality," in *Which Homosexuality?*, ed. Dennis Altman et al., 13–34 (Amsterdam: Dekker/Schorrer, 1989), 22.

7. These examples come from Greenberg, *Construction of Homosexuality*.

8. Judith Gay, "'Mummies and Babies' and Friends and Lovers in Lesotho," *Journal of Homosexuality* 11, nos. 3–4 (1985): 97–116.

9. Peter Boag, *Same-Sex Affairs: Constructing and Controlling Homosexuality in the Pacific Northwest* (Berkeley: University of California Press, 2003).

10. See A. Finn Enke, "The Education of Little Cis: Cisgender and the Discipline of Opposing Bodies," in *Transgender Perspectives in and beyond Transgender and Gender Studies*, ed. A. Finn Enke (Philadelphia: Temple University Press, 2013).

11. Evelyn Blackwood, "Sexuality and Gender in Certain Native American Tribes: The Case of Cross-Gender Females," *Signs: Journal of Women in Culture and Society* 10, no. 1 (1984): 27–42; Charles Callender and Lee M. Kochems, "The North American Berdache," *Current Anthropology* 24, no. 4 (1983): 443–56; Sabine Lang, "Lesbians, Men-Women, and Two-Spirits: Homosexuality and Gender in Native American Cultures," in *Female Desires: Same-Sex Relations and Transgender Practices across Cultures*, ed. Evelyn Blackwood and Saskia E. Wieringa, 91–116 (New York: Columbia University Press, 1999).

12. Serena Nanda, *Neither Man nor Woman: The Hijras of India* (Belmont, CA: Wadsworth, 1990); Gayatri Reddy, *With Respect to Sex: Negotiating Hijra Identity in South India* (Chicago: University of Chicago Press, 2005).

13. Don Kulick, *Travestí: Sex, Gender, and Culture among Brazilian Transgendered Prostitutes* (Chicago: University of Chicago Press, 1998).

14. René Grémaux, "Woman Becomes Man in the Balkans," in *Third Sex, Third Gender: Beyond Sexual Dimorphism in Culture and History*, ed. Gilbert Herdt, 241–81 (New York: Zone Books, 1993); Regina Smith Oboler, "Is the Female Husband a Man? Woman/Woman Marriage among the Nandi of Kenya," *Ethnology* 19, no. 1 (1980): 69–88; Joseph M. Carrier and Stephen O. Murray, "Woman-Woman Marriage in Africa," in *Boy-Wives and Female Husbands: Studies in African Homosexualities*, ed. Stephen O. Murray and Will Roscoe, 255–66 (New York: Palgrave, 1998); Ife Amadiume, *Male Daughters, Female Husbands: Gender and Sex in an African Society* (London: Zed Books, 1987). The latter is insistent that there was nothing sexual between female husbands and their wives.

15. Brigitte Ericksson, "A Lesbian Execution in Germany, 1721: The Trial Records," *Journal of Homosexuality* 6, nos. 1–2 (1980–81): 27–40.

16. See Leila J. Rupp, *Sapphistries: A Global History of Love between Women* (New York: New York University Press, 2009).

17. Martin F. Manalansan IV, *Global Divas: Filipino Gay Men in the Diaspora* (Durham, NC: Duke University Press, 2003).

18. Megan Sinnott, *Toms and Dees: Transgender Identity and Female Same-Sex Relationships in Thailand* (Honolulu: University of Hawai'i Press, 2004); Franco Lai, "Lesbian Masculinities: Identity and Body Construction among Tomboys in Hong Kong," in *Women's Sexualities and Masculinities in a Globalizing Asia*, ed. Saskia E. Wieringa, Evelyn Blackwood, and Abha Bhaiya, 159–79 (New York: Palgrave Macmillan, 2007); Y. Antonia Chao, "Drink, Stories, Penis, and Breasts: Lesbian Tomboys in Taiwan from the 1960s to the 1990s," *Journal of Homosexuality* 40, nos. 3–4 (2001): 185–209; Evelyn Blackwood, "Transnational Sexualities

in One Place: Indonesian Readings," in *Women's Sexualities and Masculinities in a Globalizing Asia*, ed. Saskia E. Wieringa, Evelyn Blackwood, and Abha Bhaiya, 181–99 (New York: Palgrave Macmillan, 2007).

19. John D'Emilio, "Foreword," in St. Sukie de la Croix, *Chicago Whispers: A History of LGBT Chicago before Stonewall* (Madison: University of Wisconsin Press, 2012). Thanks to Susan K. Freeman for this reference.

20. Ruth Vanita, "'Married among Their Companions': Female Homoerotic Relations in Nineteenth-Century Urdu *Rekthi* Poetry in India," *Journal of Women's History* 16, no. 1 (2004): 12–53.

21. Tze-lan Sang, *The Emerging Lesbian: Female Same-Sex Desire in Modern China* (Chicago: University of Chicago Press, 2003); Abha Bhaiya, "The Spring That Flowers between Women," in *Women's Sexualities and Masculinities in a Globalizing Asia*, ed. Saskia E. Wieringa, Evelyn Blackwood, and Abha Bhaiya, 69–76 (New York: Palgrave Macmillan, 2007).

22. Tom Boellstorff, *The Gay Archipelago* (Princeton, NJ: Princeton University Press, 2005).

# PART ONE

# The Challenge of Teaching Lesbian, Gay, Bisexual, and Transgender History

# Forty Years and Counting

JOHN D'EMILIO

When I started graduate school in 1971, I never expected that I would become a professor. Work-
ing in an entry-level library job after college, I stumbled on some of the
literature in U.S. history that was emerging in the 1960s. Writers such
as William Appleman Williams and Gabriel Kolko recounted a long
history of U.S. imperialism and corporate power that was completely
new to me. The Vietnam War had already changed me from the Gold-
water Republican I had been in high school to the morally outraged
but politically confused antiwar activist I became in college. "How can
my country be doing this?" I remember thinking many times in the face
of new headlines. Dipping my toes in this New Left history gave me a
framework for understanding. More, it made me believe I could never
advocate for change persuasively unless I knew U.S. history in ways
different than what I had learned in school. And so, with the unbridled
enthusiasm of a twenty-three-year-old, I entered the history graduate
program at Columbia University. During those first two years, I wrote
a master's essay on corporate liberalism and the origins of the Cold War
and eagerly consumed a critical literature in U.S. history on a broad
range of topics.

The assumption that I was not heading toward an academic career
was confirmed the year after I took my exams. I had the opportunity to
supplement my meager fellowship by teaching as an adjunct faculty
member at local colleges. Objectively, nothing bad happened. But the
stress of being in front of the classroom was so great that I would return
home and sleep for the rest of the day. I was a wreck. No more teaching
for me, I resolved. And so, for the next seven years, as I worked on my
dissertation, I supported myself as a writer for reference book publishers

and as a researcher and staffer for advocacy organizations on a range of issues, from publicly funded day care to resisting prison expansion.

Surprisingly, one of the courses I taught in that brief time in the classroom was a gay studies course. Like many schools in the early 1970s, Montclair State College in New Jersey had established an experimental unit to try out new kinds of courses and new forms of teaching. It approached Martin Duberman, at that time the highest profile academic in New York known to be gay, and he recommended me. It would be hard to claim it was a history course back then, although much of the material in the syllabus would today make good documents for teaching the United States since 1945. We read some Kinsey and a bit of the sociology that had recently been produced, some fiction by writers such as James Baldwin and Rita Mae Brown, and a lot of gay liberation literature being churned out by activists and collected in anthologies. The course should have thrilled me, but, honestly, it made that year even more stressful. I was not accustomed to being "out" in mainstream settings like that. The students were not open about their own identities and tiptoed around such matters. Despite my efforts to project great enthusiasm, I mostly recall a group of about fifteen students and me sitting in a circle and feeling awkward.

But how was it that an antiwar activist and student of corporate liberalism came to teach such a course? By 1974 my life felt thoroughly entwined with the gay liberation movement in New York. The year before, a small group of graduate students, faculty, writers, and independent researchers had come together to talk about "gay history." At that point in time, the very phrase had such a daring ring that it provoked thrills of excitement. A broader organization, the Gay Academic Union (GAU), emerged from those discussions. It quickly became a vast networking device for graduate students, faculty, and community members interested in intellectual work as a tool for activism and social change. Jonathan Ned Katz, working on what would become *Gay American History*, was deeply involved with GAU; his documentary play, *Coming Out*, was staged in New York at the time.[1] Many GAU meetings took place at Marty Duberman's home; he had recently come out in his book *Black Mountain*.[2] In this environment, it seemed preordained that I would choose to write a dissertation on gay history, even if I had almost no sense of what that would entail.

Graduate school teaches historians to embed our research in the existing literature on a topic. We are supposed to be joining a conversation,

John D'Emilio

adding our own insights, and either shifting the conversation's direction or solidifying it. In the 1970s, there was not yet a conversation in LGBT history. But neither had there been much conversation in such emerging areas as women's or working-class history, yet these fields were developing rapidly. The times seemed made for this adventure in discovery. Although I know there were moments when I thought "what the hell made me choose this path?," most of the time excitement ruled the day.

The excitement came from the context of the 1970s: the newness of coming out, of affirming one's identity, of building visible communities, and of mobilizing those communities for political resistance. Choosing visibility was still exceptional rather than typical, and it sometimes seemed as if all the out-of-the-closet activists in the seventies knew one another. For those of us doing intellectual work, especially if we were researching and writing history, the sense of connection was magnified. "Study groups" were our faculty meetings, movement newspapers our scholarly journals, and community spaces our lecture halls. I remember

giving well-attended talks on the left-wing origins of the gay movement after the Second World War, the persecution of homosexuals
during the Cold War, and the historical relationship between capitalism
and gay identity. As word got out that some of us were doing historical
work, student and faculty activists began extending invitations to lecture
on their campuses. Each talk had the feel of doing something completely
new, something that had not happened before.

Exhilarating as this was, it did not earn me a living. At some point I
realized that, my dread of teaching notwithstanding, I had to give the
academic job market a shot, because I could not think of another way to
support my passion for history. After three years of applications, I finally
landed, in 1983, a tenure-track position at the University of North Carolina at Greensboro (UNCG). My responsibilities included the second
half of the U.S. survey each semester, a course on the United States since
1945, and another on U.S. foreign policy. I also taught two of every four
semesters in a four-course American studies sequence in the campus
Residential College, an alternative education environment where students both lived and learned together. And I developed two courses of
my own: a history of sexuality in the United States and a class on the
United States in the 1960s, both of which proved popular.

I will always be deeply grateful to Allen Trelease, Loren Schweninger,
and other members of the UNCG history department for hiring me. It
was not common then for graduate students to be writing on gay and
lesbian topics, and I was one of the earliest PhDs—perhaps the first—in
gay and lesbian history to land a tenure-track position. Yes, my curriculum vitae was strong. My book, *Sexual Politics, Sexual Communities*, had
just been released when they offered me the position, and I had other
publications as well.[3] But there was little sense in the profession that
what we today call LGBT history had any depth or substance to it, or
that it was anything more than a curiosity on the margins of what really
counts as history.

The decision to hire me was even more remarkable given the context.
Until that point, I had lived only in New York City, with extended stays
in San Francisco and Los Angeles for research. Unlike those cities,
Greensboro could not claim to be a gay mecca. The Triangle area of
Chapel Hill, Durham, and Raleigh did have an activist movement that
stretched back to the early seventies. But Greensboro was different. One
member of the faculty had taught a gay-themed anthropology course in
summer session a couple of years earlier, but the experience had not

been good, and he retreated. Soon after I arrived, a local paper in the next county published a piece announcing that a "fag doctor" from New York was now teaching in Greensboro; the article conjured up fears of child molestation by mentioning that I had worked in day care. Greensboro did have a gay and lesbian social world, and a chapter of the GAU existed. But the organization was primarily a means for well-educated folks to socialize outside the bars. When my partner Jim, who volunteered to edit its newsletter, used his own name in the publication, it created quite a commotion. The failure to use a pseudonym provoked fears of exposure throughout the organization; Jim had violated some basic norm of secrecy.

Thankfully, my second foray into teaching was totally different from my earlier one. The first year, with three new preps each semester, was exhausting. But I connected well with students, and I enjoyed putting my years of reading U.S. history into lectures. Ronald Reagan's presidency was already throwing a conservative pall over public discourse, and there was something delightfully subversive about providing a view of U.S. history from the left, whether through interpretations of Reconstruction, populism, and the progressive era or of the Cold War, McCarthyism, and the Vietnam War. By the second year, as I developed a stable of courses that I reliably offered, teaching settled into a satisfying and invigorating rhythm.

It seemed natural to incorporate gay material into most of my courses, though not in any major way. It figured in lectures about the political persecutions of the McCarthy era and the social protests of the 1960s and 1970s. When I did assign readings, I tended to use primary sources. *Gay American History* was an indispensable resource, as were the anthologies of gay liberationist and lesbian feminist writing edited by Karla Jay and Allen Young.[4]

My history of sexuality course provided a more organic context for teaching LGBT history. In its first years, the class served almost as a trial run for *Intimate Matters*, which Estelle Freedman and I were then drafting.[5] Looking back, I am amazed at how thin the literature on same-sex love and desire was in comparison to today. There was Carroll Smith-Rosenberg's groundbreaking essay "The Female World of Love and Ritual" and a few other pieces that appeared in some of the alternative journals that feminists created.[6] Katz's *Gay American History* and its successor, *Gay/Lesbian Almanac*, were essential.[7] They allowed incorporation of queer stories into the history of colonial America, discussions of the Native American experience, the inclusion of gender-crossing behavior and identities, and much more. A work such as John S. and Robin M. Haller's *The Physician and Sexuality in Victorian America* exposed students to such critical scrutiny of medical ideas that, by extension, scientific theories about homosexuality suddenly became suspect.[8]

Again, context matters. In the 1980s, my presence in the classroom was at least as important as the course content. The student population at UNCG was overwhelmingly in-state. The vast majority was white, but there was a contingent of black students as well. Many were from towns and communities smaller than Greensboro. For the overwhelming majority of these students, I was the first gay person they had knowingly encountered. In those years, coming out was not a "do it once, and it's over" event. It had to happen again and again. Because of my sexuality course and the book I had written, my identity circulated as a kind of whispered rumor. Among students who took my classes and came to know me, I had the nicknames "Doctor Sex" and "the Sex Prof," both of which were spoken in my presence with affectionate humor. But for those meeting me for the first time in a course, my identity just hung there, unspoken yet present.

In my third semester, I taught a seminar section, in the Residential College's American studies core sequence, titled Sexuality, Power, and Politics since 1945. In the middle of a discussion during the first segment of the course, which covered sexuality and Cold War society and included an excerpt from *Sexual Politics, Sexual Communities*, a student raised her hand. When I called on her, she looked at me and asked, "Are you a homosexual?" It was not the question I was expecting. But, with a friendly smile and without skipping a beat, I said "Yes, I am gay" and moved on to the next student comment. That moment changed everything. Over the next week, I noticed that the whole tone of the class had shifted. Everyone became more relaxed.

The experience made me realize that I had to figure out a way to name the elephant in my classroom without making it high drama. So, beginning with the next semester, I began each new course not simply by calling roll but by asking students to introduce themselves through answering a series of questions designed to let them show themselves: "Fifty years from now, what would you like your legacy to be? What makes you a good friend? Tell us about the best day of your life. If you were President of the World for a day, what one thing would you change and why? Tell us about the most important person in your life."

I had six to eight students do it at the start of each meeting, and I varied the questions to preserve the spontaneity of the introductions. I explained that it was a good way for me to remember all their names and have each student be more than just a name on a roster. And, I told them, as a "reward" for humoring their professor by answering my questions, I would introduce myself last by answering *their* questions. It worked wondrously. Not only did their introductions help create a sense of community and connectedness, and not only did their answers produce knowing laughter and recognition from their peers, but their questions allowed me to show myself. My coming out could happen organically yet not be the main event. It was just one thing that emerged in a back-and-forth conversation.

That same Residential College class also produced one of the best teaching moments in all my years at UNCG. Besides the segment on Cold War culture, there was one on race and sexuality, taught through reading the so-called Moynihan Report of 1965 on the black family and exploring the reaction it generated; one on feminism and sexuality, taught through the debates about pornography; and one on gay liberation. Each segment required a writing assignment, and for the one on gay liberation the students had to write a "coming out" letter to their parents. The point of the assignment seemed obvious to me. At a time when gay lives were still unfamiliar to most heterosexuals, what better way to produce empathy than by asking students to imagine, and then express in words, how they would tell such a thing to their parents?

The week before the assignment was due, I passed in the hallway one of the other faculty members in the Residential College core sequence, and, with a quizzical look on her face, she said to me, "That's quite an unusual writing assignment." I smiled in a noncommittal way and went to class. When I entered the room, they all stopped talking, which was very unusual. I said "Good morning" and was getting ready to lecture a bit when a hand shot up. "I have a question about the assignment," the student said. "Do we have to mail our letters?" Before I could say anything, another hand went up and a student asked, "What if my roommate sees it?" From the other end of the table a student responded "my girlfriend DID see it, and she got very upset!" And so it went, anxieties spontaneously exploding, as I just sat there, speechless and laughing, with each new comment.

At some point, several worries later, a student suddenly blurted out, "Oh my god. I get it. Can you imagine how scary it would be to really write such a letter?" And, from there, we were off and running, having one of the most authentic class discussions I have ever sat through, as students made the leap into the experience of "the other." They emerged with a deeper appreciation of the workings of homophobia, the way it is internalized, how it affects people who claim the identity, and the courage that coming out entails. I repeated the assignment in a number of other classes I taught (though with more explanation in advance), and it always proved productive and enlightening.

Most of my teaching at UNCG was with undergraduates. The department had a master's program, and some of my courses mingled undergraduates and MA students. In my dozen years in Greensboro, three students came to the master's program specifically to work with me on gay and lesbian history. In the spring of 1993, I had a singular teaching experience. Between UNCG and Chapel Hill, there were enough graduate students interested in the subject to justify a history of sexuality topics course. The literature in LGBT history was still thin in comparison to today, but it was possible to construct a broad course stretching from early modern Europe to the mid-twentieth century. *Hidden from History*, the anthology edited by Martin Duberman, Martha Vicinus, and George Chauncey, had been published, as well as Allan Bérubé's study of the Second World War, *Coming Out under Fire*, and Lillian Faderman's *Odd Girls and Twilight Lovers*.[9] In addition, the eighties had produced a spate of memoirs and collections ranging from *Zami*, by Audre Lorde, to *Compañeras*, edited by Juanita Ramos, which added many first-person voices to the historical literature.[10] Teaching the course was a dramatically different experience from my first foray at Montclair State College two decades earlier. We were not all sitting on pins and needles as we waded into the topic; we were eager to be there and open about our interests. Of the ten students who took the course, three went on to produce significant scholarship in the history of sexuality.

In 1995 I took a two-year leave from UNCG and moved to Washington, DC, to become the founding director of the Policy Institute at the National Gay and Lesbian Task Force (NGLTF). In some ways, I had always thought of academic life as my "day" job; my strongest commitments were to activism and movement building. While in Greensboro, I had worked with the North Carolina Civil Liberties Union for a while in conjunction with the effort to develop a gay and lesbian rights project. I developed a close relationship with NGLTF, serving on its board for several years, cochairing it for two, and speaking at a number of its conferences and community meetings. By the late 1980s, a combination of the AIDS epidemic and the 1987 March on Washington had propelled a more dynamic activist scene into existence in Greensboro. I testified at hearings before the city's Human Relations Commission and became a background source for reporters who occasionally covered these issues. At a time when queer issues were finally becoming part of the warp and woof of political debate, the invitation to create a Policy Institute was irresistible.

The return to urban life and a daily engagement with LGBT politics made it difficult to imagine returning to Greensboro. When I finished at the Task Force, I also resigned from UNCG and began looking for other jobs. My applications were better received this time around, and I actually had some options. I chose the University of Illinois at Chicago (UIC) partly because it was in a big city and partly because the job had special attractions. It was based in a Gender and Women's Studies program, and I was hired specifically to teach LGBT and sexuality-related courses. My hiring was different in another way as well. Stanley Fish had recently arrived as dean of liberal arts and sciences, and he had quite a yen for upsetting orthodoxies. He loved the idea of a "gay hire," and this time around there were articles not about a fag professor but about a well-respected, policy-oriented gay scholar. What a change a decade and a half had wrought!

At UIC I continued to teach a broad-based U.S. history of sexuality course. But by the early twenty-first century, the literature had grown so dramatically that I could construct such a course around the themes of power and inequality. We studied the grand sweep of U.S. history and looked at how sexuality intersects with categories such as race, class, gender, and region. We explored how sex became a vehicle both to oppress individuals and groups and to resist oppression. Same-sex love and gender-crossing wove their way through the topics we covered.

I also taught an advanced undergraduate course on U.S. LGBT history that often drew some graduate students. Unlike in the 1980s, there was enough literature that I could choose among books, articles, and documents with an eye toward connecting LGBT topics to big themes in U.S. history. Thus, I could use Lillian Faderman's work to link women loving women to movements intended to achieve social justice, such as suffrage and urban reform in the progressive era.[11] I built on the writing of Angela Y. Davis and Kevin J. Mumford to connect the LGBT experience to the mass migrations of African Americans to northern cities in the 1910s and 1920s.[12] The work of Allan Bérubé and David K. Johnson made it easy to weave gays and lesbians into narratives of the Second World War, the Cold War, and McCarthyism.[13] And there were richly textured community studies, such as Nan Alamilla Boyd's *Wide Open Town*, that integrated social life and political resistance into a seamless whole.[14]

But my signature course, the one I taught most frequently, was an introduction to LGBT issues with the title Sexuality and Community. I think of it as a kind of Queer 101. It served as an introduction to gay and lesbian life and issues, but because I am trained as a historian, I inevitably structured it so that the first half of the course covered recent history. We moved from the "worst time to be queer" in the 1950s; through Stonewall, gay liberation, and lesbian feminism; on to the AIDS epidemic of the 1980s and 1990s; and into the new century with its explosion of visibility and the mainstreaming of LGBT issues. Readings included novels, plays, memoirs, political writings, sociological studies, and primary sources ranging from newspapers to congressional testimony. Documentary films figured importantly as well. In the last part of the course, we focused on two or three contemporary issues, such as family and marriage; youth, schools, and sex education; and religion and same-sex love. Even here the research papers I assigned were historical. When we considered religion, for instance, websites such as www.religioustolerance.org and www.lgbtran.org provided a wealth of historical background on the shifting stance of religious communities toward same-sex love and on activists whose focus has been religion.

Although the overall structure of the course remained consistent, the classroom experience changed a lot across fourteen years, reflecting a generational shift. One change was that more students in a class of forty began to come out than did so in 2000, though it was still true that a clear majority of the class identified as heterosexual. In 2000, students still belonged to what I describe as the "pre-Ellen generation." Born between the mid-1970s and early 1980s, they had reached adolescence before the sea change in visibility that Ellen DeGeneres's coming out helped provoke in popular culture. The oppression experienced by gays and lesbians was readily understandable since it was still normative in the world in which they grew up. They also were old enough to have at least some ties to the spirit of the 1960s and 1970s and its social justice movements, so that protest and rebellion also were comprehensible. Later my students were both post-Ellen and post-9/11. They took "gay" for granted, their high schools often had gay-straight alliances, and they were likely to have a member of their extended families or a close friend who openly identified as gay, lesbian, bi, trans, or queer. For them the earlier decades covered by the course seemed unimaginable; they could hardly believe the oppression had been so overt and intense. At the same time, living post-9/11, they only knew an America at war, steeped in fear of terrorism and "the foreign" and, increasingly, enduring the insecurity of economic hard times. Social movements of the Left capable of effecting dramatic change require a leap of faith. It is not that these students were conservative. Quite the contrary: they yearned for social justice. But few had seen enough to know how to make it happen.

Although these shifts were significant and telling, as time passed students continued to share something with their predecessors that is relevant to my pedagogy. They entered the class knowing nothing about the topic at hand. Despite greater cultural and social visibility and a huge expansion of historical writing, with very few exceptions undergraduates had no knowledge of a queer past. Many went to Chicago's gay parade on the last Sunday in June, but they had no idea that the event commemorated an urban uprising in New York at the Stonewall Inn. They knew AIDS existed (more than a few had had family members who were living with AIDS or had died of it), but they knew nothing about the vast devastation it had caused in the eighties and nineties and the upsurge of militant activism it provoked. Their ignorance was not their fault. Rather, it was evidence that the queer past does not circulate widely in the everyday lives or formal education of Americans.

More than most courses I have taught, this one relied heavily on primary sources, which became increasingly accessible in the digital age. Students got a sense of the 1950s and 1960s through newspaper articles from the *Chicago Tribune* about the Cold War Lavender Scare as well as the bar raids and mass arrests that were commonplace. The language of perversion, deviance, and degeneration grabbed their attention. We looked at covers of lesbian pulp novels from those decades, and again the language—"strange," "twisted," "warped"—was instructive. Within this context, images of homophile demonstrators with their picket signs brought home the courage of these early activists, even as images of gay and lesbian liberationists from just a few years later dramatized the generational gulf that the radicalism of the 1960s produced. I peppered the course with documents from the Karla Jay and Allen Young anthologies of the 1970s, such as *Out of the Closets*, as well as manifestos and calls to action produced by AIDS activists in the 1980s. The protest art generated by AIDS was also powerful and informative; similarly, images of panels from the NAMES Project Memorial Quilt personalized the epidemic. I had students read both *Bowers v. Hardwick* (1986) and *Lawrence v. Texas* (2003), the legal cases that first confirmed the constitutionality of sodomy laws and then overturned them. The contrast in the outlook of the majority opinion that the intervening years had brought was compelling. The way Associate Justice Anthony M. Kennedy in the *Lawrence* decision mobilized history as a justification for overturning sodomy laws brought home to them in a powerful way the fact that history itself can be a tool for change.

To maintain my own interest and sanity, I played around with the readings from semester to semester, using some new things and then returning a semester or two later to some old favorites. But there are three things that I used in the course every time because the response was so uniformly powerful and pedagogically effective: Rita Mae Brown's *Rubyfruit Jungle* and the documentary films *The Times of Harvey Milk* and *Common Threads*.[15] Over many years of teaching, I easily had over a thousand students read *Rubyfruit Jungle*. If a dozen students were not captivated by it, that would be a lot. Queer students loved the feistiness, the "don't mess with me" attitude that saturates every page. Straight students, female and male, found themselves identifying with and cheering for a young working-class lesbian, something they had not experienced before. *The Times of Harvey Milk* was gripping from start to finish. It provoked laughter, tears, and especially rage—rage at the injustice of the assassination and the trial verdict and rage at the fact that they had never heard of Harvey Milk before. *Common Threads* brought home the tragic devastation of the early years of the AIDS epidemic and opened a window onto its politics. I never taught another course in which, reliably, tears were shed by a substantial number of students.

Much as I have cherished my decades of teaching, nothing has compared with this course. "Joy" and "happiness" wildly understate the response it provoked in me every time. It generated an endless array of unforgettable and memorable moments for me and, I know, for the students as well. Even though I taught what I knew best in this course, I steadily learned from the reactions of my students. For instance, when I first read *Rubyfruit Jungle* in 1974, to me it seemed to be a manifesto of liberation and freedom. And, over the years, many students responded in just the same way. Later more students commented that the novel ends with its heroine, Molly, still defiant and determined, to be sure, but also alone, on her own, without community and family to support her. The first time I showed the documentary *Chicks in White Satin*, the reaction of the class completely surprised me. A majority of students, male and female alike, were weeping during the wedding. Even as I remained disturbed by the prioritization of marriage by the organized gay and lesbian movement, this classroom experience gave me an insight into the emotional power of the marriage issue to humanize gay folks to heterosexuals.

Most of all, the course provided the satisfaction of knowing that virtually everything we covered was something my students had never encountered before. I loved their excitement, I loved their outrage, and I loved the way I saw their outlooks, whatever their identities, change over the course of a semester. If anyone is skeptical of the power of history and pedagogy to change hearts and minds, I can testify that the power is real.

At the same time, I would willingly forgo some of these pleasures in exchange for a group of students who would come to my LGBT classes because they want to know more than they already do. To have the Lavender Scare, the rise of gay liberation and lesbian feminism, the AIDS epidemic, and other such topics integrated into U.S. history survey courses would prepare them for deeper explorations in specialized courses like mine. And I am also willing to wager that teachers who put some of this material into their history courses will be pleased with the surprise and interest that LGBT history generates in the classroom.

### NOTES

1. Jonathan Ned Katz, *Gay American History: Lesbians and Gay Men in the U.S.A.* (New York: Thomas Y. Crowell, 1976).

2. Martin Duberman, *Black Mountain: An Exploration in Community* (Chicago: Northwestern University Press, 1972).

3. John D'Emilio, *Sexual Politics, Sexual Communities: The Making of a Homosexual Minority in the United States, 1940–1970* (Chicago: University of Chicago Press, 1983).

4. Katz, *Gay American History*; Karla Jay and Allen Young, eds., *Out of the Closets: Voices of Gay Liberation* (New York: Pyramid Books, 1972); Karla Jay and Allen Young, eds., *Lavender Culture* (New York: Jove Publications, 1978).

5. John D'Emilio and Estelle B. Freedman, *Intimate Matters: A History of Sexuality in America* (New York: Harper and Row, 1988; 3rd ed., Chicago: University of Chicago Press, 2012).

6. Carroll Smith-Rosenberg, "The Female World of Love and Ritual: Relations between Women in Nineteenth-Century America," *Signs: Journal of Women in Culture and Society* 1, no. 1 (1976): 1–29.

7. Jonathan Ned Katz, *Gay/Lesbian Almanac: A New Documentary* (New York: Harper and Row, 1983).

8. John S. Haller and Robin M. Haller, *The Physician and Sexuality in Victorian Society* (New York: Norton, 1977).

9. Martin Bauml Duberman, Martha Vicinus, and George Chauncey Jr., eds., *Hidden from History: Reclaiming the Gay and Lesbian Past* (New York: New American Library, 1989); Allan Bérubé, *Coming Out under Fire: The History of Gay Men and Women in World War Two* (New York: Free Press, 1990); Lillian Faderman, *Odd Girls and Twilight Lovers: A History of Lesbian Life in Twentieth-Century America* (New York: Columbia University Press, 1991).

10. Audre Lorde, *Zami: A New Spelling of My Name* (Watertown, MA: Persephone Press, 1982); Juanita Ramos, ed., *Compañeras: Latina Lesbians, an Anthology* (New York: Latina Lesbian History Project, 1987).

11. Lillian Faderman, *To Believe in Women: What Lesbians Have Done for America* (Boston: Houghton Mifflin, 1999).

12. Angela Y. Davis, *Blues Legacies and Black Feminism: Gertrude "Ma" Rainey, Bessie Smith, and Billie Holiday* (New York: Random House, 1998); Kevin J. Mumford, *Interzones: Black/White Sex Districts in Chicago and New York in the Early Twentieth Century* (New York: Columbia University Press, 1997).

13. Bérubé, *Coming Out under Fire*; David K. Johnson, *The Lavender Scare: The Cold War Persecution of Gays and Lesbians in the Federal Government* (Chicago: University of Chicago Press, 2004).

14. Nan Alamilla Boyd, *Wide Open Town: A History of Queer San Francisco to 1965* (Berkeley: University of California Press, 2003).

15. Rita Mae Brown, *Rubyfruit Jungle* (Plainfield, VT: Daughters, 1973).

# Putting Ideas into Practice

*High School Teachers Talk about*
*Incorporating the LGBT Past*

DANIEL HUREWITZ

In the spring of 2013, I spoke with nine high school history teachers who had begun incorporating LGBT history into what they teach. They came from a variety of backgrounds: half taught at public schools, half at private; some taught advanced placement (AP) U.S. history, some ran the International Baccalaureate (IB) course on the Americas; some offered more narrowly defined U.S.-focused seminars, some led classes specifically on LGBT history, and most taught a combination. Yet all had been breaking new ground in their schools and communities. And while most felt that their students and colleagues supported their efforts, they all faced challenges in bringing LGBT history into their schools. As a result, these nine teachers were full of insightful strategies and approaches that others could use. As I spoke with each of them, our conversations centered around a group of recurring issues: finding topics in the U.S. survey where LGBT content could be easily incorporated, building a framework of respect in the classroom and managing strong reactions, laying the groundwork with colleagues and administrators, and incorporating innovative strategies for bringing the material to life.

What follows are excerpts from our conversations. They happened in back-and-forth dialogues on the telephone, but I've woven them together here to show the points of consensus and the range of suggestions. The passages that follow are not formal in tone. Instead they are

Daniel Hurewitz

the voices of teachers at the cutting edge who were putting these ideas into practice.

### Choosing Units Where LGBT Content Can Be Included

Most of our conversations began with a discussion of topics within the survey that could be readily expanded with LGBT content. While almost all the teachers mentioned folding LGBT material into their units on 1960s civil rights struggles, many suggested an array of additional potential topics: nineteenth-century women's activism, the frontier West, the Harlem Renaissance and Jazz Age, the AIDS epidemic, and contemporary analogies. And they also recommended materials that can be used in the classroom, which are gathered at the end of this essay.

Before turning to the topics, the interview with Will Grant, who had been a teacher for twenty years, offers a framework for thinking about what material to include. Grant had taught for the previous five years at the Athenian School, a small, private, middle and high school about thirty-five miles east of San Francisco in Danville, California. At Athenian, he taught a ninth-grade world history and cultures course, as well as electives for eleventh and twelfth graders, including African history, Chinese history, and a course on LGBT history and culture. He also advised the school's Gay-Straight Alliance (GSA) and consulted with the Santa Cruz School District about ways to incorporate LGBT content into its schools.

### Grant

First, I think that it's really important to integrate this information into units that you're already teaching rather than doing stand-alone units on GLBTQ history. And a major reason for doing that is that it normalizes it. It makes it part of history rather than being something that we hang on the side of the "real story" of history. . . . By integrating it, we start to create the understanding that gay and lesbian history is not just history for gays and lesbians, it's everybody's history. The second thing is that I try to look for elements to teach where the history brings in important and relevant information to current issues going on in our culture and society. So that the kids get that this is history that matters to them because

Will Grant

this is what they are seeing in the media, these are the conversations they're having with their friends.

Also, I really consciously try to construct historical information that's going to confront current stereotypes and narrow perceptions, because I want to change the ground of the discussion that the kids are having. I didn't look for topics where someone's sexuality is a sidebar—somebody did all this stuff and they *happen* to be gay. Instead, I was looking for history where their sexual identity or their gender identity was one of the moving factors, one of the things that actually compelled them forward....

Finally, it's important to not just tell the story about oppression. Often the narrative that people have, even folks who are in support, is that the world was dark and oppressive for all homosexuals before the Stonewall riots. And then after the Stonewall riots there was the gay liberation movement, but then there was AIDS. And maybe only in the mid-1990s did things start to look up. And that's *not* the case in so many ways in U.S. history. So I think, especially for kids who do identify as GLBTQ or kids who are questioning, it's really important for them to get that there's a history of a coherent culture, and strong identity, and especially of resilience, and even a kind of celebration. And I think doing that— even for the kids who aren't questioning and are straight identified—creates a kind of opening, that there's a strong vibrant subculture that's always been around.

### Nineteenth-Century Women's Activism and the Frontier West

While most teachers readily identified LGBT content to incorporate into twentieth-century U.S. history, Grant also had two dynamic ideas about bringing LGBT history into the nineteenth century.

#### Grant

The suffrage movement is actually one of the best examples. Because the leadership of the suffrage movement [and other reform movements] in the 1800s ... many of them were known to be involved in Boston marriages, and there's strong evidence that many of them were lesbians. One of the readings that I've done pointed out that, in the 1800s, political activism for a married woman was very difficult because they were legally controlled by their husbands [and] could be prevented from being involved in these politics.... So a lot of the women who were involved in the suffrage movement were [people we might today call] lesbians, and many were women who had made the choice not to be involved in marriage, even though that was going to cost them enormously in terms of economic security, legal standing, and social standing. So what becomes clear is that their sexual identities actually created a situation where they had mental independence but took a massive hit in terms of their social security, and being placed outside of society. But then these were the women who had the freedom to mobilize and organize....

One of the things I do with cowboys is rethinking what's going on. Why would young men in their twenties leave the comfort of society to go live in a very rough area where the only thing they will have is the company of men? The dominant narrative is "Oh, these poor men, and how they lacked a woman's touch, and how there were a few women who would go out there *eventually* after things got settled." ...And then the other interpretation, that's backed with historical information from diaries and really interesting photos, is that what you actually had was a lot of young men who ... went out west to live among other men. [I bring in these] two amazing pictures of the cowboy stag dances [which show male cowboys dancing together]. And I use this again with the goal of changing their gender stereotypes. People chuckle at the idea of gay cowboys, but these were men who loved men, who loved masculine men, and if you loved masculine men and you wanted to be around men and out from under the eyes of Victorian society on the East Coast, then you headed out to the frontier and started a life where nobody was going to pry into your private life.

### Harlem Renaissance and the Jazz Age

Several teachers suggested the 1920s and Harlem Renaissance as good places to incorporate LGBT content, drawing on research done by George Chauncey, Eric Garber, and others. (See Red Vaughan Tremmel's essay in this volume for an expanded discussion of this topic.) Eric De Lora had been teaching for five years at Maybeck High School, a private, progressive, college preparatory school in Berkeley, California, with a strong reputation for diversity. Prior to that, he had taught at community colleges in Oregon and elsewhere in the Bay Area. De Lora's courses included music history, theater history, film history, social justice, and LGBT U.S. history. In his LGBT class, he said, students connected strongly with the Harlem Renaissance material.

#### De Lora

In discussing the Harlem Renaissance, we were able to talk about African American history and the connection to LGBT history. We talked about how the Harlem Renaissance developed separately from what was going on in the rest of

Eric-Richard De Lora

New York, how there was this other place, and so people would go to Harlem to have these other experiences, whether it was to listen to jazz or explore their sexuality.... And you can weave African American and LGBT history together easily. You can talk about Zora Neale Hurston and Langston Hughes and the others and say, "By the way, you've got some gays in there, you've got some lesbians." And the students then are, "Oh! Oh, really!"

This came up repeatedly in the class, that the kids would say, "I never knew that Langston Hughes was gay." "I never knew that James Baldwin was gay." These were names that, if they had read them at all, their sexual orientation was not discussed.... Students are surprised that there is a sexual side to these celebrities and artists that they have heard about, and the sexual side is not the standard heterosexual side.... And for the students that have those other sexualities, well, you need your role models and you want your list of top-ten gay or lesbian performers, so you feel like you've got some connection: "Hey, there's a few of my people like that who are famous and important!"

Nell Hirschmann-Levy repeatedly taught a course on LGBT U.S. history at Urban Academy High School, a small public school in Manhattan built around inquiry-based learning. In her course, one of the most successful discussions focused on the Hamilton Lodge Ball, an annual drag ball that took place in Harlem for much of the 1920s and 1930s,

Nell Hirschmann-Levy

and drew thousands of participants and spectators, both white and black, and gay, straight, and otherwise. Hirschmann-Levy and Grant both drew on George Chauncey's research in *Gay New York* to give students an LGBT angle on the Jazz Age.

### Hirschmann-Levy

The Hamilton Lodge Ball was very interesting to students! What did it mean that there was a space that people were so attracted to, and yet there also seemed to be a disgust for gay people at the same time in this era? How do you explain that? It was a huge gathering of gays and lesbians, but also thousands of heterosexuals attended the ball. So what explains their attendance? Was it just to make fun of them? Does that explain its popularity? . . . And we'd also discuss the fact that there was the participation of white people and black people. What were the race dynamics at the time, in the '20s and '30s, that played obviously into sexuality but also racism? That idea of slumming, of white people going into Harlem, my students see that dynamic now. And it adds to the discussion in a very rich way, where students could bring in their own lives and make analogies.

### Grant

I also talk about speakeasy culture, which the kids find interesting because it's a little bit risqué. The idea that speakeasies became these places of social mixture, and because people were already breaking the law, they start to break the social law, and you get social mixture, gender mixture, and class mixture—and people found that fascinating. I also talk about the Pansy Craze and Gene Malin. It's really fun to let the kids get immersed in it and play with the idea of a socially subversive, but not dangerous, movement of people who decided to push the boundaries. And that, as a result of their pushing, they were breaking down social oppression through entertainment and fun. They really get that at the level of rave culture and parties, and they think, "Wow, these instincts that I've got to be adventurous, maybe they can be socially powerful."

### 1960s Civil Rights and Social Movements

Even the teachers on the tightest AP schedules felt able to include LGBT content in their 1960s/civil rights units. They did it, though, in a range of ways and for varying amounts of class time. Some of the AP teachers, such as Robert King at Palisades Charter High School in Southern California, were only able to incorporate it into part of a single lecture on "other social movements." Sarah Strauss's school had stopped following the AP U.S. history curriculum for the first time that year, and she was able to devote a full class session to LGBT activism. Strauss, who had been a teacher for over fifteen years, worked in the upper school of the Packer Collegiate Institute, a small private school in Brooklyn, and she taught tenth-grade U.S. history, constitutional law, and criminal justice.

Robert King (photograph by Benjamin Bustamante)

Sarah Strauss (photograph by Sarah
Haimes)

### Strauss

This year, for one day, we took an article by Alex Ross that was in the *New Yorker*,
called, "Love on the March." My colleague and I edited it down so that it was not
too much for the kids to read at once. We had been talking about different social
movements—civil rights, the women's movement—and then we looked at LGBT
movements....We gave them this article to read, we had some guiding questions,
and we gave them some key terms to look for. And essentially what Ross does is
lay out a sort of popular history of LGBT movements over time, starting with the
nineteenth century and early twentieth century, then Daughters of Bilitis, Mattachine Society, and getting to gay rights, marriage, and HIV/AIDS. It's sort of a
summary version of LGBT rights history. It's certainly not perfect—it's fairly male
oriented, and there's lots of stuff that I didn't necessarily agree with. But several
of the kids came into class and said things like, "This is really interesting! I didn't
know any of this before." And that validates the risks I take with the curriculum. In
essence, I am saying to kids, "You know what? Here's this whole topic that you've
never been allowed to talk about before in a high school history class, and we're
going to talk about it."

Mark Buenzle had been teaching at the Brooklyn Friends School, an
independent Quaker school in Brooklyn, for twenty-five years, working

for the last eighteen in the high school. He taught studio art, art history, and the IB history course on the Americas; he also advised the GSA. Buenzle incorporated LGBT material into the middle section of the IB course, which focused on the black civil rights movement, the women's movement, and the struggle for LGBT equality, and while the bulk of the time was devoted to black civil rights, he spent three or four weeks on the women's and LGBT movements combined.

### Buenzle

I find [the documentary *After Stonewall*] terrific to use with kids. I present it in small sections, followed by discussion. I've also given them material on Supreme Court decisions and summaries of the decisions, starting with *Griswold v. Connecticut* and *Roe v. Wade*, and talking about the relationship to the Fourteenth Amendment and the right to privacy. And then moving into the cases that were more specifically LGBT related—like *Bowers v. Hardwick* and *Lawrence v. Texas*. Certainly that part of the course keeps evolving, because of what's happening now. [See the essay by Marc Stein in this volume for further discussion of teaching Supreme Court cases.] Current *New York Times* articles are helpful, and I've used *Making History* from Eric Marcus. I think some of its first-person accounts are good.

Mark Buenzle (photograph by Melissa Eder)

Finally, Kurt Dearie, who taught both the general U.S. survey and the AP survey at Carlsbad High School in Carlsbad, California, had a more elaborate project. Carlsbad High is a large public school in a fairly affluent community in Southern California.

### Dearie

The way that I organized the civil rights unit was to look at and compare the goals, strategies, and support for different civil rights movements. We look at LGBT, African Americans, women, Native Americans, Mexican and Mexican Americans, Americans with disabilities, Japanese and Japanese Americans. I feed them documents and videos, and, using their textbook, we create this huge matrix: down one side of the page, all these movements are listed; across the top of the page—goals, strategies, support. . . . And ultimately it culminates with them writing a paper arguing what they believe are the most effective strategies for promoting civil rights.

When I structured this question of looking for effective strategies, I framed it as "either for or in opposition to." In part what I was doing there was, one, you

Kurt Dearie

always need to look at both sides, because when you're looking at strategies, everybody is always trying to adapt to the other side. But also it was my way of trying to make sure that, if I got calls from parents who want to argue that I'm promoting the gay lifestyle or forcing kids to believe a certain way, that was my out: "No, we're looking at both sides. We're not taking a moral side. We're looking at it through this objective lens." Whether that's the right or wrong thing to do, I do it so I can be ready to defend myself. . . . But when they write their research papers where they are comparing various movements, many students will choose to look specifically at gay rights.

## AIDS Epidemic

For many teachers, the AIDS epidemic was the other topic they felt they could easily fit into their survey, and some felt that it was mandatory. Will Grant and Eric De Lora spoke ardently on this theme. (For additional discussion of teaching about AIDS, see the essay by Jennifer Brier in this volume.)

### De Lora

You *have* to talk about AIDS and what happened during the epidemic, particularly in the 1980s. You're going to talk about Reagan, and you're going to talk about the Berlin Wall coming down, and all that stuff. To not talk about what happened in the first ten to twelve years of the AIDS epidemic is to not really teach what happened in the history of this country.

### Grant

Here's my framing. The dominant narrative is that AIDS was something that was incubated in the gay community and then spread because of the immoral lifestyle of gay men in the 1980s. The counter-narrative that I give [my students] is that AIDS was something that had a three- to four-year incubation period, that it was spread before anybody knew it, and then it was the political organizing among the gay men's communities, supported by the lesbians, that forced the largest, fastest public health reaction in American history. They created whole new models of medical care, they forced safe sex onto the agenda for the nation and the entire world, and they actually stopped the spread of the disease as far as it could have gone.

I use the film *We Were Here* [a documentary about the impact of the early years of the epidemic in San Francisco]. It so beautifully personalizes the story, and it tells the story of that public health reaction....And the thing about the film is that it's so devastating emotionally, and so powerful for the kids to watch. Whatever leftover lingering stereotypes they've got I think just get blown away by it.

De Lora concurred about the power of that film, suggesting that a teacher could easily show twenty minutes of it, or of *And the Band Played On*, the docudrama based on the Randy Shilts book, from which he had also assigned selections.

### De Lora

Shilts was a journalist for the *San Francisco Chronicle*, and the book came out of his reporting on what was going on. It's very much taking Reagan to task, and the CDC [Centers for Disease Control] ... in terms of where's the blame, and who are the guilty parties. And I used that until *We Were Here* came out, which is much more personal in terms of, here's what was happening to us as individuals.

### Grant

One year I also did a role-play. The idea was that we are a local community AIDS task force in the mid-1980s. I create different social roles. I've got the straight public health official. I've got the mainstream AIDS activist who's focused on mainstream acceptance. I've got the Queer Nation and the ACT UP contingent. I've got straight folks whose families have been impacted by AIDS. So I create all of these different roles for them. And then they have a debate over the right response to AIDS. It's set at a time when the scientific information was available, but the public perception was very distorted about how the disease is spread and what it means. And what I do is that I have a set of lots in front of me, and the activity runs about half an hour. Every couple of minutes, I pull a number out of the bowl, and that person dies of AIDS, and that person has to leave the simulation and just watch what's happening. The kids said it was one of the most effective things we did all year. Because by the time the fourth or fifth person disappears, the kids all said that they started to get this sense of intensity and panic, and the emotional sense of what was going on.

### *Contemporary Analogies*

A final thought about inclusion was presented by Kurt Dearie. Dearie found multiple ways to make connections to LGBT issues throughout his U.S. surveys without always carving out a moment to discuss "LGBT history." Because he believed that "you always have to make a past-to-present connection" with students, he regularly used analogies to contemporary issues to explain historical material to his students. He continually pointed to current struggles around race, class, gender, *and* sexual orientation as ways to illuminate issues from the past.

#### Dearie

For instance, early on in my class, we deal with the Constitution. So there, when we talk about federalism, we talk about gay marriage and issues of federalism. But also for separation of powers, the Fourteenth Amendment, equal protection under the law, checks and balances—I'm always using LGBT rights as examples of those. I do it because it's ongoing: kids can see it, you turn on the news at night, this is what's going on. So it's actually been very helpful [as a way to explain the Constitution].

Similarly, in my AP course, when we look at Seneca Falls, I really like there to bring up the issue of gender and connect the role that gender played in that type of society with the role of gender today—specifically if we look at the issues of transgender people today. I can make the connection to the issue of gender as a contemporary issue that still causes trouble, and that we're still trying to deal with. Fundamentally, wherever it comes up in that general survey course where I can see connections, I make them with students.

### Building a Framework of Respect and Managing Strong Student Reactions

I regularly asked the teachers if they felt worried about bringing this content into their classes and how they made it work. Most indicated that it was important to have ground rules for the students in a course that contained potentially controversial material. For some teachers, this was standard practice at their schools; for others it was something that they added because of the LGBT content. But they emphasized that, with those rules in place, their classrooms became much safer spaces. Michelle Berry, for instance, taught at St. Gregory

College Prep, a small, nonreligious, independent school in Tucson, Arizona. She taught the AP U.S. history survey for tenth graders, narrower electives for eleventh and twelfth graders on the American West and the United States from the Second World War to the 1980s, and the AP U.S. government class. She underscored the work she did with her students at the beginning of each term.

### Berry

Part of the key is just laying the groundwork in the very beginning of every course. "We're going to talk about new ideas, things maybe we've never thought about, that might be very foreign to our own values system or our own way of living our lives and how we think about ourselves. And we have to be open to listening and hearing about those ideas, not necessarily agreeing with them. And then also to have a great deal of ability to have a sense of humor about stuff."

We do pretty profound work creating our class norms, which we spend the first entire two classes of every semester doing. That includes how we're going to enter into civil dialogue with each other. We establish processes for, if things get heated or uncomfortable, what are the processes that we are going to go through as a learning community to work ourselves out of that. So if someone says something incredibly offensive to somebody else, we have something called the "ouch rule." The ouch rule is when anyone in the room thinks that what has been said

Michelle K. Berry

61

would perhaps be read as hurtful by anybody, whether they're in the room or not, you can say, "Ouch." Then the person who said "Ouch" and the person who made the offending remark are totally off the hook. They don't need to say a word after that. And then I facilitate a conversation about why what has been said could be offensive, hurtful, or inflammatory in a negative way.

Mark Rentflejs taught at Forsyth Satellite Academy, a small public high school in New York City designed for students who had failed or dropped out of their original high schools. According to him, most of his students read at the sixth-grade level. He was principally a foreign language teacher, but he regularly augmented the history department's offerings and had recently been invited by the school to teach a course divided between the history of the First World War and U.S. LGBT history. Like Berry, Rentflejs said that he did "a lot of groundwork in the first couple of days" about how "we need to be appropriate" and "what it means to be offensive." That work paid off across the rest of the semester.

### Rentflejs

I can only remember a couple of times having to say, "That wording was kind of offensive: can you reword that?" And they did; they found another way to do it.

Mark Rentflejs

And then once I modeled that a couple of times, they really self-corrected often. Or other students would say, "That was kind of mean." "OK, I'm sorry," and they would say it a different way.

⁓

Like many others, Eric De Lora described the ground rules that were present in all the classes at his school. But rather than emphasizing how the rules established limits on class discussion, he stressed the value of creating an atmosphere where students could freely express their range of reactions.

### De Lora

It really is about being open to their questions and their comments. . . . Because we're a seminar-style school, as teachers we're very comfortable saying to a student, "What did you think about that?" And we're also prepared for a student to say, "Here's what I thought about it: it was nuts!" or "It was goofy!" or "I really hated it!" The follow up question is "Why?," and that's where the conversation starts. Just trying to be really open to their questions, that was the best choice that I made, because they all came with dozens of questions. . . . As a teacher, I'm not afraid to say, "I don't know." I think that's a valid response. And coupled with that you say, "Let's go find the answer." Then it becomes a joint exploration that we're doing.

⁓

Uniquely, Will Grant saw no need for special class preparation to talk about LGBT content. He described his approach to me in discussing how he incorporated LGBT content into his ninth-grade world cultures course.

### Grant

I just start talking about it in the midst of a lecture, and actually I don't give the kids any notice. What I do is when we're studying ancient Greece, and we're talking about different elements of the society, without breaking my stride at all, I start talking about the fact that homosexuality was part and parcel of Greek society, that there were significant elements that could be equivalent to civil unions that were called "collateral adoptions." And the reason I started doing that was that I wanted to normalize it. I wanted to make homosexuality a part of history, just as when I talk about marriage and gender relationships in Greek society. . . . What I find is that there is a little bit of a blip in the class, in terms of the energy of the students, when I say that, and then they simply keep taking notes. And eventually one of them will get up the nerve to ask a question about it.

There's a lot of concern among teachers about teaching [this material to] younger students. But what we've got to remember is that these kids are totally immersed in the media world, and they are very familiar with homosexuality. There are gay characters on television; they are all on the Internet, there's stuff on Facebook. Where maybe in our generation a teacher teaching on homosexual history would have been introducing the topic, we're not introducing anything to these kids. All we're doing is normalizing it and indicating that it had a place in history.

⟶

Even the best ground rules, however, cannot stop students from having strong reactions, asking uncomfortable questions, or even making the occasional hostile comment. Researchers have underscored that teachers often feel overwhelmed at the idea of introducing discussions of sexuality, let alone homosexuality, into their classrooms. Their fears circulate around their ability to manage the discussions that will ensue, the possibility of needing to confront homophobic remarks, and the ways they will feel vulnerable as a result. Because of that, I repeatedly asked the teachers if there were homophobic outbursts in their classes and what they did about them. For instance, I asked Mark Rentflejs if there were declarations in his LGBT history class like "I don't think gay people should be allowed to get married!"

### Rentflejs

Yes, of course! But most of the time it was the students who would challenge each other's views. . . . And I would totally validate the students' views. "I don't think gay people should get married!" "OK, why not?" I would say. And I would let them explain that. And then I would say, "OK, well, imagine this scenario. How would you feel about that? Or how about this scenario?" Based on whatever argument they were making, whether it be religious or constitutional, I would lay out other options to help them see where their line of logic would go—and if their argument was a consistent argument or a prejudice. But I always invited them to argue and said, "I'm not going to take it personally, because as a teacher it's my job to make you think."

⌒

Kurt Dearie said his corrections were usually around students' tone, not content, and he had a clear response ready for someone shouting out something inappropriate.

### Dearie

I'd say, "You're certainly entitled to have whatever beliefs you want, in support of gay rights or against gay rights. But we're not going to shout out any kind of homophobic remarks, or other remarks, because that's not appropriate behavior that we're going to show in my classroom." So I steer that towards behavior. Because behavior is what I can control, and what the law allows me to control, and what I expect to have control over in my classroom. And if they use certain words, I also explain why these are inappropriate words, and why they can be hurtful, and that there are lots of words that can be hurtful to a lot of people, and we're not going to use *any* of them.

⌒

But Dearie, who also helped found the GSA at Carlsbad High, stressed the importance of the teacher responding to whatever was said and not ignoring it.

### Dearie

Everybody in class is going to be waiting to see what you do, and you better deal with it. Because one of the things that I discovered when I started working with my GSA students is how many teachers seemed to be deaf, dumb, and blind: they are hearing all of these words in their classroom, and they are pretending that they don't. And the signal that they are giving the students is that this is perfectly acceptable. But as soon as the teacher intervenes, and intervenes consistently, with the right tone and education, it starts: students adapt, and they change their behavior.

There is, right now, a huge negativity. We have all these LGBT students sitting in classrooms wondering if it's safe in here. And as soon as they hear a teacher who doesn't intervene in a remark like that, well, then they know it's not a safe place. And if you're going to change things, as a teacher, you have to first create a safe place, and that's really important. If you're going to bring in any of this material, you need to create a safe environment for all students in your classroom.

⌒

Michelle Berry, who embraced seminar-style teaching at St. Gregory, also stressed that it should not come as a surprise if something controversial is said.

### Berry

You have to recognize that it's going to happen. That's the most important thing: to recognize that these *are* controversial issues for these kids, these are things that they've never talked about before [in a classroom]. . . . And you have to meet these students where they are, and recognize that that might happen. But there's a way to get around that in a very civil, kind way. And we have to create a learning community that is full of trust and full of respect, and therefore everybody has to feel safe, including the most conservative student who thinks that homosexuality is a sin against God. They have to feel safe also. Finding that balance is not easy, and it is scary. But it's well worth doing, because inevitably what you see is students meeting each other halfway, with lots of care and consideration for one another, and you really watch students become beautiful discussants in the course of all of this.

### Grant

In terms of the homophobic comment, I think it's important for the kids to be able to disagree with what I'm saying, but to show that they can do it in a way that isn't homophobic. I think giving the kids that permission is important. So I can say, "Look, if you want to debate whether or not our society is ready for gay marriage, let's totally have that debate. But the one thing that I need to have is that there is no question about the full humanness of everybody involved on both sides. The question as to whether or not anybody should have the right to marriage, we can discuss that. But you can't question the humanness of the people on the other side of this debate. Other than that, I'm really interested in having this debate."

66

One of the things I found was that the kids were terrified of being labeled as homophobic if they wanted to raise questions like "Well, didn't gay men kind of spread AIDS?" So it's important to let them feel like they can ask that question. What I've found is that it also, de facto, shows the kids what I mean by homophobia and what the problem is, if they're saying that somebody isn't fully human.

⟳

**Will Grant also felt clear about how to keep discussions of sex out of his classroom.**

### Grant

I call it the "bright line." I explain it to the kids that what I'm talking about is sexual identity, and not sex, and sexual identity is the way in which their sexuality impacts a person's psychology, politics, their standing in the community, their political rights—that's sexual identity. Sex is something else, and I say, "That's for health class, not for this class." And I say, "We don't need to talk about sex in order to talk about sexual identity." And somebody inevitably says, "Well isn't it impossible to talk about homosexuality without talking about sex?" And I say, "No. We teach history all the time, and sexuality is a part of it, but it's just normative because it's heterosexuality, and we don't talk about sex." And the example I give is Queen Victoria and Albert—how their children became the ruling family of Europe, and World War I in many ways was a family feud between all these cousins who were all related. So their sexuality, their normative heterosexuality, was clearly a part of that history, but we never stop and talk about sex. You don't need to.

## Laying the Groundwork with Colleagues

With the exception of one teacher, all the others emphasized the importance of talking over this venture with colleagues—both fellow teachers and administrators—before beginning. Almost all suggested clearing the new content with the principal, head of school, or department chair. But most emphasized these conversations as a way to build support and community within the school. Sarah Strauss, for instance, emphasized the value of creating "a support structure" within the school by engaging in multiple conversations about the curriculum in advance of doing the teaching.

### Strauss

Talk to people, teachers, administrators within the school who are supportive. Try to let them know "This is what I'm doing" and try to get them onboard. Have an open meeting with parents. I think it really depends on your community, in terms of what is necessary. But at least then you're setting up the conversation about what's going to take place, and this is why. . . . And you can also say that there is not just a "teaching history" reason for doing this, but there are other reasons—like this is a way of fighting bullying. In other words, there is an expansive reason for doing it that is about kids.

Will Grant's department chair at Athenian had approached *him* about teaching a course on LGBT history and culture in the wake of the passage of the anti-same-sex-marriage Proposition 8 in California in 2008. Grant followed the kind of advice Strauss offered before he began teaching in order to build consensus among his colleagues.

### Grant

Once we got approval from the administration to create the course, I did a lot of work at our school. I had several meetings with the Gay-Straight Alliance, with teachers, with my department head, to talk about the course and the idea of teaching it. And I asked folks at the school, "What do you feel comfortable with me teaching, what do you not want me to go into, and what are the gray areas? Let's create a process as I set up the course because I want you to know I am not flying off in a direction you don't want me to. I recognize as a school that we are taking a step forward with this course, and I want everybody to be really comfortable with the content of the course."

In some communities and some schools, cultivating that kind of support can be very challenging work, to say the least. About six years before Kurt Dearie started including LGBT content in his U.S. history classes—both the general one and the AP—he joined a group of students to establish a GSA at Carlsbad High. Dearie grew up in Carlsbad and described it as a "very conservative Christian community" that voted overwhelmingly in favor of banning same-sex marriage. When the students' efforts were initially blocked by the school, the group had to file a lawsuit to force the school board to allow the GSA to operate, and Dearie himself met with various forms of retribution: vandalism, being called a "pedophile," and having the school targeted by the Concerned Women for America. Dearie, who is a straight married father, was very proud of how Carlsbad High changed after the GSA started. But because of his experiences, he thought it was very important that teachers understand clearly what legal support (in states such as California) or curricular support they have for incorporating LGBT content. And Dearie, who had also done teacher training for AVID (Advancement Via Individual Determination, a program that guides kids from lower socioeconomic groups into college), emphasized that teachers must rely on those frameworks as they present their proposals to school administrators.

### Dearie

Any teacher that is going down this road has to deal with educating the administration, other teachers, and the community. . . . In California we have very specific laws. So I explain that we're going to look at LGBT rights and the contributions of LGBT people, because that's what the law requires us to do. . . . For our administrators, that really freed them. Literally, when they get calls or complaints from the community—which they have in the last ten years—they can simply say, "We're following the law, but I appreciate your concerns." That's all that needs to be said, and then move on.

But also, when introducing [this content] into the classroom, you have to tie it to your state curricular framework or to the AP and their new framework. You've got to legitimize why you're doing what you're doing in the classroom: that it is educational, that it is part of our history, that the framework requires it. Outside California, if I were introducing [LGBT content], it would be in terms of the things that are identified in that state's framework—and which always include civil rights. Because when you're connecting ideas of civil rights—whether it is goals, strategies, support, etc.—and you connect past to present, gay rights are always there. You can't ignore the one civil rights movement which is in front of your face and going on at the time!

That's something that's really critical to any teacher in bringing this material into the classroom: that they be ready to defend it. Because they will have to defend it, and you can't defend it based on people's beliefs or your own beliefs.

You have to have some legal grounding or some educational grounding. I think that's a critical lesson that has really served me well over the years.

⁓

Inevitably, Sarah Strauss suggested, there will be questions raised about what is being dropped from the syllabus in order to include the new material. Given that, Strauss underscored that teachers should also feel okay about taking small steps first.

### Strauss

In spite of the rise of social history over the last half century, most people still believe that the "important" topics are traditional political, economic, and military issues. If you choose to focus on sexuality, race, and/or gender, you will necessarily "neglect" the more canonical curricula. And if teachers are in a situation where they have standardized tests, APs or state-mandated curricula, that's a lot to push back against. So the initial focus can just be on where can you find those places to create little wedges to start important conversations about LGBT issues.

I go back to the idea that just using the words *gay*, *lesbian*, or *transgender* in a positive or neutral way is a big thing. Because in some ways it's about exposing students to the information, and on another level it's about saying to kids, "You know what? If this is you, if you think this is you, if this is someone you love, it's okay." To me, honestly, it's as much about *that* as the actual content.

## Engaging Classroom Strategies

Teachers offered a variety of additional strategies for engaging students with LGBT history, including the use of dynamic sources, guest speakers, field trips, and, surprisingly enough, tests.

In Michelle Berry's post-1945 course, gender and sexuality was one of the three major themes she explored with students, and she saw exciting primary sources and selected secondary texts as essential to that work.

### Berry

For me the sources are what unite us all in common conversation, even scholarly articles that are appropriate with that particular age group. For instance, I assign excerpts from Chauncey's *Gay New York*. . . . We actually read some of the Kinsey report—that always gets them going and is a lot of fun. I pick some excerpts from a terrific book on Pachucas in LA in the '40s. Of course we read big excerpts from Betty Friedan. . . . Then we've got this beautiful document from which we're working, and from there we can have bigger conversations. "Well, how does this apply to today? . . . Are we in a Kinsey moment or in a 1950s moment or what historical moment?" And if you have that common reading—be it one primary source or an academic article—then you can begin to have these bigger conversations. And that's just enough for high school students to get them going, to get them excited, to get them really engaged. Because then they're like, "Holy crap! This is so new!" Just giving them that little bit gets them fired up, because it is so new for them—and it's so not the Bank War or Andrew Jackson!

## Nell Hirschmann-Levy loved having speakers engage with her students.

### Hirschmann-Levy

I always incorporated speakers into the class. That was a pretty crucial part of the course, being able to really talk to people. . . . One of the best parts of the course for the students was when we would go to the home of this woman, Joan, who was ninety-six and lived through most of the eras that we were talking about. She talked about being a Trotskyist, about working in a factory in Detroit for the first time during World War II, about the first time she took off her skirt and wore pants. She had a front marriage, had a kid. She was really open with the students and talked about her life in an incredible way! And for the students to see someone in the flesh talking about experiences that they had read about in Chauncey and [Lillian] Faderman just made the texts and the history come alive. You should have seen their faces: it was like they were watching a movie!

## Eric De Lora said that his Berkeley students were electrified by a Saturday field trip into San Francisco to see some of the history they had been discussing.

### De Lora

There's a visceral reaction. It makes it real for kids. Maybe in the age of Internet technology and social media, we don't have real conversations and real experiences: we have cyber-conversations and experiences. Getting out of your head and into the practical, it helps you understand that it was real, that it happened, that these people actually existed. And that's what kids respond to. . . . Getting out there really connects them to the real world.

Likewise, Hirschmann-Levy described taking her New York City students to a few of the sites described in Chauncey's book and my book of LGBT history walking tours, *Stepping Out*.

### Hirschmann-Levy

Those walks always helped ground the text in real experiences. The students got, in some ways, to experience the areas through the lens of the twenty-first century, and it always kind of made it come alive. . . . Students would go up and touch the brick, and say, "Oooh, I'm touching something from 1900!" They would talk about how different the neighborhood was. They would say, "I can't believe we're standing in front of a clothing store when it used to be" X, Y, or Z. They start to feel that there was a real history to this neighborhood, and that it's changed dramatically. . . . It allows the students to feel that the history is not just on paper, but that it's more alive than that.

Finally, several teachers talked about testing as a way to signify the importance of this material. For instance, Dearie pointed out that the College Board would begin testing on LGBT history in the 2014 AP curriculum—which would encourage more teachers to incorporate the material. Buenzle hoped that the IB might do the same, noting that if it did "it would . . . allow us to explore this content in more depth." But even without those external tests, Grant emphasized that any teacher's own tests can help underscore the significance of LGBT history.

### Grant

It's important to test the kids on this information, and to make a test question or an essay question where the kids can weave this knowledge into a larger discussion. So if you ask a question about the social impacts of World War II, then one of the things that should be in the kids' complete answers is the creation of strong gay communities along the coasts because of demobilization. It's important for teachers to think not just about the *presentation* but the *assessment* of it as well, and to angle the questions towards showing how these were social movements that impacted U.S. history.

## Concluding Thoughts

Michelle Berry, Mark Buenzle, Eric De Lora, Kurt Dearie, Will Grant, Nell Hirschmann-Levy, Robert King, Mark Rentflejs, and Sarah Strauss changed the way history was being learned at their schools and understood in their communities, and as a result, they shifted the horizons of their students. Some did it with a whole course, some with a class theme, some with a mini-lecture. But all of them courageously altered the landscape around them.

Beyond the insights they shared for this essay, three additional things became increasingly clear to me over the course of these conversations. One is the power of a single teacher to change the whole culture of a school. That was made apparent by the way Kurt Dearie's decision to help start a GSA radically transformed Carlsbad High School into a place where GSA students regularly conducted sensitivity trainings with the faculty about LGBT issues. Similarly, it became clear to me that eleventh graders at Brooklyn Friends School learned LGBT history as part of their standard curriculum simply because Mark Buenzle started incorporating that material into his social movements elective course several years earlier. These teachers' individual actions made a tremendous difference.

Second, even the smallest effort can have a large impact. At Palisades Charter High School in Southern California, Robert King included LGBT content merely as *a part* of just *one day's* lecture in his AP U.S. history class, the day he focused on "the other civil rights movements." That was all he had time to do. Nonetheless, that lecture proved to be transformative. He explained, "We were discussing the Stonewall Inn, and I had mentioned the documentary [*Stonewall Uprising*], and I was doing the best I could do, relating what the story was. And Jack Davis raised his hand and, at that moment, came out to the entire class." In an essay published later, Davis wrote that King had been his "favorite teacher" and at the time he had been "looking for a way to come out to everyone." "When a slide popped up that mentioned Stonewall and that many people were coming out at this time, I shot up my hand and said, 'I think I'll take this opportunity to come out, and say that I'm gay.'"[1] King told me that when Davis came out, "the reaction of the entire class was a round of applause. The kids just spontaneously got up out their seats and hugged him. It was truly an amazing experience." For Davis "that history class may have been the most defining moment of my coming out"; running out the classroom door afterward, "the weight of the world seemingly lifted from my shoulders . . . and I was ecstatic." That was the impact of a single mini-lecture, and for King as well, that day was "a highlight of a twenty-three-year career in teaching."

Third, as King's comment implies, taking these steps, even when daunting or difficult, can also profoundly shift the classroom experience for *teachers* themselves. Sarah Strauss, for instance, made clear that introducing this kind of new material felt risky. But when students entered her class exclaiming, "This was a really interesting article! I never knew this stuff!" she felt reassured. In part, she thought, "they appreciate that I'm taking a risk." But more important, for Strauss herself, "I would say that some of *my* most satisfying or meaningful experiences as a teacher are interconnected to this sort of risk-taking."

Interestingly, Kurt Dearie faced the hardest challenges in doing this work, and yet he also expressed the strongest sense of gratification about it for himself: "You know, you go into education to help kids. And nowhere in my professional career or my personal life have I been able to see the effect of good work as clearly. As teachers we hope that we make change, but I can really see it right in front of me with my own students. It's very rewarding work, and the more you do, the better things are, and that really rewards you. So it's become a passion for me. You can see that it's so needed, and that it really makes change."

These teachers all shared Dearie's passion to help kids, to educate them, and to make change. What made them extraordinary was that every day they were taking concrete steps to achieve those goals. And while I suspect that many of them had never been "interviewed" before about their teaching, I found each of their words and actions inspiring. Their thoughtfulness, their courage, and their insights all impressed me. It was clear to me that they were all working to transform their classes and schools and communities by their efforts. And they all proved generous and even eager to have their experiences shared with other teachers—so that other teachers could begin to imagine how the

LGBT past can become part of the shared past we all teach in our schools.

NOTE

1. Jack Davis, "Gay High School Swim Captain Makes a Splash Standing Up for Rights," *Outsports*, April 24, 2013, http://www.outsports.com/2013 /4/24/4262084/gay-high-school-swim-captain-jack-davis-makes-splash-standing-up-for-rights, accessed July 22, 2013.

OVERVIEWS OF LGBT HISTORY

Alsenas, Linas. *Gay America: Struggle for Equality*. New York: Amulet, 2008. Will Grant recommended this book as a survey pitched at the high school level: "It's a great read. He starts every chapter with individual stories, tons of pictures, and the students *loved* it. It's a fantastic resource."

Bronski, Michael. *A Queer History of the United States*. Boston: Beacon, 2012.

Eaklor, Vicki. *Queer America: A People's GLBT History of the United States*. New York: New Press, 2011.

Faderman, Lillian. *Odd Girls and Twilight Lovers: A History of Lesbian Life in Twentieth-Century America*. New York: Penguin, 1991.

Miller, Neil. *Out of the Past: Gay and Lesbian History from 1869 to the Present*. New York: Vintage, 1995. Eric De Lora recommended this work for its accessible "journalistic style," inclusion of primary sources, and extensive bibliography.

Peiss, Kathy, ed. *Major Problems in the History of American Sexuality*. New York: Houghton Mifflin, 2001. Michelle Berry recommended this text for its valuable primary sources.

Rupp, Leila. *A Desired Past: A Short History of Same-Sex Love in America*. Chicago: University of Chicago, 1999.

TEXTS AND FILMS FOR SPECIFIC TOPICS

Lesbians among Women Activists

Brownworth, Victoria. "Lesbians and Social Justice." *Curve*, July 2010, http:// www.curvemag.com/Curve-Magazine/Web-Articles-2010/Lesbians-and-Social-Justice/.

Harlem Renaissance

*Brother to Brother*. Dir. Rodney Evans. Wolfe Video, 2004. DVD, 2005. Eric De Lora recommended this feature film about a gay teen who meets an artist from the Harlem Renaissance.

Chauncey, George. *Gay New York: Gender, Urban Culture, and the Making of the Gay Male World, 1890–1930.* New York: Basic Books, 1994.

Garber, Eric. "A Spectacle in Color: The Lesbian and Gay Subculture of Jazz Age Harlem." In *Hidden from History: Reclaiming the Gay and Lesbian Past*, edited by Martin Bauml Duberman, Martha Vicinus, and George Chauncey Jr. New York: Penguin, 1991.

## LGBT Activism

*After Stonewall.* Dir. John Scagliotti. First Run Features, 1999. DVD, 2005. Focuses on LGBT activism from 1969 to 1999.

*Before Stonewall.* Dir. Greta Schiller. First Run Features, 1984. DVD, 2004. Portrays pre-Stonewall activism.

Duberman, Martin. *Stonewall.* New York: Dutton, 1993. Mark Rentflejs recommended this text and its first-person accounts as accessible, even for students with low reading ability.

Marcus, Eric. *Making History: The Struggle for Gay and Lesbian Equal Rights, 1945–1990, an Oral History.* New York: HarperCollins, 1992. Marcus updated and reformatted this book in 2002 as *Making Gay History: The Half-Century Fight for Lesbian and Gay Equal Rights* (New York, HarperCollins, 2002). Mark Buenzle recommended these oral history interviews as a dynamic source for students.

*Milk.* Dir. Gus Van Sant. Universal, 2008. DVD, 2009. Eric De Lora recommended this feature film about the career of slain San Francisco supervisor Harvey Milk, portrayed by Sean Penn.

Ross, Alex. "Love on the March." *New Yorker*, November 12, 2012. Sarah Strauss recommended this article as a brief overview of LGBT activism.

*Stonewall Uprising.* Dir. Kate Davis and David Heilbroner. PBS, 2010. DVD, 2011. Public television documentary focused on the Stonewall riots.

## HIV/AIDS

*And the Band Played On.* Dir. Roger Spottiswode. HBO, 1993. DVD, 2001. Eric De Lora used this television docudrama based on Randy Shilts's book.

Shilts, Randy. *And the Band Played On: Politics, People, and the AIDS Epidemic.* New York: St. Martin's, 1987. Eric De Lora used selected chapters from this account of the epidemic.

*United in Anger.* Dir. Jim Hubbard. Film Collaborative, 2012. DVD, 2013. Sarah Strauss screened parts of this documentary, which focuses on the organization ACT UP.

*We Were Here.* Dir. David Weissman. New Video, 2011. DVD, 2011. Both Will Grant and Eric De Lora recommended this emotionally powerful documentary about San Francisco in the early AIDS years.

# Questions, Not Test Answers

*Teaching LGBT History in Public Schools*

EMILY K. HOBSON and FELICIA T. PEREZ

In 2011 a coalition of activists, advocates, and politicians succeeded in passing California's Fair, Accurate, Inclusive, and Responsible (FAIR) Education Act (SB 48). Among other directives, SB 48 requires the state to incorporate the "contributions of lesbian, gay, bisexual, and transgender (LGBT) Americans" in K-12 social studies instruction and textbooks.[1] The individuals and groups that worked to pass this legislation—including the Gay-Straight Alliance (GSA) Network; Gay, Lesbian, and Straight Education Network (GLSEN); Equality California; National Center for Lesbian Rights; state senator Mark Leno; and State Assembly member Tom Ammiano—persistently framed it as a student safety measure. They called for a "welcoming learning environment" and defined curricular inclusion as key to the emotional well-being and academic success of LGBT and questioning students. These messages were not only well founded but also politically savvy, as they mobilized concern about harassment, dropouts, and suicides while forestalling questions about precisely what material the FAIR Education Act would require schools to address.

We were thrilled by the passage of the FAIR Education Act but struck by the challenges of implementing LGBT history in public schools in any state. Some of these challenges were predictable: the reactions of conservative colleagues, administrators, and parents. Yet even teachers committed to LGBT history encounter obstacles in developing lesson plans, finding course materials and funds to pay for them, and carving out classroom time. To mobilize support, convince themselves that the effort is worth it, and teach the subject well, teachers need to be able to see LGBT history as more than just another item in a long list of curricular requirements. Our experiences in teaching and organizing for progressive school change tell us that bringing the queer past into the curriculum requires skills beyond intervening against homophobia and justifications beyond student safety. We must explain the political and pedagogical value of LGBT history in terms that respond to the fundamental problems in education today.

Above all else, public school teachers face classrooms saturated with standardized testing. The number of tests and the time spent on them expand every year, and more and more tests carry "high-stakes" consequences for school funding and curriculum, teacher assessment and working conditions, and student retention. Supporters of testing claim victory because scores are going up. But growing numbers of educators argue that students are becoming expert test takers while losing out on skills of critical thinking and independent analysis, including reading and writing.

Our approach to LGBT history responds directly to this problem. We argue that teaching the queer past offers a powerful means of energizing the social studies curriculum and pushing back against the drive toward standardized testing in schools. This is because LGBT history operates not only as content but also as method. It engages students as a "current" topic yet also pushes them to ask creative, critical questions about the past—the kinds of questions we want them to use in approaching all aspects of history. Thinking about LGBT history as a method can help teachers think both practically and strategically about how to incorporate the subject. It may also help faculty at state universities and colleges—who train the majority of K-12 educators—make a stronger case for hiring in LGBT history and for incorporating it into survey courses.

In what follows, we explain our own relationships to K-12 teaching; describe the effects of standardized testing, especially for social studies; discuss pedagogical approaches to LGBT history in middle and high school courses; and reflect on how sexual, gender, racial, and class identities—both teachers' and students'—shape the ways we teach the queer past.

Felicia T. Perez and Emily K. Hobson (photograph by B. Hobez)

## Addressing the Politics of Public Education

From 1999 through 2012, Felicia taught U.S. and world history to high school and middle school students in the Los Angeles Unified School District (LAUSD). She spent her first ten years at the district's oldest high school, Los Angeles Senior High; from 2010 through 2012 she helped inaugurate the New Open World Academy at the district's newest campus, the Robert F. Kennedy Community Schools. Both LA High and the NOW Academy are Title I schools, meaning that over 80 percent of students' families live below the poverty line. Both also overwhelmingly serve students of color. Los Angeles Senior High is roughly evenly split between black, Asian (mostly Korean), and Latino (primarily Mexican and Salvadoran) students, while NOW is about three-quarters Latino (primarily Central American) and one-quarter Asian (Korean and Indian).

Emily teaches gender and queer studies, LGBT history, and twentieth-century U.S. history at the University of Nevada, Reno (UNR). UNR's students come primarily from Nevada, whose K-12 schools are some of the most poorly funded in the nation. However, as the institution seeks more tuition dollars, it is recruiting a rising number of students from California and other states in the U.S. West. Many at UNR are first-generation college students, and many have seen their families and communities hit hard by the recession and foreclosure crisis. The university is Nevada's land grant institution, and racially it is similar to many other public institutions in the region: about two-thirds white but with growing numbers of students of color, especially those identifying as Latina/Latino or multiethnic.

We mention the UNR context alongside that of LAUSD because we see our teaching settings as deeply interconnected. State colleges and universities offer the most accessible path to a degree for students who are poor, working class, immigrant, of color, or any combination thereof—collectively, the growing majority in public school districts across the United States. State institutions are also charged with training K-12 teachers, and students who feel mentored by their high school teachers and see education as personally and socially transformative are especially motivated to commit to the teaching profession as adults.

Other links between K-12 schools and universities are negative: attacks on education are aimed at all levels. We have both seen our students, fellow faculty, and service staff hit hard by budget cuts, privatization, and union bashing. Arts, languages, and other fields viewed as frivolous or unable to draw private funds have been slashed. Teachers in K-12 schools face larger class sizes and are pushed to adopt "scripted" curricula, sold by private companies, which are geared toward test performance and used to justify lower teacher pay. Districts have become increasingly reliant on charter schools, which minimize accountability to the public and teachers' unions. Many universities' education departments or programs in education policy have become complicit in justifying such shifts. Higher education has seen tuition hikes, salary freezes and furloughs, growing reliance on contingent faculty, outsourcing to "massive open online courses" (MOOCs) and grading services, and ever-expanding administrative growth.[2] Graduate students and the faculty members who teach them are increasingly demoralized about the future of academic research and labor yet often unaware of the connections between their problems and those in K-12 schools.

Standardized testing provides both pedagogical and political logic for these attacks on public education. Schools' reliance on standardized testing has grown steadily since the 1980s and truly exploded following 2001's federal No Child Left Behind Act (NCLB). Testing might as well be considered a "core content area": across the country, students and teachers spend several weeks every year learning test-taking techniques, running practice drills, and taking daylong tests. Under NCLB, more and more tests are "high stakes," meaning that they are used to determine student promotion and graduation, evaluate teacher success and merit pay, and produce benefits or sanctions for schoolwide funding.[3] In 2010 the National Governors Association and the corporate-dominated group Achieve, Inc., developed the Common Core Standards, national guidelines for English and math; these also require new tests. States are required to adopt the Common Core to qualify for federal "Race to the Top" funds, and the vast majority have complied (forty-six states, the District of Columbia, four territories, and the education programs within the Department of Defense had adopted the Common Core as of December 2013; Alaska, Minnesota, Nebraska, Virginia, Texas, and Puerto Rico had not).[4] While the Common Core does not set content standards for social studies, a number of historical skills are integrated into its English and language arts requirements.

Although testing has most directly affected K-12 education, it also carries consequences in college classrooms. More time spent testing means less time available for complex, skill-based, and creative instruction. In the wake of NCLB, students arrive at college with weak writing skills, little to no preparation in interpreting primary sources or scholarly arguments, and a view of themselves as consumers of educational products rather than people who can direct their own learning.[5] These problems are heightened for students from "underperforming" schools, who are tested most frequently. And while many teachers seek to undo the effects of high-stakes testing through creative curriculum, budget cuts strip away the funds that help them attend trainings or purchase materials. (High school teachers, do you expect to be reimbursed for buying this book? We didn't think so.)

Backers of the Common Core claim that its English and language arts standards promote "critical thinking" and other aspects of "college readiness." But many educators argue that its emphasis on testing fundamentally contradicts those goals. In May 2013 forty-nine New York City area principals published a letter to their state education commissioner sharply criticizing the tests administered under the Common Core. The principals found the tests poorly written and decried New York's three-year, $5.5 million contract with Pearson, the company that published the exams. They found that the reading comprehension segments relied on "granular questions about unrelated topics" rather than deeper, comparative analysis, and argued that multiple-choice questions are incompatible with teaching analytical skills: "[T]he [Common Core] standards themselves and everything we as pedagogues know to be true . . . say that multiple interpretations of a text are not only possible but necessary when reading deeply. However, for several multiple choice questions the distinction between the right answer and the next best right answer was paltry at best. The fact that teachers report disagreeing about . . . [answers] in several places . . . indicates that this format is unfair to students."[6] The Common Core responds to the antitesting backlash in the most cynical way possible: by using the concept of "critical thinking" simply as political rhetoric. We need to cultivate suspicion of such rhetoric. We need to criticize the ways in which a single-minded focus on "results" devalues engaged citizenship, previously understood as an important goal for high school graduates. We need to be aware that tactics for "college readiness" can lead students to enroll in college and then drop out because a testing-saturated curriculum has not prepared them to thrive as undergraduates.

It is unlikely that LGBT history will be added to standardized tests anytime soon. But why push for inclusion when we can queer it up? In alliance with critical ethnic studies, women's and gender studies, and labor history, LGBT history offers a way to actively resist the pedagogical practices of high-stakes testing and privatization. By demanding that students ask unexpected questions about the past, LGBT history shifts analytical skills front and center. What are the reasons people might have cross-dressed in the nineteenth century, and how did reasons for cross-dressing—and reactions to it—change over time? How were gay and lesbian people excluded from the GI Bill and targeted in the Lavender Scare, and what does that suggest about U.S. citizenship and the growth of the federal state? How did the black freedom struggle influence the gay and lesbian movement? Questions like these make history interesting (and keep students attending school), help people understand their society (and participate in the political process), and prepare students to do well in college (and earn degrees). But the skills of asking and answering these questions are left behind by high-stakes testing.

Efforts to incorporate LGBT history into K-12 schools have, and will, meet with sharp resistance. Many such assaults will read as unveiled homophobia, much as racism and xenophobia have been blatant in attacks on ethnic studies in Arizona and elsewhere. But other forms of resistance will be more skillfully coded, woven into a larger economic and social fabric that frames discussion of the LGBT past as a frivolous luxury irrelevant to "results." If we name such coding directly, we can show how it is interwoven with broader problems. Likewise, situating LGBT history as a method can help teachers, administrators, students, and parents include it within larger goals of transformative education— including, though not limited to, college success.

## Pedagogy and Curriculum

Some excellent resources for teaching LGBT history in middle and high schools have appeared in the past few years. In particular, organizations backing California's FAIR Education Act have published lesson plans and resource guides online (the GSA Network also provides an excellent tool kit students can use to push for implementation.)[7] However, most lesson plans for LGBT history focus on activism from the 1950s to the present, and this restricts them to specific grades. California, like many states, expects eighth graders to study U.S. history from the Constitution to the First World War and eleventh graders to study the twentieth-century United States.[8] Teaching LGBT history only through postwar activism limits the subject to the eleventh grade and, further, risks naturalizing homophobia as a problem that existed always and everywhere prior to the homophile and gay liberation movements. Although stories of postwar activism are essential, the queer past runs wide and deep, and its utility for teaching analytical skills is heightened when the curriculum ranges across time and space. In what follows, we offer some general thoughts on pedagogy and reflect on three topics that Felicia has used to teach LGBT history: the histories of so-called passing women in the Civil War, the growth of state homophobia during the Second World War and the McCarthy era, and Stonewall and the rise of gay liberation.

Felicia incorporated LGBT history into all her courses, in the eighth through the eleventh grades, throughout her twelve years in Los

Angeles. The queer past fit into her curriculum because she designed all her history courses around three basic concepts: social justice, perspective, and context. She taught these concepts from the beginning of a class and used them to connect material across the semester. Defining "social justice" and the ways people have worked for it framed history as a study of social power and resistance, "perspective" asked students to consider how social status and broader cultural norms shape points of view, and "context" pushed them to situate perspectives and definitions of social justice into time and place. While these concepts may seem obvious, middle and high school students are often taught history without them, particularly when the curriculum is scripted for high-stakes tests. In Felicia's courses, they gave students an analytical vocabulary, helped them identify change over time, and enabled them to consider how historical narratives are products of points of view. They helped Felicia to collaborate with colleagues (aligning world and U.S. history, for example) and to adapt her teaching for English language learners, students with learning disabilities, students in honors courses, and those in various grades. She found that LGBT history was served well by these concepts and that it helped students understand and apply them.

For example, there is widespread, easily accessible evidence of female-bodied individuals who cross-dressed to fight as men in the Civil War. Most scholars term these individuals "passing women," though that phrase is contested since some lived as men for decades. They passed for various reasons: transgressive gender identities, support for the Union or Confederacy, attachment to husbands who went to war, and the chance for self-reinvention through wartime mobility and upheaval. Middle and high school students, whose own experiences of gender are shifting so dramatically, are fascinated by the stories of Sarah Edmonds, Albert D. J. Cashier, Loreta Velazquez, and others who passed as men. They also learn a good deal from comparing these individuals' different experiences after the war. Sarah Edmonds won fame and, in the 1880s, a government pension after publicizing her story; Albert D. J. Cashier lived as a man until he was "discovered" to be female in the 1910s and spent his last years in an insane asylum. Comparing these stories helps students identify both the connections and the differences between women's and LGBT histories and to understand how sexuality and gender are historically contingent.

The photographic record of passing women makes the topic quite rich. Felicia's students tended to read photographs of Edmonds, Cashier, or Velazquez as "obviously" female and, as a result, to imagine that others in the past would have easily guessed their "real" sex and what cross-dressing meant to them. But those reactions opened the door to discussions of context and perspective. When, where, and why did pants stop becoming a way to know someone was a man? How could the absence of widely known transgender or lesbian identities make cross-dressing acceptable as just a disguise? Looking back, can we tell the difference between passing to identify as a man and passing to evade limits on women's lives? Did people cross-dress to escape slavery, and how might that have shaped cross-dressing's meaning? How was passing across gender both similar to and different from passing across the color line? These questions are complex and not easily answered, and that is the point: asking them is a skill in and of itself. Asking such questions helps students to see gender, race, and sexuality as products of history; to consider travel and mobility as products of industrialization, slavery, and war; and to think critically about how the Civil War has been remembered or misremembered over time. Passing women shake up static, "olden days" views of history and compel students to ask, "Why have we never heard this before?"

These histories also work well in the classroom because students, especially younger ones, are highly drawn to biography and can use personal accounts to focus their independent work. Felicia assigned magazine projects to conclude her eighth grade unit on the Civil War, requiring students to create annotated maps and cover stories, to write an article by a conductor on the Underground Railroad, and to compose interviews with key figures, including Sarah Edmonds. Several students chose Edmonds for their cover stories, and one made Edmonds interview other people. This assignment could be adapted to include an interview with Albert D. J. Cashier, whose life suggests something closer to a transgender identity. As an end-of-year project, it might be reformulated to analyze gender, race, and sexuality in the military over time. Felicia also frequently assigned research projects on "history makers." These projects required students to chose from a list of individuals, some well known and others unknown. Some individuals they could choose were connected to the queer past, and even students who did not select these figures gained a sense of their lives through reviewing introductory material and seeing classmates' final presentations.

Telling history through individuals does carry risks, including the possibility that students will evaluate the figure's individual character (heroic? deceitful? weak?) on the basis of sexual or gender identity.

Felicia found that students sometimes raised rumors: "Wasn't Napoléon gay?" She persistently sought to shift such questions away from individual confirmation or denial to historical context and knowledge. Why would that rumor be used to explain his failure at Waterloo, and what does that say about our assumptions? In what contexts did people begin to identify as gay, and how does that shape what we can know about the past? Similarly, when teaching on Edmonds or Cashier, she refrained from naming them using the contemporary categories "transgender" or "lesbian." Although she certainly discussed those possibilities, she worked to leave them unsettled in order to frame LGBT identities—and hostility to them—as products of historical change.

Of course the queer past includes many moments in which LGBT identities *have* been explicitly named, both as the focus of repression and as groundwork for radical change. Felicia incorporated state containment of sexuality into classroom material on the Second World War "home front" and the McCarthy hearings. Her examples included the "undesirable" discharges of gay men—and of black soldiers who challenged segregation—during and after the war, the "witch hunts" of lesbians in women's military units in the 1950s, and firings from federal jobs during the Lavender Scare. Other topics to cover here include the impact of wartime discharges on access to GI Bill benefits and the 1952 exclusion of gay men, lesbians, and communists from immigrating to the United States. If needed, teachers can point to state standards to justify this material; well before the FAIR Education Act, California called for eleventh graders to consider "the expanding role of the federal government and federal courts as well as the continuing tension between the individual and the state."[9]

Material for teaching Second World War and Cold War homophobia includes clips from the films *Coming Out under Fire* and the forthcoming *Lavender Scare*, excerpts from personal accounts collected by Allan Bérubé, and government documents reprinted in the anthology *Documenting Intimate Matters*.[10] Such material can be used to teach primary source analysis, and we urge that more be published online to make it accessible to K-12 teachers and students. Analyzing state policies helps students to understand how homophobia has been shaped by wartime nationalism, anticommunism, and debates over women's place in the work force—in other words, how homophobia has operated as an ideology about who belongs in the United States and how the society should function. This helps students see discrimination as more than personal bias and pushes them toward deeper comprehension of state power and political rights.

Finally, as suggested by the growth of online resources on this topic, LGBT history fits centrally into discussions of 1960s social movements. In teaching this era, Felicia found it key to emphasize gay liberation and lesbian feminism as connected to the black freedom struggle; the antiwar, student, Chicano, Asian American, and American Indian movements; and women's liberation. She discussed Huey Newton's call for the Black Panther Party to support gay rights (published in 1970 and easily available as a primary source) and highlighted gay and lesbian radicals who were people of color and (or) participated in antiracist movements. (The GSA Network curriculum includes a valuable module on Latina and Latino LGBT history.) When discussing the Stonewall riots, Felicia asked students to consider other settings in which they had seen police brutality: on the streets of Birmingham in 1963 or in their own city that month. This undermined fears that gay, black, Latino, or Asian identities must stand at odds and helped students develop an expansive definition of *social justice*. Of course it is far easier to advance a comparative analysis of gay liberation if similar comparisons have been explored earlier in a course.

## Talking about Personal Identities

We have defined LGBT history as both an array of content and a method for teaching historical analysis—analysis that subverts scripted, test-oriented curriculum. At the outset, we held that arguments for LGBT history must move "beyond" the goal of student safety. But it would be more accurate to say that the goals reinforce each other: critical thinking and historical understanding foster a respectful classroom, and vice versa. We refuse to reduce our teaching to the simplistic concept—dependent on a narrow and privileged view of sexual identity—that "it gets better," but we firmly believe that LGBT history is essential to every high school classroom. We literally lose people when we narrow our historical scope, and we can help everyone live fully if we allow students to see all parts of themselves in history.

We try to communicate this value by bringing ourselves more fully into our teaching. Ultimately, so much of what we teach is who we are—more accurately, how we act. Do we show respect for our students and colleagues? Do we encourage a range of students to speak up? Do we interrupt disrespectful or tokenizing behavior? Do we make room for disagreement, mistakes, humor, and joy? Are we open about our own lives and our experiences of learning?

Teachers who identify as lesbian, gay, bisexual, transgender, or otherwise queer face the question of whether and how to come out on the job. Personally, we are both out in the classroom, and we believe this is crucial—though we know from experience that it can be difficult and that being out is about more than a simple declaration. Felicia is Chicana and visibly butch, and by her first year or two of teaching her reputation preceded her. Students, to her delight, described her to each other as the "gay bald teacher with tattoos." (All true.) Still, she felt it was important to come out verbally each fall in her classes to encourage open discussion of LGBT identities. At her desk she displayed a photo of herself in heels and a dress at her high school prom, which eased the way for students who wanted to talk about personal change and self-identification.[11] In 2003 a former student sought Felicia's help in coming out to his parents as both gay and HIV positive. Felicia helped him navigate this, stayed in touch with him as he found medical treatment, and the next year walked hand in hand with his mother at the Los Angeles AIDS Walk. In 2008 a student Felicia had never imagined was queer sought help to find resources for gender transition. She realized that she had become a trans resource simply by being willing to speak about gender transgression in both personal and historical terms.

Being open about one's identity and, more broadly, one's trajectory of learning has tremendous power in the classroom. It can defuse hostile reactions and enable students to approach us as mentors. For these same reasons, we hold that straight teachers need to come out too: they need to be open about being straight and their process of learning how to teach LGBT history. When only queer teachers declare themselves, heterosexuality remains naturalized as the default way to be, and straight-identifying students are left without a model for being allies. Further, straight teachers who teach LGBT history but keep their sexuality under wraps may find that students assume that they are in the closet and therefore hypocritical or untrustworthy.

Another issue here revolves around the assumptions we make about our students. To teach LGBT history effectively, both high school teachers and college faculty must question the idea that homophobia is more prevalent, or LGBT identities more invisible, in communities of color, low-income neighborhoods, or rural places, or that LGBT recognition occurs more easily in white, suburban, or privileged schools. Our experiences directly contradict these views. Felicia's experiences at LA High and the NOW Academy suggest a different generalization: heterogeneous schools are quicker, and homogeneous schools slower, to accept "outsiders." Of Felicia's two schools, LA High was the most diverse. It included working-class Koreans who disrupted images of Asian wealth, students who identified as both black and Latino, and students from across Los Angeles who crossed neighborhood boundaries to participate in the school's band. At LA High, Felicia found it relatively easy to teach about a broad array of histories, including as related to sexuality and gender. By contrast, NOW Academy students were more alike and their discussions of LGBT life were more guarded. Vectors of difference—or homogeneity—are many, including not only race, ethnicity, and class but also religion, citizenship status, political attitudes, and subcultures.

There is one last, obvious anxiety about LGBT history: it might mean speaking about sex. The histories we have discussed teaching—and many others that can be taught, such as those of Native Americans, psychiatry and eugenics, or the Harlem Renaissance, to name just a few— address systems of knowledge, state policies, and social movements, not sexual acts. Still, we refuse to allow LGBT history to be taught without speaking of the connections between sexual desire and love. By this we mean not simply romantic love but a love of the marginalized, a love of resistance, a love of justice. If we insist on separating desire from these forms of love, we miss the opportunity to understand why sexuality has been regulated at all. But with a pedagogy centered on the love of justice, we can reclaim our classrooms for each other and our students.

### NOTES

1. Equality California and Gay-Straight Alliance (GSA) Network, "Fair Education Act (SB 48) Fact Sheet," modified December 13, 2010, http://www.eqca .org/atf/cf/%7B34f258b3-8482-4943-91cb-08c4b0246a88%7D/FAIR%20educa tion%20fact%20sheet%20final.pdf.

2. On outsourced grading, see Audrey Williams June, "Some Papers Are Outsourced to Bangalore to Be Graded," *Chronicle of Higher Education*, April 4, 2010, http://chronicle.com/article/Outsourced-Grading-With/64954.

3. Test scores have risen nationwide under NCLB, but race and class disparities remain, rooted in large part in inequities in early childhood education.

On this point, see Sean F. Reardon, "No Rich Child Left Behind," *Opinionator* (blog), *New York Times*, April 27, 2013, http://opinionator.blogs.nytimes.com/2013/04/27/no-rich-child-left-behind.

An example of how teachers might be assessed without the use of test scores can be found in San Jose, California, where faculty adopted a teacher evaluation system that relies on stringent peer assessment. John Fensterwald, "San Jose Teachers, Board Adopt Landmark Teacher Evaluation System," Edsource.org, May 23, 2013, http://www.edsource.org/today/2013/san-jose-teachers-board-adopt-landmark-teacher-evaluation-system/32542#.

4. The territories referenced here are Guam, the American Samoa Islands, the U.S. Virgin Islands, and the Northern Mariana Islands. See "In the States" and "The Standards," Common Core State Standards Initiative, http://www.corestandards.org/. For critiques, see Valerie Strauss (reposting Diane Ravitch), "Why I Oppose Common Core Standards: Ravitch," *The Answer Sheet* (blog), *Washington Post*, February 26, 2013, http://www.washingtonpost.com/blogs/answer-sheet/wp/2013/02/26/why-i-oppose-common-core-standards-ravitch/.

5. For a useful commentary, see Kenneth Bernstein, "A Warning to College Profs from a High School Teacher," *The Answer Sheet* (blog), *Washington Post*, February 9, 2013, http://www.washingtonpost.com/blogs/answer-sheet/wp/2013/02/09/a-warning-to-college-profs-from-a-high-school-teacher/.

6. Valerie Strauss, "NY Principals: Why New Common Core Tests Failed," *The Answer Sheet* (blog), *Washington Post*, May 23, 2013, http://www.washingtonpost.com/blogs/answer-sheet/wp/2013/05/23/ny-principals-why-new-common-core-tests-failed/. A related critique has been voiced in Philadelphia; see Susan Spicka, "A Major Motive behind Common Core Is Profit, Not Education," *The Philadelphia School Notebook* (blog), May 24, 2013, http://thenotebook.org/blog/136042/major-motive-behind-common-core-profit-not-education.

7. See GSA Network, www.gsanetwork.org/FAIR; www.glsen.org; and FAIR Education Act, www.faireducationact.com. It is worth noting that while the FAIR Education Act concentrates on the historical contributions of "LGBT Americans," it also refers broadly to the "social studies" curriculum, which includes world history, geography, government, economics, and electives.

8. In California a secondary social studies credential incorporates U.S. history (required in the eighth and eleventh grades), world history (sixth, seventh, and tenth grades), geography (ninth grade), and government and economics (twelfth grade). Social studies teachers may also provide electives such as ethnic studies or sociology, though few schools offer these courses.

9. "History-Social Science Standards, Adopted October 1998," Content Standards, California State Board of Education, http://www.cde.ca.gov/be/st/ss/.

10. The primary sources referenced here can be found in Allan Bérubé's essays "Marching to a Different Drummer: Lesbian and Gay GIs in World War II" and "The Military and Lesbians during the McCarthy Years," in *My Desire for History: Essays in Gay, Community, and Labor History*, ed. John D'Emilio and Estelle B. Freedman, 85–98, 125–43 (Chapel Hill: University of North Carolina Press, 2011); and Thomas A. Foster, ed., *Documenting Intimate Matters: Primary Sources for a History of Sexuality in America* (Chicago: University of Chicago Press, 2012).

11. Adult staff members' perceptions posed a bigger challenge: in her first year of teaching Felicia was routinely chased into the women's staff bathroom by security guards who thought she was a boy. She found that dressing in an even more masculine manner—slacks and dress shirts rather than androgynous polo shirts and jeans—made her more easily read as "professional." These lessons clarified the feminist stakes of authority and motivated Felicia's efforts to build community with other queer teachers, including gay men who encountered narrower room for gender expression than she did.

# Observing Difference

*Toward a Pedagogy of Historical and*
*Cultural Intersections*

KEVIN MUMFORD

L et me begin with a few personal and historical reflections that may help to situate my intellectual perspective as well as this moment in which we are teaching LGBT history.
It was the nineties, and I was attending graduate school in that brief
utopian social experiment known as California multiculturalism. As the
debates over canons and the teaching of western civilization reverberated across universities, new courses in race, class, and gender emerged
and sophisticated discourses on social constructionism shaped historical inquiries. In this tumult of progressive cultural change I took on my
first assignment as a teaching assistant, appointed to work under the
Stanford historian Estelle B. Freedman in her offering of Introduction
to Feminist Studies. As it happens, Professor Freedman later wrote an
essay, "Small Group Pedagogy: Consciousness Raising in Conservative
Times," in which she argued for the effectiveness of assigning students
to independent small groups in the form of consciousness-raising in
order to process their responses to unsettling feminist ideas. Although
the course explored many aspects of gender as a category of analysis,
we did not address questions of men in feminism, nor of queer men of
color (which is how I identified at the time). I learned a great deal about
the history of feminism and the craft of teaching. Professor Freedman
was not only rigorous but also remarkably effective.

Kevin Mumford

Yet, when I first started to teach (in several different types of departments and locations), I became discouraged by the difficulties that I encountered. I was still not ready to enter into that moment and space of the mentor, and I was unable to understand why that should be the case. I believed myself to be engaging, open, attentive, and sensitive, as well as prepared, knowledgeable, clear, and responsive. Considering my teaching evaluations over the years, it would seem that sometimes I was—and sometimes not so much. So what was the problem? Part of the difficulty may have had to do with my own misrecognition of the intersection, and underestimation of what is at stake for those invested in hegemonic difference, and part of it was that it has taken me a long time to figure out how to integrate my identity and intellectual orientation with my evolving teaching practices.

In accepting this assignment to write about teaching at the intersection, I decided against a first-person narrative that reported on my instructional experiences, presented pedagogical practices that I used, or outlined suggestions for revision of the curriculum. Instead I wanted to reach outward and find collaborators in this project of diversity, and I also wanted to educate myself. To do so, I have surveyed and organized articles and chapters from a range of major journals, books and anthologies, instructional manuals, and personal narratives that have addressed, analyzed, and theorized what I would conceive of as problems of teaching at and about the intersectional.

In this essay, drawing on that research, I seek to introduce several key concepts or perhaps present a guideline that could be useful in developing a pedagogy of the intersection. I refer to an older idea of the intersection, first formed, I believe, in the context of the rise of black feminism around the time of the 1977 Combahee River Collective statement. A genealogy of the intersection could originate in the thinking of Barbara Smith and Audre Lorde, with Smith perhaps becoming more important to academic theorizing. In the classic 1982 anthology *All the Women Are White, All the Blacks Are Men, but Some of Us Are Brave*, the editors reprinted Smith's 1977 essay "Toward a Black Feminist Criticism," in which she lamented the absence of advanced scholarship on the reemergence of black female novelists. Smith argued that a "black feminist approach to literature that embodied the realization that the politics of sex as well as the politics of race and class are crucially interlocking factors in the works of Black women writers is an absolute necessity." A second scholarly influence emerged from the writing of Kimberlé Crenshaw, the black feminist legal scholar, who stressed the invisibility of multiple subjectivities. In a powerful article on sexual violence, beyond identifying pervasive exclusion and scholarly neglect, she weighs the competing, intersecting systems that punish black men and black women through the regulation of sexual violence. Legal regimes of the state, Crenshaw suggests, intentionally separate out categories of difference and therefore overlook, misrepresent, and misconstrue black women. In a feminist academic journal, Leslie McCall surveyed a range of intersectional strategies for understanding the full complexity of multiple categories of analysis, including race, class, gender, sexuality, and others, that shape large and small, single and multiple sites in order to understand heterogeneity, comparative and cross-class phenomena, and privilege in relation to disadvantage. Here the methodology involves intercategorical or intracategorical analysis, but the main point was to grapple with multiple subjects in multidimensional systems of power that move through webs of inequality.[1]

Along those lines, I would argue for the recognition of a geography of intersectionality that sees how complicated identifications become relegated to the margins, and how these sites then become convergence points of oppression. Rather than a location of interconnectedness and multiplicity, of fluidity and coalitional possibility, the intersection confines its subjects in isolation. What this means for individual lives is not the same thing that it means for political organizing, and what this means for the classroom is different still. But a pedagogy of the intersection is less about claiming difference than diligently questioning absence, and less about diversifying the curriculum than about recognizing, indeed reveling in, the ambiguities in every text or situation. My pedagogy of the intersection is not reducible to a tool for self-expression or a mobilizing strategy, but rather it focuses on the instruction and discussion of a whole range of *connections* and *social differences* between teachers and students, among students, and between texts and contexts.

## Sensitivity and Pressure in the Classroom

Today the original founders of intersectional political activism have themselves been canonized and serve as foundational figures for diversifying curriculum. In a number of essays, teachers have reported on their use of Gloria Anzaldúa and Cherríe Moraga (*This Bridge Called My Back*), the Combahee River Collective statement, Audre Lorde (*Sister Outsider*), and Bernice Johnson Reagon, among others. One author, a recent college graduate, explained that Gloria Anzaldúa's concept of the borderlands and margin, from her classic 1988 text *Borderlands/La Frontera*, helped students to understand identity as a place of mobility, fluidity, and difference, allowing them "to destabilize analyses of marginalization." Reflecting on her first encounter with the work, she described how Anzaldúa's world became a kind of model for teaching and that studying her social experience created the conditions for feminist pedagogical praxis. In this way, hybridity of identity ought to inspire hybridity of instruction.[2] In another essay a male academic teaching a course on women explored several aspects of cross-gender teaching and the role of men in feminist studies, and the "interplay" of student perception of his identity and his personal understanding. He described feelings of discomfort when issues of gender inequality suddenly were "right in front of him," unpredictably interrupting his authority as a teacher by reminding him of his stance as an object of feminist scrutiny. In reflecting on this, he felt he lost a productive teaching opportunity by allowing dialogue about his gender to pass. In this case, reading and teaching Anzaldúa's writing on the fluidity of identity contained some of his anxiety, inspired more collective discussion of difference, and led him to turn questions of difference back on himself. He related Anzaldúa's concept of fluid identity to Eve Sedgwick's opening up of gay identification. In bringing multiple expressions of identity into play, at the very least instructors became more confident and relaxed.[3]

Some essays that focused on African American studies downplayed the disparate impact of class, gender, and body diversity. In the 1980s, there was a theoretical challenge to the state of the field that advanced new concepts of racial hybridity and racialization by authors as diverse as Hazel Carby, Paul Gilroy, and Houston Baker, but they did not necessarily situate their analysis of race at the place of intersection to examine multiple points of identification. To the extent that sexuality or masculinity entered into their analyses, the question of black gayness seemed marginalized, with the exception of the pioneering work of Kobena Mercer. In other words, in black studies intersectionality was only emerging, sexuality less so, and classroom considerations were rare. In a 1992 forum, Darlene Clark Hine charted out distinct yet overlapping traditions in black studies, but stressed that "no single category of analysis should be allowed immunity from criticism," while asserting that "dignity across categories must be maintained."[4] The best black studies pedagogy is social constructionist, and some of this considered questions of biracial identity and queer racial mixture, but my research has led me to conclude that too often single-category analyses prevail over what I would identify as truly intersectional.[5]

At the same time, some of the most informative and sensitive intersectional pedagogy was written by teachers from minority backgrounds. In one essay, a black female academic wrote about the intersection of identity and service, conceiving of her public roles as mother, activist, and professor as overlapping performances (as a minority presence, to represent difference, to participate in diversity). She understood her stance as a way to cope with the resistance, disinterest, and even racially tinged jokes that disrupted her workshops and instruction, while another instructor added categories of nation, color, and language to the course content in order to address teaching as an Asian woman at a predominantly white, midwestern university.[6] As a kind of corrective to racial essentialism, Mel Michelle Williams explored the ways in which a black queer body represented a "teachable moment" while at the same time refusing the authentic, objective, objectified authority. Teaching from the intersection, Williams experienced social difference in the class-room as intensely personal: "I have become aware that my body be-comes a text through which these intersections are read." For Williams it is possible to deploy this positioning to her advantage in the class-room, even while admitting the intense vulnerability experienced. For example, in teaching the Combahee River Collective statement Williams recounted a sense of disappointment or injury when students responded with disinterest. This is a crucial question in the pedagogy of intersec-tionality: how to defend and reposition one's own set of identities in relation to both student sensibilities and the subject matter of the mate-rial. Is objective disembodiment even possible, much less desirable, for an intersectional approach? Is it possible to pass to the lectern without recognition of one's own complicated position (both as an authority and societal subordinate), as well as the potential implications in the material?[7]

Along these lines, the essays that treated race as a socially constructed category of analysis presented some of the best strategies for addressing diversity in the classroom, with several outlining a teaching approach that "decentered whiteness." Margaret Hunter, a light-skinned black woman, deployed both her racial background and her research on strat-ification to introduce students to the subject of colorism (hierarchies of color preference within and outside racial communities) and move classroom discussion beyond the black-white binary. She contrasted knowledge of the subjugated to the unspoken knowledge of subjuga-tion, and unspoken knowledge of subjugation to the silent and invisible white male center. In the process, she attempted to link narratives of the past directly to the present—though, from my perspective, perhaps too directly. In teaching the histories of conquest, enslavement, and colonialism, she described a sort of instructional practice designed to highlight white implication. She wrote, "By making whites accountable for oppressive actions they took, we can also make visible all the resist-ance to oppression that they initiated."[8] In my experience, presenting historical material on race and racism or sexualities of the diaspora challenges students in ways that decenter not only their identities but their knowledge of the past. Therefore I favor teaching methods that avoid potential alienation or limit personal withdrawal on the part of students by reading the climate of the class at a particular moment and tuning into that vibe rather than trying to push a new or controversial subject too far. In some contexts—for example, a survey of African American history—just bringing up the topic of gay liberation or black lesbian feminist contributions is itself the objective, so as to open channels for future connections in a student's education. In recognizing its own marginality, a pedagogy of the intersection sometimes has to settle for less.

As a response to both withdrawn students and white defensiveness, Aimee Carillo Rowe and Sheena Malhotra developed the concept of the "unhinging of whiteness." In this process, they scrutinize the conflation of ideology with individuals and demonstrate the efficacy of distinguishing between and among white, whiteness, and white identity. In theory, the whiteness project of racial abolition and the renunciation of whiteness has considerable intellectual weight, perhaps even political effectiveness, particularly in advancing working-class projects for cross-racial economic justice. Yet in the classroom, calling for the "abolition" of whiteness, adopting the stance of a race traitor, and the "renunciation of whiteness" may prove entirely counterproductive. In drawing on the field of whiteness studies, Zeus Leonardo attempted to relate advocacy of political action to antiracist performativity in the classroom, and yet this strikes me as only partially successful. Although he located a productive tension between what might be understood as abolitionist and reconstruction schools of whiteness—the former seek to disarticulate and remove whiteness, while the latter seek to remake and resignify it—it seems to me that in the short span of a semester-long course, the task is more one of destabilizing an ingrained sense of entitlement and lowering defensiveness. From that initial abstract recognition of white privilege, it becomes possible to introduce the complexities of difference, including the role of white supremacy in coordinating multiple oppressions, while sharpening both communication and analytical skills.[9]

What I particularly appreciate about Rowe and Malhotra's approach is their sensitivity to class participants. By not "freezing identities" in classrooms, this pedagogy helps one avoid the mutually generative and equally disabling discourses of victimization and guilt, and destabilizes closed-down poses of authenticity and innocence. Self-awareness and diverse curricula combined with teaching through difference thereby operationalize the disentangling of whiteness—that is, the historical forces and legacies of white supremacy—from the personal identities available to blacks, Latinos, Asians, Native Americans, and whites, at the same time that white students acknowledge and learn about white supremacy without becoming the bearers of it. In the LGBT classroom, a certain disavowal of whiteness, while securing a kind of queer recognition, could advance new ways of reviving coalitional knowledge; such a mobilization might unhinge and uproot patterns of institutional incorporation mobilized by neoliberal diversity regimes. The project of decentering whiteness involves a range of strategies: inclusion of diverse writings, spaces operated for safety or neutrality, openness toward multiculturalism or pluralism, questioning of binaries, especially the black-white binary whose historical weight in the historiography can delimit attention to additional forms of difference. Intersectional pedagogy should stress knowledge of the interconnectedness of privilege and subordination and resist the temptation to claim an authentic or ahistorical experience.[10]

The least studied mode of difference in the literature—but perhaps most radical in its potential to reorient the classroom—has to do with transgender identity, studies, and pedagogy. A leader in the field, Susan Stryker, argued for seeing transgender bodies and outlooks as generative of a critical analysis of the (underscrutinized) *relations* among gender, sex, the body, and more, while another writer understood trans positionality as a pedagogical method. Some teachers recruited students to "perform" gender roles that diverged from their "natural" ones, to expose both the socially constructed nature and personal dynamics of masculinity and femininity. Yet, when one teacher attempted to build on previous classes about race and racism and asked students to consider the connections between race and gender, the students resisted. She found that some students characterized their homophobia as not serious, implicitly of less consequence than racism. In the ensuing discussions of what sounds like a fascinating class, the instructor went on to talk about gender norms, representations of power, and bodily inequalities. In reading these pieces on transgender, I identified a recurrent tension between experience and knowledge. On the one hand, Diana Courvant argued that sometimes "trans-power" holders reduce and contain the complexities of identity by inviting transgender presenters to "teach" their experience—the singular substituting for the group. Again, as with the discussion of the racially inscribed body presenting itself as a "tool" of pedagogy, employing performance for

99

pedagogical purposes runs the risk of demonstrating or performing one's identity through synecdoche, the one at the head of the class representing the complex diversities of the unknown many. At the same time, one transgender teacher, who appeared as a guest in a classroom, connected his personal transition from female to male to academic transition (from high school dropout to college honors), describing how the correction of his body, identity, and presentation catalyzed a new sense of confidence that allowed him to succeed. As a number of essays in this volume attest, there is an urgent need to consider gender variation among students, to prepare classrooms and curricula for transgender issues, and to recognize disparate, incongruously gendered learning styles.[11]

Women, for example, may have higher, softer voices than men and therefore may require encouragement to speak up in the class. Or precisely the reverse may be the case. An intersectional pedagogy ought subtly to address the problem of quietness and loudness and acknowledge that some men speak in styles associated with women. Racial and ethnic variants in voice are also apparent in the classroom. Everyone, I suppose, has preconceived ideas about how a black man or Asian woman is or is not supposed to sound and talk, and teachers have a duty to interrogate these biases and stereotypes in themselves and for their students, for not all members of minorities precisely share the same tones, accents, or lexical items. In this way, an intersectional approach moves beyond an older diversity project of bringing "forward the lives of the formerly silenced" by allowing for the complexity of citation and self-performance so that everybody can think in the classroom.[12]

In an essay on feminist sovereignty that influenced my thinking on questions of voice, Wendy Brown interrogated the feminist, and by implication multiculturalist, faith in the recognition of identity, and the assumption that marginalization operates or accomplishes its objectives by rendering complicated subjects invisible and silent. Perhaps this conception of power had its origins in gay liberation strategies of "coming out," with its attendant expectation that self-identification in public will catalyze personal and political transformation. Brown's critique was that in practice this theory of liberation becomes "compulsory discursivity." She argued, "[I]f discourses posit and organize silences, then silences themselves must be understood as discursively produced, as part of discourse, rather than opposite it." I understand her point as a critique of multicultural diversity projects that assume a direct causal connection between inclusion and diversity, between difference and pluralism, between physical representation and voice. Inspired by Michel Foucault, as well as Joan W. Scott's influential article on the problem of unmediated experience, a number of essays questioned the uses of authentic experience as a strategy for diversifying feminisms, classrooms, and curricula and considered more sophisticated and agile mobilizing practices that have the potential to reverse or subvert conservative appropriation and exclusion. To the extent that Brown was correct in arguing that the "discourse of multiculturalism has been annexed by mainstream institutions to generate new modalities of essentialized racial discourse," then I would argue that effective teaching from and about the intersection involves attention not only to the signifying of experiences but also to the sheer diversity of backgrounds, heritages, desires, and bodies that congregate in university classrooms. A more sensitive pedagogy at the intersection accepts, and possibly encourages, failures and silences, and it values the complicated, halting, messy, and uneasy contribution that marginalized students might offer as much as the loud, clear voices of the conventionally articulate.[13]

Why should all students participate in the same way and contribute the same amount to classroom discussions, and what are the consequences of recognizing only conventional conduct? I have observed an important shift in power relations when the course subject shifts toward the terrain of students from marginalized backgrounds. African American students are more likely to speak with confidence in African American history courses than in those on postwar America or the 1960s, I have observed. And LGBT students feel less vulnerable and seem more confident when they write or make presentations about LGBT history. Perhaps in another time and place, the relationship between student background and classroom performance, between identity and subject matter, would be less predictable and more fluid than it seems to be in our current situation. Yet what to do for the students at the intersection of formations of difference, and where are they to find confidence and legitimation, if this is what is promised by inclusive curriculum? Along these lines, I am not a fan of exercises, often incredibly well intentioned, that divide classes into groups based on declarations of difference: going to the front of the class if you are from a working-class background and to the back if you are from wealth, to the front of the line if you are young and to the back if you are older. It is precisely because of the inseparability of differences, their blurring into one and other, their simultaneity and mutual constitution, that these classification exercises are not only potentially painful but also misleading and reductive.

Here performance-based pedagogy engages long-standing debates between white and black feminists over the meaning and consequences of "safe space." Some of the more recent articles have developed a new critical standpoint on the question of climate in the classroom. For example, Kyoko Kishimoto and Mumbi Mwangi rejected the affective implication of security promised by safe space in part because of a presumptive essentialism already under way: "Contrary to the rhetoric of safety in feminist pedagogy, our experiences as women faculty of color teaching in a Midwestern university drive us to envision feminist pedagogical practices that embrace and validate discomfort and vulnerability as important components in learning and teaching about the experiences of women of color." Here they argue for the necessity of disclosure and discomfort that often induces anxiety and confusion, which they claim is normative in the methodological project of "learning about women of color."[14] I understand their point but also believe that discomfort may distract more than focus, shut down more than bring out conversations. Again, like the subject at the intersection, the teaching practice strikes a pose of perpetual balancing between challenge and affirmation.

When a full range of individual and group orientations and heritages becomes available for articulation in the classroom, the decentering not only of whiteness but of difference itself is possible, yielding temporary equality. One text that I return to again and again is Kevin Kumashiro's *Troubling Education: Queer Activism and Anti-Oppressive Pedagogy*, a book that explores ways to meet the needs of the Other, stressing the need to not reinscribe difference and replicate inequalities. Drawing on the writings of Judith Butler, Kumashiro understands difference to be the effect of a process of recitation in which social scripts become linked to identities and stereotypes and through which this social difference is seamlessly attached to individual students. Therefore the purpose of anti-oppressive pedagogy is to disrupt the operation of identification in our classrooms. Kumashiro questions the strategy of consciousness-raising, because, he argues, "[C]onsciousness-raising assumes that reason and reason alone is what leads to understanding." In the spirit of Paulo Freire's *Pedagogy of the Oppressed*, Kumashiro rejects a "modernist and rationalist approach" and instead suggests that short-term anxiety, uncertainty, and conflict become signs of the sort of disruption that both produces learning and leads to social change.[15]

Critical Knowledge Tool Kit

By troubling the relationship between experience and identity, knowledge and perspective, minority and difference, much of this scholarship reaffirms the value of teaching about the dynamics of the intersection while exploring methods for becoming more inclusive more effectively more of the time. When no single voice is recognized as authoritative or representative of a social difference, then no student becomes singularly responsible for "explaining" societal designations of race, class, gender, sexuality, and so on. In this way as well, the classroom refuses to become a site of recapitulating societal oppression by urgently searching for equality for all participants. Universities, especially large research institutions, have become fraught locations: that rare site in U.S. society where equalization and mobility are promised but also where the transmission of knowledge threatens to recapitulate disabling forms of difference (in uncritical and unexamined ways). The point of stressing intersectionality again is that we must not become overpowered by the university in a way that allows us to marginalize the rarities and the misrecognized, the unheard of or unheard from, the only and the multiple.

What are the prospects, then, for incorporating my research on African American gay history and activism into the classroom at a moment when the university, fractured by the defeat of identity politics since the 1980s, has become a site of misrecognition and dismaying recourse to drowning out fresh ideas in ways that eviscerate our imagination? A pioneering theorist of black feminist pedagogy, bell hooks, recounted her return to the labor of teaching (after publishing the pathbreaking *Teaching to Transgress*) in a collection entitled *Teaching Community: A Pedagogy of Hope*. After having resigned from a tenured position, she reflected on her often disappointing experiences in the classroom, like so many of the other authors that I read, with challenging normative assumptions and engaging straight, white, male students in the work of multicultural analysis. I was particularly struck by her discussion of teaching a seminar on the black gay novelist James Baldwin to predominantly nonwhite students and her surprise encounter with intense homophobia. She refused to accept the "freaked out" response of the less sophisticated students, fully recognized the LGBT and nonhomophobic students, and, finally, sought to create an environment of love. In this way, she drew on a main theme of Baldwin's fiction, transforming classroom dysfunction into a teachable moment, and explored

Baldwin's faith in the capacity of love to overcome resistance to difference at the same time that she encouraged mutual respect. "Through their work at making community, at creating love in the classroom, they could hear more intimately Baldwin's declaration of love's power," hooks discovered.[16]

I once taught a text by James Baldwin in my course on United States history since 1932 that centered reform, protest, and struggles for citizenship and rights. As usual I was a bit nervous before the class, wondering if students would attend, if this session's presenters were prepared, if my lecture would come off or suck air. I had assigned Baldwin's stirring essays in the *Fire Next Time* (1963) for discussion, and in class I had screened about ten minutes of the 1990 documentary *Price of the Ticket*. It opens with an off-screen voice asking Baldwin how he felt about his position (his location at the intersection)—about the fact that he was poor, black, and homosexual. Grinning into the camera, Baldwin replied that he'd realized he had "hit the jackpot." I then talked about Baldwin's love life, his contentious role in the movement, and his desire to speak to our consciences. I asked my students why Baldwin had chosen to write about religion, beyond the autobiographical truth that he could convey, and they surprised me with their insights. A number of students— men and women, moderate and radical, black and white—in different ways argued for the position that Baldwin was seeking a common understanding. Religion, they felt, touched many people, and although Baldwin criticized the church, he wrote about faith in a way that both expressed his opinions and entreated others to join together, because, as he prophesied, "the price of the liberation of white people is the liberation of blacks."[17] Earlier, during the hearings on same-sex marriage at the Supreme Court, I posted on the course website an editorial from the *New York Times* urging the court to proceed with caution and not rush into a decision legalizing marriage ahead of public opinion, using the backlash against *Brown v. Board of Education* as historical proof. (This is a ludicrous interpretation of the *Brown* era.) At that point in the course, we were talking about the March on Washington and Martin Luther King's declaration that the time had come for change and patient waiting was over. Nobody in the class even nibbled at the parallels, despite the breaking news story invoking the civil rights movement to delay gay rights. Helping students see connections across difference and sites of repression remains a major challenge in the humanities.

In these times, an effective intersectional pedagogy ought to draw from the best of feminist, queer, and ethnic studies work and successes, finding common ground from which to teach through and about simultaneity of oppressions, multiple differences, mutual constitutions, and irreconcilable positions and politics. Despite the rightward political turn in the United States over the past quarter century, LGBT studies is a thriving academic enterprise, and I could not be more excited by its prospects. I sit before an expensive computer with the security of academic tenure, invited to contribute to a pathbreaking volume of essays for a book series dedicated to the gay historian Harvey Goldberg (whose brilliant lectures on the French Revolution at the University of Wisconsin I never, ever skipped). Yet these are unbelievably confusing times, and surviving, indeed thriving, at this point of multiple subjectivities has given me pause. What are the terms of this kind of position—the price of my ticket, my concessions to liberal hegemony over inclusion, the hidden losses encumbered by my assertion of minority difference?[18]

I believe that one response to the current crisis is to not forget how far we have come: from the decline of feminism, the AIDS crisis, the rightward backlash, conservative racism, and more. Many brilliant teacher-scholars report on the difficult challenges that they face, yes, but also on how they have developed effective techniques and stances that continue to succeed. Another response is to not lose sight of what we have gained: from the failure of second-wave feminism to deal with race came the powerful concept of the intersection, which remains an essential tool for conceptualizing and teaching gay and lesbian history and queer studies. If we remain tentative and cautious, vulnerable and uncertain, so be it. Complaints about diversity will probably drown out those practicing it, but further collaboration, strategic unification, and more confidence will strengthen instruction in our halting, meandering, and unclear journey toward knowledge about the intersections.

## NOTES

1. Barbara Smith, "Toward a Black Feminist Criticism," in *All the Women Are White, All the Blacks Are Men, but Some of Us Are Brave*, ed. Gloria T. Hull, Patricia Bell Scott, and Barbara Smith (Westbury, NY: Feminist Press, 1982), 159; Kimberlé Crenshaw, "Mapping the Margins: Intersectionality, Identity Politics, and Violence against Women of Color," in *Foundations of Critical Race Theory in Education*, ed. Edward Taylor, Davide Gillborn, and Gloria Ladson-Billings (New York: Routledge, 2009), 213–46; Adrien Katherine Wing, ed., *Critical Race Feminism: A Reader* (New York: New York University Press, 1997);

Leslie McCall, "The Complexity of Intersectionality," *Signs: Journal of Women in Culture and Society* 30 (Spring 2005): 1771–800.

2. Katy Mahraj, "Dis/locating the Margins: Gloria Anzaldúa and Dynamic Feminist Teaching," *Feminist Teacher* 21, no. 1 (2010): 1–20; C. Alejandra Elenes, *Transforming Borders: Chicana/o Popular Culture and Pedagogy* (Lanham, MD: Lexington, 2011).

3. Nels P. Highberg, "Beware! This Is a Man!," *Feminist Teacher* 20, no. 2 (2010): 157–70. On homophobia, see Natalia Deeb-Sossa and Heather Kane, "It's the World of God: Resistance to Questioning and Overcoming Heterosexism," *Feminist Studies* 17, no. 2 (2007): 151–69.

4. Abdul Alkalimat and Ronald Bailey, "From Black to eBlack: The Digital Transformation of Black Studies Pedagogy," *Fire!!!* 1, no. 1 (2012): 9–24; Houston A. Baker Jr., *Black Studies, Rap, and the Academy* (Chicago: University of Chicago Press, 1993), 85–100; Paul Gilroy, *The Black Atlantic: Modernity and Double Consciousness* (Cambridge, MA: Harvard University Press, 1993); Hazel Carby, *Race Men* (Cambridge, MA: Harvard University Press, 2001); Kobena Mercer, *Welcome to the Jungle: New Positions in Black Cultural Studies* (New York: Routledge, 1994); on intersection of black studies and multicultural democracy, see Manning Marable, "Blueprint for Black Studies and Multiculturalism," *The Black Scholar* 22 (Summer 1992): 30–35; Darlene Clark Hine, "The Black Studies Movement: Afrocentric-Traditionalist-Feminist Paradigms for the Next Stage," *The Black Scholar* 22 (Summer 1992): 17–18; Regina A. Bernard-Carreno, "The Critical Pedagogy of Black Studies," *The Journal of Pan African Studies* 2 (June 2009): 12–28.

5. For an emphasis on biracial identification, see Bonnie M. Davis, *Biracial and Multiracial Student Experience: A Journey to Racial Literacy* (Thousand Oaks, CA: Corwin Press, 2009). For an emphasis on biracial-black identification, see Rhett Jones, "Mulattos, Freejacks, Cape Verdeans, Black Seminoles, and Others: Afrocentrism and Mixed-Race Persons," in *Afrocentricity and the Academy: Essays on Theory and Practice*, ed. James L. Conyers (Jefferson, NC: McFarland, 2003), 257–85; and Annette Henry, "Stuart Hall, Cultural Studies: Theory Letting You off the Hook?," in *Feminist Engagements: Reading, Resisting, and Revisioning Male Theorists in Education and Cultural Studies*, ed. Kathleen Weiler (New York: Routledge, 2001), 165–82.

6. Helane Adams Androne, "The 'Invisible Layers of Labor': Ritualizing a Blackwoman Experience of Service," in *Integrated but Unequal: Black Faculty in Predominantly White Space*, ed. Mark Christian (Trenton, NJ: Africa World Press, 2012), 39–66; Michiko Hase, "Student Resistance and Nationalism in the Classroom: Reflections on Globalizing the Curriculum," in *Twenty-First-Century Feminist Classrooms: Pedagogies of Identity and Difference*, ed. Amie A. Macdonald and Susan Sánchez-Casal (New York: Palgrave, 2002), 87–107.

7. Margaret Hunter, "Decentering the White and Male Standpoints in Race

and Ethnicity Courses," in *Twenty-First Century Feminist Classrooms: Pedagogies of Identity and Difference*, ed. Amie A. Macdonald and Susan Sánchez-Casal (New York: Palgrave, 2002), 251–79; Mel Michelle Lewis, "Body of Knowledge: Black Queer Feminist Pedagogy, Praxis, and Embodied Text," *Journal of Lesbian Studies* 15, no. 1 (2011): 49–57.

8. Hunter, "Decentering the White and Male Standpoints in Race and Ethnicity Courses."

9. Zeus Leonardo, *Race, Whiteness, and Education* (New York: Routledge, 2009), 92–94.

10. Aimee Carillo Rowe and Sheena Malhotra, "(Un)hinging Whiteness," *International and Intercultural Communication* 29 (October 2006): 271–98.

11. Susan Stryker, "Transgender History, Homonormativity, and Disciplinarity," *Radical History Review* 100 (Winter 2008): 145–57; Marilyn Preston, "Not Another Guest: Transgender Inclusivity in a Human Sexuality Course," *Radical Teacher* 92 (2011): 47–54; Leyden Daniels, "Erasing the Marker," *Radical Teacher* 92 (Winter 2011): 55–56; Diana Courvant, "Strip," *Radical Teacher* 92 (Winter 2011): 26–34; Nancy Sorokin Rabinowitz, "Queer Theory and Feminist Pedagogy," in *Twenty-First Century Feminist Classrooms: Pedagogies of Identity and Difference*, ed. Amie A. Macdonald and Susan Sánchez-Casal (New York: Palgrave, 2002), 175–200.

12. Frinde Maher, "Twisted Privileges: Terms of Inclusion in Feminist Teaching," *Radical Teacher* 83 (Winter 2008): 5.

13. Wendy Brown, *Edgework: Critical Essays on Knowledge and Politics* (Princeton, NJ: Princeton University Press, 2005), 85–87, 91; Joan W. Scott, "Experience," in *Feminists Theorize the Political*, ed. Judith Butler and Joan W. Scott (New York: Routledge, 1993), 22–40; Sal Johnston "Not for Queers Only: Pedagogy and Postmodernism," in *Feminist Pedagogy: Looking Back to Move Forward*, ed. Robin D. Crabtree, David Alan Sapp, and Adela C. Licona (Baltimore: Johns Hopkins University Press, 2009), 80–93.

14. Kyoko Kishimoto and Mumbi Mwangi, "Critiquing the Rhetoric of 'Safety' in Feminist Pedagogy: Women of Color Offering an Account of Ourselves," *Feminist Teacher* 19, no. 2 (2009): 89. See also Bernice Johnson Reagon, "Coalition Politics: Turning the Century," in *Home Girls: An Anthology*, ed. Barbara Smith (New York: Kitchen Table, Women of Color Press, 1983), 356–68; bell hooks, *Teaching to Transgress: Education as the Practice of Freedom* (New York: Routledge, 1994); Berenice Malka Fisher, *No Angel in the Classroom: Teaching through Feminist Discourse* (New York: Rowan and Littlefield, 2001), 137–62; Rebecca Ropers-Huilman and Kelly T. Winters, "Feminist Research in Higher Education," *Journal of Higher Education* 82, no. 6 (November–December 2011): 667–90; Martha Copp and Sherryl Kleinman, "Practicing What We Teach: Feminist Strategies for Teaching about Sexism," *Feminist Teacher* 18, no. 2 (2008): 101–24.

15. Kevin Kumashiro, *Troubling Education: Queer Activism and Anti-Oppressive Pedagogy* (New York: Routledge, 2002), 49.

16. bell hooks, *Teaching Community: A Pedagogy of Hope* (New York: Routledge, 2003), 135–36. See also Laura Quinn, "What Is Going On Here?," *Journal of Homosexuality* 34, nos. 3–4 (1998): 51–65; Lise Kildegaard, "Constructive Intersections: White Students Meet Black History in August Wilson's *The Piano Lesson*," *Radical Teacher* 80 (2007): 19–23; Mordean Taylor-Archer and Sherwood Smith, *Our Stories: The Experiences of Black Professionals on Predominantly White Campuses* (Cincinnati: John D. O'Bryant National Think Tank for Black Professionals in Higher Education on Predominantly White Campuses, 2002); Bree Brioleur, "Teaching Outside One's Race: The Story of an Oakland Teacher," *Radical Teacher* 70 (2003): 11–18; and Copp and Kleinman, "Practicing What We Teach."

17. James Baldwin, *The Price of the Ticket* (New York: Vintage, 1993), 97.

18. Roderick A. Ferguson, *The Reorder of Things: The University and Its Pedagogies of Minority Difference* (Minneapolis: University of Minnesota Press, 2012); Sara Ahmed, *On Being Included: Racism and Diversity in Institutional Life* (Durham, NC: Duke University Press, 2012).

# PART TWO

# Topics in Lesbian, Gay, Bisexual, and Transgender History

# Transforming
# the Curriculum

*The Inclusion of the Experiences*
*of Trans People*

GENNY BEEMYN

People who would be referred to today as transgender, transsexual, and gender nonconforming—trans people in contemporary popular terminology—have not only been left out of history but have been given no place to exist in history, which is constructed as the experiences of women and men. To the extent that individuals who cross-dressed or lived as a gender different from the one assigned to them at birth have been considered in historical texts, it has generally been to dismiss them as masqueraders, oddities, or degenerates. Female-bodied individuals who presented as men, for example, have been said by historians to have done so because they were seeking male privilege at a time when women had little ability to live independently or, more recently, have been said by lesbian and gay historians to have done so because they wanted to pursue same-sex sexual relationships. The possibility that they may have cross-dressed or lived cross-gendered lives as an end in itself is rarely considered. Of course we rarely have evidence of the subjectivity of people who crossed gender lines in the past, which makes teaching trans history particularly challenging. But raising questions about how we understand gender-nonconforming people historically allows for a more nuanced analysis of the construction of gender and gender systems over time.

## Conceptualizing Trans History

While it is problematic that historians have often failed to acknowledge or accept individuals who cross-dressed or lived as a gender different from the one assigned to them at birth, it would also be inappropriate to assume that "trans people," as we currently understand the term, existed throughout history. Given that "trans" is a contemporary concept, individuals in past centuries who might appear to have been trans or gender nonconforming from our vantage point would quite likely not have conceptualized their lives in such a way. But at the same time limiting trans history to people who lived at a place and time when the concept of "trans" was available and used by the individuals in question would deny the experiences of many people who would have been perceived as gender nonconforming in their eras and cultures.

Students should be introduced to these arguments so they will recognize that seemingly gender-nonconforming individuals in history cannot be claimed nonproblematically as "transgender people," "transsexuals," or "cross-dressers" if these categories were not yet named or embraced. Students should also be alerted to the difference between individuals whose actions would seem to indicate that they would be what we call "trans" today and those who might have presented as a gender different from the one assigned to them at birth for reasons other than a sense of gender difference (such as to escape narrow gender roles or pursue same-sex sexual relationships). While someone's motivations for gender nonconformity are not always simple and clear, it is important to try to make these distinctions in order to delineate a specific "transgender history."[1]

An example that demonstrates the usefulness of making these types of distinctions is the case of Hannah Snell/James Gray. According to a 1750 biography, Snell, a resident of Worcester, England, began dressing as a man in 1745 to search for her husband, a Dutch sailor who had deserted her while she was pregnant with their first child.[2] For the next five years, Snell served under the name James Gray in both the British navy and army, working variously as a servant, watchman, and deckhand aboard ship. After learning from another sailor that her husband had been executed for murder, Snell/Gray returned to England, at which point she disclosed her assigned gender to her shocked but ultimately supportive shipmates. The "female soldier" became a sensation after her story was published, and Snell/Gray took advantage of her fame to earn an income by appearing on the stage in her military uniform. On her retirement from performing, she continued to wear traditionally male apparel and purchased a "public house . . . for which [she] had a signboard painted with a British tar on one side and a brave marine on the other, while beneath was inscribed: The Widow in Masquerade or the Female Warrior."[3] Although Snell/Gray initially had little choice but to present as male in order to look for her husband, she seems to have been someone we would refer to today as a cross-dresser because she continued to cross-dress after the ostensible reason disappeared. This is an example of the kind of story, from the perspective of the British background of many early American colonists, that illustrates the complexity of gender in that time period.

Along with the difficulty of knowing someone's motivations for gender nonconformity, another challenge in constructing trans history that should be pointed out to students is the relatively limited amount of source material available because gender nonconformity was frequently not documented and, if someone was successful in presenting as a member of a different gender, he or she would not be known to history. For example, a number of female-assigned individuals were discovered to be living as men only when their bodies were examined following an injury or death. Some students may have heard of Billy Tipton, a jazz musician who lived as a man for more than fifty years and was not known to have been assigned female until his death in 1989.[4]

Tipton's case drew widespread attention because he lived in more contemporary times, but his experiences were far from unique in earlier centuries. Similar circumstances surround Murray Hall, a female-assigned individual who lived as a man for the last thirty years of the nineteenth century. He became a prominent New York City politician, operated a commercial "intelligence office," and married twice. Like Tipton, Murray was not discovered to have been assigned female until his death in 1901 from breast cancer, for which he had avoided medical treatment for several years, seemingly out of fear of disclosure. His wives apparently were aware of Hall's secret and respected the way he expressed his gender. No one else knew, including the daughter he raised, and his friends and colleagues were shocked at the revelation. While some officials and a coroner's jury subsequently chose to see Hall as female, his daughter, friends, and political colleagues continued to recognize him as a man. Said an aide to a New York State senator, "If he was a woman he ought to have been born a man, for he lived and looked like one."[5]

## Early U.S. Trans History

As Thomas A. Foster's essay in this volume points out, historical evidence exists to show that many indigenous cultures in North America recognized nonbinary genders. From the outset of their arrival in the Americas in the sixteenth and seventeenth centuries, Europeans reported on the visibility of individuals who adopted cross-gender roles, including having sexual relations with and marrying people of the same birth gender assignment. Within their respective societies, individuals who took on different gender roles were viewed as neither men nor women but as additional genders that either combined male and female elements or existed completely apart from binary gender categories. Thus partnerships between cross-gender and non-cross-gender individuals of the same birth gender assignment were considered to be what the anthropologist Sabine Lang calls "hetero-gender" relationships and not same-sex sexual relationships, as many Europeans, and later European Americans, believed.[6]

Learning about the traditional gender belief systems of Native American societies can help students better understand the complexities of gender—that different cultures constructed gender in different ways and that gender cannot be reduced to genitalia. In addition, by seeing how some white cultural outsiders read gender very differently from the Native Americans themselves, students can recognize the unintentional biases that we all bring to studies of cultures and times different from our own. This history can also be used as an example of the deep cultural conflicts that arose between Native American people and European and other U.S. settlers.

The acceptance of nonbinary genders in some Native American societies stands in contrast to the general lack of recognition within the white-dominated American colonies in the seventeenth and eighteenth centuries, despite the fact that, as the Hannah Snell/James Gray story makes clear, secret gender-crossing existed in European societies. To the extent that individuals who cross-dressed or lived as a gender different from the one assigned to them at birth were acknowledged in the colonies, it was largely to condemn their behavior as unnatural and

114

sinful. For example, the charges filed in Middlesex County, Massachusetts, in 1692 against a female-assigned individual named Mary Henly for wearing "men's clothing" stated that such behavior was "seeming to confound the course of nature."[7]

Given the illegality and social stigma faced by individuals who assumed different genders in many areas of what would become the United States, relatively few instances of gender nonconformity are documented in the colonial and revolutionary periods. Perhaps most famous is the case of Deborah Sampson, who joined the Continental Army and fought in the American Revolution.[8] More is known beginning in the mid–nineteenth century, as a growing number of single people left their communities of origin to earn a living, gain greater freedom, or simply see the world. Able to take advantage of the anonymity afforded by new surroundings, these migrants had greater opportunities to fashion their own lives, which included presenting as a gender different from the one assigned to them at birth. This is part of the story of geographic mobility so central to U.S. history.

Some headed to the West, where, according to the historian Peter Boag, "[C]ross-dressers were not simply ubiquitous, but were very much a part of daily life on the frontier." Among these individuals was Sammy Williams, a lumberjack and cook for nearly two decades in Montana logging camps in the late nineteenth century, who was only discovered to have been assigned female when his body was examined on his death.[9] Such examples can challenge students' perceptions of the Old West as primarily the domain of "manly men" and their assumption that gender transgression was limited or nonexistent in rigidly gendered settings. For it was not in spite of but because frontier societies were coded as places "where men are men" that cross-dressing, particularly among female-assigned individuals, could be so prevalent. A female-assigned individual who could present as a masculine man would unquestionably be seen as a man. Historians have long noted that homosocial environments such as frontier communities facilitated same-sex sexual relationships; the nature of these environments likewise enabled individuals to live cross-gendered lives.[10] Individuals who presented as a gender different from the one assigned to them at birth also moved from rural to urban areas, often to pursue wage labor. In the same way that the growth of cities in the nineteenth century made it possible for individuals who pursued same-sex sexual relationships to create their own cultures, similar circumstances likely benefited individuals who lived cross-gendered lives, enabling them to meet and socialize with others like themselves. Not that the two groups were entirely separate; there was significant overlap between the communities, and together they created and frequented some of the same social spaces.[11]

Given the prevalence of the stereotype that all trans people are gay, it is important in teaching trans history to make distinctions, where possible, between the two groups while noting the substantial commonalities and instances of shared history. One such place of intersection was masquerade balls, or "drags," as they were commonly known. Adapting the tradition of costume balls from the larger society, individuals who might be referred to today as gay men, transsexual women, and female-presenting cross-dressers began to organize and participate in drags in large U.S. cities in the late nineteenth century.[12] By the 1920s, drag balls began to attract thousands of participants and onlookers—many of whom were African Americans—and received significant and sometimes surprisingly positive coverage in the black press. For example, in a 1934 story on Harlem's Hamilton Lodge Ball, the country's largest drag event, the reporter for the *Amsterdam News* weighed in on his choices for the best-dressed participants, among them "a dreamy looking creature arrayed in a carnival outfit of rhinestones and a jeweled star-pointed crown." He described some of the others as "stunning," "cute," "attractive," and "smart[ly]" dressed.[13] Teaching about the popularity and visibility of drags can serve to challenge students' assumption that most trans and gay people were in the closet and lacked self-pride prior to Stonewall. This history can also be included in material on the effects of urbanization to provide students with a fuller picture of late-nineteenth-century gender norms and leisure activities in the United States (see Red Vaughan Tremmel's essay in this volume).

### The Classification of Trans People and the Rise of a Movement

Another place of intersection between same-sex sexual and cross-gendered communities was in the fact that those who first studied sex failed to differentiate between them. Medical professionals and researchers in Europe and the United States began to focus on cross-gendered identities in the late nineteenth century in response to the growing visibility of urban communities of people who lived at least part time as a gender different from that assigned to them. These sexologists considered such individuals to be "gender inverts"—that is, to have a gender the opposite of or inverted from what was expected. Included in this group were individuals whose primary expression of inversion was considered to be their attraction to others of the same sex. Not until the early twentieth century did sexologists begin to separate sexual identity from gender identity and recognize that individuals who transgressed gender norms were not necessarily what they described as "homosexuals."

The central figure in developing the concept of gender identity was the German sexologist Magnus Hirschfeld, who coined and popularized the term *transvestism* (Latin for *cross-dressing*) in his 1910 book *The Transvestites*. Hirschfeld argued that transvestites were not fetishists but were overcome with a "feeling of peace, security and exaltation, happiness and well-being . . . when in the clothing of the other sex."[14] Challenging the claim by other sexologists that transvestites were homosexuals and almost always men, Hirschfeld demonstrated that transvestites could be male or female and of any sexual orientation. He did not, however, distinguish between people who cross-dressed but identified as the gender assigned to them at birth ("transvestites," now referred to as "cross-dressers") and people who identified as a gender different from their assigned gender who lived cross-gendered lives, which included cross-dressing.

The latter group began to be categorized as "transsexuals" in the medical literature in the late 1940s and early 1950s, largely through the work of the American endocrinologist Harry Benjamin. Unlike many of his contemporaries, Benjamin recognized that psychotherapy could not change someone's inner sense of gender and therefore advocated that transsexual individuals be given access to hormones and gender-affirming surgeries to bring their bodies into harmony with their minds. As more and more transsexual individuals became known and studied, Benjamin's position gained greater acceptance, and the dominant medical view gradually began to shift to today's understanding: that gender identity and not biological sex is the critical element of someone's gender and is immutable. Providing students with this history enables them to better grasp the concept of gender and how it developed and to recognize that individuals who became known as transsexual existed well before the medical processes for transitioning were developed.[15]

The concept of transsexuality entered western popular discourse in 1952 when Christine Jorgensen made headlines around the world as the first person from the United States widely known to have undergone a "sex change." Most students today would be astounded to learn that someone could become internationally famous simply for altering her appearance through electrolysis, hormones, and surgeries. This surprising historical moment can provide an interesting and useful entrée into teaching about the United States in the mid-twentieth century.

Part of the reason Jorgensen became such a sensation was her dramatic transformation: a U.S. serviceman, the epitome of masculinity in post–Second World War America, was reborn as a "blonde bombshell," the symbol of 1950s white feminine sexiness. Her popularity also reflected the public's fascination with the power of science in the mid-twentieth century. A tidal wave of remarkable inventions—from television and the transistor to the atomic bomb—had made scientists in the 1950s seem capable of anything, so why not the ability to turn a man into a woman? However, in the aftermath of the first use of nuclear weapons, Jorgensen's "sex change" was also pointed to as evidence that science had gone too far in its efforts to alter the natural environment. Jorgensen thus served as a symbol of both scientific progress and the fear that science was attempting to play God.[16]

Another way in which trans history can be incorporated into U.S. history courses is by including trans activism as part of an examination of movements for civil rights in the postwar period and beyond. Transsexual individuals began to organize in the late 1960s to assist others in finding support and gaining access to services, but most of these efforts were small and short-lived. More successful were spontaneous acts of resistance by trans individuals to harassment and police brutality. Most famous were the 1969 Stonewall riots in New York City, which have become legendary as the beginning of LGBT militancy and the birthplace of the LGBT liberation movement. However, as Susan Stryker points out in *Transgender History*, Stonewall was not a unique event but the culmination of more than a decade of militant opposition by poor and working-class LGBT people to discriminatory treatment and police brutality. She recounts two conflicts with the police that for many years were largely unknown: a May 1959 confrontation at Cooper's Donuts in Los Angeles and an August 1966 confrontation at Compton's Cafeteria in San Francisco. In both cases, young drag queens, many of whom were Latino/Latina or African American, fought back when harassed

Trans March, San Francisco, June 22, 2012 (photograph by Jill Schneider, reprinted with permission)

by police officers. "Back then we were beat up by the police, by everybody," remembers Sylvia Rivera, a Puerto Rican trans woman who was a leader in the Stonewall riots. "You get tired of being just pushed around."[17] Teaching this history of trans resistance can serve as an important corrective to the popular belief that LGBT people did not become militant until the Stonewall riots and address the common erasure of trans people from involvement in Stonewall itself.

A large-scale trans rights movement began to develop in the 1990s, facilitated by the growing use of the term *transgender* to encompass all individuals whose gender identity or expression differs from the social norms of the gender assigned to them at birth. This understanding of *transgender* became most strongly associated with the socialist writer and activist Leslie Feinberg, who called on all people who face discrimination for not conforming to gender norms to organize around their shared oppression. The expansive meaning of the term was further popularized by writers such as Kate Bornstein and Martine Rothblatt, and this usage became commonplace by the late 1990s.[18]

At the same time, many younger trans people who described themselves as "genderqueer" began challenging the dominant trans paradigm—that individuals recognize themselves as of the "opposite" gender and start to identify and present as that gender. Refusing to accept a gender binary, genderqueer individuals do not feel that they have to transition completely or at all. Instead, they may blend or bend gender in appearance, dress, and/or expression, which may include wanting to be referred to by gender-inclusive pronouns. Genderqueer individuals use a wide variety of terms to characterize their gender and sexual identities, including *third gendered, bigendered, nongendered, gender blender, boygirl, trannyboi,* and *androgyne.*[19]

## The Importance of Transgender History

More and more people have been coming out publicly as trans since the outset of the twenty-first century, and often doing so at younger and younger ages, due to information and support being more readily available through websites, social media, and, in many places, local trans and trans-supportive youth groups. It is becoming increasingly common today for high school, junior high, and even elementary school students to be open with their friends and family about their trans identities and to express these identities in a myriad of ways. As a result, trans communities are not only expanding in size, but also becoming more diverse and visible.

The growing number of students openly identifying as trans means that it is even more important not to assume that everyone in the classroom is cisgender (i.e., non-transgender) or fits gender norms. Both faculty and students should respect the gender identity and expression of trans individuals by using the names and pronouns that they request be used and by avoiding language that reinforces a gender binary. But to be truly inclusive, the content of history courses must also recognize gender diversity, and not only by including lessons that consider gender issues and trans people. Just as we do not presume that everyone in history was white, male, and Christian, we cannot take for granted that everyone identified as women or men.

Teaching about trans people and being trans inclusive in the classroom can help trans students feel more welcome at school and increase support on the part of cisgender students. The growing visibility of gender-nonconforming people in society is also likely to lead to greater support, as many cisgender people will find that individuals they care about—friends, coworkers, and family members—are trans.

Trans activists and allies in the United States have succeeded in having trans-supportive laws and policies enacted by a growing number of states, municipalities, schools, and corporations; the years ahead should see even more progress made toward the recognition and full inclusion of people of all genders.

NOTES

1. For more on making this distinction, see Genny Beemyn, "Transgender History," in *Trans Bodies, Trans Selves*, ed. Laura Erickson-Schroth (New York: Oxford University Press, 2014).

2. Anonymous, *The Female Soldier; or, The Surprising Life and Adventures of Hannah Snell* (Los Angeles: William Andrews Clark Memorial Library, [1750] 1989).

3. C. J. S. Thompson, *The Mysteries of Sex: Women Who Posed as Men and Men Who Impersonated Women* (New York: Causeway Books, 1974), 105.

4. Diane Wood Middlebrook, *Suits Me: The Double Life of Billy Tipton* (New York: Houghton Mifflin, 1998).

5. Jonathan Ned Katz, *Gay American History: Lesbians and Gay Men in the U.S.A.* (New York: Thomas Y. Crowell, 1976), 234. See also Jason Cromwell, *Transmen and FTMs: Identities, Bodies, Genders, and Sexualities* (Urbana: University of Illinois Press, 1999), 77.

6. Sabine Lang, *Men as Women, Women as Men: Changing Gender in Native American Cultures* (Austin: University of Texas Press, 1998), 210.

7. Elizabeth Reis, "Hermaphrodites and 'Same-Sex' Sex in Early America," in *Long before Stonewall: Histories of Same-Sex Sexuality in Early America*, ed. Thomas A. Foster (New York: New York University Press, 2007), 152.

8. Leila J. Rupp, *A Desired Past: A Short History of Same-Sex Love in America* (Chicago: University of Chicago Press, 1999), 28.

9. Peter Boag, *Re-dressing America's Frontier Past* (Berkeley: University of California Press, 2011), 1–2.

10. Katz, *Gay American History*, 508–12.

11. Susan Stryker, *Transgender History* (Berkeley, CA: Seal Press, 2008), 33.

12. George Chauncey, *Gay New York: Gender, Urban Culture, and the Making of the Gay Male World, 1890–1940* (New York: HarperCollins, 1994), 292–93.

13. Edgar T. Rouzeau, "Snow and Ice Cover Streets as Pansies Blossom Out at Hamilton Lodge's Dance," *Amsterdam News*, February 28, 1934, 1–2.

14. Magnus Hirschfeld, *Transvestites: The Erotic Drive to Cross Dress*, trans. Michael A. Lombardi-Nash (Buffalo: Prometheus Books, 1991), 125.

15. Harry Benjamin, *The Transsexual Phenomenon* (New York: Julian Press, 1966); Joanne Meyerowitz, *How Sex Changed: A History of Transsexuality in the United States* (Cambridge, MA: Harvard University Press, 2002), 6.

16. Meyerowitz, *How Sex Changed*, 62.

17. Leslie Feinberg, *Trans Liberation: Beyond Pink or Blue* (Boston: Beacon Press, 1998), 107–8. See also Stryker, *Transgender History*, 60–61, 65.

18. Leslie Feinberg, *Transgender Liberation: A Movement Whose Time Has Come* (New York: World View Forum, 1992); Leslie Feinberg, *Transgender Warriors: Making History from Joan of Arc to RuPaul* (Boston: Beacon Press, 1996); Kate Bornstein, *Gender Outlaw: On Men, Women, and the Rest of Us* (New York: Routledge, 1994); Martine Rothblatt, *The Apartheid of Sex: A Manifesto on the Freedom of Gender* (New York: Crown, 1994).

19. Sue Rankin and Genny Beemyn, "Beyond a Binary: The Lives of Gender-Nonconforming Youth," *About Campus* 17, no. 4 (2012): 2–10.

# Sexual Diversity in Early America

THOMAS A. FOSTER

When I teach the history of same-sex sexuality in early America, I am acutely aware of the multiple perspectives from which my students approach the subject. I cover same-sex sexuality within my survey of the history of sexuality in early America. The course counts for the LGBTQ Studies Program minor and is cross-listed with the American Studies Program, so the forty-student class has already self-selected. But the course also meets university-wide, general education requirements for history, and many students take it because sex sounds more interesting to them than the standard survey. As a result, some students come to the topic of same-sex sexuality in early America with a background in theory; some are deeply inculcated with the notion that sexuality in early America was simply "acts" before "orientations" were developed; some are lesbian, gay, bisexual, transgender, or queer and seeking to learn about their own history; some have studied Stonewall and modern histories and think of early America as irrelevant to contemporary political concerns; some are blindsided by the topic, having expected the course to be a history of heterosexuals; and some approach it with reservations stemming from negative religious doctrines or personal homophobia. Teaching the history of same-sex sexuality offers an object lesson in being sensitive to one's audience.

## Teaching about Essentialism and Social Constructionism

I generally begin the course with a brief overview of how scholars have differed on the development of modern sexual identities

123

and end that first lesson with an emphasis on what is at stake in that debate. To illustrate the essentialist model, I use Rictor Norton's statement that "Homosexuality is a broad stream which continues to run despite being dammed up and channeled off by social control." I also show students a slide with his lamentation that it is "tragic that homosexuals have been subsumed totally under the idea of the homosexual" and his conclusion that the "result is little better than intellectual ethnic cleansing."[1] I ask them to consider the parallel being drawn between sexual orientation and ethnicity, and we discuss why the stakes are so high for Norton. I remind students that for some it is about having a history. It is about real people who lived and died.

To illustrate the social constructionist model, I use Jeffrey Weeks, who wrote, "Sexuality is not a head of steam that must be capped lest it destroy us; nor is it a life force we must release to save our civilization."[2] I note the critique here of the idea that we must attempt to get at the alleged truth of sexuality and somehow liberate it if society is to be healthy. We discuss the nature references in the quote itself. I make the analogy of discovering planets that no one knew existed before, pointing out that the essentialist view would be that they were there before science discovered them. The social constructionist would argue that we created the very category of planet and could point to the example of Pluto, which was once defined as a planet and is no longer one. Definitions have histories all their own. After this initial discussion, we turn to the historical record.

## Native American Gender-Crossing

Documented instances of same-sex sexual behavior in early America date back to the sixteenth century. In 1528 Álvar Núñez Cabeza de Vaca wrote that he observed "one man married to another" while he was held captive among Indians in Florida. European explorers and traders noted similar instances of same-sex sexuality in other regions of North America. Such documented occurrences of same-sex sexuality were not limited to Native American practices. Indeed, just one year after the establishment of the Spanish in Saint Augustine, Florida, in 1565, a French Lutheran interpreter was condemned to death as a "sodomite."[3]

Native practices of same-sex sexual behavior have most notably been captured by scholarly and popular work on what Europeans called the "berdache." A fair amount of work by anthropologists and historians on the phenomenon of gender-crossing has argued that within a wide range of traditional Native American societies there existed a third gender or a cultural, social, and religious space for a blurred gender category. Such individuals have been referred to as "third sex," "fourth sex," "two-spirited persons," and "man-woman." Those who were male bodied generally wore women's clothing and did women's work but blended male and female qualities and held revered spiritual positions within their communities. In some communities women took on traditional male clothing and roles.

Some scholars argue that the recent view of Native American gender-crossing is overly romanticized and that activists who use the phenomenon as an example of queer tolerance that western society should adopt misread the extant sixteenth-century documentary evidence. These scholars argue that virtually all berdaches were male prisoners of war subjected to a degrading status, as women, as a result of being conquered—and that the misuse of romanticized Native American history has fueled the depiction of the berdache as an example of liberated genderqueer individuals from which modern society can learn.

How does one reconcile the conflicting scholarly interpretations? Virtually all agree on Native American gender blurring, so that topic is one way to introduce to students the varieties of ways that past societies constructed sex and gender differently than we do today. The general point that one should not romanticize the past is also a useful reminder of how to approach people and subjects in a way that allows for complexity and respect rather than simply serving the needs of the present. Introducing alternative interpretations also provides a place for students to critically examine how histories have been crafted and used for political purposes.[4] It is also important to remind students that Native American cultures, even those aspects of them deemed "traditional," are dynamic, and of course the influence of white intrusion cannot be discounted. The sixteenth-century documents that some scholars have used may well document a different tradition than the one observed by nineteenth-century anthropologists such as Matilda Coxe Stevenson, who studied We'wha, a Zuni *lhamana*, or "man-woman," whose image graces this essay.

Recorded European observations of Native American queer practices are not limited to cross-gender individuals. One eighteenth-century

We'wha, Zuni *lhamana* ("man-woman")

German Moravian missionary wrote about Weibe-Town, where only women lived. Hunting-women communities were not unheard of and were also described by Europeans in other regions, including among the Illinois. In some communities, women eschewed marriage, prompting even more concern on the part of European missionaries.[5] In eighteenth-century New Mexico, Spanish authorities investigated a case of sodomy involving two Native American men, reminding us that European observations and policing of same-sex sexual behavior among Native Americans had implications for the colonial project. That is, sexuality played an important role in the process of conquering Native peoples.[6]

## Same-Sex Sexuality in Early America

Despite the shock of Europeans in encountering same-sex sexuality among the indigenous peoples of the Americas, the practice was not unknown in their own societies. One of the best-documented court cases involving a seventeenth-century arrest for sodomy comes from Windsor, Connecticut. Nicholas Sension was a wealthy, established member of this small town when he was charged with attempted sodomy. Perhaps most astonishing about the resulting depositions is the fact that Sension had a long-standing reputation among his servants and others in the community as a man who held an expressly sexual and romantic interest in young men. Sension was married, never had children, and was well respected in the larger community, although he had been investigated and reprimanded by the town elders in the 1640s and 1660s. In 1677 he found himself before the General Court charged with a capital crime. The charges were eventually reduced to attempted sodomy, and he was fined, whipped, publicly shamed, and disenfranchised. The case provides students a chance to grapple with several apparent contradictions, including what they think they know about Puritan communities and a lack of tolerance for deviant behavior.[7]

The early laws against sodomy were almost exclusively aimed at men, although we do know of women who were punished for "uncleanness" in seventeenth-century New England. An important lesson to be learned in looking at some of the colonial statutes is that women did not figure in many of them. Does this mean women never had sex with other women so there was no need for a law? Or does it mean that women went undetected? Or that sex between women simply was not important? Such questions are vitally important for students to wrestle with as they begin to understand the nature of interpreting not only the extant records but the *silences* in the archives.

Students should also be made aware of the broader Atlantic context of the mainland colonies. Molly house culture, for example, emerged in London and other European capital cities in the eighteenth century. Men interested in sex with other men gathered in certain taverns for sexual intimacy but also for camaraderie and socializing. Some adopted feminine nicknames, dressed as milkmaids and in other costumes, and performed mock childbirths and marriages. I remind students that most, if not all, of these men were married and that it would be anachronistic to label them as "gay" given that this identity, as such, did not yet exist.

Because much of what is described in the accounts is playful and campy, it is important also to point out that men were imprisoned for such behavior and some were executed for sodomy.[8]

Eighteenth-century newspapers in Boston and elsewhere reported on molly house culture, and I have students read one or two notices to attempt to glean all the information they can.[9] I argue that such notices have radical implications for the spread of information about same-sex sexuality. Even condemnatory notices that circulated in a culture that largely viewed sodomy as a sin and not part of a politicized identity had the potential to confront readers with the realization that not everyone configured their affective, romantic, and physical lives in the same way. Finally, I teach molly house history as the history of "heterosexuality" (as anachronistic as it is to use that term). As important as I think it is to focus on minority history for the LGBT community, I bristle at the students who see that as being about "them" and "their" history. I remind them that the concepts of homosexuality and heterosexuality developed in tandem in the late nineteenth century: there are no heterosexuals without homosexuals, and vice versa. I introduce students to the development of the concepts of heterosexuality and homosexuality that occurred at the tail end of the time period covered in my class and situate molly house history in the narrative of the development of heterosexuality.

The same-sex erotic and romantic orientation expressed in the form of the molly house culture was limited to the urban centers of Europe; we do not know of eighteenth-century molly houses in North America. However, the sharing of romantic bonds between members of the same sex was ubiquitous in early America (as the essays in this volume by David D. Doyle Jr. and Dáša Frančíková make clear). Love between members of the same sex was acceptable and even idealized in the late eighteenth and nineteenth centuries. These relationships cut across class and race. Visual representation of love between African American men, for example, is captured in some of the photos that are part of an online exhibit of men in romantic relationships. In class we look at the images, discuss romantic friendships, and interrogate ways to understand that world and what we may have lost.[10]

As the case of Nicholas Sension and the example of cross-gender Native Americans indicate, it is important to contextualize same-sex intimacy in the hierarchical world of early America. This is an important corrective for students who may be accustomed to thinking of gay and lesbian love as rooted in the equitable partnerships of modern discourse. Sexual exploitation and abuse was undoubtedly as prevalent as intimacy among peers. Although we know little about the same-sex experiences of men and women of African descent in this early period, we do have handfuls of references to abuse that can be used to broach the subject, and we do know of at least one seventeenth-century sodomy charge involving an African American man and a ten-year-old boy.[11] Jamaican planter Thomas Thistlewood wrote in his diary about a white man who was accused of committing sodomy with his slave and about "strange reports" about a parson and his male slave. That such occurrences would almost certainly have been kept secret suggests that the documentary record is no indicator of the number of instances of both affectionate same-sex embraces among free and enslaved people and exploitative sexual encounters involving same-sex sexual exploitation and abuse of male and female slaves.[12]

Although I teach the history of same-sex sexuality in a broader course on the history of sexuality, these histories can help us better understand any number of traditional narratives and as such can be useful in standard survey courses. As the above examples show, studying same-sex sexuality in the context of slavery and servitude in early America expands our understanding of those institutions and the experiences of those who lived within their confines. Other aspects of early American history can be better understood by incorporating the history of LGBT America, including Native-European interactions and culture clashes, the gendered and hierarchical world of early America, and the stock understanding of Puritan culture. A focus on early America also upsets the overwhelming association of same-sex love with post-Stonewall activism and modern sexual liberation.

Studying the history of same-sex sexuality in early America requires that students question a historical narrative of liberation, of progress. Teaching LGBT history is especially challenging in this regard, given that so many of us recognize the valuable gains in legal equality that have occurred in recent decades. Students are conditioned to see a history of liberation, but I push them to think about the history of social construction and the constraints of regimes of binary sexual orientation and homophobia that prevent same-sex love. Much smug tittering can occur in a class on the history of sexuality in early America, but I work hard to get students to enjoy the material while not "othering" those in the past, a lesson that I think applies to the embrace of diverse cultures in our own world. Students think of themselves as advanced and liberated in their thinking today, so it is vitally important to unsettle those notions and historicize the present. I ask students to envision history classes fifty to a hundred years from now and imagine what things those students of the future will snicker about when learning about us.

### NOTES

1. Rictor Norton, "Essentialism," *A Critique of Social Constructionism and Postmodern Queer Theory*, June 1, 2002, updated June 19, 2008, http://www.rictor norton.co.uk/social03.htm.

2. Jeffrey Weeks, *Sexuality* (New York: Routledge, 1986), 15, 19.

3. For useful documents see Jonathan Ned Katz, *Gay American History: Lesbians and Gay Men in the U.S.A.* (New York: Thomas Y. Crowell, 1976); Jonathan Ned Katz, *Gay/Lesbian Almanac: A Documentary* (New York: Harper and Row, 1983).

4. For positive views of Native American gender-crossing, see Will Roscoe, *The Zuni Man-Woman* (Albuquerque: University of New Mexico Press, 1991); Will Roscoe, *Changing Ones: Third and Fourth Genders in Native North America* (London: Macmillan, 1998); Walter Williams, *The Spirit and the Flesh: Sexual Diversity in American Indian Culture* (Boston: Beacon, 1986). For negative views, see Ramón Gutiérrez, *When Jesus Came, the Corn Mothers Went Away: Marriage, Sexuality, and Power in New Mexico, 1500–1846* (Berkeley: University of California Press, 1991); Richard Trexler, *Sex and Conquest: Gendered Violence, Political Order, and the European Conquest of the Americas* (Ithaca, NY: Cornell University Press, 1995).

5. Gunlög Fur, "Weibe-Town and the Delawares-as-Women: Gender-Crossing and Same-Sex Relations in Eighteenth-Century Northeastern Indian Culture," in *Long before Stonewall: Histories of Same-Sex Sexuality in Early America*, ed. Thomas A. Foster (New York: New York University Press, 2007), 32–50.

6. Tracy Brown, "'Abominable Sin' in Colonial New Mexico: Spanish and Pueblo Perceptions of Same-Sex Sexuality," in *Long before Stonewall: Histories of Same-Sex Sexuality in Early America*, ed. Thomas A. Foster (New York: New York University Press, 2007), 51–77.

7. Richard Godbeer, "'The Cry of Sodom': Discourse, Intercourse, and Desire in Colonial New England," in *Long before Stonewall: Histories of Same-Sex Sexuality in Early America*, ed. Thomas A. Foster (New York: New York University Press, 2007), 81–113.

8. Rictor Norton, *Mother Clap's Molly House: The Gay Subculture in England, 1700–1830* (London: Gay Men's Press, 1992); Randolph Trumbach, "The Birth of the Queen: Sodomy and the Emergence of Gender Equality in Modern

Culture, 1660–1750," in *Hidden from History: Reclaiming the Gay and Lesbian Past*, ed. Martin Bauml Duberman, Martha Vicinus, and George Chauncey Jr. (New York: New American Library, 1989), 129–40. I have occasionally used the documentary *Paris Is Burning* to jar students into thinking about and imagining gender performance and in-group/out-group sensibilities, the broader context of danger and death (from hostile outsiders but also from AIDS in this period), and mocking and parodying a dominant culture.

9. "The Boston News-Letter on 'Sodomitical Clubs,'" in *Documenting Intimate Matters: Primary Sources for a History of Sexuality in America*, ed. Thomas A. Foster (Chicago: University of Chicago Press, 2012), 25.

10. John D'Emilio and Estelle Freedman, *Intimate Matters: A History of Sexuality in America*, 3rd ed. (Chicago: University of Chicago Press, 2012); Richard Godbeer, *The Overflowing of Friendship: Love between Men and the Creation of the American Republic* (Baltimore: Johns Hopkins University Press, 2009); Karen V. Hansen, "'No Kisses Is Like Youres': An Erotic Friendship between Two African-American Women during the Mid-Nineteenth Century," *Gender & History* 7, no. 2 (1995): 153–82; Lisa L. Moore, "The Swan of Litchfield: Sarah Pierce and the Lesbian Landscape Poem," in *Long before Stonewall: Histories of Same-Sex Sexuality in Early America*, ed. Thomas A. Foster (New York: New York University Press, 2007), 253–78; "Dear Friends: American Photographs of Men Together, 1840–1918," Museum of the International Center of Photography, http://museum.icp.org/museum/exhibitions/dear_friends.

11. Katz, *Gay American History*, 22–23.

12. Trevor Burnard, *Mastery, Tyranny, and Desire: Thomas Thistlewood and His Slaves in the Anglo-Jamaican World* (Chapel Hill: University of North Carolina Press, 2004), 216; Thomas A. Foster, "Sexual Abuse of Black Men under American Slavery," *Journal of the History of Sexuality* 20 (September 2011): 445–64.

# Nineteenth-Century Male Love Stories and Sex Stories

DAVID D. DOYLE JR.

In the early nineteenth century, the United States under-
went enormous change; not only were the political
implications of the Revolution and the resulting new Republic profound,
but the economic and social changes affecting the young country were
also unprecedented. In the move toward industrialization and a developed market economy, increasingly distinct spheres emerged, dividing
the population by social class, race, and gender. It was in this new world
that two phenomena developed: intimate same-sex friendships among
men and erotic male same-sex relationships both on the frontier and in
a nascent urban culture.

## Male Romantic Friendships

Close male same-sex friendships flourished as part of
middle-class life on a scale never seen before or since. These romantic
friendships allowed men to be in publicly accepted, indeed sanctioned,
relationships with peers. From the end of the eighteenth century to the
beginning of the twentieth, U.S. culture embraced these idealized
same-sex relationships—although myriad variations of male same-sex
love coexisted, dependent on region, social class, and ethnicity.

The middle-class ideology that emerged early in the century increasingly segregated men and women; the former went out into the
workplace or marketplace, while the latter remained in the home. Such

132

Daguerreotype of two men, ca. 1853 (from John Ibson, *Picturing Men: A Century of Male Relationships in Everyday American Photography* [Smithsonian Institution Press, 2002])

separate spheres had not existed in the preindustrial United States, when men and women tended to work in a household or farmstead in tandem. Indeed, as Carroll Smith-Rosenberg illustrated in her pioneering article, those of the same sex spent the majority of their time together, and it was into organically emerging same-sex relationships that people poured their passions.[1] (On women's romantic friendships, see the essay by Dáša Frančíková in this volume.) It is important to understand that middle- and upper-class antebellum society operated under a sexual system quite distinct from our own. Our twenty-first-century tendency to make companionate marriage the primary location for satisfying human emotional and sexual needs, for example, would not have made sense to our ancestors. More often a union of interests or estates, people entered into marriage with a more pragmatic set of expectations, such as financial stability, especially among the middle and upper classes. Alongside marriage, same-sex romantic friendships were central to many people's lives—married or unmarried. Some evidence indicates that for men these romantic friendships were more common among the young.

This nineteenth-century sexual and gender system allowed for many male practices not seen today: open declarations of passion from one male friend to another, a willingness to show emotion without shame or stigma, and a fluid sense of romantic love that allowed a man to proclaim his love for both men and women openly. In short, the definition of what was "manly" was far removed from our own. After all this was a world without the discrete identities of heterosexual, bisexual, and homosexual.

Similar to newly emerging romantic ideals surrounding marriage, the construct of romantic friendship was one that emphasized the spiritual and eschewed the physical.[2] Middle-class culture in general sought to downplay the physical, and romantic friendships were no exception. The sexual ideology of the middle classes conceptualized women as pure and removed from the erotic, and relegated sexual desire to racial and ethnic minorities, the working class, and immigrants. Available evidence suggests that romantic friendships were most common among white Anglo men and women. Limited sources reveal loving friendships among African Americans, immigrants, and working-class people, although it is especially difficult to learn about the intimate lives of people who left behind no written records. For the white middle and upper classes, romantic friendship was the primary way that same-sex relationships took shape in the decades after the American Revolution up until the First World War.

Throughout the nineteenth century there are examples of romantic friendships, among the famous as well as the obscure. For instance, both James Buchanan and Abraham Lincoln, the fifteenth and sixteenth U.S. presidents, were involved in well-documented friendships with other males. Following a broken engagement in his twenties with the daughter of the wealthiest man in Pennsylvania, Buchanan never married or again actively courted a woman. Much later in life, however, he formed a romantic friendship with Senator (and later Vice President) William R. King of Alabama. The two roomed together in Washington and attended society events as a couple, remaining virtually inseparable from 1840 until King's death in 1853. Buchanan himself referred to their relationship as a "communion" of central importance in his life. Evidence as to the physical side of the relationship is limited, however, as Buchanan's niece Harriet Lane, who served her uncle as the official White House hostess, burned most of the two men's correspondence.[3] This very public relationship gives us significant insight into the era's belief that romantic friendships were spiritual and noble—and far re-moved from the uncontrolled sexual instincts of the less civilized classes or races.

Lincoln, Buchanan's successor in the White House, is also known for his long, intense romantic friendships with other men—most im-portantly with Kentucky native Joshua Speed, who befriended him in his twenties. Indeed, many biographers and scholars have noted that Lincoln found greater contentment in his male friendships than in his tumultuous marriage to Mary Todd. His friendship with Speed was typical of his time and place; the two roomed together in Springfield, Illinois, sharing the same bed for over four years, and relied on one another as the emotional constant or center of their lives. "Lincoln 'loved this man more than anyone dead or living,'" said his later law partner, Robert Herndon, including Mary. Significantly, Lincoln always had a large circle of male friends and was uncomfortable socializing with single women—characteristics easily accommodated by the homo-social and gender-segregated world of the nineteenth-century United States.[4]

If romantic friendship ideology privileged the spiritual union over the physical, there were those who clearly embraced the physical aspect of these relationships. Writing in 1826, a nineteen-year-old Thomas Jefferson "Jeff" Withers chided his friend and peer James Hammond (later congressman, senator, and governor of South Carolina): "I feel some inclination to learn whether you yet sleep in your shirt-tail, and whether you yet have the extravagant delight of poking and punching a writhing bedfellow with your long fleshen pole—the exquisite touches of which I have often had the honor of feeling?"[5] It is significant to note that the sexual act is not only discussed but done so with no sense of em-barrassment. Similar to Lincoln, both Hammond and Withers's youth-ful romantic involvements with other men did not preclude a later marriage and children. Others at midcentury, such as Walt Whitman, were likewise outspoken about their physical attraction to young men and did not shy away from the physical. Writing in the 1890s to his close friend Arthur Little, the architect Ogden Codman was equally specific, and bold, in describing his attraction to and conquests of men he met in his native Boston.[6] Not many extant sources from this century are this frank; whereas Withers and Codman wrote with an eye to the physical, most men were far more ambiguous in their language, focusing most often on the spiritual side of the relationship.

A review of the lives and letters of such figures as presidents Buchanan and Lincoln, politician Daniel Webster, writer and philosopher Ralph Waldo Emerson, or poet Fitz-Greene Halleck—to name only a few prominent examples—will bring home immediately a world distinct from the one students live in today.[7] Examples of loving male couples can be found in studies of the Mormons, the abolitionists, the southern planter class, the clergy, and political and social reformers. Similarly, the excerpts found in Axel Nissen's anthology of the period's best romantic friendship fiction—written by some of the country's best-known writers—will further emphasize how central to men's lives such relationships once were.[8]

More than anything else, it is the ambiguity surrounding sexuality that presents historians with the most formidable challenge of interpretation. Typical of their nineteenth-century world, the majority of middle- and upper-class men involved in romantic friendships demurred at specifics when it came to sexuality. There are enough clear examples to illustrate that sexual acts did often take place in the context of these friendships; the construct certainly allowed for this possibility. The historian William Benemann has found some examples of sex acts among nineteenth-century romantic friends, but not enough to back his claim that they are prototypes of the modern homosexual. His work does have great value, though. It looks beyond the construct of the romantic friendship—a type of relationship that was, after all, only one among many—and questions the distinction between love and sex, a distinction that essentially obscures the era's views.[9] When teaching students about this nineteenth-century sexual system, distinct in its parameters from current norms, it is more productive to focus on the romantic love between men openly professed and celebrated than to engender a guessing game about sexual consummation.

The rise and fall of romantic friendship is well documented in the primary materials left behind, including private letters and diaries, literary works, and photographic images.[10] As John Ibson has shown, photographs of men from the middle of the nineteenth century reveal friends holding hands or embracing without shame or stigma. Photographs from the twentieth century, especially those from the 1930s and later, provide visual evidence of how men separated themselves from one another—standing in rows, hands crossed, and rarely allowing their bodies to touch. Such images and their chronology illustrate the rise and fall of male romantic friendships in American life.[11]

If same-sex love and attractions exist across the centuries and conti-
nents, romantic friendships do not. They were a result of specific conditions in the nineteenth-century western world, and they need to be
properly placed in their historical context. These relationships reveal
how institutions such as marriage and friendship are not static but are
constantly in flux and under revision and renegotiation. This variation
is an important point to emphasize to our students.

If a history class is truly to understand nineteenth-century life, then
the era's sexual system and gender roles must be addressed. An assignment that uses primary documents to delve into separate spheres, romantic friendship, sexuality, and marriage is a key way to draw students
into the study of the past. Readings that convey both the atmosphere of
these friendships and their ubiquity will go a long way toward illuminating a world with values removed from our own. Primary documents
from romantic friends, such as letters, a novel or short story that highlights a friendship, or an article titled "Was Abraham Lincoln Gay?,"
can really bring a classroom discussion alive.[12] Along these lines, I have
often used texts by the writer Henry James in my history classes, as his
letters and novels have been an exciting, and effective, way to delve
into this other world and its values.

### Erotic Relationships on the Frontier and in the City

In thinking about nineteenth-century U.S. history, it is
equally important to convey a sense of the myriad sexual systems and
norms that coexisted with the ideal of romantic friendship. Historical
themes integral to all basic surveys of U.S. history can be examined
with a fresh approach by relating them to significant variations in male
same-sex intimacy. Western settlement, most famously in the 1849 California Gold Rush, privileged relationships between men in an almost
all-male world. Similarly, the proliferation of railroad lines across the
country, symbolized by the famous meeting of the Central and Union
Pacific railroads in Promontory, Utah, in 1869, fostered the all-male
world of transient hobos, men who could travel anywhere the railroad
went by just hopping aboard. Among the Chinese population in the
western states, men vastly outnumbered women as a result of immigration policies designed to prevent family settlement, fostering Chinese
bachelor societies in which male same-sex sexuality may have flourished.

And for centuries men attracted to their own sex were drawn to the all-male world aboard ships at sea.

Significantly, many of the erotic relationships between men were not between equals. Whereas the romantic friendships of the popular imagination were typically developed between men of the same age and class, a number of pairings featured an older, sexually dominant man and a younger, passive one. Yet common to all these relationships was a direct acceptance, often even celebration, of male-to-male sexuality.[13] This represents an important difference from the idealized romantic friendship's marginalization of the sexual. Sodomy laws, though focused narrowly on anal sex between men, were used almost exclusively to regulate the sexuality of racial, ethnic, and class "others." Such selective enforcement helped to solidify racial and class boundaries.[14]

As Thomas A. Foster points out in his essay in this volume, historians of sexuality have located highly developed subcultures of men attracted to their own sex in early modern European cities. Evidence points to such nascent subcultures in Venice, Paris, London, and Amsterdam at least by the eighteenth century, and many had already been in existence for a century or more.[15] As late as the American Revolution, however, U.S. cities still lacked the large urban populations found in Europe. With the first Industrial Revolution this situation began to change. Work by Jonathan Ned Katz, Timothy J. Gilfoyle, and others traces a newly emerging male subculture—often centered on drinking establishments and prostitution—back to the 1820s and 1830s in New York City.[16] Despite the overlap in time between romantic friendship and the emergence of a male sexual culture inclusive of working-class prostitutes and effeminate males seeking masculine partners, any connection between the two would not have occurred to most people.

By the time the century came to an end, and urbanization followed industrialization, U.S. cities had grown enormously. New York City had a population of 3.5 million, Chicago 1.7 million, and Philadelphia 1.3 million according to the 1900 census. In these vast urban landscapes, the population was further divided by social class, and gender segregation began to wane as women entered the work force and public sphere in unprecedented numbers. As Red Vaughan Tremmel's essay in this volume indicates, a male sexual underworld flourished in this tumultuous era. Closely tied to a burgeoning commercialized sexuality, especially prostitution, this world was centered on such sites as

the saloon or bar and semipublic spaces such as Turkish baths.[17] The
architect Ogden Codman traveled frequently into this world, yet he
always remained aloof due to social class blinders, whether he was in
Boston, New York, London, or Paris, during the last two decades of the
century.[18]

With its laissez-faire, hands-off government and the nearly constant influx of migrants and immigrants on a massive scale, the bustling
late-nineteenth-century city spawned a great deal of hardship, inequality, and desperation. In the controversy over these conditions the progressive movement came to prominence as a top-down effort to alleviate
some of capitalism's most egregious excesses. Reformers worked to
eradicate such urban ills as alcohol consumption, crowded housing,
unsafe working conditions, broken educational systems and prisons,
and finally the vices most apparent in the city's streets, including the
relatively open sexual subculture of working-class districts. This effort,
while seeking to promote change, nonetheless perpetuated prejudices
about the sexually voracious lower classes. It was here that many
middle-class men, such as those studied by Kevin Murphy, found their
life's work by fusing ideals of romantic friendship with progressive
noblesse oblige in their efforts to ameliorate the lives of young men in
the slums, schools, and prisons.[19]

## Same-Sex Intimacy Reconceived

By the end of the century, another influence was being
increasingly felt in the United States—namely, the work of the sexologists, those scientists who had turned to the study of sexuality. Although
the word *homosexual* was coined in 1869, it would be the last decade of
the century before the writings of European sexologists had an influence on U.S. culture. The 1895 sodomy trials of Oscar Wilde in London
were well publicized in the United States and brought home to the respectable middle classes the fact that male same-sex relationships of
any social class were not simply spiritual but could involve sexual acts.
These messages were received unevenly, however, as is evidenced by
the shock that greeted news of an extensive middle-class, male homosexual subculture in Portland, Oregon, in 1912.[20] The efforts of urban
progressives and moral reformers, and the growth of a vibrant working-
class sexual culture, led to a gradual sexual transformation of the
middle class in the United States—a process that began in the 1890s and

culminated in the Roaring Twenties. By the early twentieth century, there were many visible reminders that male romantic friendships held the possibility of physical consummation, and as a result these relationships were increasingly shunned.

For several years I have taught a seminar on the history of marriage in the United States that traces the institution from the earliest colonies up to the present—concluding with the gay marriage debate. After reading monographs and primary documents that reveal how marriage has been altered according to historical conditions, students begin to question the assertion that the sacrosanct institution has been impervious to change over time. The semester's final examination essay asks the students to take a position on gay marriage by placing their answers in careful historical context. Having read that marriage was not legally allowed for slaves or later allowed between people of different colors, that women's legal rights often were limited, and that both women and men enjoyed widespread and accepted romantic friendships (along with other forms of same-sex relationships) in many time periods, the students are almost inevitably passionate about the need for same-sex marriage. Indeed, they often remark on how well informed about the subject they feel. This process—of understanding that norms, assumptions, and patterns of intimacy change depending on ever-evolving historical conditions—is a powerful one, and it reveals the importance of history in the classroom. It is for these reasons that learning about romantic friendships and erotic relationships on the frontier and in the cities in the context of the nineteenth-century sexual system is vital and needs to be incorporated into the central narrative of U.S. history.

### NOTES

1. Carroll Smith-Rosenberg, "The Female World of Love and Ritual: Relations between Women in Nineteenth-Century America," *Signs: Journal of Women in Culture and Society* 1, no. 1 (1975): 1–29.

2. Steven Seidman, *Romantic Longings: Love in America, 1830–1980* (New York: Routledge, 1991); E. Anthony Rotundo, "Romantic Friendship: Male Intimacy and Middle-Class Youth in the Northern United States, 1800–1900," *Journal of Social History* 23, no. 1 (1989): 1–25; E. Anthony Rotundo, *American Manhood: Transformations in Masculinity from the Revolution to the Modern Era* (New York: Basic Books, 1993), 75–91.

3. Jean Baker, *James Buchanan* (New York: Henry Holt, 2004), 19–27.

4. Jonathan Ned Katz, *Love Stories: Sex between Men before Homosexuality* (Chicago: University of Chicago Press, 2001), 3–25; C. A. Tripp, *The Intimate World of Abraham Lincoln* (New York: Free Press, 2005); Michael Ferguson, "Was Abraham Lincoln Gay?," *Journal of Homosexuality* 57, no. 9 (2010): 1124–57. A work that argues that Lincoln was heterosexual is David Herbert Donald, *"We Are Lincoln Men": Abraham Lincoln and His Friends* (New York: Simon and Schuster, 2003).

5. Martin Duberman, "'Writhing Bedfellows' in Antebellum South Carolina: Historical Interpretation and the Politics of Evidence," in *About Time: Exploring the Gay Past* (New York: Meridian/Penguin Books, 1986), 3–23.

6. On Walt Whitman, see Katz, *Love Stories*, 148–77, 221–31, 235–87; David S. Reynolds, *Walt Whitman's America: A Cultural Biography* (New York: Alfred A. Knopf, 1995); David D. Doyle Jr., "'A Very Proper Bostonian': Rediscovering Ogden Codman and His Late Nineteenth Century Queer World," *Journal of the History of Sexuality* 13, no. 4 (2004): 446–76.

7. Caleb Crain, *American Sympathy: Men, Friendship, and Literature in the New Nation* (New Haven, CT: Yale University Press, 2001), 148–237; John W. M. Hallock, *The American Byron: Homosexuality and the Fall of Fitz-Greene Halleck* (Madison: University of Wisconsin Press, 2000).

8. D. Michael Quinn, *Same-Sex Dynamics among Nineteenth-Century Americans: A Mormon Example* (Urbana: University of Illinois Press, 1996); Donald Yacavone, "Abolitionists and the 'Language of Fraternal Love,'" in *Meanings for Manhood: Constructions of Masculinity in Victorian America*, ed. Mark C. Carnes and Clyde Griffens (Chicago: University of Chicago Press, 1990), 85–95; George Chauncey Jr., "Christian Brotherhood or Sexual Perversion? Homosexual Identifies and the Construction of Sexual Boundaries in the World War I Era," in *Hidden from History: Reclaiming the Gay and Lesbian Past*, ed. Martin Bauml Duberman, Martha Vicinus, and George Chauncey Jr. (New York: New American Library, 1989), 294–317; Kevin Murphy, *Political Manhood: Red Bloods, Mollycoddles, and the Politics of Progressive Era Reform* (New York: Columbia University Press, 2008); John Donald Gustav-Wrathall, *Take the Young Stranger by the Hand: Same-Sex Relations and the YMCA* (Chicago: University of Chicago Press, 1998); Axel Nissen, ed., *The Romantic Friendship Reader* (Boston: Northeastern University Press, 2003).

9. William Benemann, *Male-Male Intimacy in Early America: Beyond Romantic Friendships* (New York: Harrington Park Press, 2006). See also Graham Robb, *Strangers: Homosexual Love in the Nineteenth Century* (New York: W. W. Norton, 2003).

10. Crain, *American Sympathy*; Axel Nissen, *Manly Love: Romantic Friendship in American Fiction* (Chicago: University of Chicago Press, 2009).

11. John Ibson, *Picturing Men: A Century of Male Relationships in Everyday American Photography* (Washington, DC: Smithsonian Institution Press, 2002).

12. Examples include Henry James's novels *Roderick Hudson* (1875) and *The Bostonians* (1886); Susan E. Gunter and Steven H. Jobe, eds., *Dearly Beloved Friends: Henry James's Letters to Young Men* (Ann Arbor: University of Michigan Press, 2004); Ferguson, "Was Abraham Lincoln Gay?"

13. Susan Johnson, *Roaring Camp: The Social World of the California Gold Rush* (New York: W. W. Norton, 2000), 99–140; B. R. Burg, *Sodomy and the Pirate Tradition: English Sea Rovers in the Seventeenth Century* (New York: New York University Press, 1983); B. R. Burg, *The Erotic Diaries of Philip Van Buskirk, 1851–1870* (New Haven, CT: Yale University Press, 1994); Peter Boag, *Sex Affairs: Constructing and Controlling Homosexuality in the Pacific Northwest* (Berkeley: University of California Press, 2003), 1–86.

14. William Eskridge Jr., *Dishonorable Passions: Sodomy Laws in America, 1861–2003* (New York: Viking, 2008), 1–72.

15. Kent Gerard and Gert Hekma, eds., *The Pursuit of Sodomy: Male Homosexuality in Renaissance and Enlightenment Europe* (New York: Harrington Park Press, 1989); Rictor Norton, *Mother Clap's Molly House: The Gay Subculture in England, 1700–1830* (London: CMP Publishers, 1992); David Higgs, ed., *"Queer Sites": Gay Urban Histories since 1600* (New York: Routledge, 1999).

16. Katz, *Love Stories*, 34–90; Timothy J. Gilfoyle, *City of Eros: New York City, Prostitution, and the Commercialization of Sex, 1790–1920* (New York: W. W. Norton, 1992), 135–41.

17. George Chauncey, *Gay New York: Gender, Urban Culture, and the Making of the Gay Male World, 1890–1940* (New York: Basic Books, 1994); Kevin J. Mumford, *Interzones: Black/White Sex Districts in Chicago and New York in the Early Twentieth Century* (New York: Columbia University Press, 1997); Katz, *Love Stories*; St. Sukie De La Croix, *Chicago Whispers: A History of LGBT Chicago before Stonewall* (Madison: University of Wisconsin Press, 2012).

18. Doyle, "'A Very Proper Bostonian,'" 458–63.

19. Murphy, *Political Manhood*.

20. Boag, *Same-Sex Affairs*; Jay Hathaway, *The Gilded Age Construction of Modern American Homophobia* (New York: Palgrave Macmillan, 2003).

# Romantic Friendship

*Exploring Modern Categories of Sexuality,*
*Love, and Desire between Women*

DÁŠA FRANČÍKOVÁ

While exploring a multitude of expressions of female same-sex sexuality across time and space, students in my course on the global history of love between women busily imagined the historical accounts in the context of their present-day lives: having boyfriends but suddenly finding themselves attracted to their girlfriends; resisting modern categories of heterosexuality, bisexuality, and homosexuality, which they found problematic and limiting, especially when talking to their families and friends; and not wanting to spend their lives taking care of husbands and children. And then we read *Dear John, I Love Jane,* a collection of stories by women who left men for other women, set in the context of psychologist Lisa Diamond's notion of sexual fluidity, which emphasizes shifts in the desires, behaviors, and sexual identities of women.[1] My students could not stop talking about *Dear John, I Love Jane,* relating the stories to their own experiences, as well as discussing them in terms of romantic friendship. A quaint and intriguing concept, romantic friendship now seemed to have come to life through these contemporary narratives.

A term used in the eighteenth and nineteenth centuries, *romantic friendship* refers to a particularly close and socially accepted type of same-sex relationship. Most frequently formed between women, romantic friendships provided companions with support and nurturance in their personal and professional lives. That such relationships allowed a degree of same-sex intimacy while remaining compatible with hetero-sexual marriage is unfathomable for many twenty-first-century students. The contemporary stories brought the notion of romantic friendship closer to my students' lives, helping them connect the present and the past and identify possibilities they would not have imagined otherwise. But, as my students realized, the lens of romantic friendship has histori-cal significance beyond the pairing of two women or two men. Under-standing these relationships alters the ways in which we imagine, learn about, and understand the construction of modern gendered social scripts, women's pursuit of work, and definitions of sexuality. By grasp-ing the possibilities of romantic friendship, students also learned about the historical dimensions of gender, sexuality, and even U.S. history more generally.

## Romantic Friendship and Separate Spheres

Incorporating romantic friendship into U.S. history courses allows us to reconsider a number of issues, including the ideas of "separate spheres" and "opposite sexes," both prevalent ways to conceptualize gendered social scripts and gender relations in the eigh-teenth and nineteenth centuries. Modern science, medicine, and culture since the eighteenth century established women and men as polar opposites: women defined by the heart, men by the head and hand. Heterosexual marriage was supposed to unite the two opposites into a whole. The binary opposition between women and men also meant that, at least for the middle class, eighteenth- and nineteenth-century women and men were supposed to occupy two different and separate spheres. Men were expected to have jobs outside the home and partici-pate in public activities; women were supposed to devote their lives to domestic duties, their families, and their households, a relegation to the private sphere that made them invisible in the more highly valued public sphere.

The lens of romantic friendship, however, offers a different, queer perspective on this narrative. Historian Carroll Smith-Rosenberg's "The Female World of Love and Ritual" and literary historian Lillian Faderman's *Surpassing the Love of Men* first revealed a fascinating world of intimacy among women. The authors demonstrated how middle- and upper-class women spent their lives in the company of other women and formed close, often physically affectionate and lifelong relationships that played a central role in their lives.[2] Describing a typical female friendship, Smith-Rosenberg, who based her study on an analysis of correspondence and diaries written between the 1760s and the 1880s, told the story of Helena and Molly. The two friends met in 1868 at the Cooper Institute School of Design for Women in New York City and developed a long-term friendship. Like many other female friends, they visited each other's families and, when they were apart, wrote frequent letters, expressing longing to be together. In one letter, Molly wrote to Helena, "I was happy with you during those few so incredibly short weeks but surely you do not need words to tell you what you must know." "Imagine yourself kissed many times by one who loved you so dearly," she ended the letter.[3]

The documents and analysis in Smith-Rosenberg's essay point not only to one-on-one relationships but also to networks of relationships, which provided women with help and support in their daily activities and tasks. Helena, Molly, and many others readily accepted such companionship and community as a welcome alternative to relationships with men. This also enables us to connect the historical phenomenon of romantic friendship and worlds of women with Adrienne Rich's concept of "compulsory heterosexuality," which has challenged the presumption of women's heterosexuality and shown the significance and possibilities of women's communities.[4]

Although Smith-Rosenberg's and Faderman's work drew from a relatively homogeneous and privileged group of women, romantic friendships were not limited to white middle-class women in the arena of domesticity. In antebellum Philadelphia, New York, Baltimore, and Boston, African American women involved in antislavery projects created friendship albums that point to strong ties and relationships. Their affectionate connections with other women supported them not only in their domestic duties but also in their activities outside their homes.[5] The mid-nineteenth-century correspondence between Addie Brown, a domestic worker, and Rebecca Primus, who helped to found an educational institute for freed blacks in Royal Oak, Maryland, where she also taught, suggests that the two women shared a close and passionate friendship. Like other romantic friends, Brown expressed her yearning for Primus with reference to their physical closeness. She longed to be near Rebecca, "breathing the same air, with your arm gently drawn around me, my head reclining on your noble breast in perfect confidence and love," and wrote that she will "never be happy

*Summer Evening on Skagen's Southern Beach*, 1893, painting by Peder Severin Krøyer

again unless I am near you." Rebecca, in turn, assured her that their "love will not grow cold," stating, "I will always love you and you only."[6] But the focus of Brown and Primus's correspondence extended beyond their affectionate bonds. They also exchanged news and commented on social issues, making clear that their relationship encompassed not only emotional and physical ties but also intellectual and political affinities.

Heterosexual marriage did not mean an end to romantic friendships between women. Some female friends nevertheless considered marriage to be a strain on their romantic friendships. In 1873, when Helena was getting ready to marry, Molly wrote to her friend's fiancé, stating "that until you came along I believe that [Helena] loved me almost as girls love their lovers. *I know I loved her so.* Don't you wonder that I can stand the sight of you."[7] But marriage did not necessarily break up women's relationships. Even after she married, Sarah Butler Wister would write to Jeannie Field Musgrove, "I shall be entirely alone [this coming week]. I can give you no idea how desperately I shall want you." Jeannie reciprocated by assuring Sarah, "I love you & how happy I have been! You are the joy of my life."[8]

When marriage or other circumstances physically separated them, women often found ways to maintain their friendships. Those who could afford to would spend summer vacations together. One young woman in the late eighteenth century wrote her friend, "I hear Aunt is gone with the Friend and won't be back for two weeks, fine times indeed" and complained that "we poor young girls must spend all spring at home," deprived of each other's company.[9] Women would also make visits to see one another, when possible. When they did, much to the surprise of students today, they would sometimes move their husbands out of the bedroom so they could be together.[10] In the context of separate spheres and opposite sexes, where women were supposed to understand and relate to each other better than to their husbands, romantic friendships between women were compatible with and complementary to heterosexual marriage. Although marriage to a man was not inevitable, the vast majority of women in romantic friendships with other women did eventually marry.

## Romantic Friendship, Education, and the Professions

In addition to having an impact on our perception of the ideology of separate spheres and opposite sexes, the perspective of romantic friendship also makes an important contribution to the ways in which we consider women's pursuit of education and careers in the second half of the nineteenth century. Girls' schools fostered romantic friendships between classmates, as well as between students and teachers in the United States and in other countries around the world.[11] As women increasingly gained access to education and moved into professions, including social work, many found it difficult to combine their lives with heterosexual marriage. Instead, many educated and independent women formed relationships that came to be known as Boston marriages. Named after the geographic location on the East Coast where such relationships were most frequently found, Boston marriages allowed women not only to pursue their careers but also to live with other women in socially condoned relationships.

The social reformer and founder of Hull House in Chicago, Jane Addams, for example, had several close female friends. For over four decades, beginning in the early 1890s, she maintained a particularly close relationship with Mary Rozet Smith. Smith financially, physically, and emotionally supported Addams in her work at Hull House, "following [her] around with a shawl, pocket handkerchief, crackers if she thought Miss Addams might be hungry," as well as "feeding her raw oysters and providing 'delightful rubbings.'"[12] As Addams and Hull House are indispensible features of the progressive era in U.S. history courses, teachers might raise historical questions through the lens of romantic friendships. Is it significant that Addams did not marry a man? How might heterosexual marriage and motherhood have been incompatible with her work? Were Mary Rozet Smith's attention, affection, and money essential to Addams's accomplishments?

Undergraduates, as well as college-preparatory high school students, are likely to be interested in the possible career trajectories for their generation versus an earlier generation of college students and professional women. Another couple whose lives highlight change over time, Mary Woolley and Jeannette Marks, met at Wellesley College in 1895, where Marks was a student and Woolley taught history. The two lived together until Woolley's death in 1947. Woolley served as the president of Mount Holyoke College and Marks was a professor in the English department. One of Marks's colleagues in the National Woman's Party who had to resign because of her husband's health compared her own situation to Marks's inability to travel because of Woolley's health.[13] Using this example in the classroom, teachers might ask students to contemplate whether Marks and Woolley's colleagues might or might not have accepted the two as a married couple.

## Romantic Friends and the Invention of Lesbianism

As with other topics in queer history, it is important to balance evidence of acceptance and possibility in the past with instances of repression. In the late nineteenth century, new scientific knowledge establishing the category "homosexual" put a damper on social tolerance of women's same-sex intimacy. In this light, formerly respectable middle- and upper-class romantic friendships were aligned with pathological and criminal behavior. In January 1892, U.S. newspapers reported that in Memphis, Tennessee, nineteen-year-old Alice Mitchell from a well-off middle-class family slit the throat of her seventeen-year-old friend Freda Ward. The relationship, including Mitchell's plans to marry Ward and live with her, resembled accounts of other close eighteenth- and nineteenth-century female friends. But when Ward hesitated and returned her engagement ring, Mitchell killed her because, as she admitted in court, she "loved her and [Ward] did not want to marry [her]."[14]

The story of Mitchell and Ward has immediate appeal for students, although teaching it requires careful attention to harmful stereotypes about same-sex sexuality. One effective way to introduce the subject is to put it in the context of the journalism of this era. Students can examine U.S. newspaper stories, which cited jealousy as a motive, called the relationship a "misfit affection," and discussed Mitchell's—and, in typical nineteenth-century fashion, also her mother's—mental and physical instability in order to explain the murder. Historian Lisa Duggan, who analyzed the case in *Sapphic Slashers*, suggested that the confluence of emerging mass media and new scientific knowledge yielded the cultural narrative of a "lesbian murder," simultaneously discouraging women's pursuit of careers and independent lives. *Sapphic Slashers* includes two appendices—a hypothetical case and letters—that hold promise for classroom use as well.[15]

Modern scientific knowledge had a complex impact on the ways in which women thought about their own sexual subjectivity. The relationships of Miriam van Waters, a prison reformer and superintendent of the Massachusetts Reformatory for Women, with Geraldine Thompson, and first lady Eleanor Roosevelt with the Associated Press journalist Lorena Hickok illustrate how. Van Waters, who lived with Thompson between the late 1920s and late 1940s, was familiar with the new scientific discourse on homosexuality, even though she did not consider herself or her relationship with Geraldine Thompson in these terms.[16] Yet in 1948, during the rise of McCarthyism, she faced accusations of condoning homosexual behavior in prison. A subsequent investigation led to her dismissal from her job, and she burned the letters she thought would point to a romantic relationship with Thompson. Rather than keeping Thompson's letters, which, as she herself put it, could have been an "inspiration, history, joy, style—to me in 'old age,'" her awareness of the negative perception of homosexuality and fear of the consequences of being associated with homosexual behavior led van Waters to conceal the evidence.[17]

Similarly, the relationship between Eleanor Roosevelt and Lorena Hickok reminds students that sources may be elusive. Roosevelt met Hickok when Hickok was reporting on Franklin Delano Roosevelt's New York gubernatorial campaign, and later she began writing about Eleanor. Hickok was instrumental in designing Eleanor Roosevelt's media presence, encouraging her to hold her own press conferences, making her the only first lady to do so, and write her own newspaper column. After Roosevelt became first lady, the women began an extensive correspondence, writing thirty-five hundred letters before Roosevelt's death. Hickok destroyed all of her own and most of Roosevelt's letters written during the most intense phase of the relationship.[18] But the preserved correspondence includes letters in which Roosevelt missed "the feel of [Hickok's] hair," and Hickok remembered "the feeling of that soft spot just northeast of the corner of [Roosevelt's] mouth against [her] lips."[19] When the correspondence was opened to the public, journalists and scholars fiercely debated whether Roosevelt was a lesbian or bisexual. But the letters that the two women exchanged, along with evidence of other, similar relationships in the past, allow us to think of the ways in which women's sexuality and sexual activity have been defined, and even whether or not it is important if the relationships included a physical/erotic component.[20] Such documents point to a rather close relationship that was mutually significant for both their personal and professional lives and that persisted despite the stigma romantic friendship had developed due to its association with homosexuality.

## Conclusion

Romantic friendship thus offers a different and nuanced perspective not only on women's lives and relationships in the past but also on histories of community building, professionalism, education, journalism, politics, and more. It adds to our understanding of the ways in which modern gendered social scripts were constructed. The lens of romantic friendship shows that in the context of separate spheres women's relegation to domesticity enabled bonds and relationships that provided them with support that extended beyond the mundane world of domesticity. The imagined polarity between men and women facilitated a great deal of same-sex intimacy, which was, at least for women, reconcilable with heterosexuality and marriage. At the same time, the complementarity of the homosocial and heterosocial worlds that enabled romantic friendship invites us to think not only about how norms of sexuality and gender are defined and redefined over time but also about what constitutes sexual activity. Finally, the persistence of romantic friendship between women into the twentieth century shows that however powerful the new scientific knowledge on homosexuality and its impact on popular perception was, women's complex understandings of their own sexual identities drew from multifaceted desires, ideologies, and norms.

As my students in the class on the global history of love between women pointed out, romantic friendship remains highly significant today. As they noted, the concept allows us to examine the ways in which we perceive relationships and the limits and possibilities of friendships, specifically same-sex friendships. At the same time, my students found their learning experiences both encouraging and liberating. Exploring the historical phenomenon of romantic friendship in connection with present-day realities offers a number of possibilities, options, and alternatives to our modern categories of sexuality and our seemingly predefined lives.

## NOTES

1. Candace Walsh and Laura André, eds., *Dear John, I Love Jane: Women Write about Leaving Men for Women* (Berkeley, CA: Seal Press, 2010). For Lisa Diamond's concept of sexual fluidity, see *Sexual Fluidity: Understanding Women's Love and Desire* (Cambridge, MA: Harvard University Press, 2009).

2. Carroll Smith-Rosenberg, "The Female World of Love and Ritual: Relations between Women in Nineteenth-Century America," *Signs: Journal of Women in Culture and Society* 1, no. 1 (1975): 1–29; Lillian Faderman, *Surpassing the Love of Men: Romantic Friendships and Love between Women from the Renaissance to the Present* (London: Women's Press, 1991).

3. Quoted in Smith-Rosenberg, "Female World of Love and Ritual," 5, 6.

4. Adrienne Rich, "Compulsory Heterosexuality and Lesbian Existence," *Signs: Journal of Women in Culture and Society* 5, no. 4 (1980): 631–60.

5. Erica R. Armstrong, *A Fragile Freedom: African American Women and Emancipation in the Antebellum City* (New Haven, CT: Yale University Press, 2008). See also Erica R. Armstrong, "A Mental and Moral Feast: Reading, Writing, and Sentimentality in Black Philadelphia," *Journal of Women's History* 16, no. 1 (2004): 78–102.

6. Quoted in Karen V. Hansen, "'No Kisses Is Like Youres': An Erotic Friendship between Two African-American Women during the Mid-Nineteenth Century," *Gender & History* 7, no. 2 (1995): 159, 160. See also Farah Jasmine Griffin, ed., *Beloved Sisters and Loving Friends: Letters from Rebecca Primus of Royal Oak, Maryland, and Addie Brown of Hartford, Connecticut, 1854–1868* (New York: Knopf, 1999).

7. Smith-Rosenberg, "Female World of Love and Ritual," 7–8.

8. Ibid., 4.

9. Ibid., 11.

10. Ibid., 10.

11. See Leila J. Rupp, *Sapphistries: A Global History of Love between Women* (New York: New York University Press, 2009).

12. Victoria Bissell Brown, *The Education of Jane Addams* (Philadelphia: University of Pennsylvania Press, 2007), 257.

13. Leila J. Rupp, "'Imagine My Surprise': Women's Relationships in Historical Perspective," *Frontiers: A Journal of Women Studies* 5 (Fall 1980): 63.

14. *New York Times*, January 29, 1892, http://tinyurl.com/c89ugyn, accessed December 20, 2012. For an analysis of the case, see Lisa Duggan, *Sapphic Slashers: Sex, Violence, and American Modernity* (Durham, NC: Duke University Press, 2000).

15. See Duggan, *Sapphic Slashers*, 213–31.

16. Estelle B. Freedman, *Maternal Justice: Miriam Van Waters and the Female Reform Tradition* (Chicago: University of Chicago Press, 1996).

17. Quoted in Estelle B. Freedman, "'The Burning of Letters Continues': Elusive Identities and the Historical Construction of Sexuality," *Journal of Women's History* 9, no. 4 (1998): 182.

18. Rodger Streitmatter, ed., *Empty without You: The Intimate Letters of Eleanor Roosevelt and Lorena Hickok* (New York: Free Press, 1998), xiv, xxii.

19. Ibid., 77, 52.

20. See Martha Vicinus's concept of "erotic friendship" in Martha Vicinus, *Intimate Friends: Women Who Loved Women, 1778–1928* (Chicago: University of Chicago Press, 2004), as well as the discussion in the *Journal of Women's History* 20, no. 4 (2008): 132–59.

# Industrial Capitalism and Emergent Sexual Cultures

RED VAUGHAN TREMMEL

Urbanization profoundly altered the erotic lives of Americans, and it was as thrilling to some as it was alarming to others. At the end of the nineteenth century, in the electric times and improvised spaces of the industrializing city, new sexual and gender cultures emerged and conventional familial structures disintegrated. As divorce rates increased each decade after the Civil War, city dwellers attended unchaperoned dance halls, burlesque shows, brothels, annual drag balls, and dimly lit parks and theaters known for affording privacy. Late at night, in theater districts, city dwellers walked through streets animated by the painted faces of off-work vaudeville performers, burlesque dancers, and drag queens. Still in makeup and costumed attire, performers brought theater to the streets, creating a liminal space where millions of young people experimented with a widening variety of intimacies, sexual practices, and gender expressions. In cities such as New York, Chicago, San Francisco, New Orleans, and Los Angeles, the sexual and gender customs that had long organized agrarian life were utterly transformed. Many embraced the city as a site for social daring, autonomy, and culture building. The city offered opportunities to move in unusual ways, dance with strangers, invent new styles, pursue romantic and sexual desires, and try on modern identities—including queer ones.[1] Examining the rise of these new gender and sexual cultures, as well as the critiques they sparked, offers a richer understanding of urbanization and the inextricable ties between economic transformations and social ones.

In response to transformations in urban sexual and gender cultures, a small but powerful group of social reformers, medical professionals, industrialists, evangelical moralists, and government officials coalesced into "crusades for sexual order."[2] By the 1930s, after decades of organizing, reformers institutionalized their campaigns in city ordinances, law enforcement agencies, and culture industries, such as those in Hollywood and on Broadway. Believing that patriarchal sexual and gender conventions undergirded their prosperity as a class, race, and nation, crusaders created an aura of criminality and pathology around dance hall patrons, divorcees, burlesque dancers, sex workers, queer people, and their associates. The historian George Chauncey argues that urban reformers were so threatened by the emerging cultures that they built a closet and forced a whole host of people, practices, and histories into it.[3]

This essay offers one way to bring those histories out of the closet. Summarizing the most significant research findings of the last several decades, I suggest here one way to incorporate these hidden histories into a survey course. I begin, as my teaching does, with an examination of the effects of industrial capitalism on agrarian patriarchal conventions. I then examine the broad range of sexual and gender cultures that emerged in industrializing cities and place the rise of queer cultures within that context. I conclude with an examination of the crusades for social-sexual order that were institutionalized in the 1930s. This trajectory emphasizes the historical diversity and variability of sexual and gender practices, the correlation between changing economies and shifting sexual and gender identities, and the role of racial and class politics in shaping sexual and gender identities and communities.

We can expect students to be highly engaged and eager to learn about these hidden histories—perhaps more so than any other type of history we teach. Not unlike the young people who lived through the industrial age, students today are living through tremendous economic, technological, and social transformations. The generational gap between young people and their parents and grandparents is similarly wide. And those differences are particularly pronounced when it comes to sexuality and gender. In this age of biotechnological sexuality and embodiment, young people are evolving new gender and sexual orders, often without the guidance or support of their elders. As such, they are eager for analytical tools with which to contextualize the sexual and gender politics of their own age. Each semester it is quite common for at least a few students to vocalize a visceral frustration that they had not learned the history of gender and sexuality sooner. One student, practically in tears, used the word *cheated* to describe her lack of education. Others commonly ask, "Why didn't we learn this history in high school?" I use these questions to ask them to go deeper. Why do they believe these histories are useful? What did you learn about sexuality and gender that you did not know before? What do these hidden histories teach us about the politics of history and knowledge production itself?

## Out from under the Family's Watch

In order for students to understand the degree of social revolution that was stimulated by industrialization, they must be able to describe the transformations in the nation's most powerful institution — the family.[4] In the emerging industrial economy, millions of rural people, in the United States and Europe, found it increasingly difficult to cultivate land, manufacture goods for sale, and purchase household necessities competitively. As a result, many families were forced to uproot or send their adult children to cities in search of jobs. As the primary site where elders socialized their young into the ways of the world, the family's profound transformations led to dramatic changes in society.

On their arrival in cities, most young men and women spent the majority of their waking hours beyond the household — in a mill, factory, port, or shop, or on boats and trains — under the influence of elders who were not their mothers, fathers, or neighbors. City dwellers experienced unprecedented opportunities to pursue sexual and romantic desires beyond the watchful eyes of their family. Many chose to socialize away from tenements and other makeshift city dwellings, which were overcrowded, dimly lit, and often unsanitary. After work and on weekends, millions of young people from diverse racial and ethnic backgrounds spilled out onto street corners, boulevards, and parks to socialize, dance, mingle, flirt, and otherwise experiment with sexuality and gender.[5]

With so much time spent away from their families, young adults and children, many of whom were wage earners, began developing their own youth culture, which deviated from their parents' values. For centuries sexuality and gender were inextricably entangled with the sustenance of households. The more children one had, the more laborers a household could rely on. Because the economic success of the household, and therefore the wealth of nations and churches, was dependent on reproductive sexuality, parents, religious leaders, and public figures had long valorized procreative, patriarchal sexuality as ideal.

In the industrializing economy, reproductive sexuality and patriarchal households posed new challenges. A large family was increasingly burdensome in urban areas, and it was expensive to feed, house, and clothe children on the wages offered by employers. Additionally, employers in many extraction and processing zones preferred an all-male labor force because men without families would be less likely to demand a "family wage." It was in these zones that industrialists often supported the establishment of brothels. In this new economy, the imperative to reproduce declined and sexuality was released from its practical and economic obligations to procreate. While families were still invested in how and with whom their relatives had sex, the stakes of sexuality were very different. By the end of the industrial era, sex shifted from an act primarily associated with familial reproduction to an act associated with pleasure, happiness, and business.[6]

Attuned to the desires of pleasure-seeking city dwellers, thousands of amusement developers in every industrializing city opened dance halls, burlesque houses, cabarets, interracial clubs known as "black and tans," nickelodeons, bathhouses, brothels, jazz clubs, nightclubs, gambling halls, and amusement parks. Unlike the situation in agrarian and small town sites of socialization, urban venue owners and managers generally did not care if their customers were moral family members, good workers, or upstanding citizens. As such, young people experienced a new freedom to experiment. For a small price, city dwellers could find sexual partners of their choice, express unique genders, and engage in anonymous intimacies, voyeurism, and sexual barters.[7]

## Emerging Queer Worlds

Contrary to popular belief, turn-of-the-century queer cultures were quite visible and woven into the fabric of everyday urban life. As early as the 1860s, reports of "women dressed in masculine attire" regularly began appearing in city newspapers.[8] By the end of the century, in every major U.S. city, feminine men and masculine women strutted their genders with dazzling confidence in widely publicized drag balls that attracted thousands. During the 1920s, as many as six or seven large-scale drag balls operated annually in New York City, with many smaller balls taking place in saloon halls. They became so popular

Drag ball at Greenwich Village's Webster Hall, 1920s (*Greenwich Village History*, http://gvh.aphdigital.org/items/show/947, accessed December 23, 2014)

in Manhattan that some observers felt they surpassed the balls in Chicago and New Orleans. Feminine men, who often dressed as such and identified as "fairies," could be found any day of the week in many working-class bars and saloons. Queer life also formed on boulevards and beaches, in parks, and at boardinghouses such as Young Men's Christian Associations (YMCAs). Established nationwide during the 1840s and 1850s, YMCAs were built to offer rural men a family-like experience in the city, yet they often served as a key gateway where newcomers were introduced to the "gay world." Chauncey argues that there was no one gay space in the city. Rather, there were places throughout the city where queer people created worlds for themselves.[9]

Queer women often created social-sexual cultures in private spaces—in apartments or private social clubs. The public sphere had long been the domain of men, the place where fathers, husbands, and brothers engaged in political and economic transactions with other men. After work men found camaraderie in saloons, clubs, and restaurants that catered to male pleasures. As such, well into the twentieth century, city streets and venues were rough masculine spaces where women sometimes entered but not without fear of sexual harassment or sexual assault. In western societies, women and girls had long been conceptualized, in law and custom, as the property of husbands and fathers. Men derived their sense of masculinity from the acquisition of and authority over property. As women became increasingly independent from families, walking city streets alone, living in rooming houses, and earning wages, men's sense of authority, independence, and privilege was challenged. Men often saw women walking alone as fair game for sexual advances, presuming that such women were not the property of another.[10] Finances also played a role in the development of women's sexual cultures. Employers usually paid women starvation wages, making it difficult for them to have the spending money required to enjoy commercial amusements and entertainments. Additionally, parents often expected young women to turn over their paychecks to the household. The gendered nature of the new economy gave young men a distinct advantage in the sexual cultures of cities.[11] In this environment, many queer women, unaccompanied by men, chose to socialize in private spaces.

There were, of course, exceptions. African American and bohemian neighborhoods were known for their relative openness to gender and sexual diversity and were fertile sites of cultural and social experimentation—and mixed gatherings. Masculine women, drag queens, studs, bulldykers, and bulldaggers were much more likely to engage in queer practices in bars, clubs, resorts, and buffet flats in neighborhoods such as Greenwich Village and Harlem.[12] In bohemian areas of cities, outcasts of the middle class embraced nonconformity, cultural critique, eccentricity, and the creation of alternative worlds. There women, queer and otherwise, developed critiques of the institution of marriage and materialism, formed the feminist group Heterodoxy, valued sexual experimentation, and rejected gender conventions. Margaret Chung, the first Chinese American woman physician, in the late 1920s opened a practice in Chinatown in San Francisco, a bohemian neighborhood where she could pursue her penchant for male attire and her homoerotic interests.[13] Men as well as women considered places such as the West Village in New York and the Near North Side in Chicago, with their cafés, bars, and streets, to be meccas for queer people.[14]

During the 1920s, writers, intellectuals, visual artists, blues singers, novelists, and musicians increasingly amplified this visibility by reflecting queer cultures in their work. Blues singers such as Alberta Hunter, Ma Rainey, Bessie Smith, Ethel Waters, and Mabel Hampton plainly sang about "the life" in songs such as "Prove It on Me Blues," "Bulldykers Women's Blues," "Down Hearted Blues," and "Sissy Blues." Gladys Bentley was well known for singing the blues while in masculine attire. And such Harlem Renaissance writers as Langston Hughes and Richard Bruce Nugent incorporated the life into their novels.[15]

Fascinated by the increasingly rich, expressive, and queer nature of working-class, bohemian, and African American neighborhoods, middle-class European Americans began "slumming" there. During the 1920s, in places such as Harlem and the South Side of Chicago, pleasure-seeking slummers patronized white-owned nightclubs and other gathering places in African American neighborhoods in order to experience sensations of adventure and freedom from bourgeois America. Following on the heels of what came to be called the Negro craze, white middle-class pleasure-seekers became interested in queerness as spectacle. Drag queens became so popular with tourists in the late 1920s and early 1930s that contemporaries described the phenomenon as a pansy crazy. Taboo in a conventional milieu, the spectacle of African Americans, fairies, pansies, "inverted" women, and interracial sexuality offered white middle-class city dwellers a feeling of escape and freedom from the conventions of their own cultures as well as the feeling of being more modern, transgressive, metropolitan, and liberal than others in their class.[16]

Significantly, cities were not yet worlds divided into homosexual or heterosexual, gay or straight. Likewise, there was no one queer culture. Rather, there were multiple cultures composed of a diverse array of social types, gender practices, languages, and developing customs and informed by the distinct forces of race, class, and gender. Fairies and drag queens, for example, developed a witty style that came to be known as "camp"—a wit so sharp that it functioned to combat public hostility.[17] And a distinctive culture was fostered in bohemian areas of cities, such as Greenwich Village and the Near North Side of Chicago, where people collectively developed critiques of marriage, promoted free love, and generally fostered queer visibility.[18] It was within this multiplicity of spaces that a wide variety of people gathered, shared experiences, and developed distinct cultures that later fueled a coalition-style political movement for LGBT rights.

## Crusades for Urban Sexual Order

While some experienced the kaleidoscope of change brought about by industrial capitalism as exciting, others described it as social-sexual anarchy. Moralists, lawmakers, and reformers were alarmed by the sea change in social conventions that followed the massive arrival of workers in the nation's port cities. They watched with alarm as young people mingled with one another across racial, class, and ethnic divisions; traded sexual favors for access to cheap amusements; wore clothing that moralists considered inappropriate to their sex; and engaged in sexual activities with people of the same sex. For many, especially members of the new middle class, which was managing the incorporation of U.S. businesses, working-class youth culture was quite troubling.

A variety of campaigns sought to eliminate prostitution, risqué entertainment, interracial sex, pornography, birth control, and the visibility of queer people and cultures. Naming everything from divorce to the "mongrelization" of the nation by indiscriminate youths as threats to the social fabric, reformers doggedly targeted sites where they believed social-sexual anarchy flourished: saloons, brothels, dance halls, nickelodeons, burlesque houses, theaters, and even the scripts of films and plays. The broad critique of modern sexual cultures resonated among parents of all backgrounds, who similarly searched for ways to navigate the shift in their authority over their young.

Marriage, a key institution through which the state and religious institutions influenced the lives of citizens, seemed to be disintegrating. In every successive decade after the Civil War, the number of divorced people increased, causing some vocal religious, civic, and political leaders to liken divorcees to anarchists.[19] During the 1920s, critics of divorce pleaded with the public to place spiritual and civic obligations above individual desires, arguing that the social welfare of the entire community was at stake. Roman Catholic churches, among the most vehement critics of divorce, refused to remarry divorcees and banned them from receiving sacraments. Most states regularly recommitted to laws that discouraged divorce.

In another campaign, reformers advocated the establishment of cross-dressing laws. Between 1863 and 1900, legislatures sponsored and passed anti-cross-dressing laws in thirty-four cities in twenty-one states; between 1900 and 1914, eleven more states passed such laws.

According to Clare Sears, by relegating these gender practices and expressions to the private sphere, not only did public officials censor individuals, but they began creating an artificial public sphere where only a narrow range of gender practices was permitted. To the next generation, the limited number of gender expressions allowed in public exaggerated the citizenry's commitment to "normal" male and female representations; the legislation pushed a variety of desires, practices, and expressions out of sight. After generations of enforcement, transgender practices were effectively criminalized, causing the display of those behaviors to seem abnormal, extraordinary, and beyond traditional conventions.[20] Nonetheless, it was difficult for authorities to control the number of people who were engaging in transgender practices. While the authorities had stigmatized them, they could not administratively thwart the emergence of new gender practices.

During the 1930s, crusades for social-sexual order in urban areas were reenergized. The expansion of the industrial economy failed to provide labor and food to its participants, and a widespread panic over the market's unpredictability and its forcible rearrangement of family and gender roles swept the nation. As jobs, routines, and incomes were lost and daily roles and ranks mutated, the social and economic distinctions that gave meaning and order to life disintegrated. With a "disdain for chaos," many people began scrutinizing themselves and others for idiosyncratic social behavior; they examined events, language, opinions, and activities that seemingly caused or amplified chaos.

Unable to affect the major downturn in the economy, politicians promised voters that they would combat sexual, social, and political disorder. Government officials in major urban areas ordered the police to shut down commercial amusements where burlesque dancers, fairies, bulldaggers, and prostitutes gathered. Although these groups were engaged in disparate activities, they were similarly charged with being seductive, deceitful, and unpredictable and amplifying the familial disorder of the time. Because the scope of the perceived social-sexual threat was enormous and it was impossible for the state to target and regulate the behavior of millions of individuals, the state focused on recreational sites. In New York, it threatened bar and cabaret owners with the revocation of their liquor and amusement licenses if they did not regulate the activities of their customers. During "cleanup" campaigns, plainclothes police fanned throughout the city bars where queer people gathered, arresting patrons who visibly violated gender or sexual norms. Seeking to further eliminate queerness from the public sphere, New York City mayor Fiorello La Guardia ordered the police to clear all queer people from the streets, parks, and any other public space between 14th and 77th Streets. Fairies in midtown became invisible where they had once openly socialized.[21]

Reformers also sought to use the state to influence the sexual and gendered content of theatrical performances. City officials ordered the police to raid burlesque houses and drag shows, and performers were sent to jail; the authorities also hired censors to ensure that theaters were in compliance. By the end of the 1930s, legislatures had banned "female impersonation" in Chicago, New York, New Orleans, Detroit, Los Angeles, and many other large cities.[22] In San Francisco drag shows continued but only in upscale nightclubs.[23] Seeking to control all theatrical performances that reflected the emerging sexual order, the New York state legislature passed the Padlock Bill in 1927, which required that all representations of prostitution, burlesque, and queer cultures be portrayed in a negative light or be censored altogether. At the same time in Los Angeles, the Motion Picture Producers and Distributers of America anticipated that the state would soon regulate their productions. To avoid similar censorship, corporate heads created their own code of self-regulation, known as the Hays or Hollywood Production Code. In 1934 they established an office whose sole purpose was to monitor the content of movies for "repellant subjects," which included crime, profanity, religion, and sex. According to the code, "The sanctity of the institution of marriage and the home shall be upheld. Pictures shall not infer that low forms of sex relationship are the accepted or common thing."[24]

## Resistance and Persistence

Although there had been efforts to police queer cultures prior to the 1930s, it was in this decade that the ruling classes of modern cities built a closet and began forcing city dwellers into it. Sears's and Chauncey's research demonstrates that the state sought nothing less than to exclude queer life from the public sphere. By way of raids, employment discrimination, censorship, and biased representations, reformers used the state actively to infuse the nation with the social-sexual ideals of European American middle-class reformers. Through the 1960s, arrests and raids on bars were commonplace, and entertainment producers created an aura of criminality and abnormality around many working-class gender and sexual practices. The vast numbers of gender and sexual practices that emerged in urban areas were increasingly categorized as abnormal or normal, criminal or legal, and homosexual or heterosexual. In the meantime, political and business elites pointed to the arrests, ordinances, and laws targeting gender practices and sexual subcultures as evidence that they were establishing order out of chaos, stabilizing the marketplace, and protecting the patriarchal heterosexual monogamous family.

The eclectic sexual geographies of cities began to take shape just as the agriculturally based patriarchal household, which had typified the early American economy, began to collapse. Not only were families splitting apart as a result of migration, women's entrance into the labor force, and the Great Depression, but the gender roles that had long been tied to labor organization were also coming undone. In the new economy, women and children increasingly took wage-earning jobs beyond the household and successfully advocated for suffrage, birth control, and increased power within the government and economy. In the era of the New Woman, increasing numbers of men experienced a new dependence on women's wages and the corporations that determined the nature, availability, and value of their labor. The era when native-born boys grew up to become heads of agricultural, patriarchal households was over, and a new era had begun in which most boys would grow up to work for a man who was neither his father nor a neighbor but a manager who sought to extract as much labor from him as cheaply as possible. Through the 1960s, cultural debates broke out about the role and power of men and women in the new economy, and a strong line emerged between normal and degenerate sex, legal and criminal gender expressions, and heterosexual and homosexual people. This utter upheaval of gender relations and hierarchies, historians argue, fueled decades of panic about the nature of manhood, female autonomy, and heteronormative sexuality, leading to crusades for gender and sexual order.[25]

The use of the state by reform groups to assert sexual and gender norms and ideals had widespread and devastating consequences. The campaigns sent a message to everyone in the United States: if you do not watch yourself, you may be the next target. Millions of city dwellers, not only those who identified as queer, entered the post–Second World War period under stricter regulations and heightened sexual and gendered pressures. Most were likely to think twice before dancing too intimately or without inhibition in public; dressing in a style too akin to that of fairies, bulldaggers, or prostitutes; or otherwise associating with anyone who might be stigmatized. Many parents enforced strict codes of behavior, especially in public, to ensure that their children would not face degradation, discrimination, or criminalization. And, while queer people continued to create social networks and develop new gender cultures after the 1930s, it was often in clandestine, marginal, or mobile spaces to avoid discovery.[26] People who would come to identify as lesbian, gay, bisexual, and transgender in future decades moved in increasingly marginal public spaces and were cut off from their own history, leaving many to feel a sense of isolation, invisibility, and personal failure. While challenges to criminalization and stigmatization began to emerge in the 1950s, it was not until the Compton Cafeteria riot in San Francisco and the Stonewall Inn riots in New York City that LGBT-identified people would boldly and collectively assert their right to exist and assemble in the public sphere.

NOTES

1. I am using *queer* to describe a wide variety of nascent sexual practices and gender embodiments that significantly diverged from western patriarchal norms. Those who engaged in queer practices and embodiments came to be known as fairies, studs, bulldykers, bulldaggers, wolves, punks, trade, queens, inverts, homosexuals, transsexuals, or otherwise "in the life."

2. John D'Emilio and Estelle B. Freedman, *Intimate Matters: A History of Sexuality in America* (New York: Harper and Row, 1988), chap. 29.

3. George Chauncey, *Gay New York: Gender, Urban Culture and the Making of the Gay Male World, 1890–1940* (New York: Basic Books, 1994), chap. 12.

4. John D'Emilio, "Capitalism and Gay Identity," in *The Lesbian and Gay Studies Reader*, ed. Henry Abelove, Michèle Aina Barale, and David Halperin (New York: Routledge, 1993), 467–78.

5. Lewis A. Erenberg, *Steppin' Out: New York Nightlife and the Transformation of American Culture, 1890–1930* (Westport, CT: Greenwood Press, 1981); David Nasaw, *Going Out: The Rise and Fall of Public Amusements* (New York: Basic Books, 1993).

6. D'Emilio and Freedman, *Intimate Matters*, chap. 11. On the development of queer communities in rural areas, see Colin R. Johnson's essay in this volume.

7. Kathy Peiss, *Cheap Amusements: Working Women and Leisure in Turn-of-the-Century New York* (Philadelphia: Temple University Press, 1986), chaps. 1–2.

8. Clare Sears, "Electric Brilliancy: Cross-Dressing Law and Freak Show Displays in Nineteenth-Century San Francisco," *WSQ: Women's Studies Quarterly* 36 (Fall–Winter 2008): 170–87.

9. Chauncey, *Gay New York*.

10. Christine Stansell, "Male License and Working-Class Women's Sexuality," in *Major Problems in the History of American Sexuality*, ed. Kathy Peiss (New York: Houghton Mifflin, 2001), 120–31.

11. Peiss, *Cheap Amusements*.

12. Chauncey, *Gay New York*; Eric Garber, "A Spectacle in Color: The Lesbian and Gay Subculture of Jazz Age Harlem," in *Hidden from History: Reclaiming the Gay and Lesbian Past*, ed. Martin Bauml Duberman, Martha Vicinus, and George Chauncey Jr. (New York: New American Library, 1989), 318–31.

13. See Judy Tzu-Chun Wu, *Doctor Mom Chung of the Fair-Haired Bastards: The Life of a Wartime Celebrity* (Berkeley: University of California Press, 2005).

14. Christine Stansell, *American Moderns: Bohemian New York and the Creation of a New Century* (Princeton, NJ: Princeton University Press, 2009); Chauncey, *Gay New York*; St. Sukie de la Croix, *Chicago Whispers: A History of LGBT Chicago before Stonewall* (Madison: University of Wisconsin Press, 2012).

15. Eric Garber, "Gladys Bentley: The Bulldagger Who Sang the Blues," *Out/look* 1, no. 1 (Spring 1988): 52–61; Hazel Carby, "'It Just Be's Dat Way Sometime': The Sexual Politics of Women's Blues," in *The Jazz Cadence of American Culture* (New York: Columbia University Press, 1998), 471–82; Chad Heap, *Slumming: Sexual and Racial Encounters in American Nightlife, 1885–1940* (Chicago: University of Chicago Press, 2000), chap. 5; De la Croix, *Chicago Whispers*, chaps. 9, 10.

16. Chauncey, *Gay New York*; Heap, *Slumming*.

17. Chauncey, *Gay New York*, chaps. 1, 10.

18. Stansell, *American Moderns*; Heap, *Slumming*.

19. Nancy Cott, *Public Vows: A History of Marriage and the Nation* (Cambridge, MA: Harvard University Press, 2000).

20. Sears, "Electric Brilliancy," 170–74, 184. See also Genny Beemyn's essay in this volume.

21. Chauncey, *Gay New York*, 333.

22. Thomas Bolze, "Female Impersonation in the United States, 1900–1970" (PhD dissertation, State University of New York, Buffalo, 1994), 197.

23. Nan Alamilla Boyd, *Wide Open Town: A History of Queer San Francisco to 1965* (University California Press, 2003), 53–56.

24. Chauncey, *Gay New York*, 352–55.

25. Ibid., 111–27, 331.

26. The exception to this was San Francisco, where queer practices remained visible in the city's North Beach area. See Boyd, *Wide Open Town*, chap. 2.

# Men and Women Like That

*Regional Identities and*
*Rural Sexual Cultures in the South and*
*Pacific Northwest*

COLIN R. JOHNSON

ities occupy a prominent place in the story of American LGBT life for good reason, but focusing exclusively on urban contexts can distort students' understanding of the history of gender and sexual diversity in the United States. At best doing so leaves out a great deal. At worst it can leave students with the impression that gender nonconformity and same-sex desire are somehow *products* of metropolitan culture—a notion that arguably has some basis in fact, but one that too easily gives way to the reactionary and historically inaccurate belief that nonnormative genders and desires are merely the result of secularization, postmodern disaffectedness, or a general sense of moral permissiveness often associated with urban life. Additionally, limiting accounts of the history of LGBT life in America to the history of life as it was lived in cities also has the unfortunate effect of drawing attention away from distinctively regional stories of struggle and survival that can help to illustrate both the many challenges LGBT Americans have faced and the various strategies such individuals have employed to overcome them. In my experience, asking students to think critically about the history of gender and sexuality in nonmetropolitan America has another benefit as well. Namely, it provides them with an excellent opportunity to think carefully about binaries and the role they play in our thinking about virtually everything, including race, gender, sexuality, and even the character of space itself. So, for example, one of the hidden opportunities that talking about LGBT history in "rural" America provides is the opportunity to challenge students to think twice about what they mean when they use familiar terms such as *urban* and *rural*. In a similar vein, discussions about nonmetropolitan LGBT history can also afford students the chance to reflect on the complicated relation between gendered or sexual *behaviors* and gendered or sexual *identities*.

## Being Queer Outside the City

These days the nature of behavior's relation to identity often appears to be quite obvious to students, at least initially. Yet throughout much of U.S. history the question of how what one did sexually related to one's identity was a contextually specific and therefore surprisingly open one. To be sure, in some nonmetropolitan contexts, individuals who engaged in same-sex sexual behavior or failed to conform to established gender norms were thought to be distinctly different from their neighbors and therefore out of place in much the same way that LGBT Americans are sometimes made to feel unwelcome or out of place today. But in other rural and regional contexts, it was precisely the nonmetropolitan circumstances under which people lived that allowed them to depart from gendered conventions or act on same-sex desires.

As a way to get students thinking about how rural life might figure into U.S. history, I often start by inviting them to contemplate the sex-segregated conditions under which most wage-paying labor was performed in the United States through at least the first half of the twentieth century, particularly in agricultural and extractive industries. In the wake of director Ang Lee's 2005 Hollywood blockbuster *Brokeback Mountain*, many students' minds run immediately to sheepherding, a reasonable enough and yet oddly specific place to begin the discussion. But the conversation tends to open up quickly to other subjects, including cattle ranching, mining, and the timber trade, all of which depended heavily on the labor of young, unmarried men throughout much of the nineteenth and twentieth centuries. And appropriately enough. For it was these men—"ranchmen, cattle men, prospectors [and] lumbermen"—to whom the noted sex researcher Alfred C. Kinsey was mostly referring when he reported, in 1948, that "the highest frequencies

Rancher and sheepherder, Madison County, Montana, 1939 (photograph by Arthur Rothstein, Farm Security Administration—Office of War Information Photograph Collection, Library of Congress)

of the homosexual which we have ever secured anywhere have been in particular rural communities in some of the more remote sections of the country."[1] According to Kinsey, men who had sex with other men in the context of all-male rural labor communities seldom thought deeply, or possibly even at all, about what engaging in such activity said about them as people.

Others were less sanguine regarding such behavior, however. As sex generally became a topic of widespread national concern during the late nineteenth and early twentieth centuries, progressive era moral reformers grew increasingly concerned not only about the urban dwellers Red Vaughan Tremmel discusses in this volume but also about the moral laxity of men who worked in agriculture and extractive industries. In response they began targeting such workers for surveillance and legal prosecution whenever they turned up in towns and cities. In so doing, urban reformers and law enforcement officials effectively extended the reach of a newly emerging understanding of "homosexuality" as a substantive form of physiological and psychological pathology to an enormous group of people previously untouched by such an idea. As both Peter Boag and Nayan Shah have shown, this was especially true in the Pacific Northwest, where urban reformers in cities such as Portland worried increasingly about the perversity of timber industry workers and South Asian migrants, many of whom were arrested, imprisoned, or even institutionalized as "sexual psychopaths" under the terms of various antisodomy statutes.[2] This is a part of the story of progressive reform that is not commonly recounted in survey classes.

Given the oft-commented-upon prevalence of what is sometimes referred to as "situational homosexuality" in prisons and other sex-segregated environments even today, it is relatively easy for students to understand why it is actually unreasonable to assume that working-class men who lived and labored in entirely homosocial labor communities in rural areas remained sexually chaste. One does have to be careful about presenting the history of same-sex sexual behavior in this way, however—which is to say as a routine consequence of sex segregation—since doing so can create the mistaken impression that same-sex desire and gender nonconformity occurred only in rural areas when people lacked the opportunity to abide by social and cultural norms that have otherwise remained stable over time. Nothing could be further from the truth.

In fact, rural and small-town communities in the United States have a long history of accommodating, and in some cases even encouraging, gender and sexual nonconformity. These traditions of accommodation and encouragement were rarely politicized or politicizing in the same way that the postwar urban social movements were. Nor were they necessarily even understood as efforts to acknowledge or enfranchise LGBT people. But many LGBT individuals did experience them as opportunities to express their gender and sexual differences openly, if somewhat tacitly, while also making these differences visible to anyone else in the community who might share them. For example, Pete Daniel has suggested that "womanless weddings," in which men were married to one another in heavily attended mock ceremonies, provided a surprisingly public form of cover for those who enjoyed cross-dressing throughout much of the South. Brock Thompson, a historian of lesbian and gay life in Arkansas, has recently affirmed this theory, noting that he himself both attended and participated in womanless weddings for precisely these reasons as a young man growing up in the "Natural State."[3]

With the possible exception of a few small bohemian communities such as Eureka Springs, Arkansas; Key West, Florida; and Provincetown, Massachusetts, all of which made concerted efforts to attract artists and other free thinkers at various points in time, LGBT Americans have seldom constituted distinctive subcultures in rural areas and small towns in quite the same way they have in densely populated cities.[4] Rather, they tended to occupy particular social positions in rural and small-town communities, some of which were explicitly stigmatized, others of which were not. As we shall see, adults' ability to secure a place for themselves within the landscape of many rural and small-town communities depended on a number of factors, including their family history. On the other hand, children and adolescents who were perceived as different or strange often faced considerable stigmatization and harassment by their peers.

## Rural and Small-Town Queer Experiences

Regrettably, stigmatization and harassment comprise one aspect of the history of LGBT life in rural and small-town America with which many students today can easily identify, regardless of where they live. At the same time, the fact that there are so many commonalities in people's childhood experiences across time and over space provides an excellent opportunity to raise important questions about how Americans tend to encounter gender and sexual norms for the first time. It also clears the way to draw on literature, an expressive form that can provide valuable insights into how people felt about gender and sexual difference at various moments in American history.

For example, many of the United States' best-known regional authors have written eloquently about the challenges faced by gender-variant youths in small towns and rural areas. The most famous of these may be Carson McCullers, whose prize-winning novel *The Member of the Wedding* chronicles the anguished adolescence of Frankie Addams, a twelve-year-old "tomboy," as she confronts the dismal prospect of having to outgrow what theorist J. Jack Halberstam would refer to as her "female masculinity" in order to assume a more respectable version of adult femininity.[5] Similarly, the midwestern regionalist Sherwood

Anderson recalled that when he was growing up in the small town of Camden, Ohio, during the 1880s and 1890s, there were "certain men and boys who were somewhat feminine as there were women and girls who seemed somewhat on the masculine side. We others had called such boys 'sissies.'"[6]

These days American adolescents are far more likely to chide their peers for being "fags" or "dykes" than "sissies" or "tomboys," quite often regardless of whether there is any reason to believe that those they are attempting to humiliate and police might actually be gay or lesbian, as the sociologist C. J. Pascoe has shown.[7] But there are some notable similarities between Anderson's account of adolescent life in small-town Ohio during the late nineteenth century and the accounts of many young people of what it is like to attend an American primary or secondary school today. For one thing, it seems clear that athleticism and intellect have long been at odds in American youth culture, and in ways that have contributed directly to the ranking in value of different forms of gender expression.

Of course, adolescent "sissies" and "tomboys" obviously did not remain adolescents indefinitely; eventually, they grew up, in rural areas and small towns as much as anyplace. When they did, some moved to cities, especially during periods when rates of rural-to-urban migration were already high for other reasons. Others remained where they were, however, either because they had to do so for economic reasons or because they chose to do so. When they chose to stay, the lives such women and men led tended to be understood and sometimes even rationalized by themselves and their neighbors in light of a number of factors.

For those who came from families of wealth or influence, or families whose history stretched far back in local memory, living in a small community was often surprisingly easy, especially under circumstances in which their privileged social positions effectively guaranteed that neighbors would limit public criticism of those many undoubtedly regarded as their "betters," whether in theory or in fact. Such was clearly the case for gay male poet William Alexander Percy, for example. The son of a U.S. senator from Mississippi, Percy enjoyed broad latitude to live more or less as he pleased in Greenville, Mississippi, the place of his birth and the place where he remained throughout most of his adult life.[8] Such was also the case for Julia Boyer Reinstein, a lesbian heiress who spent much of her youth and young adulthood living without incident or significant difficulty in the decidedly provincial town of Deadwood, South Dakota.[9]

Lesbians and gay men who were less well heeled than Percy and Reinstein could also make a place for themselves within rural and small-town communities. But without wealth or pedigree to stand behind, these individuals were often considerably more vulnerable to the moralizing judgment and recriminations of those around them. As was the case in cities, some people who were "not the marrying type" deflected disapprobation by explaining their decision to eschew matrimony and procreation in terms of their chosen profession. Teaching, for example, was a vocation that tended to attract a disproportionate number of single women by the end of the nineteenth century—partly because such work was poorly paid, which meant that men were less likely to want to do it, and partly because it was seen as a relatively respectable way for a young woman to spend her time before becoming engaged. Once a women gained a teaching position in a small town, however, she could easily justify her ongoing attachment to spinsterhood by claiming her work in the classroom as her calling and all the school-age children in her community as her own.

Other lesbians and gay men in small towns and rural areas simply settled for being branded as "eccentric" or even "queer." Indeed, as the essayist and literary critic Mab Segrest notes, southern communities have a long history of making space for gender and sexual difference under the sign of *queerness*, a term that now carries with it a sense of theoretical or political sophistication thanks to the fact that it was appropriated for use by radical activists and academic theorists during the 1990s. In the South, however, the term *queer* was used to mean strange or different for decades before that, sometimes disparagingly, sometimes not.

*Particular* is another term that was used in many small southern communities throughout the twentieth century to describe men or women who managed to resist social pressure to conform to gender and sexual conventions. "Daisy, in her late fifties, is unmarried. This means that she is particular," Segrest explains, recalling one of the women her mother played bridge with every Tuesday morning back in the small Alabama town where she grew up during the 1960s. "Part of this particularity, as far as I am concerned, is that she is too particular to catch a man. (I suspect that because I did perhaps the same thing in that town through my adolescence. I carefully liked only the boys who didn't like me, and did not like the ones who did, to my mother's warnings that I couldn't afford to be so choosy.)"[10]

Thus, while being "particular" clearly was not exactly the same thing as being "out and proud," it was a way of being lesbian in a small southern town, for Segrest as much as Daisy. It was limiting, at times even painful, no doubt. But it was also clearly survivable in much the same way that discrimination, extortion, routine harassment by the police, and the experience of living in perpetual fear for one's physical safety proved to be survivable, if exhausting and profoundly unpleasant, for many lesbians and gay men who lived in American cities.

Indeed, if there is one lesson that students can learn from studying the history of gender and sexuality in rural and small-town America, it must certainly be the error of presuming that diversity has only existed under conditions that favored it, or that people have necessarily been quick to abandon ways of life that were familiar to them simply because those ways of life could sometimes be hard. If that were the case, it is unclear how the members of any stigmatized group of people ever would have been able to gain greater freedom or increased social equality. And yet gender and sexual minorities have made considerable strides in both areas, often by openly contesting ill-informed misconceptions regarding who they are, what they do, and where they do or do not properly belong.

## Mobility and Movement

Certainly one of the most widely held misconceptions about the spatial dimension of LGBT life during the post–Second World War era, even among many lesbians and gay men themselves, is the notion that movement between the country and the city was entirely unidirectional.[11] It was not. In fact a chief characteristic of postwar life in the United States has been the centrality of what the historian John Howard refers to as "automobility" in the lives of all Americans, including LGBT Americans.[12] Especially during the late 1960s and early 1970s, as car ownership became increasingly affordable and construction work on the sprawling Eisenhower interstate highway system reached its peak, movement back and forth *between* urban centers and more remote parts of the country became a relatively routine aspect of everyday life in the United States. For many LGBT Americans with long-standing connections to rural and small-town communities, this technological development meant they no longer had to choose between moving to the city and remaining where they were. Rather, they were able to build extended social networks that allowed them to visit densely populated urban areas, and even take part in the various sub-cultural scenes emerging there, and yet still return home at the end of the weekend or day. We know that in many cities businesses catering to members of the LGBT community depended heavily on the patronage of "weekenders" and tourists as much as the patronage of their "regulars."[13] Thus automobility is an important part of the story of postwar life.

We also know that gay men especially made use of the spaces between cities in order to find sexual partners and make other sorts of connections with people who shared their sexual proclivities. As Brock Thompson has shown, particular highway rest areas in states such as Arkansas became well known as sites for sexual assignations between men precisely because their remoteness allowed for much the same kind of anonymity that densely populated urban areas provided.[14] Furthermore, even public facilities situated *within* towns and small cities located near major highways sometimes became active gay male cruising spots during this period. Possibly because respectable members of the local community were often involved in the sexual cultures that took shape in these spaces, small-town authorities were often surprisingly reluctant to intervene. Occasionally, however, a particular incident might cause evidence of what was going on in these spaces to surface in a way that simply could not be contained or denied. When it did, local police would begin making arrests, partly for the purpose of protecting the community's welfare and partly to make a public display of their effectiveness as law enforcers.

Such was arguably the case during the summer of 1962 when police in the comparatively small midwestern town of Mansfield, Ohio, arrested no fewer than sixty men on sodomy charges following a month-long sting operation conducted in a public men's room located beneath one of the town's public parks. Although some of the men involved were Mansfield residents, many lived in neighboring villages. Others hailed from much larger municipalities such as Akron.[15] In short the history of LGBT life in rural and small-town America is not just a history of stasis and departure; it is also a history of arrival and passing through, and in this way it contributes to a deeper understanding of urbanization.

Indeed, there have even been moments when rural areas represented sites of utopian optimism for some LGBT individuals, particularly those who felt discouraged by the sexism, heterosexism, and outright homophobia that pervaded American culture during many periods in the twentieth century. For instance, during the 1970s some women who were involved with the women's liberation movement chose to experiment with various forms of woman-centered communal living, often on remotely located parcels of land they were able to rent or purchase for a fraction of what they would have had to pay to acquire adequate accommodations in a city. While most of these women considered themselves feminists, many also identified as lesbians or, in some cases, lesbian separatists, which typically meant that they advocated complete physical separation from men and male-dominated society. Known collectively as "Women's Land," the spaces these women created were sometimes wracked with controversy, including disagreements over the presence of male children. But they were often also described as life sustaining by women who experienced urban spaces as toxically sexist or physically threatening.[16]

Similarly controversial was the much publicized plan of the Los Angeles Gay Liberation Front (LA GLF) in 1970 to seize political control of California's least populous county for the purpose of establishing the first gay-majority electoral district in the United States. Although the LA GLF's Alpine County Project never actually came to fruition, mostly because of internal disagreement within the organization over whether the plan was a legitimate undertaking or a simple publicity stunt, this curious episode does show that it is not always gender or sexual difference per se that disturbs people in rural areas and small towns. Sometimes it is simply the idea of having unfamiliar values imposed on them by people they perceive to be outsiders. When asked several years after the Alpine County incident how he felt about the prospect of his community being overrun by members of yet another radical group, this time a radically *conservative* group of militant antigovernment tax objectors, one longtime Alpine County resident declared, "We'd much rather have the gays up here than those right-wingers."[17]

In sum, while it is probably fair to say that nonmetropolitan areas in the United States have tended to be more socially conservative than metropolitan ones on average, it would be a mistake to assume that people who live in small towns or rural communities have felt nothing but antipathy toward LGBT Americans. Rather, and very much like

175

their city-dwelling peers, rural and small-town Americans' feelings about same-sex sexual behavior and gender nonconformity have usually been shaped by a number of different factors. These include their personal familiarity with people who might be described as "queer" in some way and, crucially, the relative unruliness of their own genders and desires.

It is essential that students of U.S. history understand this, especially in an era in which the seemingly insuperable divide between urban values (read progressive) and rural ones (read traditionalist) looms large as a site of increasing conflict in American life. Indeed, and in much the same way they need to understand that urban sexual subcultures are social and cultural accomplishments rather than historical inevitabilities, students need to appreciate the fact that traditionalism is itself socially and culturally produced and therefore historically contingent. As such, blatantly homophobic positions that are held in traditionalism's name can be challenged in intellectually substantive ways, particularly when the traditionalism in question depends on a highly selective, and therefore distorted, vision of rural American life in both the present and the past.

## NOTES

1. Alfred C. Kinsey, Wardell B. Pomeroy, and Clyde E. Martin, *Sexual Behavior in the Human Male* (Philadelphia: Saunders, 1948), 457.

2. Peter Boag, *Same-Sex Affairs: Constructing and Controlling Homosexuality in the Pacific Northwest* (Berkeley: University of California Press, 2003); Nayan Shah, *Stranger Intimacy: Contesting Race, Sexuality, and the Law in the North American West* (Berkeley: University of California Press, 2012). See also Colin R. Johnson, "Casual Sex: Subaltern Sexuality 'on the Road' in Early Twentieth Century America," in *Subaltern Citizens and Their Histories: Investigations from India and the United States*, ed. Gyanendra Pandey (London: Routledge, 2010), 63–76.

3. On "womanless weddings," see Pete Daniel, *Lost Revolutions: The South in the 1950s* (Chapel Hill: University of North Carolina Press, 2000), 154–60. See also Brock Thompson, *The Un-Natural State: Arkansas and the Queer South* (Fayetteville: University of Arkansas Press, 2010), especially 17–19.

4. On the history of Eureka Springs as a seemingly unlikely and yet undeniably real haven for LGBT life in the Ozarks, see Thompson, *The Un-Natural State*, 131–82. On the history of Key West's emergence as a mecca for LGBT tourists from around the United States and the world, see Leila J. Rupp and Verta Taylor, *Drag Queens at the 801 Cabaret* (Chicago: University of Chicago Press, 2003), especially, 47–54. On Provincetown, see Karen Christel Krahulik,

*Provincetown: From Pilgrim Landing to Gay Resort* (New York: New York University Press, 2005).

5. Carson McCullers, *The Member of the Wedding* (New York: Mariner Books, 2004); Judith Halberstam, *Female Masculinity* (Durham, NC: Duke University Press, 1999).

6. Sherwood Anderson, *Sherwood Anderson's Memoirs: A Critical Edition*, ed. Ray Lewis White (Chapel Hill: University of North Carolina Press, 1969), 339.

7. C. J. Pascoe, *Dude, You're a Fag: Masculinity and Sexuality in High School* (Berkeley: University of California Press, 2011).

8. On the history of Percy's life in Greenville, see especially Benjamin E. Wise's masterfully researched and written biography *William Alexander Percy: The Curious Life of a Mississippi Planter and Sexual Free Thinker* (Chapel Hill: University of North Carolina Press, 2012).

9. On the life of Julia Boyer Reinstein, see Elizabeth Lapovsky Kennedy, "'But We Would Never Talk about It': The Structures of Lesbian Discretion in South Dakota, 1928–1933," in *Inventing Lesbian Cultures in America*, ed. Ellen Lewin (Boston: Beacon Press, 1996), 15–39.

10. Mab Segrest, *My Mama's Dead Squirrel: Lesbian Essays on Southern Culture* (Ithaca, NY: Firebrand Books, 1985), 67.

11. Kath Weston, "Get Thee to a Big City: Sexual Imaginary and the Great Gay Migration," in *Long, Slow Burn: Sexuality and Social Science* (New York: Routledge, 1998), 29–56; Colin R. Johnson, "The Theory of Sexual Dormancy," in *Queering the Countryside: New Directions in Rural Queer Studies*, ed. Brian J. Gilley, Mary L. Gray, and Colin R. Johnson (New York: New York University Press, forthcoming).

12. On the importance of postwar automobility to LGBT life in the United States, see John Howard, *Men Like That: A Southern Queer History* (Chicago: University of Chicago Press, 1999), 49, 96, 100–106, 112, 115.

13. Michael Warner, *The Trouble with Normal: Sex, Politics, and the Ethics of Queer Life* (New York: Free Press, 1999), 184–93.

14. Thompson, *The Un-Natural State*, 75–130.

15. Colin R. Johnson, *Just Queer Folks: Gender and Sexuality in Rural America* (Philadelphia: Temple University Press, 2013), 183–87.

16. On the history of lesbian separatism and the Women's Land movement, see Dana R. Shugar, *Separatism and Women's Community* (Lincoln: University of Nebraska Press, 1995). For a wide selection of primary source material, see Sarah Lucia Hoagland and Julia Penelope, eds., *For Lesbians Only: A Separatist Anthology* (London: Onlywomen Press, 1992).

17. On the history of the LA GLF's failed Alpine County Project, see Colin R. Johnson, "Homosexuals from Haystacks: Gay Liberation and the Specter of a Queer Majority in Rural California, circa 1970," in *Subalternity and Difference: Investigations from the North and the South*, ed. Gyanendra Pandey (London: Routledge, 2011), 41–56.

# The Other War

*Gay Men and Lesbians
in the Second World War*

MARILYN E. HEGARTY

The Second World War represents a major turning point in the history of the United States, offering a perfect opportunity to connect the history of gay men and lesbians to major themes in an introductory history course. The war not only reconfigured the global balance of power; it also had profound consequences on the home front, spurring the movement of millions of African Americans from the rural South to urban areas, confining Japanese Americans in relocation camps, admitting Mexicans into the country to fill jobs vacated by American citizens, and recruiting white middle-class housewives to work in the war industry. The massive mobilization for war moved men and, for the first time, some women into the military, opened opportunities for women to enter previously male civilian occupations, and in both of those ways introduced soldiers and war workers to new social and sexual environments. Soldiers, sailors, and women war workers recruited to work in boomtowns moved from rural areas and small towns to port and industrial cities. In addition, sex segregation in the military and war industry increased the chances that those with same-sex desires would meet others like themselves. The state apparatus, which both mobilized and policed women's heterosexuality, in a similar way inadvertently created the conditions for the growth of gay communities while cracking down on homosexuality.[1]

As a result, the wartime impact on gay men and lesbians was both positive and negative, serving as an excellent illustration of the ways in which wartime has complex social consequences.

## Gay Men in the Military

The issue of homosexuality emerged most forcefully in the military, as the work of Allan Bérubé has shown.[2] Millions of men found themselves drafted into the military, where, for the first time, they faced a stringent screening process devised by doctors and psychiatrists with the aim of weeding out homosexuals. According to government policy, homosexuals were unfit for military service because they would damage morale and interfere with military cohesion. All branches of the military had policies excluding homosexuals. Psychiatrists trained by the Selective Service took charge of examining draftees, who were subjected to questions such as whether they dated girls and engaged in sports—in other words, acted like men. Draft boards also looked for certain stereotypical homosexual mannerisms, such as whether draftees walked on tiptoe, had limp wrists, or spoke in high voices or with a lisp. Doctors examined men's bodies for evidence of anal sexual activity and gave those suspected of being homosexual the so-called gag test, which consisted of inserting a tongue depressor into the mouth to see if it produced a gag reflex. If a man did not gag, that could be a result of the fact that he engaged in fellatio. Any of these signs might result in a man being identified as a homosexual and therefore declared unfit for military service.

Some gay men lied to get into the service, while others answered questions honestly or appeared too feminine and found themselves rejected and labeled as homosexuals. Nevertheless, the screening did not keep gay men out. If discovered, men already in the armed forces could be imprisoned, sent to psychiatric hospitals, or dishonorably discharged, leaving a stain on their records with lasting consequences. The need for more soldiers on the battlefield, however, often overrode these policies, allowing numerous gay men to serve in the military. Some found a community in the casts of the "soldier shows" performed across the theater of war, where the absence of women led to the need for men to dress in drag. One gay man stationed at the San Diego Naval Training Station remembered encountering what he called "rather 'sensitive'

Snapshot of off-duty soldiers enjoying R&R, ca. 1942 (from John Ibson, *Picturing Men: A Century of Male Relationships in Everyday American Photography* [Smithsonian Institution Press, 2002])

boys" and thinking, "'Oh, these are more my kind of people.' . . . We became very chummy, quite close, very fraternal, very protective of each other."[3]

As a result of the screening policies, homosexuality became part of wartime discourse. Questions about homosexual desire and behavior ensured that every man inducted into the armed forces had to confront the possibility of homosexual feelings or experiences. This was a kind of massive public education about homosexuality. Despite—and because of—the attempts to eliminate homosexuals from the military, men with same-sex desires learned that there were many people like themselves.

### Lesbians in the Military

In contrast, women recruits escaped the scrutiny applied to men until late in the war, as Leisa D. Meyer has shown.[4] Women military personnel, who were recruited rather than drafted, represented a novelty during the war, since the only women who had been admitted to the military previously were nurses. In 1941 Edith Nourse Rogers, a

Massachusetts congresswoman, introduced legislation to establish a Women's Army Corps (WAC). She wanted the new organization to be part of the regular army and to have all the benefits of such service, although this was controversial enough that it did not happen right away. The formation of the Women's Army Auxiliary Corps (WAAC) represented a compromise and was finally approved only after the attack on Pearl Harbor increased the need for military personnel. In 1943 Rogers's dream came true when the Women's Army Corps replaced the WAAC. Thousands of women, including many lesbians, would ultimately join the armed forces. In addition to the WAC, women served in the navy as Women Accepted for Volunteer Emergency Service (WAVES), in the Coast Guard Women's Reserve, in the Marine Corps Women's Reserve, in the Army Air Forces (later the Women's Army Air Corps), and in the Air Transport Service, where they flew and delivered airplanes across the country.

Despite the establishment of the women's services, there was a significant amount of opposition to the very idea of women in the military. The masculinization of women in uniform troubled many observers. Other critics disliked women working in traditionally male fields and ignoring their assigned roles as housewives and mothers. Some men even threatened their wives, sisters, or girlfriends with dire consequences should they disobey and enter the armed services. Recruiters for the WAC sought to ensure the respectability of their military personnel by seeking out white, educated, middle-class women. In an attempt to downplay the challenge to the gender order that women in the military could represent, recruits with masculine body types, deep voices, or other masculine traits were not supposed to be admitted to the armed services. Policies did not specifically name lesbians as undesirable, but the attempt to root out masculine women no doubt had some effect. Nevertheless, lesbians signed up in significant numbers.

When the WAC achieved military status, the controversy heightened. Heated debates emerged within the military and in public venues, and rumors circulated about sexual promiscuity and lesbianism among WACs. Any sexual agency on women's part threatened the legitimacy of the corps, and official policy forbade any sexual relations on the part of women in the services. Yet administrators were worried enough about interracial heterosexual relationships and masculine women coming on to other women that they sometimes encouraged intraracial heterosexual dating and even tolerated non-gender-differentiated same-sex relationships. In other words, a hierarchy based on race, class, sexuality, and gender presentation guided military authorities in their responses to sexual relationships in their services.

The fear that military women were usurping male privilege, behaving like men, and adopting male behaviors such as drinking, partying, and sexual activity contributed to continuing hostility. Many officials, both military and civilian, believed the rumors about promiscuity and lesbianism and used them to make their case that women were unfit for military service. Oveta Culp Hobby, who headed the corps, staunchly defended WACs as respectable women who performed critical jobs in support of the war effort. She worked to suppress lesbianism without calling public attention to the issue. In conjunction with advertisers and magazine publishers, the corps took to publicizing images of attractive military women as a way to counteract the rumors.

In the early years, the WAC refrained from removing too many servicewomen accused of lesbianism because it would seriously damage the reputation of the entire corps. As the rumors of lesbianism persisted, the corps put more stringent screening procedures in place. In 1944 the War Department issued new guidelines, warning psychiatrists to "be on guard against the homosexual who may see in the WAC an opportunity to indulge her sexual perversity."[5] Some straight WACs pointed the finger at their suspected lesbian compatriots. While accusations could be difficult to prove, some WACs were urged to resign and others were ensnared by charges of conduct unbecoming a solider such as insubordination, refusing an order, or drunkenness. Even refusing male sexual advances could result in rumors of lesbianism. Yet the WAC rarely initiated proceedings against servicewomen on the grounds of homosexuality out of fear of the resultant bad publicity. The largest investigation, at Fort Oglethorpe, Georgia, began in 1944 when the mother of a WAC private found love letters a sergeant had written to her daughter. Outraged, the mother contacted officials to report that the base was "full of homosexuals and sex maniacs" and threatened to go public if the military did not act quickly.[6] In the course of the investigation, some women admitted their desires while others turned on each other, claiming to be the victim of seduction. Still working hard to avoid negative publicity and taking into account the class backgrounds and masculinity of the women charged, the authorities asked the woman named as the ringleader to resign and sent others for psychiatric evaluation to determine whether they could be restored to duty.

## The Complex Impact of the War

Both female and male soldiers charged with homosexual activities or conduct could be sent to psychiatrists, subjected to lengthy and intense interrogations, and pressured to name other homosexuals. If court-martialed, military personnel received dishonorable discharges. Beginning in 1942, homosexuals and others, including African Americans who protested discrimination within the military, could receive Section 8 discharges, known as "blue discharges" because they were printed on blue paper. These were neither honorable nor dishonorable, but the consequences were severe. Those with blue discharges lost all veterans' benefits and were excluded forever from military and government employment. And since employers requested information on military records, it was very difficult to gain any kind of employment.

At the same time that the military sought to root out homosexuals until the need for military personnel became so pressing that officials tended to look the other way, the ban on service members patronizing commercial establishments catering to gay people facilitated the spread of information about places to go and inadvertently helped to build gay communities in port cities such as San Francisco. The military police, in the interest of fighting vice and venereal disease, posted certain establishments as off limits, thus calling their existence to the attention of those interested in finding places in which to socialize. Public commercialized forms of entertainment began to replace private parties as the preferred venue for a young and mobile population. Geographic mobility disseminated gay slang across the country and started the process of nationalizing lesbian and gay subcultures. For lesbians the movement of women into factory jobs loosened restrictions on what they could wear in public, making it possible for butch women to wear pants for the first time without attracting too much attention. Working-class lesbian bars in the 1940s and 1950s played an important role in the creation of a public lesbian culture, as the pioneering work of Elizabeth Lapovsky Kennedy and Madeline D. Davis has shown.[7]

This dynamic of the complex consequences of wartime mobilization for the gay and lesbian population can easily be integrated into lectures on and discussions of the Second World War in U.S. survey courses. For many years I taught a survey course in U.S. history at Ohio State University. Early on I decided to add sexual identity to the categories of race, ethnicity, and class that intersect in defining some people as "other." Focusing on the gay and lesbian experience in the military during the war allowed us to take up the question of the rights of citizenship, an important issue for marginalized groups in general. I asked whether the Constitution excluded homosexuals from citizenship: could one find any evidence of that? So why, then, were some citizens deprived of their right to serve? Margot Canaday, in her book *The Straight State*, traces the attempts to weed homosexuals out of the military to the early twentieth century, showing how, along with welfare and immigration policy, military policy came to define the citizen as resolutely heterosexual.[8] The Second World War and its aftermath played an important role in this process while also setting in motion the process of organizing within the gay community that would challenge heterosexuality as a basis for citizenship.

In all these ways, then, integrating the experience of gay men and lesbians during the Second World War allows students to understand how important the war was not only in terms of defeating fascism and launching the rivalry between the United States and the Soviet Union but also on the home front. The need for bodies in the military and industry opened up opportunities for groups previously denied them on the grounds of race, ethnicity, and gender, but after the war pressure to return things to normal increased. Yet social change could not so easily be reversed. Despite the postwar Lavender Scare discussed by David K. Johnson in this volume—the crackdown on homosexuals in government and the military that accompanied the anticommunist hysteria of the 1950s and 1960s—the wartime experience facilitated individual and collective "coming out under fire," to use Allan Bérubé's memorable phrase.[9] This is an important part of the story of the war, as well as the story of queer community and the queer movement, and it helps students to understand the complex consequences of an event as momentous as the Second World War.

NOTES

1. On the regulation of women's sexuality, see Marilyn E. Hegarty, *Victory Girls, Khaki-Wackies, and Patriotutes: The Regulation of Female Sexuality during World War II* (New York: New York University Press, 2008).

2. Allan Bérubé, *Coming Out under Fire: The History of Gay Men and Women in World War II* (New York: Free Press, 1990).

3. Ibid., 64.

4. See Leisa D. Meyer, *Creating GI Jane: Sexuality and Power in the Women's Army Corps during World War II* (New York: Columbia University Press, 1996).

5. Ibid., 159.

6. Ibid., 173.

7. Elizabeth Lapovsky Kennedy and Madeline D. Davis, *Boots of Leather, Slippers of Gold: The History of a Lesbian Community* (New York: Routledge, 1993).

8. Margot Canaday, *The Straight State: Sexuality and Citizenship in Twentieth-Century America* (Princeton, NJ: Princeton University Press, 2009).

9. Bérubé, *Coming Out under Fire*. See also David K. Johnson, *The Lavender Scare: The Cold War Persecution of Gays and Lesbians in the Federal Government* (Chicago: University of Chicago Press, 2004).

# The Red Scare's Lavender Cousin

*The Construction of the Cold War Citizen*

DAVID K. JOHNSON

The story of Senator Joseph McCarthy and his quick rise from backbench obscurity to national media prominence in 1950 is a standard feature of lesson plans on Cold War domestic politics. The story of his Lincoln Day speech in Wheeling, West Virginia, and his charge that hundreds of "card-carrying Communists" were working in the U.S. State Department under the eye of the secretary of state is well known. "I hold in my hand a list," McCarthy told the Women's Republican Club, seeming to offer concrete support to vague suspicions that had been rumored for years. As with the recently concluded Alger Hiss spy case—where budding communist hunter Richard Nixon went before television cameras holding microfilm allegedly containing highly classified State Department documents—the claim of tangible evidence caught the public imagination and put Joseph McCarthy on a path that would make his name synonymous with the decade.

But few who teach about Cold War anticommunism remember that McCarthy's charges kept changing. The list that first offered 205 names later had only 57 or 81, depending on the day. And the label "card-carrying Communist" changed to "loyalty risks," "security risks," or simply "bad risks." Two weeks later, when McCarthy finally provided specifics to his Senate colleagues, he highlighted two cases that he thought explained all the others. Although most on his list were accused of "palling around with Communists," joining communist front organizations, or acting as Soviet agents, these two were less about political than sexual deviance. One involved a "flagrantly homosexual" translator who had been dismissed as a "bad security risk" but was later reinstated. Another case involved a cadre of homosexual employees allegedly hired en masse. These two cases were important, McCarthy explained, because, as a high government intelligence officer had told him, "If you had been in this work as long as we have been, you would realize that there is something wrong with each one of these individuals. You will find that practically every active Communist is twisted mentally or physically in some way." McCarthy's explanation captured a common understanding in 1950s America: that homosexuality was evidence of the sort of psychological weakness that made one susceptible to communist indoctrination. It showed that the Red Scare was tinged with lavender—the color then associated with homosexuality.[1]

## Linking Political and Sexual Deviance

Incorporating the Lavender Scare into a standard history survey is as effortless as it was for Senator McCarthy to enlarge his list of targets from communists to queers. Indeed, pretending that communists were McCarthy's only targets distorts the historical record. Exploring what the terms *loyalty risk* and *security risk* meant is a good place to start. In the Cold War context, "loyalty" involved a current state of mind, a willful desire to betray secrets or overthrow the government, while "security" involved behaviors or associations that might lead one inadvertently or unwillingly to betray secrets in the future. Classroom discussions might focus on what types of persons were considered threats during the Cold War compared to today. How do students make sense of newspaper headlines from the period that declared "Perverts Called Government Peril" or "Sex Perverts in Government Said Weak Link as Spy Prey"?[2] Why would gays and lesbians in the 1950s be singled out as security risks?

McCarthy was not the only one to link political and sexual deviance. The Truman administration's response to his allegations drew further attention to the connection between homosexuality and national security. Secretary of State Dean Acheson initially denied employing or dismissing any communists. But when grilled by McCarthy's Republican colleagues, he admitted to firing 202 "security risks." Then his assistant, also under intense questioning, revealed that among these were 91 homosexuals. This revelation seemed to substantiate McCarthy's otherwise groundless charges. It unleashed a flurry of newspaper columns, constituent mail, public debate, and congressional investigations. Letters from outraged citizens poured into the White House, the State Department, Capitol Hill, and news outlets. Journalists sampling McCarthy's mail revealed that only a quarter of the twenty-five thousand writers expressed concern about "red infiltration." Most expressed "shocked indignation at the evidence of sex depravity." As one woman from Long Island wrote to the *New York Daily News*, "The homosexual situation in our State Department is no more shocking than your statement that 'they are uncertain what to do about it.' Let every American who loves this country get behind McCarthy or any committee which will thoroughly investigate and expose every one of these people . . . [for] we must rid our Government of these creatures."

## Why Homosexuals Were Dangerous

One of the best sources available for giving students an understanding of the Lavender Scare is a report issued by a U.S. Senate committee investigating "The Employment of Homosexuals and Other Sex Perverts in Government." It was the culmination of a series of hearings in the summer of 1950 held behind closed doors in which security officers, law enforcement officials, and military intelligence experts testified. All unanimously agreed that homosexuals posed a threat to security because they could be blackmailed into revealing state secrets. But what sort of proof did they offer? The report pointed to only one example: Colonel Alfred Redl, head of Austrian intelligence during the run-up to the First World War, a homosexual and notorious double agent. The committee considered this sufficient proof, and its final report asserted categorically that homosexuals posed a threat to national security and that the Soviets were actively engaged in a program to optimize this vulnerability. Ask students to assess this evidence and place it in today's context. What would they think of a government report that suggested that group X posed a threat to national security based on the activities of one of its members some thirty-five years ago in a foreign country?

Given the lack of evidence for the blackmail rationale, students might consider what seems to be the real motivation for excluding gay men and lesbians from government positions during the Cold War. The Senate committee conveniently offered another justification: homosexuals were violators of "normal accepted standards of social behavior" and were therefore "unsuitable" for government employment. The report argued that homosexuals engaged in acts of moral perversion that weakened their "moral fiber" and "emotional stability" to such an extent that they could not be trusted in positions of responsibility. They tended to "gather other perverts" into the government, create dangerous cliques, and even exert a "corrosive influence" on coworkers. As the report summarized it, "One homosexual can pollute a Government office."[3]

After considering the logic of government officials, ask students to consider what else was going on in American culture that made the "homosexuals in government" scandal resonate with average citizens—how official rationales concerning blackmail meshed with larger cultural concerns. Pay particular attention to language. While some, like McCarthy, used the language of psychological weakness to link communists, homosexuals, and similar threats to American democracy, others used the language of morality. Many feared that the United States was in a state of moral decline due to the "anything goes" mentality engendered by the Second World War—a fear seemingly confirmed by the 1948 Kinsey Report, which revealed that 85 percent of U.S. men engaged in premarital sex and 37 percent had had sex with another man. Given the Cold War context, some saw this moral decline as a communist plot. As Bernarr Macfadden warned in his popular tabloid *Vitalized Physical Culture*, "COMMUNISTS ARE NOW CONVERTING AMERICAN YOUTH TO HOMOSEXUALITY TO DEFEAT US FROM WITHIN!" Homosexuality, he asserted, was "Stalin's Atom Bomb." Like many in the United States, he saw the Cold War as a moral crusade between a free, Judeo-Christian West and an atheist, communist dictatorship, the latter imagined as a paradise of free love, strong working women, and weak or nonexistent families. Encouraging strong heterosexual family structures and marginalizing sexual deviance thus became weapons that could be used to defeat communism. Bring in other elements of this "moral rearmament" in the 1950s, including the push to remove women from the work force and the addition of "under God" to the pledge of allegiance.

## The Politics of the Lavender Scare

Get students to also consider the political motivations behind the Lavender Scare: who stood to gain votes? Although concerns with national security were mostly bipartisan, the Republican Party, which had not controlled the White House since 1932, had much to gain by accusing the Truman and Roosevelt administrations of being havens for homosexuals. Seizing on the revelation that the Truman administration had dismissed ninety-one homosexuals, the chairman of the Republican National Committee warned, "Perhaps as dangerous as the actual Communists are the sexual perverts who have infiltrated our Government." Columnist John O'Donnell called the homosexual charges "a new type of political weapon—never used in this republic." He predicted it would destroy public confidence in the Truman administration, then being criticized for hiring and protecting homosexuals. Newspaper editorials were already suggesting that Republicans would be railing against "queer goings-on in the State Department" in the fall campaign. "If we were writing Republican campaign speeches," the *New York Daily News* editorialized, "we'd use the word 'queer' at every opportunity."

By 1952 the Lavender Scare even began to influence the campaigns of presidential candidates. Issues of gender and sexuality permeated that year's contest between Republican nominee Dwight Eisenhower and Democrat Adlai Stevenson. Stevenson was a divorced former diplomat publicly derided by his enemies as an intellectual "egghead." The *New York Daily News* said he had a "fruity" voice. Claiming FBI reports of an arrest on a morals charge in New York, Republicans privately floated the rumor that Stevenson was queer. The rumors had such nationwide currency that one tabloid magazine ran a story titled "How That Stevenson Rumor Started," suggesting it had originated with a story told by the former Mrs. Stevenson, which "reflected on the manhood of the father of her three sons." By contrast, Republican campaign pamphlets stressed how their candidates were "regular guys" and "God-fearing men"—even though Eisenhower was unbaptized and had no official church affiliation. To visually highlight the claim that they were "for morality," Republicans in 1952 initiated what has become a staple of American presidential politics: campaign appearances with photogenic wives and children, or grandchildren in the case of the Eisenhowers. Images of both Eisenhower and his running mate

Eisenhower and Nixon campaigning as the candidates of morality, 1952 (Division of Po-litical History, National Museum of American History, Smithsonian Institution, reprinted with permission)

THEY'RE GOD-FEARING MEN

A **vote** for Ike and Dick is a vote **for morality**

Richard Nixon with their families were ubiquitous. They called attention to Stevenson's divorce and implicitly raised questions about the reasons behind it. After looking at images of the candidates and their campaign literature, students might discuss how the notion of family values continues to be a central feature in presidential campaign politics.

## The Consequences of the Lavender Scare

Unfortunately, the Lavender Scare was more than a campaign tactic; it had real consequences for thousands of Americans. Once in office, Eisenhower fulfilled his campaign slogan to "clean house" by issuing an executive order that replaced Truman's loyalty system with a more far-reaching security system focused on general character and suitability. Executive Order 10450 banned homosexuals from all positions within the federal government—the nation's largest employer—thus institutionalizing a practice that had begun in the military during the Second World War and spread to agencies such as the State Department. It would remain standard government policy until the early 1970s, during which time federal security officers interrogated thousands of gay men and lesbians about their sex lives, forced them to name names, in a purge that rivaled that of suspected communists and leftists. It had the political advantage of inflating the number of "security risks" uncovered in Eisenhower's program. With few if any communists left in government, homosexuals proved easier targets.[4]

Highlighting the personal stories of victims of the Lavender Scare is an effective way to draw in students. Madeline Tress was one such victim, typical of the thousands of men and women impacted by Executive Order 10450. We know of her experience through both her FBI file, which she acquired through a Freedom of Information Act request, and oral history interviews conducted by a new wave of historians who have begun to document the lives of the LGBT community. Documentary filmmakers have also begun to capture these stories. It is important to point out that had these efforts not been made stories such as these might have gone unrecorded.[5]

In 1958 Tress was a twenty-four-year-old business economist at the Department of Commerce beginning what she hoped would be a long and distinguished career in international economics. A graduate of Georgetown University, Tress had been working for the Department of Commerce for only a few months, but, like all civil servants under the Eisenhower administration, she had to pass a security investigation. One day in April 1958, when Tress reported for work, she was met by two civil service investigators who took her to a private room to ask her some questions. "Miss Tress," one investigator began, "your voluntary appearance here today has been requested in order to afford you an opportunity to answer questions concerning information which has been received by the U.S. Civil Service Commission." The investigator asked Tress if she objected to taking an oath before they began to take her statement. Realizing the seriousness of the situation, Tress asked if she could consult an attorney and was told that she could but that the attorney could not be present in the room during the "interview." Tress took the oath and began to answer mundane questions concerning her name, address, and date of birth. Then came the question, the reason she had been summoned to this dingy room: "Miss Tress" the investi-gator intoned, "the Commission has information that you are an ad-mitted homosexual. What comment do you wish to make regarding this matter?"

Tress froze. Which would be worse, she wondered, admitting being gay or lying? Tress told the security officers that she had no comment and adamantly refused to discuss the matter. Undeterred, the investi-gators posed more subtle questions. "Were you ever at the Redskins Lounge?" one of them demanded to know. Figuring there was nothing illegal involved, she admitted to frequenting Washington's best-known lesbian bar. Tress insisted that she "enjoyed the orchestra there" but denied she went there to make homosexual contacts. The investigator then named a host of her gay friends, demanding to know if she asso-ciated with any of them. Tress admitted knowing what the investigators termed "known homosexuals." Under intense questioning, Tress, like most other victims of such interrogation tactics, tried to mollify her interrogators. She admitted to homosexual activity in her youth but insisted she had broken away from it since coming to Washington. In the eyes of the Civil Service Commission her admission to early homo-sexual activity, visiting lesbian bars, and associating with known homo-sexuals was sufficient proof to bar her from federal employment. At the end of the interrogation she refused to sign a prepared statement but knew that she had only one option. The next day she submitted her resig-nation. She never worked as an economist again and soon left Washing-ton for California. The State Department even vetoed a Fulbright Fel-lowship she won to study abroad because her file had been flagged with the note "questionable loyalty and morals (lesbian)." Because of that one day, Tress later noted, "My whole fucking life had changed."

Tress's experience raises interesting questions about the power and scope of the national security apparatus and the methods and tactics used to identify security risks. You might ask students to discuss what evidence they might use to detect sexual orientation and if those signs have changed over time. During the Lavender Scare a broad network of FBI investigators, agency security personnel, and private informants was constantly on the lookout for signs of homosexuality among government personnel. Authorities looked for gender deviation in dress or manner, close associations with known gay people, or other eccentricities. In their routine background investigation of Tress, FBI agents had interviewed dozens of her friends, coworkers, and neighbors.

A male coworker told the FBI she was "unstable" in dress and thinking, "bohemian" in lifestyle, and received calls from many single women. Others suggested she was "mannish," "a tomboy," or had "personality problems." A State Department secretary known to history only as Miss Blevins informed on her boss because she had "odd-shaped" lips and a close relationship with an older female coworker with a "mannish voice." Even the vaguest of suspicions would prompt the government to begin a special investigation. Men who frequented known gay cruising areas such as Washington, DC's Lafayette Park or Los Angeles's Pershing Square were even more at risk, since arrest records in such locations served as proof of homosexuality. The level of fear and suspicion was so intense that even nongay people began to monitor their behavior. Male employees of the State Department were careful not to be seen alone together in pairs for fear they might be mistaken for a gay couple—a nice illustration of the way queer history affects all society.

Victims of the Lavender Scare were not simply collateral damage from the Red Scare. In scope and size, the Lavender Scare rivaled its better known cousin. The total number of suspected gays and lesbians who lost their jobs during the more than twenty years in which the Lavender Scare held sway is impossible to determine. However, a State Department official admitted in 1961 that his department alone had terminated fourteen hundred employees for homosexuality.[6] The total number across the federal bureaucracy is probably five to ten times that amount. The purges also spread to the private sector, as corporations, especially those with government contracts, tended to follow the lead of the government in its hiring and retention practices. Faced with public embarrassment, unemployment, and sometimes exclusion from one's chosen profession, an untold number of gay men and lesbians committed suicide. After two days of intense interrogations about his sex life at the U.S. Embassy in Paris, where he worked as a code clerk, thirty-four-year-old Andrew Ference used the gas stove of his Paris apartment to asphyxiate himself. The State Department covered up the reason for the suicide, claiming that Ference was despondent about his health. After he was arrested on a morals charge in downtown Washington, DC, in 1957, civil servant Delbert Sandercook hung himself in his S Street apartment. The Washington newspapers were full of stories of young government employees taking their own lives for no apparent reason.[7]

The federal government's efforts to marginalize and exclude gay men and lesbians from positions of public trust were not limited to the civil service. Gay men and lesbians were also excluded from serving in the U.S. military, a policy initiated during the Second World War, as Marilyn E. Hegarty's essay in this volume points out. Although the policy's name and rationale have changed over time—unfitness to serve, vulnerability to blackmail, threat to "unit cohesion"—the exclusion of openly gay service members remained essentially in place until it was repealed by an act of Congress in 2011 (see Aaron Belkin's essay on "don't ask, don't tell" in this volume). During the more than half century in which this policy endured, the military drummed out hundreds of highly trained gay men and lesbians every year, in times of peace and times of war. The 1952 Immigration Act also prevented anyone from entering the country who exhibited a "psychopathic personality," a term the Immigration and Naturalization Service and the courts continually used to exclude gay men and lesbians. Relying on a determination of identity or inclination rather than proof of a particular act, these provisions enhanced the federal government's ability to exclude or deport suspected homosexuals. Some states, such as Florida, established new legal or administrative mechanisms to purge their public payrolls, particularly those of public schools and universities, of homosexuals.[8]

Teaching about the Lavender Scare raises an important opportunity to discuss how systematic oppression can lead to resistance. Never before had the apparatus of the national security state and the welfare state been used to exclude an entire class of people based on whom they loved. The level of surveillance and oppression was so great that it ignited a new level of collective activism. Frank Kameny was one of the first of the thousands of persons who lost their jobs for being gay to publicly challenge his dismissal. With a PhD in astronomy from Harvard University, Kameny worked for the Army Map Service helping to calculate distances between the United States and potential missile targets around the world. But when he was fired in 1957 for homosexuality, Kameny found little support among the few timid homophile organizations then headquartered in California. When he lost his legal appeal in the courts, his attorney abandoned his case. Forced to write his own brief to the U.S. Supreme Court, he articulated the revolutionary idea that he was being treated as a second-class citizen. He argued that antigay

discrimination was "no less illegal and no less odious than discrimination based upon religious or racial grounds." This was not an issue of
morality or national security, he argued, but of human rights. When the
Supreme Court rejected his claim, he founded a gay rights organization
called the Mattachine Society of Washington. Its members set about
lobbying government officials, testifying before Congress, and, by 1965,
picketing in front of the White House for an end to the federal government's antigay policies. They labeled themselves "homosexual citizens,"
arguing that political rights should not depend on one's sexual identity.
Emboldened by these actions, other fired gay employees began to file
suit, and in 1969 the U.S. Court of Appeals ordered the federal government to end its antigay exclusion practices. It would take the government another six years to formally change its policies, twenty-five years
after Joseph McCarthy first made headlines talking about the communists and queers in Washington.

## Conclusion

Because the mechanics of the Lavender Scare—the interrogations, resignations, and even suicides—happened largely behind
closed doors, these stories have not made it into the historical record.
Unlike the Red Scare, we have no news footage of accused homosexuals
under Capitol Hill klieg lights facing their accusers. But the story is
perhaps all the more powerful because it has been hidden for so long.
Those who already teach about McCarthyism and the Red Scare will
find inclusion of its lavender cousin not a burden but an advantage. It
helps provide a more complete and nuanced understanding of the overall fear of subversives that characterized Cold War political culture. It
helps explain how Reverend Billy Graham, defending McCarthy in 1954
against Senate censure, praised him for his work "exposing the pinks,
the lavenders, and the reds who have sought refuge beneath the wings
of the American Eagle."[9] By demonstrating how fear of political subversives overlapped with fear of sexual immorality, and how both had
political motivations, it clarifies how and why Truman's loyalty program
expanded into the Eisenhower security program. It raises timely issues
about the scapegoating of a disaffected minority, about real or imagined
threats to national security, and about the risks and benefits of the expanding apparatus of the national security state. Ultimately it raises the
issue of who is granted full citizenship rights in the United States and

the constant historical tension between preserving both freedom and security.[10]

NOTES

1. Unless otherwise identified, sources for this essay may be located by referencing David K. Johnson, *The Lavender Scare: The Cold War Persecution of Gays and Lesbians in the Federal Government* (Chicago: University of Chicago Press, 2004).

2. For visual images and headlines, see The Lavender Scare, http://www.thelavenderscare.com.

3. U.S. Congress, Senate, Committee on Expenditures in the Executive Departments, *Employment of Homosexuals and Other Sex Perverts in Government*, Senate Doc. 241, 81st Cong., 2nd sess., 1950, 4. The report is available many places online, including as evidence in the U.S. District Court, Northern District of California, *Perry v. Schwarzenegger* "Proposition 8" case at https://ecf.cand.uscourts.gov/cand/09cv2292/evidence/PX2337.pdf.

4. Executive Order 10450 is available through the U.S. National Archives and Records Administration at http://www.archives.gov/federal-register/codification/executive-order/10450.html.

5. David K. Johnson, interview with Madeleine Tress, November 11, 1998; Len Evans, interview with Madeleine Tress, April 16, 1983, GLBT Historical Society (San Francisco); Madeline Tress FBI file. The Lavender Scare website (thelavenderscare.com) provides interviews with other victims.

6. This figure of fourteen hundred firings from the State Department is substantially larger than the thousand I reported in *The Lavender Scare*. State Department statistics generally represented about 20 percent of total firings across the entire government. Further research will likely confirm that my estimate of five thousand total homosexual firings was conservative. See U.S. Congress, Senate, Committee on the Judiciary, Subcommittee to Investigate the Administration of the Internal Security Act, *Communist Threat to the United States through the Caribbean*, 87th Cong., 1st sess., part 12, Testimony of Assistant Secretary of State Robert C. Hill, June 12, 1961; and Mary McGrory, "Facts on Enemy's Marked Man," *Washington Star*, March 12, 1962.

7. Delbert Sandercook's is an additional suicide documented since the publication of *The Lavender Scare*. See *Washington Newsletter* 2, no. 6 (June 1957), Folder 11, Box 778, ACLU Records, Princeton University Library.

8. Allan Bérubé, *Coming Out under Fire: The History of Gay Men and Women in World War II* (Chapel Hill: University of North Carolina Press, 2010); Margot Canaday, *The Straight State: Sexuality and Citizenship in Twentieth-Century America* (Princeton, NJ: Princeton University Press, 2011), 214–50; Marc Stein, *Sexual Injustice: Supreme Court Decisions from "Griswold" to "Roe"* (Chapel Hill: University

of North Carolina Press, 2010); Karen Graves, *And They Were Wonderful Teachers: Florida's Purge of Gay and Lesbian Teachers* (Urbana: University of Illinois Press, 2009); Stacy Braukman, *Communists and Perverts under the Palms: The Johns Committee in Florida, 1956–1965* (Gainesville: University Press of Florida, 2012).

9. Billy Graham, quoted in K. A. Cuordileone, *Manhood and American Political Culture in the Cold War* (New York: Routledge, 2004), 37.

10. For a fuller discussion of the Lavender Scare in the context of the post-9/11 war on terrorism, see Corey Robin, *The Reactionary Mind: Conservatism from Edmund Burke to Sarah Palin* (New York: Oxford University Press, 2011), particularly his chapter "Potomac Fever."

# Public Figures, Private Lives

*Eleanor Roosevelt, J. Edgar Hoover, and a Queer Political History*

CLAIRE BOND POTTER

Eleanor Roosevelt, wife of four-term U.S. president Franklin Delano Roosevelt, probably thought about J. Edgar Hoover, the director of the FBI, only occasionally. But he was very aware of her. Beginning in 1936, when FDR authorized Hoover to keep tabs on "subversive" political movements—this category eventually embraced many Americans, including communists, civil rights activists, peace activists, homophile groups, and feminists—the conservative director kept his eye on the progressive first lady. Eleanor Roosevelt's papers at the FDR Presidential Library reveal no indexed references to Hoover, but a visit to the FBI's Freedom of Information Act Reading Room would reveal thirty-seven thick folders of reports on Mrs. Roosevelt, her friends, and her political allies.[1]

Roosevelt and Hoover can be a good pairing for a political history class, however. Their complex erotic lives allow teachers to introduce students to themes in the history of sexuality, challenging them to think about why sex might matter to the study of power and how the words that describe sexual identity changed over the course of the twentieth century. These two political brokers—who could not have been more different in terms of class background, ethics, political roles, and social vision—can be identified from the present as homosexual, bisexual, or,

199

in the case of Hoover, said to have cross-dressed, perhaps transgender. However, historians also need to think about how they would have described themselves. Mrs. Roosevelt might have pointed out that she was married to one man for most of her adult life. The hardworking Hoover would have deflected attention from his sexuality by insisting that he was a bachelor and "married" to his work. Neither statement is untruthful, but there is certainly more to be said.

Before we begin to untangle these important historical issues, let's begin with what the biographers agree, and disagree, about when they discuss two figures that helped shape twentieth-century politics in the United States.

### The Facts Ma'am, Just the Facts

This line, spoken by Detective Joe Friday on the 1960s TV show *Dragnet*, reminds us that before leaping into guessing games about a historical figure's queer private life, students should address what is well known. Much of this information is now available on the Internet. When students are alert to what is, and is not, a reliable source, they can assemble a chronology, agreed-upon facts, and dominant interpretations. They can mark gaps and disputed aspects of that person's biography for further investigation. They can establish keywords to show how descriptions of intimate life have changed over time. Students will want to *avoid* incorporating social media or fan websites that lack documentation, although these sites should be bookmarked for later conversations about how popular culture and history differ.

What might such an exercise about Eleanor Roosevelt and J. Edgar Hoover reveal?

Over seven thousand volumes describe Roosevelt, her politics, and her intimate life.[2] Born in 1884 to Elliott and Anna Roosevelt, Eleanor was the niece of President Theodore Roosevelt. When she was ten her mother died of diphtheria; subsequently, her alcoholic father committed suicide. Raised by her grandmother and tutored at home, she was in England between 1899 and 1902 attending a school run by the feminist Marie Souvestre. She fell in love with and married her fifth cousin Franklin in 1903. Unlike other female New Dealers, Roosevelt did not attend one of the private women's colleges where intense female friendships and the desire for careers blossomed. Despite that, in the early years of her marriage she was swept up in New York's progressive movement. As Dáša Frančíková's essay indicates, in these highly femi-nized, and feminist, social work and labor circles, educated women committed their lives to ending poverty and to friendships with each other. Few of these activists would have embraced the term *lesbian*, a word associated with sexual perversion, prostitution, or mental illness, but many viewed loving female partnerships as a moral and social equivalent to marriage.[3]

Eleanor gave birth to six children between 1906 and 1916; one died in infancy. Yet her sexual relations with Franklin, though frequent enough to result in pregnancies, may have been unhappy. Her daughter Anna told historian Doris Kearns Goodwin that Eleanor viewed sex as an "ordeal to be borne," a quote Goodwin understood to mean that Roosevelt was asexual.[4] Franklin may have been equally unhappy, however. The Roosevelts' relationship foundered when Eleanor dis-covered in 1918 that her husband and her personal secretary were lovers. The marriage barely survived, and their intimate life did not. Often living apart, they subsequently forged a partnership and deep friend-ship based on shared political ambitions. Following FDR's paralysis from polio in 1921, Eleanor helped her husband to rebuild his political career and win the presidency in 1932: he served until his death in 1945. With Eleanor's help, he created the New Deal welfare state, challenged racial segregation, won a world war, and crafted a modern liberal vision for a global twentieth century.

Eleanor played a crucial part in this national history. She trans-formed the role of the first lady by taking on political issues that her critics thought were inappropriate for a woman. If FDR moved far too slowly on racial issues, Eleanor challenged white women of her own class to address their racism by choosing to sit with African American delegates at women's political meetings. Many of the women who rose to prominence in the Democratic Party during the New Deal were drawn from her feminist circles, among them Mary Dewson, who made her life with Polly Porter; the educator Mary McLeod Bethune, a member of FDR's Black Cabinet; and Frances Perkins, the first woman secretary of labor. Both of the latter were married to men.[5]

Students might well ask how a president and his wife could have separate lovers (in Franklin's case, perhaps several at once) without their arrangement becoming the source of personal friction, not to mention public censure. One answer might be found in the friendships and love that can develop outside sexual relations, another in a press corps that saw politicians' private lives as off limits, that agreed never to publish pictures of Roosevelt that would reveal his disability, and that drew a veil across what we might call the Roosevelts' "queer," non-monogamous marriage. Could this brilliant political alliance, with its complex domestic life, survive contemporary media scrutiny today?

Probably not. The Roosevelts' political marriage coincided with the rise of radio, "talking" film, and newsreels, which, added to newspaper coverage, expanded the media environment dramatically much as the Internet would sixty years later. However, public figures understood the danger of losing control of one's image by the 1920s, and the profession of public relations evolved to counter that. The Roosevelts employed a former newspaperman, Louis M. Howe, who expanded the Roosevelts' press coverage but also created rules the press had to follow. Around the same time, J. Edgar Hoover created a public relations department that churned out carefully controlled stories about and images of the director, as well as books and movies about G-men aimed at all audiences. Hollywood studios not only installed "morals clauses" in performers' contracts to protect themselves from scandal, but they too employed large staffs of publicists to groom stars as properly heterosexual. They cultivated the goodwill of gossip columnists and sometimes arranged sham marriages to divert the public's attention from bisexual, lesbian, and gay rumors surrounding stars such as Rock Hudson, Cary Grant, Joan Crawford, Sal Mineo, Montgomery Clift, and Marlene Dietrich.[6]

It was not unusual for celebrity wives to live apart from their husbands; nor was it odd for a woman of Eleanor Roosevelt's background to be seen with intimate female friends. Private estates, discrete servants, and ideas about respectability also conspired to make sexual arrangements well known to the Roosevelts' family and friends invisible to others. In the 1930s, Eleanor was almost certainly having an affair with the progressive journalist Lorena Hickok; later she may have also been romantically involved with New York state trooper Earl Miller, her bodyguard from 1928 to 1941. Her FBI file also links her romantically to her friend and biographer Joseph Lash.[7] After FDR's death, Eleanor, who continued to be powerful within the Democratic Party, serving in three different posts at the United Nations before her own death in 1962, never remarried. That, too, was not unusual.

J. Edgar Hoover's trajectory was slightly different. When he began his professional career, he called himself a bachelor, but as he hit the crest of his career in the mid-twentieth century, the meaning of that word changed. A respectable identity for a young man in 1916, to be a bachelor was socially suspect by the time of the Second World War, when unmarried men were closely scrutinized for signs of homosexuality. However, the nature of Hoover's private life is a challenge to the best researchers.[8] Compared to the small library of work available on the first lady, there are fewer than two hundred volumes about J. Edgar Hoover, a man who was known for gathering information on others—and expunging information about his own past.[9] (Here students might be urged to think about how subjects try to shape political memory: on the day of his death, Hoover's loyal secretary, Helen Gandy, destroyed volumes of her boss's personal files.) Unlike Eleanor Roosevelt, Hoover was not protected by social privilege as a young man. He was born into a family of middle-class Washington, DC, bureaucrats in 1895, worked his way through college, forming close friendships with his Kappa Alpha fraternity brothers. After earning a law degree in 1916, Hoover went to work for the Justice Department, creating innovative information systems to track "enemy aliens" and domestic radicals during the First World War. By 1924 he had survived two scandals—the Palmer Raids and the Teapot Dome Affair—and become director of the Bureau of Investigation (renamed the Federal Bureau of Investigation, or FBI, in 1936). He kept that job for forty-eight years, serving six presidents and creating a modern surveillance apparatus that, as David K. Johnson explores in his essay in this volume, worked to purge homosexuals from the government in the 1950s.[10]

Rumors about Hoover's homosexuality persisted throughout his career. Here students might be taught the delicate art of reading evidence for insinuation, coded language, and planted news items. In 1927 one Washington columnist smirked about Hoover's "light" step (gay men were said to be "light in the loafers") and his recreational antique shopping. If Roosevelt's class position allowed privacy, Hoover's profession allowed him to craft publicity that deflected speculation about his private life. In 1930 he was named one of Washington's most eligible bachelors, perhaps something he arranged through one of his publicists, a newspaperman named Courtney Riley Cooper. In exchange for tips about high-profile arrests, gossip columnist Walter Winchell treated him like a Hollywood star, publishing items that paired him with female celebrities. By Hoover's side in every nightclub, and in the car on the way home, was handsome Clyde Tolson, his closest professional assistant

J. Edgar Hoover in an unguarded moment of intimacy with Clyde A. Tolson, probably in the 1940s. The pair loved horse racing, fishing, and going to night clubs. (© Corbis, reprinted with permission)

and constant companion after 1928.[11] They ate lunch together, they vacationed together, and as they aged Tolson sometimes spent the night at Hoover's house when he was unwell.

Although the grand themes of Hoover's career include wars on crime, anticommunism, infiltrating the civil rights and antiwar movements, and the creation of a modern surveillance state, increasingly he is also remembered as a gay man who harbored a special animus toward other LGBT people. Early biographers such as Athan Theoharis and Richard Gid Powers suggest psychological links between what they view as Hoover's divided self and his ethical failures in the public sphere. In 1993 a third biographer altered the conversation about Hoover forever by publishing one woman's memory that she had seen Hoover, dressed as a woman, perform a series of sexual acts with male prostitutes. Yet this evidence, like so much of the evidence we have about sexuality, requires classroom scrutiny. Students will want to discuss the nature of secondhand observation and whether Hoover, a secretive person, would engage in transgressive public sex. More important, the story is uncorroborated by any other source and the witness was paid for the interview, something that neither oral historians nor journalists view as a good practice.[12]

But might it still be true? As lurid as this story seems, it is a good moment for students to discuss the ways in which contemporary political reporting also mixes the personal and the political. Reporters and political enemies elevate one fact (New York governor Eliot Spitzer used campaign funds to buy time with sex workers) over another fact (Spitzer had a long and proud history of prosecuting white-collar crime) in ways that can seem only judgmental. But does a focus on sexual controversies deflect public scrutiny from more significant achievements? Does it hide, or highlight, serious abuses of the public trust?

Together Roosevelt and Hoover present a series of other interesting questions for teachers and students interested in the intersections of political biography and the history of sexuality. Is it accurate to write into LGBT history sexually complex people who would not have recognized themselves as part of that past? What does it mean for LGBT people to "claim" a homophobic and reactionary figure like Hoover? Is it reasonable to privilege Roosevelt as part of our lesbian or bisexual history, given that she privileged her social identity as a wife and mother?

## We Are Everywhere, but Who Are We?

Because of his antiradicalism and homophobia, J. Edgar Hoover became the kind of homosexual that gays disavow. What used to be understood as justifiable privacy is now often thought to be dishonest. As Joshua Gamson has argued, "The ultimate slimeball is not so much the gay man as the gay man who *lies* about his sexual desires."[13] The equally closeted Eleanor Roosevelt, however, has been embraced as a lesbian by many queers. For decades members of the Lesbian Herstory Archives were at the front of New York's Gay Pride Parade with large posters of women they claimed as theirs, and Roosevelt was among them.

In itself this difference tells a story about politics that teachers should emphasize. The story of LGBT politics in the United States has been crafted as part of a progressive tradition of inclusion and fairness that Eleanor Roosevelt exemplifies. Students might even see the New Deal itself as part of a lesbian feminist past; as did the "political lesbians" of the 1970s, many of Roosevelt's female political allies viewed marriage and childbearing as incompatible with a life of work. One provocative discussion could be organized around the question of whether lesbians and feminists of Roosevelt's generation would have viewed legal gay marriage and the rearing of children in LGBT families as progress or— as some queers do today—a distraction from the important work of radical change.[14]

Does J. Edgar Hoover's story give us similar insight into the history of conservatism? Students could pair public statements by such right-wing figures as Andrew Sullivan and Mary Cheney, or organizations such as the Log Cabin Republicans, with Hoover's policy positions on a range of issues: "foreign" radical influences, crime, sexual disorders, and the importance of domesticity and monogamy. Like Roosevelt's, Hoover's biography raises the question of whether sexuality can facilitate right-wing political networks. Hoover's allies included Roy Cohn, a closeted gay man on the staff of Senator Joseph McCarthy in the 1950s; the senator himself, though married, was rumored to have done so to quash gossip about his own sexuality. In other words, if Hoover fits the stereotype of a self-hating gay man, he may also offer us insight into gay male conservative networks whose political work behind the scenes includes keeping each other's secrets.[15]

Of course students might come to the conclusion that Roosevelt is a hero and Hoover a villain and they deserve different treatment by historians. During the AIDS crisis, gay activist and journalist Michelangelo Signorile came to this conclusion when he announced in 1992 that he would begin "outing" closeted queers, but only those who used their power against other LGBT people.[16] Connecting Roosevelt's and Hoover's secrecy about their sexuality to Signorile's controversial tactic can provide an opportunity for a conversation about when, and under what circumstances, it is ethical to reveal facts about other people's lives that they clearly prefer to keep private. A related task would be to ask students excited about modern queer identities and political movements to understand historical figures in *their* context. Sexual identities—like all identities—have evolved over time. They often present differently within a time period as well; naming practices, for example, can signal an individual's attachment to a *particular* queer community defined by class, race, region, education, military service, or incarceration.

The stakes for secrecy about Eleanor Roosevelt and J. Edgar Hoover were also set by twentieth-century medical experts and psychiatrists who viewed sexuality outside procreative marriage as immature, undisciplined, criminal, and/or a sign of mental illness. To publicly claim a lesbian or gay identity was not impossible, but it was incompatible with the virtues associated with public service in the mid-twentieth century. It is no accident that Harry Hay, a founder of the first homophile organization, the Mattachine Society, was a communist, not a New Deal or Fair Deal Democrat, and an artist and organizer, not a politician or a civil servant.

Nevertheless, teachers who want to encourage students to make strong arguments will want to emphasize the fact that historians have disagreed for decades about whether, and how, to assemble evidence about the sex lives of public figures. Ongoing, and different, controversies surround politicians as well known as Thomas Jefferson and Abraham Lincoln. One excellent classroom exercise would be to look at political and cultural interests in keeping sexual secrets that emerge after an individual's death. For example, it was presumed in Jefferson's lifetime that he had fathered children with his slave and half sister Sally Hemings. A century later, however, historians and white descendants who viewed interracial sex and the realities of slavery as shameful scrubbed these events from the record as incompatible with the virtues of a founding president. Only recently has the legal historian Annette Gordon-Reed decisively changed public opinion—returning it to what Jefferson's contemporaries commented on openly.[17]

This brings us to an important issue. Film dramatizations can suggest to students that disputed sexualities are documented fact. *Hyde Park on Hudson* (2012), for example, proposes that all speculation about Eleanor's sexuality and the Roosevelts' open marriage is settled. While clips from these films usefully illustrate aspects of a political history course, when students view them in their entirety they will see that the stakes for historical fiction are different from the stakes for historical scholarship. These stakes include the nature of the story and the capacity of the audience to understand complexity.

Students should also be urged to discuss whether representations of a subject's queerness, though true, are presented in a way that is potentially homophobic. In Clint Eastwood's movie *J. Edgar* (2011), Hoover and Roosevelt are pitted against each other as queer figures, one evil and one virtuous. Eastwood portrays Hoover's career as shaped by his tortured efforts to contain a sexual nature that he understands to be deviant. (As a useful aside, the good-looking Leonardo DiCaprio allows us to imagine Hoover as a reasonable object of male desire as well.) In one scene, after the death of his mother, we see Hoover draping himself in her lingerie before a mirror, a clear reference to gender confusion and cross-dressing. In another scene, Hoover announces with glee to an astonished Clyde Tolson that he has secured a now famous letter that Roosevelt wrote to Lorena Hickok, describing her memory of "that soft spot just northeast of the corner of your mouth against my lips."[18]

The powerful pair giggle like boys, and Hoover vows to use the threat of lesbian scandal to blackmail the first lady into curtailing her activism. The class can be asked to scrutinize a scene such as this for the ways in which the filmmaker weaves together real archival evidence with unproven gossip and outright fiction to depict the political struggle between liberals and conservatives within the New Deal. By making this conflict so personal, Eastwood's argument also erases the real po-litical stakes of the period. Unless the instructor urges them to view this scene through an historical, rather than presentist, view, students may be inclined to see Roosevelt only as a sympathetic victim and Hoover's blackmail as simply an example of why homophobia is wrong.

The scene (which most certainly would not have occurred, as Hoover kept his most dangerous and sexual evidence in a closed file) also portrays Hoover as a hypocrite and bully rather than the committed conservative he was. Viewers already *know* that Hoover lusts after his best friend and is doing his best to conceal it from himself. In an equally invented moment, Hoover loses control, kisses Tolson, then attacks him in a panic and insists that Tolson initiated the kiss. This fictional scene is confirmation that Hoover will lie and hurt even his dearest friend to protect his own political power and influence by remaining in the closet. As a scene that speaks to many queer students' contemporary experi-ence of homophobic violence, teachers might want to discuss it in ad-vance to avoid triggering anxiety. However, they will also want to alert students to the risk of over-identification with this character. Tolson's unrequited love and loyalty mark him as a sympathetic figure for the rest of the film. In reality, he was implicated in all Hoover's targeting of liberal and radical political groups.

In historical fiction, sexuality frames a character in addition to con-veying information. Whereas a middle-class, striving bureaucrat such as Hoover is portrayed as shamed and anxious, in *Hyde Park on Hudson* the polyamorous sexual arrangements of the upper-class Roosevelts are—if complex—a sophisticated, fun backstory to facilitating America's entry into the Second World War on the side of Great Britain. If Eastwood's film shrinks the context for understanding Hoover's sexuality, *Hyde Park on Hudson* reduces Eleanor Roosevelt's sexuality and politics to one theme in a heterosexual bedroom farce. Early in the film, Bill Murray's FDR refers to Eleanor's clique of progressive women as "she-men," a slang term for lesbians.[19] This puts the audience on notice that the president is a liberated husband. As we also quickly learn, Roosevelt's paralysis is no bar to vigorous heterosexual couplings with a loving group of women who see to his professional and sexual needs. One of them is a distant cousin, Margaret "Daisy" Suckley, later the president's first archivist, whose private journals and letters formed the basis for a book, a radio play, and the film script.[20]

Both films should serve to remind students that fiction can provoke us to revisit well-known public figures with new questions. They also give us ammunition for deflecting questions about whether homosexuality is too controversial for our history curricula. Surely if the sexual lives of Roosevelt and Hoover are discussed in major motion pictures, they belong in the classroom! But the films do not answer the question: what's the intellectual payoff for students, particularly students of political history, in thinking critically about sexuality?

In the earliest days of LGBT history, the editors of one volume argued that it could be "reassuring for gay people, raised in a society with no positive images of themselves, to claim gay heroes."[21] But teachers need to help students account for the queer figures that make us uncomfortable and angry, too. It is unlikely that anyone will ever carry a poster of J. Edgar Hoover in a gay pride parade. But learning more about him not only helps us understand the history of the closet, but it helps us trace a long history of men who have sex with and/or love men but reject the idea that they are gay. It also helps us think about the ways in which gossip about sexuality should point us to other political and social dynamics that shape history.

Empowering education for LGBT students and their allies is important, as is educating heterosexual teachers and students about the ways they might unconsciously reinforce homophobia by ruling the private lives of LGBT people out of bounds for classroom discussion. However, unlike Dan Savage's hugely popular It Gets Better Project, in which queer adults speak from the heart to teenagers about overcoming prejudice, or campus activisms that build empowering communities, history is not social work. True, understanding the past enhances our political and ethical lives, but uncovering must be accompanied by the search for meaning. As one edited collection frames its mission, queer history should "illuminate how sexual politics has organized social relationships in differing and contradictory ways over time."[22]

In a contemporary moment when the private lives of politicians and celebrities are constantly scrutinized, students will almost surely be hooked by the sexual secrets of powerful people. The teaching challenge is to make queer political history more than an opportunity to pull back the heterosexual curtain. The language used and diversions created by the most powerful among us can teach us a great deal about how other, far less important individuals might have protected themselves during the twentieth century, as homophobia became more pronounced in law, medicine, and psychiatry. Teaching about closeted lesbian and gay identities also allows students to discuss the ways in which sexual and erotic networks can provide political language and become an aspect of political networking. As strange a pair as they make, Eleanor Roosevelt and J. Edgar Hoover demonstrate that queer history intersects the history of formal politics. Students who accept the challenge of such complex lives will surely become better readers, researchers, and political thinkers when they have the confidence to embrace the challenges of this field.

### NOTES

1. See the Franklin Delano Roosevelt Presidential Library and Museum, http://www.fdrlibrary.marist.edu/. Selections from the thirty-seven volumes of documents on Eleanor Roosevelt can be found at the FBI's Freedom of Information Act (FOIA) website, http://vault.fbi.gov/search?SearchableText=eleanor+roosevelt.

2. Of these, aside from Mrs. Roosevelt's autobiographical writings, seven volumes stand out. Joseph P. Lash wrote two: *Eleanor and Franklin: The Story of Their Relationship* (New York: W. W. Norton, 1971); and *Eleanor: The Years Alone* (New York: W. W. Norton, 1972). The others are Doris Kearns Goodwin, *No Ordinary Time: Franklin and Eleanor Roosevelt, the Home Front in World War II* (New York: Simon and Schuster, 1994); Blanche Cooke's series *Eleanor Roosevelt*, vol. 1: *1884–1933* (New York: Penguin Books, 1992), and vol. 2: *The Defining Years, 1933–1938* (New York: Penguin Books, 1999), with a third projected volume forthcoming; Hazel Rowley, *Franklin and Eleanor: An Extraordinary Marriage* (New York: Farrar, Straus and Giroux, 2011); Maurine H. Beasley, *Eleanor Roosevelt: Transformative First Lady* (Lawrence: University Press of Kansas, 2010).

3. John D'Emilio and Estelle Freedman, *Intimate Matters: A History of Sexuality in America* (Chicago: University of Chicago Press, 1988), 227; Lisa Duggan, *Sapphic Slashers: Sex, Violence, and American Modernity* (Durham, NC: Duke University Press, 2000); Sharon Marcus, *Between Women: Friendship, Desire, and Marriage in Victorian England* (Princeton, NJ: Princeton University Press, 2007).

4. Goodwin, *No Ordinary Time*, 19.

5. Susan Ware, *Beyond Suffrage: Women in the New Deal* (Cambridge, MA: Harvard University Press, 1985); Susan Ware, *Partner and I: Molly Dewson, Feminism, and New Deal Politics* (New Haven, CT: Yale University Press, 1989).

6. Jennifer Frost, *Hedda Hopper's Hollywood: Celebrity Gossip and American Conservatism* (New York: New York University Press, 2011); William J. Mann, *Behind the Screen: How Gays and Lesbians Shaped Hollywood, 1910–1969* (New York: Viking, 2001); Vito Russo, *The Celluloid Closet: Homosexuality in the Movies* (New York: Harper and Row, 1987); Claire Bond Potter, *War on Crime: Bandits, G-Men, and the Politics of Mass Culture* (New Brunswick, NJ: Rutgers University Press, 1997).

7. Hickok's papers can be found at the Franklin Delano Roosevelt Library, http://www.fdrlibrary.marist.edu/archives/pdfs/findingaids/findingaid_hickok.pdf. Private papers that were opened in 1978 contain substantial evidence of her relationship with Eleanor Roosevelt; three hundred of them have been collected in Rodger Streitmatter's *Empty without You: The Intimate Letters of Eleanor Roosevelt and Lorena Hickok* (New York: Free Press, 1998).

8. Howard P. Chudacoff, *The Age of the Bachelor: Creating an American Subculture* (Princeton, NJ: Princeton University Press, 1999).

9. Prominent biographies that address Hoover's sexuality include Richard Gid Powers, *Secrecy and Power: The Life of J. Edgar Hoover* (New York: Free Press, 1988); John Stuart Cox and Athan G. Theoharis, *The Boss: J. Edgar Hoover and the Great American Inquisition* (Philadelphia: Temple University Press, 1988); Anthony Summers, *Official and Confidential: The Secret Life of J. Edgar Hoover* (New York: Pocket Books, 1993); Ronald Kessler, *The Bureau: The Secret History of the FBI* (New York: St. Martin's Press, 2002).

10. See also David K. Johnson, *The Lavender Scare: The Cold War Persecution of Gays and Lesbians in the Federal Government* (Chicago: University of Chicago Press, 2006).

11. Potter, *War on Crime*, 48, 129.

12. Claire Bond Potter, "Queer Hoover: Sex, Lies, and Political History," *Journal of the History of Sexuality* 15, no. 3 (September 2006): 355–81.

13. Joshua Gamson, *Freaks Talk Back: Tabloid Talk Shows and Sexual Nonconformity* (Chicago: University of Chicago Press, 1999), 68.

14. J. Jack Halberstam, *Gaga Feminism: Sex, Gender, and the End of Normal* (Boston: Beacon Press, 2012).

15. Andrea Friedman, "The Smearing of Joe McCarthy: The Lavender Scare, Gossip, and Cold War Politics," *American Quarterly* 57, no. 4 (2005): 1105–29;

Athan Theoharis, "Operation Adlai/Adeline: How the FBI Gaybaited Stevenson," *The Nation*, May 1990.

16. Michelangelo Signorile, *Queer in America: Sex, the Media, and the Closets of Power* (Madison: University of Wisconsin Press, 2003).

17. See Annette Gordon-Reed, *The Hemingses of Monticello: An American Family* (New York: W.W. Norton, 2009); for Lincoln's intimate friendship with Jonathan Speed, see Jonathan Ned Katz, *Love Stories: Sex between Men before Homosexuality* (Chicago: University of Chicago Press, 2001).

18. Cooke, *Eleanor Roosevelt*, 2:195.

19. Slang that signals gender inversion is highly changeable. In the twenty-first century, the phrase seems to have reemerged in Japan as a way to describe transsexual men (see YouTube, http://www.youtube.com/watch?v=rGfFv1GwOCc), in the United States in 1990s rap to describe black men who conform to white social ideals (see Paris, "Bush Killa [Hellraiser Mix]," *Sleeping with the Enemy*, Scarface Records, 1992), and in twenty-first century England to describe male-born women whose genitals do not conform to their gender identities. See Zoe O'Connell, "The NHS Governance Group: Debates on 'Unintentionally Creating She-Men,'" *Complicity* (blog), March 2012, http://www.complicity.co.uk/blog/2012/03/unintentionally-creating-she-men/.

20. Barbara Ireland, "At the Home of FDR's Secret Friend," *New York Times*, September 7, 2007, http://travel.nytimes.com/2007/09/07/travel/escapes/07daisy.html; Geoffrey C. Ward, *Closest Companion: The Unknown Story of the Intimate Friendship between Franklin Roosevelt and Margaret Suckley* (New York: Simon and Schuster, 1995).

21. Martin Bauml Duberman, Martha Vicinus, and George Chauncey Jr., eds., *Hidden from History: Reclaiming the Gay and Lesbian Past* (New York: Meridian, 1990), 3.

22. Jennifer Pierce, "Introduction," in Twin Cities GLBT Oral History Project, *Queer Twin Cities* (Minneapolis: University of Minnesota Press, 2010), xii.

# Community and Civil Rights in the Kinsey Era

CRAIG M. LOFTIN

Histories of lesbians and gay men who lived during the 1950s and early 1960s tend to paint a negative portrait of the period. They describe how the federal government purged and blacklisted its homosexual employees because of Cold War national security hysteria. They discuss how homosexuality was illegal at the time and detail how police used undercover entrapment techniques to ensnare gay men in particular into an unsympathetic criminal justice system. Other studies analyze the medical profession's inclusion of homosexuality in the *Diagnostic and Statistical Manual*, the official designator of mental illness, from 1952 to 1973. Isolation, paranoia, and victimhood dominate these narratives. The perceived experience of being gay in the 1950s resembles a film noir movie from the time, complete with shadowy tension, sexual temptation, fear of discovery, anxiety that one's life could unravel at any minute, and the sense that disaster lurks around every corner.

Gay people undoubtedly suffered in the years following the Second World War, as David K. Johnson's essay in this volume makes clear, but that is only part of the story. There were also major leaps forward in gay consciousness, activism, and visibility. As the front cover of the August 1958 issue of *ONE* suggests, a gay pride ethic was beginning to circulate throughout a national gay community with its own publications and advocacy organizations. This ethic even spread beyond urban gay subcultures into suburban and rural spaces. Despite widespread persecution, political hysteria, and police surveillance, gay men and lesbians were asserting themselves individually and collectively in bolder ways than the picture of relentless persecution allows.

213

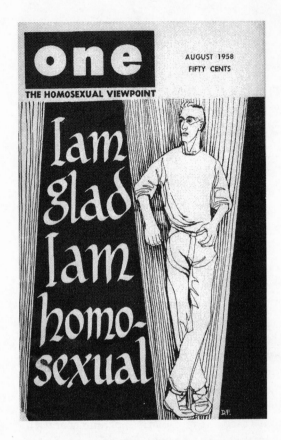

Homophile pride, *ONE* magazine, August 1958 (courtesy of the ONE National Gay & Lesbian Archives)

As Marilyn E. Hegarty's essay in this volume points out, the Second World War brought lesbians and gay men all across the country in contact with one another on an unprecedented scale. This experience clarified and sharpened their individual and collective sense of sexual identity. Despite military crackdowns against homosexuality in the later stages of the war, lesbians and gay men developed a stronger sense of national community through their service. Similar to the experiences of African Americans, wartime service fueled a determination among some gay and lesbian military personnel to fight for rights and better treatment in a hostile society after the war. This point of overlap between the black and gay experiences—keeping in mind that there were black gay men and lesbians in the military—can be useful in the classroom when discussing the impact of the Second World War on U.S. society.

## The Kinsey Report

After the war, in 1948, the release of Alfred Kinsey's controversial *Sexual Behavior in the Human Male*, better known as the male Kinsey Report, further fostered the political consciousness of a national gay community. This large book, filled with charts, graphs, and tables documenting every imaginable facet of sexual behavior, challenged myths of sexual prudery and helped bring more honest and open discussion of sexuality into the public sphere. Kinsey published a similar volume on women in 1953. Both books revealed a wide gap between the expectations and realities of sexual behavior in the United States. Premarital sexual intercourse was rampant, for example. Half of all husbands cheated on their wives. Masturbation, long stigmatized as shameful and harmful, was virtually universal among adult men. Most surprising, though, was the frequency of homosexual behavior. Over one-third of Kinsey's male case studies (37 percent) had experienced orgasm with another man during their adult lives; for women, these numbers were slightly lower but no less startling.[1] Kinsey's data not only questioned puritanical fantasies about chastity but challenged the very idea of sexual normality itself by depicting sexuality as infinitely and astonishingly diverse.

Alfred Kinsey was himself a fascinating man. Raised in a strict religious household with a minister for a father, he became a zoologist at Indiana University and subsequently one of the world's foremost experts on gall wasps. He was fascinated by the wasps' diversity. No matter how many thousands of specimens he collected, no two were ever quite the same. He would later come to the same conclusion about human sexuality. When he began teaching a course dealing with sex and relationships, he found that most research on sexuality was based on murky psychological theories rather than empirical data about actual sexual behavior. Further, such research tended to be moralistic in tone and was rife with unexplained presumptions about what constituted "normal" sexual behavior.

Kinsey and several research associates spent years collecting thousands of sexual case histories to create an empirical database of human sexual behavior. The two Kinsey Reports were the result of this work. Given his findings, a backlash predictably ensued. Kinsey's research funding was cut off after the volume on women was published, and the stress of his work probably shortened his life. He died in 1956 at age sixty-two. Two excellent biographies have been written about him, and the 2004 film *Kinsey,* starring Liam Neeson, provides a good overview of his life, with many useful clips for the classroom. "Kinsey," a 2005 PBS *American Experience* documentary, provides a more accurate and less sensationalist account of his life and historical significance, and the program's accompanying website includes several primary documents.[2]

Kinsey can be positioned in an American history class alongside the beat poets, Hugh Hefner, Grace Metalious's popular novel *Peyton Place,* or Tennessee Williams as part of a broader postwar trend that challenged traditional sexual morality. Bring in a volume from your library and share some of Kinsey's data with your students. They will be mesmerized. Discussing Kinsey's intentions, methods, and conclusions is a great way for students to practice having civil, rational, and intelligent conversations about sexuality. It helps them get over the giggling and blushing.

Some critics over the years objected to the way Kinsey boiled human sexuality down to cold statistical orgasm counting. Others pointed out that when he was collecting sex case histories he relied disproportionately on homosocial environments such as prisons, the military, or gay bars, where homosexual behavior was more common. Nonetheless, Kinsey's data on homosexuality remain provocative today. No one had ever suggested that homosexual behavior was so common and widely practiced. Kinsey was *not* suggesting, though, that 37 percent of men were "gay" or "homosexual" as a fundamental orientation or identity—in fact, he questioned the very idea of "homosexual" as a discrete category of identity. "It would encourage clearer thinking on these matters if persons were not characterized as heterosexual or homosexual," Kinsey wrote, "but as individuals who have had certain amounts of heterosexual experience and certain amounts of homosexual experience."[3]

To clarify his theory of sexual fluidity, Kinsey created his famous Kinsey Scale (easily found on Google), a 0 to 6 scale measuring the ratio of sexual experiences with same-sex versus opposite-sex partners. A 0, for example, was a person who had exclusive sexual behavior with the opposite sex, a 2 was someone with mostly heterosexual experiences but also "more than incidental" homosexual experiences, and a 6 (about 4 percent of his case studies) had exclusive sexual behavior with the same sex. Kinsey's data highlighted an unexpectedly large number of people in the middle of the spectrum.[4] Most students grow up with rigidly distinct notions of "gay" and "straight," as though a person must be entirely one or the other, despite increasing recognition of women's sexual fluidity and the contemporary adoption of bisexual and other fluid identities. Kinsey's complex thinking about sexuality can be very enlightening for students.

Kinsey's books had a major impact on American culture in the 1950s and a particularly important impact on gay men and lesbians. Individuals who felt lonely or isolated from other gay people became aware of how many millions of others felt an attraction to their own sex and dared to act on it. Kinsey's rigorous statistical data normalized gay people's lives, made them feel more comfortable in their own skins, and gave nascent activists empirical data with which to begin challenging repressive institutional policies that demonized homosexuality. The books' immense popularity meant that Kinsey's revelations about homosexuality would not go unnoticed by the general public.

However, not everyone shared Kinsey's interpretation that the widespread existence of homosexuality was evidence of its normality. Many people looked at Kinsey's graphs but never read his analysis. In particular, anticommunist crusaders interpreted his data in an alarmist manner consistent with the broader rhetoric of the Red Scare. Homosexuality must be on the rise, they argued, signaling a decline in national strength and morality. They cited Kinsey's data showing that most homosexuals were visually indistinguishable from heterosexuals, and thus difficult to detect, when demanding broader and deeper investigations into the sex lives of government employees, teachers, and defense workers. Thus, the Kinsey Reports reinforced a greater sense of community and strength in numbers among gay people, but they also contributed to the era's antigay hysteria because of the ways people misconstrued Kinsey's data.[5]

## Gay and Lesbian Lives in the Postwar Period

The mixed legacy of the Kinsey Reports reflects a basic paradox facing homosexuals during the 1950s and early 1960s: gay people felt emboldened after the Second World War, but their increasing visibility as a distinct subculture helped trigger the McCarthyite backlash against them, making their lives tense and anxious. To cope with the anxieties of the McCarthy era, many homosexuals wore metaphorical masks of heterosexuality as they figured out how to negotiate their social lives and meet one another. These masks allowed them to participate in mainstream social life while cultivating their own unique sense of lesbian or gay identity. A man who appeared to his neighbors and co-workers as the consummate white-collar professional with wife, kids, and a suburban home, for example, might secretly go to gay bars, cruise parks at night for male sex partners, or have a long-term male lover on the side. A woman who married young and had children, like so many others during the baby boom, might only later realize her deeper attraction to women and thus explore her lesbian identity surreptitiously as a married woman. Fitting in and passing as heterosexual were important survival strategies for most gay people, especially those who identified as middle class.[6]

Bars were probably the most important social spaces in these years for lesbians and gay men. Gay bars serving an exclusively homosexual clientele were a new trend after the war, replacing more bohemian pre-war spaces where gays drank alongside artists, political radicals, and other socially marginalized groups. Gay bars emerged in large and medium-sized cities throughout the country after the war, and some-times in smaller towns and out-of-the-way places as well. They were often run by organized crime syndicates and subject to police raids, but for many patrons it was worth the risk to be in a gay environment. This was the heyday of a working-class, lesbian bar culture, where distinctions between fems (feminine women) and butches (masculine women) challenged mainstream gender conventions and made public the erotic relations between women.[7]

Gay bars were hardly the only place to meet other gay people, though. Public parks were common meeting grounds for gay male sexual encounters or just friendly conversation. Certain theaters attracted gay men. Softball fields, bowling leagues, and certain bookstores served as a basis for many lesbian friendship networks. Indeed, despite all the police surveillance and crackdowns, a camouflaged gay social life suffused 1950s American culture if one knew where to look. Every large city had gay areas, and clandestine gay networks and institutions existed in suburbs and small towns throughout the country as well.[8]

Even churches (especially church choirs) could be important spaces for homosexual bonds and liaisons during the 1950s. Although most mainstream Christian churches officially condemned homosexuality along with other nonprocreative sexual behaviors, churches were less vocal about the issue compared to the years after the emergence of the modern Religious Right in the 1970s and 1980s. Same-sex love thus could flourish as an open secret. This was especially true in the South and among African American churches.[9] In Detroit, for example, a prominent black minister named Prophet Jones who had his own popular television show lived a relatively open gay life. During the civil rights movement's peak years, however, many prominent gay African Americans, including Jones, were marginalized so that the group as a whole would appear sexually "normal" (hence respectable) in an attempt to overcome the historical legacy of disparaging stereotypes that characterize African Americans as hypersexual or promiscuous.[10]

## The Rise of the Homophile Movement

Targeted by McCarthyism, police raids, and general hostility, these expansive yet camouflaged gay social networks incubated a gay political consciousness during the 1950s. This consciousness led to the creation of the country's first gay civil rights organizations, referred to as "homophile" organizations because activists thought the word "homosexual" held too many negative associations. Gay rights activism had first appeared in Germany during the late nineteenth century and spread elsewhere in Europe during the early twentieth century. After the Nazis wiped out this movement during the 1930s, nearly a dozen newly organized homophile groups emerged throughout Western and Northern Europe during the late 1940s. In the United States, after a few failed attempts, the first major organization, the Mattachine Society, began in 1950 in Los Angeles. Mattachine recruited politically conscious gay men (and a few women) into discussion group cells. In these clandestine cells, Mattachine members discussed strategies to improve their status as a minority. One strategy that emerged from these discussions was to challenge police entrapment cases in court. Another was to reach out to influential persons in professions such as medicine, law, and religion in order to mobilize a vanguard of heterosexual sympathizers who would influence others in their profession. During the early 1950s, Mattachine chapters emerged in New York, Chicago, Boston, San Francisco, Detroit, and Washington, DC, creating the first national gay activist network.

The Mattachine Society was founded by a left-wing aspiring actor named Harry Hay. Hay used his experience as a member of the Communist Party to come up with the organization's clandestine cell structure—secrecy, after all, was important to communists as well as homosexuals.

Hay's leftist past, however, proved to be his undoing in the organization. In 1953, after Mattachine received local press coverage following a successful court challenge of an entrapment arrest, the organization was flooded with new members. Many were worried about losing their jobs in Southern California's booming defense industry. When they learned that their leader, Hay, was a former communist, they voted to expel him from the organization over fears that his communist past increased the chances of a backlash against the organization. Thus Hay was kicked out of the organization he had founded, and others, such as Hal Call, led Mattachine until it faded away in the late 1960s.[11]

As the coup against Hay was brewing in late 1952, another group of Mattachine members, frustrated with the organization's secretive nature, broke away and formed ONE, Inc., the second major U.S. homophile organization. From 1953 until the late 1960s, ONE, Inc. published the first openly gay magazine, *ONE*, in order to explore gay culture and facilitate a national discussion about the status of gays in American society. *ONE*'s leadership, like Mattachine's, was predominantly white, although ethnic and racial minorities contributed to the magazine in important, though often behind the scenes, ways. The name of the magazine, for example, was thought up by an African American member, and a Latino founder of ONE, Inc. also occasionally drew cover art for the magazine. *ONE* published essays on science, literature, employment, police, and politics; it also published poetry, movie reviews, artwork, and advertising. It was available on newsstands in large cities throughout the country (and in several foreign countries), reaching several thousand readers every month. It represented an important step forward in the public visibility of homosexuals as a distinct minority group.[12]

Like Mattachine, *ONE* also tended to be male-dominated, but women made important contributions to the magazine. They did most of the illustrations, and a woman served as chief editor for several years in the mid-1950s. Women regularly wrote for the magazine, and each issue contained a column called "The Feminine Viewpoint." Despite these efforts, most of *ONE*'s readers were male and most of its content geared toward men. In response, women protested in letters to the editor that their voices were being marginalized.

Partly in response to the male dominance of Mattachine and ONE, Inc., women created the Daughters of Bilitis, the first lesbian rights organization, in San Francisco in 1955. The Daughters began publishing *The Ladder* in 1956, a magazine similar in structure and content to *ONE*

(Mattachine began publishing *Mattachine Review*, also similar to *ONE*, in 1955). The Daughters hosted discussion groups and guest speakers in San Francisco and established a few chapters in other cities. In contrast to the male-dominated organizations, Daughters of Bilitis members were more interested in discussing family issues, relationships, child rearing, loneliness, and isolation. During the 1960s, the organization became an important source of lesbian feminism before dissolving in the 1970s, bridging the homophile period and the more radical gay liberation era.[13]

Two of the founders of the Daughters, Del Martin and Phyllis Lyon, provide an excellent classroom opportunity to connect the pre-Stonewall past with more recent events. Nearly fifty years after forming the Daughters, both women were featured on the front pages of dozens of newspapers when San Francisco mayor Gavin Newsome declared in 2004 that the city would begin to give marriage licenses to same-sex couples. Martin and Lyon were first in line and the first to be married in California. A court eventually overturned Newsome's declaration, annulling their marriage, but when the California State Supreme Court legalized same-sex marriage in 2008 (before Proposition 8 temporarily overturned the court's decision), Martin and Lyon were once again first in line to wed in San Francisco and once again on the front pages of many newspapers. As Nicholas L. Syrett's essay in this volume demonstrates, the documentary *No Secret Anymore: The Times of Del Martin and Phyllis Lyon* is a tremendous teaching tool, introducing students to a lesbian couple whose relationship spanned more than five decades and whose story is connected to many chapters in LGBT history.

In the 1960s, new gay activist groups emerged with a younger and more militant tone, eventually transforming the assimilationist homophile movement into a more radical gay liberation movement, which favored street demonstrations, sit-ins, and radical new forms of visibility, as Ian Lekus's essay in this volume points out. A similar pattern occurred on a larger scale in the black civil rights movement as Black Power militants challenged the assimilationist strategies of Martin Luther King Jr. and other civil rights leaders. The gay liberationists, who drew inspiration from Black Power, the counterculture, and women's liberation, often dismissed the earlier homophile activists as apologetic fuddy-duddies who failed to accomplish anything of importance. But the mere survival of these first organizations represented a major accomplishment, and they succeeded beyond their wildest expectations in creating a national discussion about gay rights that continues to this day.

## Conclusion

At a broader historical level, the homophile movement's visible (if understated) presence in 1950s American political culture, along with myriad new manifestations of gay culture, undermines the notion of the postwar United States as a country of unrelenting conservatism, consensus, and domesticity. The Second World War had changed the country in many ways, and perhaps one of the most unexpected consequences was the awakening of a gay rights consciousness, an awakening nourished by the Kinsey Reports and Cold War national security hysteria. The homophile movement's presence also demonstrates the influence of African American activism on other social movements. Often narrowly described as a struggle for racial integration, the civil rights movement of the 1950s and 1960s in fact represented a deeper reimagining of the nature of equality itself, a reimagining involving race, ethnicity, gender, and sexuality. This early phase of gay rights activism provides an essential context for and perspective on the current debates about queer rights being played out in the mass media, at the polls, and in legislatures and courtrooms throughout the country.

### NOTES

1. Alfred Kinsey, Wardell Pomeroy, and Clyde Martin, *Sexual Behavior in the Human Male* (Philadelphia: W. B. Saunders, 1948), 610–66; Alfred Kinsey, Wardell Pomeroy, Clyde Martin, and Paul Gebhard, *Sexual Behavior in the Human Female* (Philadelphia: W. B. Saunders, 1953), 446–500.

2. James H. Jones, *Alfred C. Kinsey: A Public/Private Life* (New York: W. W. Norton, 1997); Jonathan Gathorne-Hardy, *Sex the Measure of All Things: A Life of Alfred C. Kinsey* (Bloomington: Indiana University Press, 1998). Gathorne-Hardy's book tends to be favored by scholars, and both Gathorne-Hardy and Jones were consultants for the PBS documentary. William Condon wrote and directed the critically acclaimed 2004 film.

3. Kinsey, Pomeroy, and Martin, *Sexual Behavior in the Human Male*, 617.

4. Ibid., 638.

5. David K. Johnson, *The Lavender Scare: The Cold War Persecution of Gays and Lesbians in the Federal Government* (Chicago: University of Chicago Press, 2004), 53–54.

6. Craig M. Loftin, *Masked Voices: Gay Men and Lesbians in Cold War America* (Albany: State University of New York Press, 2012), 10–14.

7. Elizabeth Lapovsky Kennedy and Madeline D. Davis, *Boots of Leather, Slippers of Gold: The History of a Lesbian Community* (New York: Routledge, 1993).

8. Loftin, *Masked Voices*, 54–58.

9. John Howard, *Men Like That: A Southern Queer History* (Chicago: University of Chicago Press, 2001).

10. Tim Retzloff, "'Seer or Queer?' Postwar Fascination with Detroit's Prophet Jones," *Gay and Lesbian Quarterly* 8, no. 3 (2002): 271–96.

11. John D'Emilio, *Sexual Politics, Sexual Communities: The Making of a Homosexual Minority in the United States* (Chicago: University of Chicago Press, 1983); Stuart Timmons, *The Trouble with Harry Hay* (Boston: Alyson, 1990).

12. Loftin, *Masked Voices*, 17–62; C. Todd White, *Pre-gay L.A.: A Social History of the Movement for Homosexual Rights* (Urbana: University of Illinois Press, 2009).

13. Marcia M. Gallo, *Different Daughters: A History of the Daughters of Bilitis and the Rise of the Lesbian Rights Movement* (New York: Carroll and Graf, 2006).

# Queers of Hope, Gays of Rage

*Reexamining the Sixties in the Classroom*

IAN LEKUS

While roughly four decades have passed since the sixties drew to a close, the meanings and legacies of that period remain hotly contested in U.S. politics.[1] One need only consider the intense debates during presidential campaigns over the last twenty years, from Bill Clinton's Vietnam draft deferment to Barack Obama's alleged relationship with Bill Ayers of the Weathermen, for evidence of the still contested understanding of this era.[2] When asked for the first images that come to mind when hearing the phrase, "the sixties," my undergraduate students generally mention "sex, drugs, and rock and roll." For students studying the sixties, it was an atypical "time of upheaval" or a "war at home, war abroad," at least according to numerous textbook chapter titles.

In teaching the sixties, I challenge the long-standing scholarly and popular narratives that frame the era as an exceptional, aberrant—even queer—moment in U.S. history. In this mythology, the chaos and conflict of the decade stand in stark contrast to the purported conformity of the fifties and the supposed return to normalcy in the seventies. Both in my U.S. survey lecture classes and in my course dedicated to the period, I explain how the sixties emerged gradually and organically out of the early postwar years. From the nuclear family to nuclear weapons, from suburbanization, gender roles, and media culture to Cold War liberal expert ideology, I re-anchor the political and cultural transformations of the sixties firmly in the full sweep of post-1945 U.S. history. In doing so, I show my students the connections between, for example, the middle-class rhetoric of women's domesticity in the suburbs of the fifties and the marginalization of women in the civil rights and antiwar movements that inspired second-wave feminism. Likewise, explaining the Lavender Scare and the early homophile movement (see the essays by David K. Johnson and Craig M. Loftin in this volume) sets the stage for discussions of both the homophobia that LGBT activists encountered in the New Left and the birth of the gay liberation and lesbian feminist movements.

For all the references to sex and sexual revolution in the sixties, by and large the history of this era continues to be written—and thus taught—in resolutely heterosexual terms. This is especially striking given the culture wars waged since the seventies, in which the question of LGBT rights continues to be one of the hottest flashpoints.[3] Both survey text chapters and resources specifically dedicated to the sixties tend to add very brief references to the June 1969 riots at the Stonewall Inn and the subsequent emergence of a national gay liberation movement.[4] At times this gap can offer a pedagogical opportunity, such as when I screen the 1990 documentary *Berkeley in the Sixties*. The relegation of women's liberation to just a couple of minutes at the end of the film, and the virtual absence of gay liberation and lesbian feminism— from a documentary on protest and social change set in the San Francisco Bay Area—unmistakably illustrates for students how the original narrative of sixties history fails to address sexuality and gender.[5]

So my agenda in teaching recent U.S. history is twofold: to anchor discussion of the sixties in the broader coverage of post–Second World War society; and, like my coauthors in this volume, to integrate LGBT people, communities, politics, and culture into the U.S. historical narrative. When teaching the sixties, I seek to include LGBT material throughout the era rather than reducing gay liberation and lesbian feminism to postscripts. Moreover, I apply the central question of queer history to the history of the sixties: how are the ideas and practices of what we consider to be "normal" constructed and maintained, resisted and reshaped? That is to say, how does political and cultural change happen, and what are the limits of that change?

Looking back at the sixties, I encourage my students to inquire why some activists who dedicated their lives to ending Jim Crow, economic injustice, and the Vietnam War found it so difficult to question the sexual and gender norms of the society against which they rebelled. Huey Newton's 1970 letter endorsing women's and gay liberation (though not lesbian feminism) offers an excellent tool for discussion, illustrating how some male activists reconsidered those norms as part of their political agenda. I also assign Carl Wittman's "A Gay Manifesto," Charlotte Bunch's "Lesbians in Revolt," and other critiques of marriage, monogamy, and military service in order to prompt debate over whether today's LGBT leaders are more conservative than their sixties forebears.[6]

## The Politics of Authenticity

Throughout the sixties, LGBT people played critical roles in local and national movements for freedom and justice. Following the Stonewall riots, the gay liberation movement's sweeping vision of democratic social transformation and ardent espousal of "coming out" derived directly from its members' experiences in the civil rights movement and the white New Left. In particular, activists attempted to live out what Doug Rossinow describes as "the politics of authenticity," wherein expanding democratic participation and achieving personal wholeness were inextricably intertwined.[7] For much of the decade, however, the movements for civil rights, Black Power, women's liberation, and ending the Vietnam War were not comfortable spaces for LGBT members.

The story of Bayard Rustin provides an obvious entry point for introducing LGBT people into the history of the sixties. The African American peace and civil rights activist is best known as the chief organizer of the August 1963 March on Washington for Jobs and Freedom. A Quaker and pacifist, Rustin was imprisoned during the Second World War for draft resistance. After the war, he became perhaps the leading advocate for Gandhian nonviolence in the United States, and he introduced Gandhian principles and strategies to the black freedom struggle during the Montgomery, Alabama, bus boycott of 1955–56, during which he became a mentor to the Reverend Dr. Martin Luther King Jr. Rustin was also an openly gay man during the intense homophobia of the early Cold War. After a 1953 arrest on a morals charge in Pasadena, California, Rustin lost his position with the Fellowship of Reconciliation, a Christian pacifist organization. He was soon thereafter hired by the War Resisters League and helped launch *Liberation*, the highly influential magazine of the New Left.

The video documentary *Brother Outsider: The Life of Bayard Rustin* offers one teaching resource covering both the accomplishments of this pioneering activist and the political homophobia that he encountered from would-be allies and adversaries alike.[8] In 1960 Rustin and King planned civil rights demonstrations outside of the Democratic National Convention in Los Angeles. Harlem congressman Adam Clayton Powell Jr., who viewed King's rising prominence as a threat to his own place in the black political establishment, told the press of "an immoral element" in the civil rights movement's leadership. Powell privately phoned King and threatened to expose him and Rustin as lovers if King did not cancel the demonstrations. King acquiesced and publicly dissociated himself from Rustin. Three years later, after A. Philip Randolph chose him to organize the 1963 March on Washington, Rustin came under fire once again. Strom Thurmond, the prominent segregationist senator from South Carolina, tried to discredit the event by publicizing Rustin's brief membership in the Communist Party. By 1963, however, McCarthyite tactics of red baiting had lost their efficacy, and Thurmond instead read the reports of Rustin's arrest in Pasadena into the Senate record. But Randolph stood firmly by Rustin, who successfully organized the march, which drew more than 250,000 people to Washington and climaxed with King's "I Have a Dream" speech. Because of the stigma associated with Rustin's sexual identity at the time, however, his work in organizing the largest demonstration in American history to that point—in just seven weeks—went unacknowledged by King and other civil rights leaders who spoke on that famous day.

Inspired by the civil rights movement and alarmed by the persistence of poverty during the tremendous postwar economic expansion, a white student movement grew throughout the 1960s. The members of Students for a Democratic Society (SDS) and other New Left groups shared similar goals: ending poverty and racism, organizing disenfranchised citizens to improve the material conditions of their lives, stopping the Vietnam War, and curbing the excesses of the American military-industrial complex. But, despite the self-proclaimed radicalism of many in the New Left, they frequently shared the antigay attitudes of the Cold War society in which they grew up.

Heterosexual male movement leaders often gay baited their opponents and cajoled male recruits into proving their normative masculinity. They frequently ushered women in and out of the movement based on whom they were dating at a given moment, effectively dividing New Left women into girlfriends who mimeographed and made coffee, on the one hand, and desexualized leaders who were essentially accepted as "one of the boys" on the other. Frequently, these white middle-class men justified their antigay and antifeminist rhetoric and practices by portraying the homophobia and misogyny that they perceived as inherent to the white working-class, Black Power, and Third World movements and cultures as authentic revolutionary attitudes. Such hostile movement cultures were further exacerbated by FBI infiltrators and other government authorities, whose agents spread rumors about the sexual orientation of specific activists in order to discredit them.

Gay baiting took its toll on unknown numbers of LGBT people, compelling some to lie and hide their sexual orientation while driving others from the movement altogether.[9] Gay and bisexual men endured slurs from their movement comrades, as heterosexual men disparagingly called their male rivals "fags," bragged about their prowess with women, and joked about pretending to be gay to avoid the draft. Such behavior deflected mainstream condemnation that equated their opposition to the Vietnam War with being insufficiently masculine. At the same time, women who challenged the male chauvinism in the New Left risked being labeled lesbians—although relatively few came out as such until after their immersion in the women's liberation movement.

Carl Wittman's experience in SDS illustrates the challenges faced by some LGBT movement participants. A pioneering student leader at Swarthmore College, Wittman authored "An Interracial Movement for the Poor?" with Tom Hayden, the lead author of the Port Huron Statement. Wittman and Hayden's document, which became the template for SDS's Economic Research and Action Projects (ERAP), outlined the strategy of building social movements through local community organizing against racism and poverty. The two led ERAP organizing in Newark, New Jersey, but after Hayden reportedly declared that homosexuals were not welcome on the project, Wittman—then closeted about his sexual orientation—withdrew and launched a similar venture in nearby Hoboken.

Charlotte Bunch and Amber Hollibaugh's journeys through the sixties reveal the challenges that lesbians negotiated in their political and personal lives. Both Bunch, from a middle-class, Methodist, New Mexico family, and Hollibaugh, from an impoverished family in California's Central Valley, cut their organizing teeth in civil rights and antiwar work before rising to prominence in women's liberation and lesbian feminism. Bunch, as an undergraduate at Duke University, threw herself into the Methodist Student Movement, marched from Selma to Montgomery, read Betty Friedan's *The Feminine Mystique*, and protested the war outside the Durham, North Carolina, post office. Hollibaugh, for whom the movement offered upward class mobility, organized for the Student Nonviolent Coordinating Committee and the United Farm Workers in New York. While Bunch married one of her male movement comrades after graduation, following him to Cleveland for his studies, Hollibaugh earned money for activism through sex work. She traveled throughout North America, smuggling draft evaders, army deserters, and Black Panthers into Canada, while Bunch moved to Washington, DC, spoke at the 1968 Jeannette Rankin Brigade antiwar rally, traveled to Hanoi with the National Mobilization to End the War, and cofounded D.C. Women's Liberation.

The "personal is political," the women's liberation movement declared, expanding on the politics of authenticity to critically examine the connections between lived experience and structures of power, especially with regard to gender and sexuality. Bunch came out as a lesbian in 1971, as she came to understand her attraction to other women through her participation in consciousness-raising groups and other women-only spaces. D.C. Women's Liberation suffered the "gay-straight divide" that split many second-wave feminist groups, and Bunch cofounded the short-lived but highly influential lesbian feminist organization the Furies. Hollibaugh represented the minority of lesbians in the movement who discovered their attraction to other women before becoming involved in feminism. When she became romantically involved with a female housemate in a Berkeley commune in the mid-1960s, she and her housemate were told that their behavior was unacceptable and they were asked to leave the commune. Half a decade later, while sheltering members of the Weather Underground on the run from the government, she was amazed to find herself lectured, in her own home, about the political error of her homosexuality by the very radicals she was hiding.[10]

While many New Leftists brought to the movement the antigay attitudes instilled in them while growing up in the fifties, the trust and candor developed while organizing provided some heterosexual activists with the opportunity to rethink these homophobic assumptions. Helen Garvy, the first woman elected to SDS's national leadership, recalled watching the difficulties Carl Wittman encountered in coming out to his old leftist parents. Similar transformations of consciousness took place during the Chicago Seven conspiracy trial following the 1968 Democratic National Convention. During the trial, government prosecutor Thomas Foran relentlessly gay baited the white defendants, as well as defense witness Allen Ginsberg, lamenting that "we've lost our kids to the freaking fag revolution." In other words, Foran cast the entire generation of New Left and countercultural youths as "freaking fags" disloyal to the conventions of white middle-class heteronormativity. His laments prompted Tom Hayden and other movement leaders to consider that gay liberation might be integral to their overarching vision of social transformation.[11]

### Get Up, Stand Up: Gay Liberation, Lesbian Feminism, and Late Sixties Radicalism

In the spring of 1969, months before the Stonewall riots, Carl Wittman began writing "A Gay Manifesto," an essay that became the seminal theoretical outline of the new gay liberation movement. Drawing heavily on his experiences in civil rights, economic justice, and antidraft organizing, Wittman's manifesto applied the lessons learned by sixties organizers to the issues facing lesbians and gay men. He denounced gay male chauvinism, rejected marriage and the mimicry of other heterosexual institutions, and condemned discrimination by legal, psychiatric, and government authorities. He called for the formation of coalitions with the women's, black, and Chicano movements, other white heterosexual radicals, homophiles, and members of the counterculture and issued a call to "free ourselves: come out everywhere; initiate self defense and political activity; [and] initiate counter community institutions."[12]

In the wake of Stonewall, and as the protest movements of the sixties became increasingly decentralized and splintered, LGBT New Leftists began organizing gay liberation across the United States. In taking the name Gay Liberation Front, GLF members paid homage to South Vietnam's rebel National Liberation Front (more commonly referred to as the Viet Cong). Activists in GLF took part in antiwar demonstrations in New York, Washington, San Francisco, and elsewhere under banners such as "Gays Unite against the War." They also took part in pro-Cuba projects and supported the Black Panther Party.[13]

Black Panther leaders, to whom many white radicals looked for role models, were divided over the question of homosexuality. In his 1968

Gay Liberation Front march, New York City, June 28, 1970 (© Ellen Shumsky / The Image Works, reprinted with permission)

book *Soul on Ice*, Eldridge Cleaver venomously attacked James Baldwin and other African American gay men, who were "acquiescing in this racial death-wish . . . bending over and touching their toes for the white man." But in 1970 Black Panther Party leader Huey Newton declared his support for the gay liberation movement and exhorted his comrades to reject their antigay attitudes and eliminate words such as *faggot* and *punk* from their everyday vocabularies. For many white New Leftists, Newton's proclamation helped legitimize homosexuality and prompted them to reconsider the place of gay liberation in progressive politics.

Lesbians struggled with similar hostility from some of their heterosexual sisters in the women's liberation movement. Betty Friedan of the National Organization for Women (NOW) raised the specter of a "lavender menace" threatening that movement. In 1970, when *Time* outed the bisexual feminist literary critic Kate Millett (dubbed "the Mao Tse-Tung of Women's Liberation" by the newsmagazine) as a lesbian, some NOW members rushed to her defense while others sought to distance the organization from the growing lesbian movement. (The

*Time* news story would make a productive prompt for a discussion about what has and has not changed regarding celebrities coming out or being outed by the media.)

In the post-Stonewall era, LGBT organizers regularly faced resistance from fellow radicals who did not consider sexuality to be a central political issue. Lesbian feminism faced skepticism within the broader feminist movement, for example, when women's peace groups in the United States and Canada arranged for a delegation of Southeast Asian women to visit Toronto and Vancouver to meet with North American activists. In the planning for the North American–Indochinese Women's Conference, squabbles erupted along racial, national, and generational lines. Those lesbian feminist organizers who sought representation at the event—including both Charlotte Bunch in Washington and Amber Hollibaugh in Toronto—met with intense opposition. Bunch, then "coming out rather rapidly as a militant lesbian," in her own words, recalled being told by movement leaders that "we were trying to introduce something that was irrelevant" to the Indochinese visitors. At that point, Bunch dropped out of antiwar activism. Like many others alienated by the homophobia they encountered in women's liberation, the New Left, and other radical movements, she committed her energies to lesbian feminism for the next few years.[14]

While gay liberationists and lesbian feminists dedicated themselves to antiracism and anti-imperialism, many LGBT people of color chafed at the "inherent racism" of these movements' white leadership. In 1970 a group of LGBT African Americans and Latinos split off from GLF to found Third World Gay Liberation, a short-lived but highly influential organization that linked struggles against racism, capitalism, sexism, and homophobia. Their manifesto demanded full inclusion in both the Third World revolutionary and LGBT movements. The statement, directly modeled on the Black Panther Party's Ten Point Platform, articulated what theorists would later describe as an intersectional model of politics.[15]

Activists of color recognized from their own personal LGBT histories that race, class, gender, sexuality, and other forms of oppression were fundamentally interlocking and could not be understood or confronted in isolation. This intersectional approach synthesized Black Power ideology, feminist personal politics, and New Left authenticity, connecting ever more clearly the intricate webs of power that shape politics, culture, and lived experience. Black lesbian activists in the Combahee

River Collective articulated a model of identity politics, arguing in "A Black Feminist Statement" that "our liberation is a necessity, not as an adjunct to someone else's but because of our need as human persons for autonomy." For the teacher looking to connect the sixties to more recent history, the collective provides an invaluable opportunity to interrogate how activists have wrestled with identity and difference in building effective coalitions to transform U.S. politics and culture.[16]

## Pedagogical Strategies

A broad range of primary and secondary sources are available that emphasize personal narratives from the sixties.[17] Students, not surprisingly, often find it relatively easy to empathize with young activists, whether out of admiration for their causes or curiosity about how differently an earlier generation of students experienced their time in college. Comparing and contrasting the experiences of different activists, and the choices they debated and then made, helps students to better understand the contexts in which these movements took place and to resist a single, uncritical narrative of heroic people just doing the right thing.

Few exercises make history as relevant and accessible to students as conducting oral history interviews. (See the essay by Nan Alamilla Boyd in this volume.) Whether interviewing parents, grandparents, or other family members, older neighbors, teachers, coaches, school staff, religious or civil figures, or other members of their communities, oral history provides an experience that often remains with students long after the details of their readings have begun to fade. Moreover, oral history is especially well suited to exploring the history both of LGBT people so long "hidden from history" and of the sixties, given the emphasis on giving voice to "the people." In completing an interview with someone who lived through the sixties, writing a critical analysis of the interview, and then discussing their interviews with their classmates, students should quickly come to understand that the pace and intensity of change during the sixties varied dramatically from region to region, and that the movement occurred within the context of an often skeptical, anxious, and even hostile broader local and national political climate. They should also develop an understanding of the heterogeneity of movement activism and how participants' involvement related to their personal experiences.

The popular culture of the sixties provides another entry point for discussing how some notable activists and artists of the era inherited the prejudices of their parents' generation. I have students listen to two classic antidraft anthems, Arlo Guthrie's "Alice's Restaurant" and Phil Ochs's "Draft Dodger Rag," both of which advise male listeners to feign homosexuality to escape conscription. I also show them a short selection from the film *The Gay Deceivers* in which the two straight male characters pretend to be a couple to their draft board while simultaneously reminding their families and girlfriends of their heterosexuality. This sets up a discussion of how the folksingers and movie characters sought to convince the military authorities that they were psychiatrically unfit for military service while still using humor to reassure others that they were actually "normal." Furthermore, Ochs's advice to "always carry a purse" and the conflation of male homosexuality with effeminacy in *The Gay Deceivers* reveal to students how the postwar discourse on gender deviance persisted into the protests and counterculture of the sixties.[18]

Besides *The Gay Deceivers* and other films from the sixties that I use in class, I juxtapose excerpts from two much more recent documentaries, *Screaming Queens* and *Stonewall Uprising*. (See the essay by Nicholas L. Syrett in this volume.) Shown together, the documentaries spur a discussion of why the 1966 Compton Cafeteria riot stimulated local LGBT and transgender-specific activism but not a national movement. Screening *Stonewall Uprising* in conjunction with other accounts of the homophile, gay liberation, and other late sixties movements prompts students to articulate what is almost entirely omitted from the documentary: the organizing that turned a riot by mostly working-class African American and Latino drag queens and transgender people into the inspiration for a predominantly white, middle-class, lesbian and gay movement in the seventies and beyond.

Teaching the sixties remains exciting and vital even as the period itself recedes farther into the past. That distance presents a challenge insofar as popular culture offers little more than songs, slogans, and heroic caricatures stripped of the context of political and social transformation. But that distance also offers opportunities for teachers to bury once and for all that other sixties cliché: "You had to be there." For some students, this history offers political and cultural role models, showing them how earlier generations resisted injustice and wrestled with the challenge of securing the promise of U.S. democracy. For most students, the acceleration of grassroots conservative activism in the sixties comes as a surprise; the discovery that for most of the period conservatives paid relatively little attention to LGBT rights, or to sexuality and gender more generally, is even more startling. That latter pair of lessons is yet one more example of how to lead our students beyond their assumptions about the era.

Such instruction shatters one further popular myth: that LGBT history began in 1969 at the Stonewall Inn. We can understand those riots, and the emergence of the gay liberation and lesbian feminist movements, far more fully when we anchor them in the social movements of the sixties and in the postwar decades more generally. The queer riots and open rebellions appear as chapters in a story of everyday people resisting the prejudicial and arbitrary use of state power and demanding to be treated with respect and dignity. Stonewall no longer magically ushers in gay liberation and lesbian feminism. Instead, LGBT people who had developed skills and frameworks in working for racial, economic, and gender justice and against the Vietnam War organized new movements fundamentally informed by a sweeping progressive vision of political transformation. In challenging the homophobia of their fellow comrades, they revealed how a generation of radicals inherited the sexual and gender norms of the fifties. By organizing movements to dismantle those norms and secure justice and civil rights for LGBT citizens, gay liberation and lesbian feminism ensured that the queer legacy of the sixties would live on.

### NOTES

1. Portions of this essay were adapted from my "The Long Sixties," *Organization of American Historians Magazine of History* 20, no. 2 (March 2006): 32–38; from my entries "Antiwar, Pacifist, and Peace Movements" (1:72–74), "New Left and Student Movements" (2:325–29), and "Carl Wittman" (3:285–87), in *Encyclopedia of Lesbian, Gay, Bisexual, and Transgender History in America*, ed. Marc Stein (New York: Charles Scribner's Sons, 2003); and from my *Queer and Present Dangers: Masculinity, Sexuality, and the Sixties* (Chapel Hill: University of North Carolina Press, forthcoming).

2. I refer to the sixties rather than the 1960s to emphasize the political, social, and cultural trends of this historical period.

3. Robert O. Self, *All in the Family: The Realignment of American Democracy since the 1960s* (New York: Hill & Wang, 2012).

4. Mark Hamilton Lytle's *America's Uncivil Wars: The Sixties Era from Elvis to the Fall of Richard Nixon* (New York: Oxford University Press, 2006), offers the most extensive material on LGBT history of any broad sixties histories to date.

Also helpful are Alexander Bloom and Wini Breines, eds., *Takin' It to the Streets: A Sixties Reader*, 2nd ed. (New York: Oxford University Press, 2003); and Van Gosse, *The Movements of the New Left, 1950–1975: A Brief History with Documents* (Boston: Bedford, 2005).

5. *Berkeley in the Sixties*, dir. Mark Kitchell, Kitchell Films and P.O.V. Theatrical Films, New York, 1990.

6. Charlotte Bunch, "Lesbians in Revolt," Carl Wittman, "A Gay Manifesto," and Huey Newton, "A Letter from Huey to the Revolutionary Brothers and Sisters about the Women's Liberation and Gay Liberation Movements," all in *Come Out Fighting: A Century of Essential Writing on Gay and Lesbian Liberation*, ed. Chris Bull (New York: Thunder's Mouth Press, 2001), 126–31, 67–79, 89–91.

7. Doug Rossinow, *The Politics of Authenticity: Liberalism, Christianity, and the New Left* (New York: Columbia University Press, 1998).

8. *Brother Outsider: The Life of Bayard Rustin*, dir. Nancy Kates and Bennett Singer, California Newsreel, San Francisco, 2003. See also John D'Emilio, *Lost Prophet: The Life and Times of Bayard Rustin* (New York: Free Press, 2003).

9. See Lekus, *Queer and Present Dangers.*

10. Charlotte Bunch, *Passionate Politics: Feminist Theory in Action* (New York: St. Martin's Press, 1987); Amber Hollibaugh, *My Dangerous Desires: A Queer Girl Dreaming Her Way Home* (Durham, NC: Duke University Press, 2000); Ian Lekus, "Interview with Amber Hollibaugh," *Peace and Change* 29, no. 2 (April 2004): 266–321. The documentary film *Passionate Politics: The Life and Work of Charlotte Bunch* (dir. Tami Gold, AndersonGold Films, New York, 2011) is an excellent resource for the classroom.

11. Lekus, *Queer and Present Dangers*; and Ian Lekus, "Losing Our Kids: Queer Perspectives on the Chicago Seven Conspiracy Trial," in *The New Left Revisited*, ed. Paul Buhle and John McMillian (Philadelphia: Temple University Press, 2003), 199–213.

12. Wittman, "A Gay Manifesto," 79.

13. Ian Lekus, "Queer Harvests: Homosexuality, the U.S. New Left, and the Venceremos Brigades to Cuba," *Radical History Review* 89 (Spring 2004): 57–91.

14. Charlotte Bunch, quoted in Lekus, *Queer and Present Dangers*. See also Judy Tzu-Chun Wu, *Radicals on the Road: Internationalism, Orientalism, and Feminism during the Vietnam Era* (Ithaca, NY: Cornell University Press, 2013).

15. Third World Gay Revolution, "The Oppressed Shall Not Become the Oppressor," reprinted in *We Are Everywhere: A Historical Sourcebook of Gay and Lesbian Politics*, ed. Mark Blasius and Shane Phelan (New York: Routledge, 1997), 400–401.

16. Combahee River Collective, "A Black Feminist Statement," in *This Bridge Called My Back: Writings by Radical Women of Color*, ed. Cherríe Moraga and Gloria Anzaldúa (Watertown, MA: Persephone Press, 1981), 210–18. Also see Anne Enke, *Finding the Movement: Sexuality, Contested Space, and Feminist*

*Activism* (Durham, NC: Duke University Press, 2007); Stephanie Gilmore, *Groundswell: Feminist Grassroots Activism in Postwar America* (New York: Routledge, 2012); and Anne M. Valk, *Radical Sisters: Second-Wave Feminism and Black Liberation in Washington, D.C.* (Urbana: University of Illinois Press, 2008).

17. There are far too many memoirs of sixties activists to cite here. On LGBT activists from the sixties, see Bettina Aptheker, *Intimate Politics: How I Grew Up Red, Fought for Free Speech, and Became a Feminist Rebel* (Emeryville, CA: Seal Press, 2006); Rachel Blau DuPlessis and Ann Snitow, eds., *The Feminist Memoir Project: Voices from Women's Liberation* (New York: Three Rivers Press, 1998); Karla Jay, *Tales of the Lavender Menace: A Memoir of Liberation* (New York: Basic Books, 2000); and Tommi Avicolli Mecca, *Smash the Church, Smash the State! The Early Years of Gay Liberation* (San Francisco: City Lights, 2009).

18. Arlo Guthrie, "Alice's Restaurant," *Alice's Restaurant*, Reprise RS-6267 (stereo), 1967; Phil Ochs, "Draft Dodger Rag," *I Ain't Marching Anymore*, Elektra EKL-287, 1965; *The Gay Deceivers*, dir. Bruce Kessler, Fanfare Films, 1969.

# Sexual Rights and Wrongs

*Teaching the U.S. Supreme Court's Greatest Gay and Lesbian Hits*

MARC STEIN

In the twenty-first century, U.S. Supreme Court cases have repeatedly provoked wide-ranging debates about sexual freedom and equality, but these discussions are rarely informed by knowledge of the long history of Supreme Court decisions that addressed gay and lesbian rights. Since 2006 I have regularly considered these decisions in a university course on constitutional law and equal rights in U.S. history. I developed the course in part because I thought it would support one of my major research projects, which was published in 2010 as *Sexual Injustice: Supreme Court Decisions from "Griswold" to "Roe."*[1] I also wanted to introduce students to important episodes in U.S. history, enrich their understanding of law and politics, broaden their perspectives on freedom and equality, and help them see the past as a resource that can be useful in today's political struggles. In this essay I reflect on how Supreme Court decisions on gay and lesbian rights can be used in introductory courses on U.S. history.

My course focuses on gay and lesbian cases only in its final two weeks, but our consideration of earlier equal rights decisions, most of which concern African Americans, Asian Americans, Native Americans, people with disabilities, and women, helps my students understand these cases. By the time we reach the final weeks, for example, my students are familiar with the notion that the relationship between the U.S.

Constitution and the Supreme Court is analogous to the relationship between the rules and referees in sports. When they dislike a ruling, I sometimes ask if they blame the rules or the referees. In a survey course, too, discussions of gay and lesbian cases can build on earlier lectures and readings about the Constitution and the Supreme Court.

Supreme Court decisions are excellent primary sources for teaching students about U.S. history and the history of sexuality. In each case, there are two opposing sides with conflicting arguments, although it can be illuminating to look for points of agreement. After working with students to identify the opposing arguments, I help them understand the legal reasoning and legal outcome. In many cases, there are majority, concurring, and dissenting opinions, so students can consider multiple perspectives on equal rights. I work with students to locate the decisions in their historical moments, explore change over time, and consider relationships between different types of cases. We treat the Court's opinions as cultural texts that are filled with rich and revealing language about the justices' perspectives and prejudices, their rhetorical strategies, and their interactive relationships with other social, cultural, and political developments. Supreme Court decisions, which are available online through findlaw.com, justia.com, and other websites, generally begin with a summary, although this is not part of the formal ruling. After this comes the majority opinion, followed by concurring and dissenting opinions. Rather than assigning entire decisions, which can be lengthy and difficult for nonspecialists, I often provide excerpts. More advanced students benefit from access to lower court rulings, legal briefs, oral arguments, media coverage, and other materials, some of which is available online and in law libraries, but some of which can only be found in historical archives.

When I talk with students about these cases, I emphasize that legal reform is just one component of gender and sexual liberation, but I also show that the Supreme Court has played a major role in gay and lesbian struggles. Many activists have argued that changes in law are a necessary precondition for broader social transformation, and many have seen legal debates as critical arenas for larger discussions about sex, gender, and sexuality. For example, by the time the Court announced major rulings about sodomy law in 1986 and 2003, sodomy prosecutions were rare, but as long as these statutes existed they influenced discussions of sexual rights and freedoms. And in fighting for the decriminalization of same-sex sex, legal advocates were able to present powerful arguments to the U.S. public about gay and lesbian lives, loves, and lusts.

It also can be helpful to address the reasons that the gay and lesbian movement has turned to the Supreme Court specifically. In many situations, the movement has achieved law reform not through the courts but through electoral politics, executive policy making, and legislative action. For a variety of reasons, however, gay and lesbian activists have often appealed to the Supreme Court. One reason is that they were influenced by the judicial victories achieved by African American activists, especially in the 1954 *Brown v. Board of Education* decision, which overturned racial segregation in public schools.[2] A second reason is that when the gay and lesbian movement has lacked majority public support, it sometimes has turned to the Court, whose members are less vulnerable to popular opinion because they are appointed for life (unlike officials who are elected for fixed terms). A third reason is that the U.S. political system constrains the powers of the legislative and executive branches of government. For example, there was no direct way in which the Congress or president could force states to repeal their sodomy laws, but the Court could invalidate them. Finally, many gay and lesbian activists have focused on the Court because of their confidence in the Constitution and their belief that there is constitutional language that can be applied to sexual and gender matters.

The remainder of this essay introduces six key decisions on gay and lesbian rights, links these decisions to major themes in U.S. history, and offers suggestions for how these decisions could be taught in U.S. history survey courses. In these cases, the Supreme Court focused more on men than women, partly because of sex differences in sexual cultures and sexual policing, partly because the gay and lesbian movement privileged the concerns of men, and partly because some of the main targets of litigation—immigration restriction, military discrimination, sexual censorship, and sodomy law—seemed to affect men more than women. While some of these rulings had important implications for transgender rights, there has yet to be a major Supreme Court decision that addresses these rights directly, which in and of itself is historically significant. Notwithstanding these limitations, the Court's decisions on gay and lesbian rights have much to teach us about freedom, equality, and democracy. Together they show that "progress" on gay and lesbian rights has been impressive but inconsistent, partial, and limited.[3]

### An Early Victory: *ONE v. Olesen* (1958)

In the context of the complicated politics of the 1950s, the Supreme Court's first major gay and lesbian rights decision was a qualified victory for the homophile movement.[4] In this case, ONE, Inc., the publisher of *ONE* magazine, challenged Los Angeles postmaster Otto Olesen, who had refused to mail the periodical's October 1954 issue. *ONE*, the first magazine produced by the U.S. homophile movement, was hardly the most risqué publication in the United States: its contents were not sexually explicit, it was not as homoerotically stimulating as were male physique magazines or lesbian pulp novels, and it was far less racy than countless books and magazines marketed to straight men. Nevertheless, Olesen refused to distribute *ONE* based on a federal law that prohibited the mailing of obscene materials. He singled out a lesbian-themed short story, a poem titled "Lord Samuel and Lord Montagu," and an advertisement for European gay magazines.[5]

As David K. Johnson's and Craig M. Loftin's essays in this volume make clear, the 1950s was a time of promise and danger for gay and lesbian activists. On the one hand, gender and sexual repression escalated during the Red and Lavender Scares. On the other hand, the homophile movement was established, civil rights activism strengthened, and the Supreme Court responded favorably to some equal rights arguments. Meanwhile, obscenity law was in flux. Just one year before *ONE* was decided, the Court had affirmed its position that obscenity was not protected by the Constitution. According to *Roth v. United States* (1957), a text could be classified as obscene if "the average person, applying contemporary community standards," would conclude that "the dominant theme of the material taken as a whole appeals to prurient interest."[6] One year later the Court considered the question of whether the October 1954 issue of *ONE* could be classified as obscene.

When the justices announced their decision, the results were a qualified victory for gay and lesbian rights. Overturning two lower court decisions, the Supreme Court ruled five to four in favor of *ONE*. Without explaining its reasoning, the Court simply cited *Roth*, which presumably meant that the government had not proved that *ONE* met *Roth*'s definition of obscenity. This was an important victory; without this ruling it would have been more difficult for gay and lesbian activists to communicate, organize, and mobilize. Nevertheless, the victory was limited. First, the decision did not endorse the libertarian notion that all

241

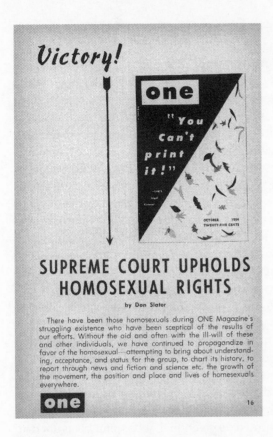

*ONE* magazine announces Supreme Court victory, February 1958 (courtesy of the ONE National Gay & Lesbian Archives)

sexual censorship is unconstitutional. Second, it was based on *Roth*'s definition of obscenity, which discriminated in referring to "average people," "community standards," and "prurient interest." Third, since *ONE*'s lawyers emphasized that the magazine did not advocate homosexuality and did not publish sexually explicit materials, the implications of the decision were unclear.

In the next several years, homophile activists and their allies appealed to the Supreme Court to overturn negative lower court rulings in cases concerning sexual censorship, immigration restriction, employment discrimination, police harassment, and sodomy law. Most of the time, the justices dismissed or declined to consider the case, which happens with most decisions appealed to the Supreme Court. In a few instances, the justices ruled in favor of gay and lesbian litigants, but the grounds were narrow and the decisions did not establish promising precedents.

Many saw signs of hope in the *Griswold v. Connecticut* decision (1965), which recognized marital privacy rights in a birth control case, but the language used by the justices suggested that they believed that laws prohibiting nonmarital sex were constitutional. Along similar lines, some were hopeful about the decision in *A Book Named "John Cleland's Memoirs of a Woman of Pleasure" v. Attorney General of the Commonwealth of Massachusetts* (1966), commonly referred to as *Fanny Hill*, which specified that only materials with no "redeeming social value" could be classified as obscene. On the same day, however, the Court upheld an obscenity conviction in *Mishkin v. New York* (1966), which concerned depictions of sadomasochism, fetishism, and homosexuality.[7] In the early years of the sexual revolution, this did not bode well for gay and lesbian rights.

In U.S. history survey courses, *ONE v. Olesen* can be addressed in lectures on gender and sexuality in the post–Second World War era, the Red and Lavender Scares, the sexual revolution, gay and lesbian politics, and the Supreme Court. Because the Court did not produce a detailed decision, the ruling is not useful as an assigned reading, but showing students a copy of a homophile magazine from the 1950s can be educationally effective. Covers of *ONE*, *Mattachine Review*, and *The Ladder* can be viewed online, and some of the contents are available in digitized format, which means that students can see the issue of *ONE* that was censored. This can be juxtaposed with covers of *Playboy*, physique magazines, and lesbian novels to highlight the discriminatory character of sexual censorship. *ONE v. Olesen* can also be used to challenge the myth that the U.S. gay and lesbian movement began with the Stonewall riots of 1969.

### A Major Setback: *Boutilier v. Immigration and Naturalization Service* (1967)

While the homophile movement secured its first significant victory at the Supreme Court in the 1950s, which is generally regarded as a conservative period in U.S. history, it suffered its first major defeat in the 1960s, which is commonly associated with liberal and radical politics. The Court's decision in *Boutilier v. Immigration and Naturalization Service* (1967), which focused on antihomosexual immigration restriction, was a major blow to gay and lesbian activists.[8] In the mid-1960s, several homophile organizations, influenced by the civil rights movement, decided that constitutional litigation was a promising avenue for promoting social change. In *Boutilier*, the Philadelphia-based Homosexual Law Reform Society worked with radical immigration lawyers and the American Civil Liberties Union (ACLU). Together they defended Clive Boutilier, a Canadian who had been living in New York since 1955. Boutilier had applied for U.S. citizenship in 1963, but he was turned down after he revealed that in 1959 he had been arrested, though not convicted, on a sodomy charge. The Immigration and Naturalization Service (INS) then began deportation proceedings based on the 1952 Immigration and Nationality Act, which provided for the exclusion and deportation of aliens "afflicted with psychopathic personality." According to the INS, Congress intended for this provision to be used against homosexuals. Boutilier's lawyers challenged this interpretation of the legislative history. They also argued that the law was unconstitutionally vague, that the INS had failed to establish that Boutilier was a homosexual, and that most scientific experts rejected the notion that homosexuality was psychopathological.

If *ONE* was a qualified victory for gay and lesbian rights, *Boutilier* was a devastating loss. In a six-to-three decision, the Supreme Court upheld the immigration statute and the deportation of Boutilier. Systematically rejecting the arguments made by Boutilier's lawyers, the Court held that Congress intended to provide for the exclusion and deportation of homosexuals, the law was sufficiently clear, the INS was justified in classifying Boutilier as a homosexual, and the expert testimony was irrelevant since legislative authority trumped scientific knowledge. In a revealing analogy, the Court stated that just as it had deferred to Congress when it upheld the Chinese Exclusion Act in the nineteenth century, it was deferring to Congress now by upholding the antihomosexual provisions of the Immigration and Nationality Act.

Over the next two decades, as gay and lesbian activists mobilized in unprecedented ways, their movement won many legal victories in the lower courts and in legislative and executive decisions made at the state and local levels, but Supreme Court litigation was less successful. Lower court rulings reduced the scope of employment discrimination by the federal government, and in a few exceptional circumstances there were victories in military discrimination cases. Challenged by the gay and lesbian movement, many state and local governments curtailed their most egregiously antihomosexual police practices. Some state sodomy and local cross-dressing laws were repealed or overturned, and some state and local governments amended their human rights codes to restrict discrimination based on sexual orientation (and some-times gender identity as well). There were also occasional victories in family law and parental custody cases.

Until the mid-1980s, however, the Supreme Court refused to accept for argument any major gay and lesbian rights appeals. Gay and lesbian activists and their allies, led by Lambda Legal Defense and a network of similar groups, brought dozens of cases to the Supreme Court, but the justices generally turned them away. In several instances they signaled that laws against nonmarital sex and same-sex sex were constitutional. While the Court overturned various forms of sex discrimination (mean-ing discrimination against women or discrimination against men) in this era, the justices rejected most appeals that concerned discrimination against gays and lesbians. In this situation, gay and lesbian reformers confronted two major problems: (1) there was great local variability in the recognition of gay and lesbian rights and freedoms, and (2) gay and lesbian rights and freedoms were limited even in the most favorable jurisdictions.

In a survey course, *Boutilier* can be addressed in all the lectures men-tioned above for *ONE* and in discussions about immigration reform. When I teach *Boutilier*, I assign the text of the ruling, but I also often show students a copy of *Drum* magazine, the popular gay periodical that helped fund the litigation in *Boutilier*; one issue of *Drum* reprinted the Homosexual Law Reform Society's *Boutilier* brief alongside erotic photographs of men. I also share with my students feature stories about gay and lesbian law reform in the *New York Times Magazine* in 1967 and the *Wall Street Journal* in 1968; these help challenge the myth that the gay and lesbian movement was publicly invisible until the Stonewall riots of 1969.[9] *Boutilier* can also be paired with *Quiroz v. Neelly*, a lower court ruling against a Mexican woman classified as a psychopathic per-sonality.[10] Another approach is to teach *Boutilier* alongside *Griswold* on birth control, *Loving v. Virginia* on interracial marriage, and *Roe v. Wade* on abortion; this highlights the heteronormative character of sexual liberalization.[11] *Boutilier* can also be used when discussing the American Psychiatric Association's 1973 decision to declassify homosexuality as a mental illness.

## A Devastating Loss: *Bowers v. Hardwick* (1986)

The decade of the 1980s was not a favorable time to pursue gay and lesbian reform through constitutional litigation. The Supreme

Court was dominated by Republican Party appointees, and the Republicans, influenced by the Christian Right and New Right, were hostile to gay and lesbian rights. This was also the first decade of the AIDS epidemic, which contributed to a rise in sexual prejudice and discrimination. Many activists nevertheless believed that overturning state sodomy laws would remove the most important lynchpins of sexual oppression. Sodomy laws in this period typically criminalized anal and oral sex. Some applied to same-sex and cross-sex sex, some only to same-sex sex. The laws were rarely enforced, but the criminal status of same-sex sex was commonly used to justify other forms of sexual prejudice and discrimination. Many activists thought it was critical to overturn these laws in the twenty-four states that still had them.

In *Bowers v. Hardwick* (1986), Michael Hardwick, who had been arrested for engaging in oral sex with another man in his home (which police discovered while serving an arrest warrant for public drinking), challenged Georgia's sodomy law, which criminalized oral and anal sex (homosexual and heterosexual).[12] According to Hardwick's ACLU lawyers, Georgia's law violated his privacy rights and this was in conflict with the Court's decisions about sexual privacy in cases concerning birth control, pornography, and abortion. While they acknowledged that the Constitution does not explicitly refer to privacy, they pointed to various provisions of the Constitution, including its language about liberty and its limitations on state power, that implicitly recognize privacy rights. According to Georgia, the constitutional right to privacy applied to family, marriage, and procreation but not homosexual sodomy. In fact the state argued that homosexuality was immoral, unnatural, and a threat to family and marriage.

In a five-to-four decision, the Supreme Court upheld Georgia's sodomy law. According to the majority, the Constitution does not recognize a "fundamental right to engage in homosexual sodomy" and the privacy precedents only applied to family, marriage, and procreation. Adding insult to injury, the majority declared, "To claim that a right to engage in such conduct is 'deeply rooted in this nation's history and tradition' or 'implicit in the concept of ordered liberty' is, at best, facetious." After deciding that the law did not violate a fundamental constitutional right, the Court ruled that Georgia could defend its sodomy law on the basis of morality.

While *Boutilier* was met with great disappointment by gay and lesbian activists, *Bowers* was greeted with fury. The fact that the decision occurred in the early years of the AIDS epidemic, when government responses to the health crisis seemed to be marked by callous indifference and antihomosexual animus, intensified the reaction. *Bowers* was one of the reasons that hundreds of thousands of people participated in the 1987 March on Washington for Lesbian and Gay Rights. Two days after the march, hundreds of activists signaled their opposition to *Bowers* by committing civil disobedience at the Supreme Court. Over the next decade, the Court continued to turn away most gay and lesbian rights appeals, although there were occasional minor victories and a few significant defeats. Nevertheless, activists continued to fight for legal reform, compiling a mixed record of success and failure on the federal, state, and local levels.

*Bowers* can be used in U.S. history survey courses in discussions about the rise of New Right conservatism, the influence of the Christian Right, and the politics of the Reagan era. Considered alongside conservative campaigns against abortion, pornography, sex education, and women's rights and linked to other moments in the history of antihomosexual backlash, the majority opinion in *Bowers* can help students consider the significance of gender and sexuality in this period's politics. *Bowers* can also be used to challenge the notion that liberals invariably favored and conservatives invariably opposed "big government"; conservatives in this era may have claimed that they wanted to shrink the size of government, but in policy areas such as abortion, homosexuality, and pornography they favored strong government policing of "private" matters. At the same time, the dissenting opinions in *Bowers*, media coverage of the ruling, visual images of the 1987 March on Washington, and the story of mass civil disobedience at the Supreme Court can help illustrate the importance of dissent during the Reagan era.

## A Victory against Backlash: *Romer v. Evans* (1996)

Ten years after *Bowers* and in the context of the complex politics of the Clinton era, the Supreme Court announced its next major gay and lesbian rights decision, which addressed Colorado's ban on state or local government measures to limit discrimination on the basis of homosexuality or bisexuality.[13] By 1996 nine states and dozens of cities and counties had passed laws that restricted discrimination on the basis of sexual orientation (and sometimes gender identity) in housing, employment, and/or public accommodations. For two decades, however,

247

conservatives had campaigned against these laws, winning victories in various locations. Adopted in a popular referendum in 1992, Colorado's constitutional amendment not only invalidated antidiscrimination laws in various municipalities but also prohibited all government recognition of discrimination claims based on homosexuality or bisexuality within the state.

In 1996 conservatives had good reasons to expect a positive outcome in *Romer*. Seven of the nine justices had been appointed by Republican presidents, the Republican Party continued to oppose LGBT rights, and many Republicans were critical of antidiscrimination legislation in general. Nevertheless, six justices, including four of the seven Republican appointees, voted to overturn Colorado's amendment. According to the majority, the state had gone well beyond repealing antidiscrimination measures; it had deprived gays and lesbians of legal protection against discrimination. In this respect, the amendment imposed "a special disability" on homosexuals and constituted "a denial of equal protection of the laws in the most literal sense."

*Romer* was a great victory for the LGBT movement, but its significance should not be exaggerated. The decision did not change the criminalization of same-sex sex in many states. Nor did it force the federal government, state governments, or local municipalities to limit discrimination based on sexual orientation or gender identity. In 1998 the Court declined to consider an appeal of a lower court ruling that allowed Cincinnati to repeal its law against sexual orientation discrimination. In 2000 the Court ruled that the Boy Scouts, because it is a private organization, could exclude homosexuals.[14] Anti-LGBT discrimination remained pervasive in U.S. society.

*Romer* can be used in U.S. history survey courses in several ways. The majority and dissenting opinions can be used to illustrate conflicting perspectives on sexual politics, equal rights, and democratic governance in the late twentieth century. The case can also be used to consider the limitations of liberalism and conflicts within conservatism in the Clinton era. For a lecture on LGBT politics, *Romer* can be situated between *Bowers* and *Lawrence v. Texas* (2003, discussed below) or it can be discussed in relation to grassroots conservative campaigns against LGBT rights. Alternatively, the case can be considered in broad lectures about gender and sexuality, equal rights, or the politics of the Supreme Court in this period.

## Victory and Its Discontents: *Lawrence v. Texas* (2003)

By 2003, when the Supreme Court decided its next major gay and lesbian rights case, thirteen states still criminalized same-sex oral and anal sex and nine of these still criminalized all oral and anal sex. In *Lawrence*, the Court revisited many of the questions it had considered in *Bowers*, although one important difference was that in Texas the law applied only to same-sex sex.[15] In 1998 Harris County police officers had entered John Lawrence's Houston home based on a false report of an armed black man on the premises. According to the information presented to the Supreme Court (although it was subsequently challenged by witnesses and scholars), the officers found Lawrence and Tyron Garner engaging in same-sex sex and arrested them for violating the Texas "homosexual conduct" law. Assisted by Lambda Legal Defense and supported by an influential brief prepared by historians of sexuality, Lawrence and Garner challenged the constitutionality of the law on two principal grounds: (1) it violated their constitutional rights of liberty and privacy and (2) it violated their constitutional equality rights.

In a six-to-three decision, the Supreme Court ruled that the Texas law was unconstitutional. Six justices did so on the basis of equal protection; five did so on the basis of liberty and privacy. Reversing its decision in *Bowers*, the Court invalidated the use of state sodomy laws to criminalize private sex by consenting adults. According to the majority, the Texas law violated fundamental rights of liberty, privacy, and equality. Lawrence and Garner, the majority declared, "are entitled to respect for their private lives" and Texas "cannot demean their existence or control their destiny by making their private sexual conduct a crime."

Many people regard *Lawrence* as the crowning achievement of the LGBT movement. In some respects, this is true, but in teaching students about *Lawrence* it is important to emphasize the limitations of the ruling. First, the Court made it clear that its decision did not apply to sex involving minors (including sex between teenagers), public sex, or prostitution. Second, insofar as many sex laws are enforced in ways that discriminate against LGBT people and same-sex sex, the Court did not affirmatively reject sexual discrimination. Third, the Court emphasized that the decision did not address the question of whether Texas or the federal government had to grant formal recognition (presumably in the form of marriage) to same-sex relationships. Fourth, by suggesting that Lawrence and Garner were long-term and committed partners, which was not true, the court privileged certain types of sexual relationships over others. Finally, the decision, while it reflected and promoted increased acceptance of LGBT people, did not and could not lead to full freedom and equality.

*Lawrence* can be used in U.S. history survey courses in several ways. It pairs well with *Bowers, Romer,* and *United States v. Windsor* (2013). It can be used in broad discussions of the LGBT movement, the sexual revolution, and sexual politics in the late twentieth and early twenty-first centuries. For a lecture on recent developments in civil rights activism and equal rights struggles, *Lawrence* can illustrate important shifts and new challenges. The majority, concurring, and dissenting opinions can be helpful when considering conflicts on the political left, conflicts on the political right, and conflicts between the left and right. Because of the significant role played by the historians' brief in this case, which is available online, *Lawrence* can also be used to explore the influence of history and historians on political reform and social change.

## Marriage In(equality): *United States v. Windsor* (2013)

On the tenth anniversary of *Lawrence,* the Supreme Court announced its decision in a constitutional challenge to the Defense of Marriage Act (DOMA), which had been passed by Congress and signed into law by President Bill Clinton in 1996.[16] Gay and lesbian activists had been campaigning for the right to marry since the 1950s, and there were significant lower court cases on this subject beginning in the 1970s, but DOMA was passed at a time when a few states seemed to be on the verge of legalizing same-sex marriage. It defined marriage as "a legal union between one man and one woman," affecting more than a thousand federal laws that restricted rights, benefits, and responsibilities based on marital status. Several foreign countries, Native American tribes, and U.S. states, beginning with Massachusetts in 2003, subsequently legalized same-sex marriage, but these marriages were not recognized under U.S. federal law, which had major implications for immigration rights, Social Security benefits, inheritance taxes, and many other rights, benefits, and responsibilities.

In 2007 U.S. citizens Edith Windsor and Thea Spyer, a wealthy lesbian couple living in New York, were married in Toronto, Ontario.

After Spyer died in 2009, Windsor inherited her estate. By this time, New York State recognized same-sex marriages performed in other jurisdictions, but because of DOMA Windsor owed $363,053 in inheritance taxes. As Spyer's spouse, she would not have owed any inheritance taxes if her marriage had been recognized by the federal government. In *Windsor*, she challenged DOMA, claiming that the law was invalid because it violated her constitutional right to equal protection. By the time the case was decided by the Supreme Court in 2013, twelve states, the District of Columbia, and several Native American tribes had legalized same-sex marriage, but many states had passed state constitutional amendments or laws that rejected same-sex marriage. The main question presented to the Supreme Court in *Windsor* was not whether all states had to recognize same-sex marriages but whether the U.S. federal government could withhold recognition and deny benefits to same-sex couples whose marriages were recognized within their states, tribes, or the District of Columbia. Another interesting aspect of this case is that because the executive branch, led by President Barack Obama, refused to defend DOMA, the United States was represented before the Court by the Republican-controlled Bipartisan Legal Advisory Group of the U.S. House of Representatives.

In a five-to-four decision, the Supreme Court ruled that DOMA was unconstitutional. According to the majority opinion, it imposed "a disadvantage, a separate status, and so a stigma upon all those who enter into same-sex marriages." In the majority's view, "Interference with the equal dignity of same-sex marriage, a dignity conferred by the States in the exercise of their sovereign power, was more than an incidental effect of the federal statute. It was its essence." On this basis, the Court ruled that DOMA violated Edith Windsor's right to equal protection. On the same day, the Court let stand a lower court ruling that had overturned a California law, passed narrowly in a popular referendum, that banned same-sex marriage in that state.[17] The combined results of the two decisions meant that Windsor was entitled to a tax refund, California soon legalized same-sex marriage, and millions of U.S. Americans became eligible for rights and benefits that had been denied to them based on their sexual orientation.

*Windsor* can be used to teach students about LGBT rights and sexual politics in the early twenty-first century and the changing nature of marriage, family, and reproduction in this period. The majority and dissenting opinions allow students to better appreciate and understand the contested nature of arguments about sexual rights and freedoms in this era. Because the decision touches on major debates about the role of the state and religion in society, the nature of democracy in the United States, and the shifting politics of the Republican and Democratic parties, the New Right, the Christian Right, and the Tea Party, *Windsor* can be used to consider important continuities and discontinuities in U.S. history. In teaching students about *Windsor*, it can be helpful to emphasize that there are more than two positions on same-sex marriage in the United States; in particular, many LGBT activists and sex radicals, as explored in the essay by Shannon Weber in this volume, see marriage as a normative and heteronormative institution, believe that the state should have no role in recognizing and regulating marriage, and are critical of laws that discriminate against the unmarried. Because historians authored two influential briefs that were presented to the Supreme Court in this case, *Windsor* can be used alongside *Lawrence* to teach students about the politics of history and the roles played by historians in the public sphere. Finally, *Windsor* can provide opportunities to reflect on ongoing struggles for LGBT freedom and equality, which include but extend well beyond the right to marry.

### NOTES

1. Marc Stein, *Sexual Injustice: Supreme Court Decisions from "Griswold" to "Roe"* (Chapel Hill: University of North Carolina Press, 2010). For teaching purposes, see also Marc Stein, "The U.S. Supreme Court's Sexual Counter-Revolution," *Organization of American Historians Magazine of History* 20, no. 2 (March 2006): 21–25; Marc Stein, *Rethinking the Gay and Lesbian Movement* (New York: Routledge, 2012).

2. *Brown v. Board of Education*, 347 U.S. 483 (1954).

3. For a useful discussion of these cases and others, see Joyce Murdoch and Deb Price, *Courting Justice: Gay Men and Lesbians v. the Supreme Court* (New York: Basic Books, 2001).

4. *ONE v. Olesen*, 355 U.S. 371 (1958).

5. On *ONE* magazine, see Craig Loftin, *Masked Voices: Gay Men and Lesbians in Cold War America* (Albany: State University of New York Press, 2012).

6. *Roth v. United States*, 354 U.S. 476 (1957).

7. *Griswold v. Connecticut*, 381 U.S. 479 (1965); *A Book Named "John Cleland's Memoirs of a Woman of Pleasure" v. Attorney General of the Commonwealth of Massachusetts*, 383 U.S. 413 (1966); *Mishkin v. New York*, 383 U.S. 502 (1966).

8. *Boutilier v. Immigration and Naturalization Service*, 387 U.S. 118 (1967). For teaching purposes, see also Marc Stein, "*Boutilier* and the U.S. Supreme Court's Sexual Revolution," *Law and History Review* 23, no. 3 (Fall 2005): 491–536.

9. Webster Schott, "Civil Rights and the Homosexual: A 4-Million Minority Asks for Equal Rights," *New York Times Magazine*, November 12, 1967, 44–45, 49–54, 59; Charles Alverson, "U.S. Homosexuals Gain in Trying to Persuade Society to Accept Them," *Wall Street Journal*, July 17, 1968, 1, 22.

10. *Quiroz v. Neelly*, 291 F.2d 906 (1961). On this case, see Eithne Luibheid, "'Looking Like a Lesbian': The Organization of Sexual Monitoring at the United States–Mexican Border," *Journal of the History of Sexuality* 8, no. 3 (1998): 477–506.

11. *Griswold v. Connecticut; Loving v. Virginia*, 388 U.S. 1 (1967); *Roe v. Wade*, 410 U.S. 113 (1973).

12. *Bowers v. Hardwick*, 478 U.S. 186 (1986). See also William Eskridge, *Dishonorable Passions: Sodomy Laws in America* (New York: Penguin, 2008).

13. *Romer v. Evans*, 517 U.S. 620 (1996).

14. *Equality Foundation of Greater Cincinnati v. City of Cincinnati*, 518 U.S. 1001 (1996); *Boy Scouts of America v. Dale*, 530 U.S. 640 (2000).

15. *Lawrence v. Texas*, 539 U.S. 558 (2003). See also Dale Carpenter, *Flagrant Conduct: The Story of "Lawrence v. Texas"* (New York: W. W. Norton, 2012).

16. *United States v. Windsor*, 570 U.S. ____ (2013).

17. *Hollingsworth v. Perry*, 570 U.S. ____ (2013).

# Queer Generations

*Teaching the History of Same-Sex Parenting since the Second World War*

DANIEL RIVERS

Contrary to the popular perception that sees same-sex parenting as a novel phenomenon, lesbians and gay men in the United States have been raising children for generations. Before the advent of the liberation era, they did so underground, knowing that if their sexual orientation was discovered they could easily lose their parental rights, and then in the 1970s and 1980s they struggled to maintain those rights, both in custody courts and through political organizing. The history of same-sex parenting since the Second World War can be a valuable addition to the U.S. history curriculum, enabling new insights into histories of sexuality, gender, reproductive rights activism, the family, and LGBT postwar experiences. Incorporating lesbian mothers, gay fathers, and their children into LGBT history also brings into focus the ways in which same-sex intimacy and child rearing have been constructed as antithetical to one another and highlights how what has been thought of as the "sexual revolution" often also revolved around changes in the American family.[1] This essay guides teachers in implementing this material in the U.S. history classroom.

Introducing the history of lesbian and gay parents and their children in the modern U.S. survey course provides a complex illustration of how sexuality and the family have been culturally and legally intertwined. This history can be easily incorporated into other material on gender, sexuality, and the family in the survey class and can help challenge the notion that the family is only a traditional, conservative structure that is separate from the history of sexuality. For example, linking the history of lesbian and gay parenting to topics such as the treatment of immigrant families by social reform movements can encourage students to think about how ideologies of sexuality and the family have been mutually constitutive.

## The Mandate of the Heterosexual Family

One useful way to incorporate these topics into a survey course is by addressing the custody struggles of lesbian mothers and gay fathers and the presumptions of pathology they faced in the courts. Lesbian and gay parental custody cases from 1967 to 1985 offer students clear evidence that a vision of the family as categorically heterosexual stripped LGBT individuals of their civil and domestic rights; this both allows for a discussion of connections between histories of sexuality, gender, and the family in the twentieth century and introduces students to the ways LGBT individuals in the United States struggled against social and legal oppression. Judges told lesbian mothers and gay fathers that to maintain custody, or even any parental rights at all, they would have to agree never to be in the presence of their same-sex partners and their children at the same time, nor to take their children to any gay or lesbian social or political activities. They were routinely accused in the courtroom of deviancy, sexually molesting their children, and emotional immaturity based on their sexual orientation.

Teachers can assign material from landmark cases, available in abbreviated form in legal databases, in conjunction with secondary material on lesbian mother and gay father custody struggles. For example, students can read about the 1967 case of Ellen Nadler. Nadler lost custody of her children, and in the course of the custody rehearing where Nadler was trying to get back custody of her children, the judge forced her to speak graphically about what she did sexually with other women. Overruling the objections of her attorney in reaction to invasive questions by her ex-husband's attorney, the judge argued that he needed to know the details of her deviancy. In the same hearing, he asked her if she had ever had sex with another woman in front of her children and forced her to name all the women with whom she had been in relationships, arguing that under the state's sodomy laws they and Nadler were criminals. Although some of this detail is absent from the published

Blue Lunden and her daughter Linda, New Orleans, 1955 (courtesy of Linda Lunden)

case record, the judicial bias against lesbian motherhood remains clear. Combining this kind of published primary text with secondary scholarship based on archival collections that preserve more of what transpired in the courtroom can facilitate useful conversations about absences in publicly available materials.[2]

The history of custody cases serves as a compelling opening for classroom discussions about cultural injunctions involving queer people and children. These can include the rhetoric of Anita Bryant's "Save Our Children" campaign, the persecution of LGBT teachers, and the "sex-crime" panics of the 1950s, among other examples discussed in the essays in this volume. In a class on U.S. history, gay and lesbian custody cases connect readily to other expressions of the cultural assumption of queer childlessness and anxieties about exposing children to same-sex relationships. In addition, an analysis of the rhetoric of "family values" and the rise of the new conservatism in the 1970s and 1980s can further illustrate the connections between family and sexuality in U.S. history. In the classroom, we can ask students to think about why various cultural manifestations of homophobia across decades have been structured around an imagined and enforced dissonance between children and same-sex relationships; such a discussion might reveal, for instance, the ways this dissonance has prohibited children from seeing same-sex intimacy as a viable option while also justifying the legal and social vilification of LGBT adults.

Undergraduate and graduate topical research seminars provide opportunities to explore these connections in even more depth. When I teach seminars on the history of the family, race, and sexuality in the postwar United States, I use material on lesbian mothers and gay fathers in the 1950s and 1960s in conjunction with the work of scholars such as Rickie Solinger, Dorothy Roberts, Ellen Herman, Elaine Tyler May, Elizabeth Pleck, and Thomas Sugrue to explore how postwar definitions of a "fit family" upheld and policed racial, sexual, gendered, and class boundaries.[3] This literature also demonstrates how families became places where individuals and communities implicitly and explicitly resisted this policing. I draw connections between various historical experiences and institutional practices, such as the struggle of African American families against Federal Housing Administration redlining practices and the collusion of urban renewal policies with white supremacist investments in segregation; the postwar emergence of the adoption industry, imbued with normative ideas of the "fit family"; and the underground struggles of lesbian mothers and gay fathers in an era dominated by the ideologies of heteronormative domesticity.

Such concepts are well illustrated by historical examples of queer families. Vera Martin, who raised her children as a black lesbian mother in Los Angeles in the 1950s, lived in fear of exposure, and the loss of her job and children that would result, because she knew that racism, homophobia, and sexism would operate together to strip her of her employment and parental rights.[4] Comparative work on the experiences of individuals who struggled with the policing of families in this period, and the way this policing was grounded in a middle-class, white, heterosexual, nuclear, patriarchal, and biological ideal of the family, can help students see how categories of reproduction and sexuality have operated intersectionally. It can also give them a framework for understanding the later social and cultural changes in the family and reproduction of the 1960s and 1970s.

## A "Reproductive Rights" Revolution

The history of lesbian mothers and gay fathers provides an excellent way to introduce students to the complex story of reproductive rights activism that grew out of the women's movement of the 1960s. In women's history we often encourage students to think in more nuanced ways about reproductive rights, to see coalitions and divisions that came out of different models of reproductive activism, and to recognize the importance of an intersectional analysis of race, class, gender, and sexuality for understanding this history. New work on women's activism in the 1970s has shown that grassroots political movements for welfare rights, against sexual harassment in the workplace, and for women's health reform forged coalitions that brought diverse communities of women into common political struggle.[5] One critical place where this happened was in the development of a broad-based reproductive rights movement. Material about lesbian mother activist groups can bring this history into focus for students and illustrate the ways in which the so-called sexual revolutions of the 1960s and 1970s can also be understood as "reproductive revolutions."

Lesbian mother activist groups first emerged in the early 1970s and are a clear example of a reproductive, grassroots political movement that grew out of a second-wave politics of the family. Lesbian mother groups were formed nationwide at this time, both to help women who were losing custody of their children because of their lesbianism and to provide social outlets for lesbian mothers. They were founded primarily in lesbian feminist communities in urban areas, although groups also emerged in more rural areas, where lesbian mothers lacked the resources and lesbian feminist communities of the metropoles. The activists who founded these organizations often had extensive experience in earlier social justice movements, including the African American freedom struggle, the women's movement, the antiwar movement, and the homophile movement, and brought knowledge and analytical tools from these movements into their work in lesbian mother activist groups.[6] These groups were an important part of the reproductive rights revolution of the 1970s, and their history illustrates a complex politics that linked the family to issues of race, class, gender, and sexuality.

Dykes and Tykes, a lesbian mother activist organization founded in New York in 1976, was one such group that developed an intersectional political perspective informed by an antiracist, anticlassist vision of reproductive rights. As its members argued for the rights of lesbian mothers and gay fathers, they also demanded an end to the forced sterilization of poor women and women of color, opposed welfare cuts under President Jimmy Carter and the 1978 anti-affirmative-action *Bakke* Supreme Court decision, and demanded access to legal abortion and contraception for all women. They also organized social events for lesbian mothers in the New York area and operated a custody center in conjunction with the National Lawyers Guild, where feminist attorneys and law students gave legal advice to lesbian mothers fearful of losing their children. Studying this grassroots activism can help students understand how women have linked reproductive struggles to a radical vision of the family through an intersectional political analysis that challenged compulsory heterosexuality, state racism, and attacks on reproductive freedom.[7]

## Reevaluating Gay and Lesbian Liberation and the Family

The history of same-sex parenting is an important component of understanding LGBT experiences in the post–Second World War era. In teaching the emergence of the gay liberation and lesbian feminist movements after the Stonewall riots, for example, the activism of gay fathers and lesbian mothers complicates a polarizing, simplistic historical perspective that sees these movements as being "antifamily." Gay fathers who were a part of gay liberation organizing in cities such as New York, Detroit, and San Francisco developed a radical, feminist vision of gay fatherhood, arguing that it held the potential to transform masculinity by claiming the power of fathers to be nurturing and to raise sons and daughters outside traditional gender norms. This, they theorized, could be a fundamental element of a revolutionary shift away from homophobia and sexism in American society.[8]

During the same years, lesbian mothers in lesbian feminist enclaves across the country raised children in lesbian-feminist-identified families that were explicitly antihomophobic and antipatriarchal. Lesbian feminist mothers of male children challenged and expanded lesbian separatism, sometimes even while identifying as separatists themselves, by integrating a nonbiologically determinist vision of a lesbian feminist

259

future into the separatist critique of the violence of a male-dominated society. They envisioned a time when all the children of lesbians would be welcome to participate in lesbian feminist communities and would be a part of the transformation of patriarchal society and its ideologies of family. These visions of and experiments with nonheteronormative family organization add complexity to our understanding of early lesbian and gay politics and are an important component of understanding the social and political dimensions of lesbian and gay activism in these critical years.

In the classroom, a case study of how gay father groups evolved—from their initially radical liberationist view of sexuality and the family toward a politics of respectability—and contrasting this development with the continued radicalism of lesbian mother groups, illustrates the tension between assimilationist and revolutionary political impulses in late-twentieth-century LGBT history. Such a discussion not only enriches students' understanding of sexual and reproductive politics but also expands and challenges their notions of the relationship between "liberal" and "radical" political approaches in social movement history, not to mention the particular ways these different strategies have played out in the post-liberation-era LGBT freedom struggle.

Tracing the history of gay father groups into the 1980s illuminates many core themes of the era, including "family values" and AIDS. As more middle-class, professional, married or previously married gay fathers came out and moved into gay communities, they infused gay father groups with concerns specific to this demographic. They posited gay fathers and their children as an antidote to homophobic depictions in the 1980s of gay communities as "antifamily." Yet, because most gay men could not hope to gain custody of their children in this period, even if they managed to keep their sexuality hidden, gay fathers often maintained relationships with wives and ex-wives, who sometimes participated in gay fathers groups as advocates and formed support groups among themselves. Gay fathers formed local support groups and developed vibrant nationwide networks throughout the 1970s and 1980s. Although the membership of these groups was devastated by the AIDS crisis, the national networks continued into the 1990s and beyond.[9] Teaching students about the complex legacies of liberation era radical and feminist re-visioning of fatherhood and the later development of a family politics of respectability, together with the lesbian feminist intersectional critique of patriarchy, capitalism, and racism, illustrates the true complexity of the history of both reproductive and LGBT civil rights politics in the United States.

## Marriage Equality and the Politics of Family

A history of lesbian mothers, gay fathers, and their children also contributes to the teaching of postwar LGBT history by putting today's focus on family, domestic rights, and especially same-sex marriage into long-term historical context. (See the essay by Shannon Weber in this volume for a discussion of marriage equality.) The struggle for same-sex marriage arose in part out of the decades-long political organizing of lesbian and gay parents, beginning with early articulations and explorations within the homophile movement and then more openly expressed through the decades of the 1970s and 1980s in the form of local and national gay and lesbian parental activism. This history and the current movement for same-sex marriage are both grounded in a struggle against cultural assumptions of queer childlessness and the family as by definition heterosexual. Against the backdrop of these false cultural assumptions, lesbian mothers, gay fathers, and their children have long lived invisible, underground lives, have marched in the streets since the very first years of the liberation era, and in the 1970s and 1980s persuaded major LGBT organizations, such as the National Center for Lesbian Rights, the National Gay and Lesbian Task Force, and Lambda Legal Defense and Education Fund, Inc., to be increasingly attentive to the issues of LGBT domestic, parenting, and marital rights. I have found that offering this historical perspective in the classroom radically shifts students' ways of thinking about what had previously appeared to them to be a very recent political debate around same-sex marriage.

Beginning in the mid-1980s, mainstream LGBT civil rights organizations began to make family and domestic partnership rights a core focus of their lobbying and legal advocacy efforts. In doing so, they were influenced by both the tradition of legal activism that grew out of the lesbian mother custody movement and the advocacy efforts and organizing networks of the gay fathers movement. In 1989 both Lambda Legal and the National Gay and Lesbian Task Force, in partnership with the National Center for Lesbian Rights, initiated projects specifically aimed at securing family and domestic rights. Over the next few years, activists with experience in gay fathers and lesbian mothers groups worked with these organizations to secure passage of domestic partnership laws at the municipal and state levels. In 1993, however, after the Hawaii Supreme Court ruled that the state constitution protected same-sex marriage rights, the movement for same-sex parental and domestic rights increasingly focused on same-sex marriage.[10] Other legal struggles that have been a part of the postwar attempts to secure full civil rights for LGBT individuals, such as the movement to overturn sodomy laws or ban gender and sexual minority employment discrimination, have also affected nonheteronormative families. In a class on postwar LGBT history, these legal and social histories can complicate and nuance students' understandings of family, sexuality, race, gender, and the line between the personal and the political.

## Conclusion

A history of same-sex parenting contributes to the teaching of LGBT history across the curriculum in many ways as it encourages students to interrogate and question the assumptions of queer childlessness and the inevitability of parenting as exclusively heterosexual. Through the histories of lesbian mothers, gay fathers, and their children, students can examine the intersectional connections between sexuality and the family, as well as race, ethnicity, gender, and class, in twentieth-century U.S. history. At the same time, studying the diversity of lesbian and gay child rearing relationships since the Second World War can help students see that lesbian and gay parenting and activism for parental rights have taken many forms over the decades; this can then help them to look critically at the ways in which same-sex parenting is currently represented in the media and political campaigns, both for and against LGBT marital, domestic, and parental rights. From a historical perspective, we can provide our students in a variety of U.S. history classes with ways to explore how the family in the United States has been, and continues to be, both a site of regulation and a site of vibrant resistance.

Bringing the history of lesbian mothers, gay fathers, and their children into the classroom will not only enrich our understanding of histories of the family, sexuality, and social movements, but it will also be invaluable for individual students whose families had not been previously reflected in their education. Growing up in the lesbian feminist community in the San Francisco Bay Area of the 1970s, my best friend

Shem and I were proud of our families and defiantly opposed homo-phobia, but we also knew the dangers of revealing our lives to outsiders and felt separated from the world that saw same-sex relationships and families as antithetical. We felt as if we were at the edge of history, that we were the only children to have ever grown up outside of what we thought of as the "straight world." Unbeknownst to us, however, les-bians and gay men had raised children for decades before us, and these families, though not all "out," as ours were, had grappled with similar struggles. At each place I have taught LGBT history—Stanford Univer-sity, Smith College, Princeton University, and Ohio State University—I have had students who were children of lesbians and gay men; some were younger than I and some older, but all understood what I meant when I spoke of the need for a history that includes our families and life experiences. Such a history enriches and nuances all students' under-standing of U.S. history, but for these students it also begins to rectify their experience of silence and exclusion.

### NOTES

1. Daniel Rivers, *Radical Relations: Lesbian Mothers, Gay Fathers, and Their Children in the United States since World War II* (Chapel Hill: University of North Carolina Press, 2013).

2. Ibid., 53, 57–58.

3. Rickie Solinger, *Wake Up Little Susie: Single Pregnancy and Race before Roe v. Wade* (New York: Routledge, 1992); Dorothy Roberts, *Killing the Black Body: Race, Reproduction, and the Meaning of Liberty* (New York: Pantheon, 1997); Ellen Herman, *Kinship by Design: A History of Adoption in the Modern United States* (Chicago: University of Chicago Press, 2008); Elaine Tyler May, *Homeward Bound: American Families in the Cold War Era* (New York: Basic Books, 1988); Elizabeth Pleck, *Not Just Roommates: Cohabitation after the Sexual Revolution* (Chi-cago: University of Chicago Press, 2012); Thomas Sugrue, *Origins of the Urban Crisis: Race and Inequality in Postwar Detroit* (Princeton, NJ: Princeton University Press, 1996).

4. Vera Martin, interview with the author, Apache Junction, Arizona, Sep-tember 22, 2006.

5. Stephanie Gilmore, ed., *Feminist Coalitions: Historical Perspectives on Second-Wave Feminism in the United States* (Urbana: University of Illinois Press, 2008); Carrie Baker, *The Women's Movement against Sexual Harassment* (New York: Cambridge University Press, 2008).

6. Rivers, *Radical Relations*, 80–110.

7. Ibid., 96–102.

8. Ibid., 113–21, 143–47. Gay liberationist perspectives on child rearing appear in movement publications such as *Rat*, *Gay Liberator*, and *Gay Sunshine Journal*.

9. Ibid., 111–38.

10. Ibid., 193–97.

# The New Right's Antigay Backlash

WHITNEY STRUB

The ascent of modern conservatism was one of the most important political developments of the late twentieth century, and sexual politics played a significant driving role in the mobilization of what became known as the New Right. In particular, hostility to LGBT rights and visibility has occupied a central position in the platform of the modern conservative movement. Although Anita Bryant's 1977 Save Our Children campaign in Miami–Dade County often receives credit for the birth of modern antigay politics, in fact political homophobia runs deeper, and longer, than might first be evident. Although a devastating New Right backlash to the queer advances of the 1970s coalesced around Bryant and ran all the way through the presidency of George W. Bush, the roots of the backlash predate the New Right—and, indeed, play a formative role in its emergence. To teach the history of the New Right, then, one must situate it within the broader currents of national homophobia and show how the harnessing of this widely shared sentiment paid political dividends, particularly for the Republican Party. Important to note too, however, is the persistent acquiescence and complacency of the Democrats on matters of antigay politics; indeed, sexual politics provides an extremely useful avenue for encouraging students to think critically about the ways heteronormativity as a social force has crossed party lines, even as the harshest political homophobia has undeniably emanated from the Right. Put plainly, homophobia has been a crucial foundation of modern conservative politics, even as heteronormativity has remained largely unchallenged by liberal politics.

## Antigay Politics

As David K. Johnson shows in his essay on Cold War sexual citizenship in this volume, the heteronormativity of the 1950s was never a strictly conservative disposition but rather was deeply embedded in the sexual politics of postwar liberalism. As the sexual revolution of the 1960s forced liberals to confront and often transcend the boundaries of their oppressive framework, however, increasing polarization set in. The crucial lesson for students here is that homophobia was not new, but sexuality took on newly partisan hues. On gay rights, the Democratic Party moved tentatively toward increasing support. By the 1972 election cycle, the Democratic National Convention in Miami allowed thirty-two-year-old lesbian Madeline Davis the unprecedented opportunity to address the crowd and advocate a gay rights platform. Despite the plank's failure, the very fact of Davis publicly describing the "gamut of oppression" faced by gay people powerfully signaled advancing gay visibility.[1] Discernibly wary of embracing gay rights, Democratic presidential candidate George McGovern conveyed a general opposition to discrimination that nevertheless could be understood as gay friendly.

McGovern lost the general election to incumbent Richard Nixon by a landslide, one early sign of the Republican Party's rebuilding through conservative sexual politics. The Democrats had lost their Solid South after embracing African American civil rights, and, although the Republicans picked up alienated white voters, progress in black voting rights precluded the overt fanning of racial flames. Meanwhile, growing public ambivalence over the military quagmire in Vietnam made 1950s-style anticommunist rhetoric a tougher sell. The greatest continuity in the Republican Party was opposition to the New Deal social welfare programs and organized labor; however, neither of these was an optimal campaign issue. Thus sexual and gender politics moved into greater prominence as conservatives regrouped around them.

By the time of Richard Nixon's first successful campaign in 1968, conservatism was increasingly associated with resistance to the sexual revolution, as embodied in feminism, abortion rights, and pornography. Antipathy toward homosexuality saturated much of this rhetoric. Contemporary students can dig through the primary documents of the era and see that concerns about homosexuality were never far from the surface of conservative sexual politics. For instance, in *Perversion for*

*Profit*, a short 1963 propaganda film by the antiporn group Citizens for Decent Literature, narrator George Putnam frequently invokes homosexuality as one of the dangers posed by smut, warning of "your daughter, lured into lesbianism." Surveying a rack of male physique magazines, he also notes that "prolonged exposure" to their images can "pervert" even the "normal male adult."[2] Available on YouTube and the Internet Archive (Archive.org), *Perversion for Profit* makes an excellent teaching resource; students inevitably begin by laughing at its perceived campiness but can then unpack its ideological assumptions and sexual politics.

This antigay sentiment reverberated through other forms of conservative sexual and gender politics as well. Debate over the Equal Rights Amendment (ERA) provided one such venue. Passed by Congress in 1972 a half century after its first appearance, the ERA was intended to write gender equality into the U.S. Constitution. Although states initially rushed to ratify it, a strong backlash developed, spearheaded by activist Phyllis Schlafly and her group STOP ERA. Opponents of the ERA used a multitude of arguments: it would force women into military combat duty, it would undermine traditional gender roles, and it would mandate unisex bathrooms in schools. Another tactic was to link the ERA to "homosexual marriage," as Schlafly did in her 1977 book *The Power of the Positive Woman*.[3] Indeed, students today are often interested to learn that President Nixon himself had already stated his opposition to same-sex marriage in 1970, forecasting, somewhat prematurely, "that's [for] the year 2000."[4] The political cartoons in conservative newsletters such as *The Phyllis Schlafly Report* can easily fit into classroom lectures, providing not only vivid examples of this discourse but also useful reminders to students of the sites where important political contestations were played out. Short analytical assignments based on surveying political cartoons in mainstream media outlets such as *Newsweek* or the *New York Times* can be effective exercises in identifying sexual norms, since homosexuality was a frequent motif in the 1970s.

## Mobilizing Antigay Sentiment

A more overt and aggressive attack on gay and lesbian rights and visibility emerged in South Florida, where the Save Our Children crusade began a mass mobilization of homophobic sentiment. After Dade County passed a nondiscrimination ordinance protecting

San Francisco Gay Freedom Day Parade, 1977 (© Rink Foto, reprinted with permission)

sexual orientation in 1977 (reflecting the advances gays and lesbians had made since Stonewall), country singer Anita Bryant was selected to serve as the public face of the opposition group, spearheading a repeal movement. Invoking long-held antigay tropes, Bryant focused on the alleged risks of employing gay teachers. "A particularly deviant-minded teacher could sexually molest children," she claimed, while even mere public acceptance could "encourage more homosexuality by inducing pupils into looking upon it as an acceptable life-style."[5] Bryant's scare tactics worked, and the antidiscrimination ordinance was decisively repealed by a two-thirds majority later that year.[6]

Bryant's activism built on preexisting antigay sentiment but also pointed toward the future; in the wake of Save Our Children, local sexual orientation nondiscrimination laws came under attack across the nation. The most visible backlash took place in California, where state legislator John Briggs, a conservative Orange County Republican, sought to ban gays, lesbians, and vocal allies from holding teaching positions in the state's public schools. The Briggs Amendment, as it became known, seemed slated to pass in polls leading up to the 1978 election.

Opposition to the Briggs Amendment was organized by several prominent gay and lesbian activists, including, most famously, San Francisco County Supervisor Harvey Milk. Thanks to the amendment's harsh stance, the opposing coalition was able to find bipartisan support that ranged from Democratic president Jimmy Carter to Republican ex-governor Ronald Reagan and managed to turn public opinion around. In November 1978, the Briggs Amendment was defeated by a nearly twenty-point margin. Its defeat nonetheless marked the arrival of an antigay backlash that would be sustained for three decades. Perhaps more telling were the contemporaneous repeals of gay rights ordinances in Wichita, Saint Paul, and Eugene, Oregon, all modeled on the Florida Save Our Children mobilization.

For contemporary students, the rhetoric of the antigay backlash can be both jolting and instructive. Although in later years such efforts would avoid language and claims that could be labeled homophobic, in its early years the movement bore no such self-awareness. The subtitle of *The Anita Bryant Story*, the activist's 1977 account of the Dade County struggle, situated her work as *The Survival of Our Nation's Families and the Threat of Militant Homosexuality*. Militant, to Bryant, was any and all publicly visible homosexuality. Legal protection in housing, public accommodations, or employment constituted "special privileges," a phrase that would circulate for decades. She even suggested that gay rights laws might discriminate against her *own* children's rights to "grow up in a healthy, decent community."[7] This was a critical aspect of the antigay backlash: inverting social power dynamics so that *heterosexuals* were the victims of so-called militant homosexuals.

Not only did Save Our Children launch a national antigay political movement, but it generated a torrent of discourse as well. San Diego–based minister Tim LaHaye's 1978 *The Unhappy Gays* best exemplified the emerging framework. A two-hundred-page litany of perversions and moral turpitude, the book rejected even the very label *gay* in its third chapter, "Gay It Isn't!" LaHaye offered a compendium of antigay beliefs, attributing the "cause" of homosexuality to such factors as "a passive or absent father," "permissive childhood training," "childhood sexual trauma," and even youthful masturbation. Some of these ideas reflected Cold War ideas of only a few decades back, while others reached back to Victorian sexual anxieties.[8] Homosexuality was a sin, something to be overcome, and it was marked by extreme promiscuity, venereal disease, and, as Bryant had warned, an interest in "the recruitment of children and young people into homosexuality." As LaHaye nonsensically but confidently wrote, "[I]f some homosexuals didn't recruit, they would become extinct because they do not procreate." So intense was LaHaye's fear that he opened the book with the explicit claim that rape by a male teacher would be less detrimental to the development of a young girl than a "conditioning process" by a gay teacher, which might lead her to "think favorably about homosexuality."[9]

### The Christian Right

Because LaHaye went on the next year to become a founding member of the New Right evangelical group the Moral Majority, *The Unhappy Gays* merits close scrutiny, both as a foundational text and because its empirical claims were so frequently demonstrably false. As with Bryant's book, this makes an excellent primary source with which students can engage. Critical thinking exercises about *how* these discourses work—their logic, rhetoric, and affective appeals—help students understand *why* antigay positions proved so effective. Although the Reverend Jerry Falwell would become the public face of the Moral Majority, the group's entire history embodied LaHaye's casual assertion, "Homosexuality is not just a sexual experience; it is a total life style. Homosexuals think differently than straights, they act differently."[10] Making this distinction a social reality became a centerpiece of the Moral Majority's policy agenda.

The Moral Majority helped create what observers labeled the Christian Right against the backdrop of Jimmy Carter's presidency. Elected in 1976 as the first born-again Christian president, Carter had nonetheless alienated conservative evangelicals with his relatively liberal social politics, including his tenuous endorsement of abortion rights. On matters of gay rights, Carter allowed quiet but unprecedented administration communications with the National Gay Task Force, but even the most tentative of presidential gestures met with Christian Right outrage, as when the president shifted the name of a planned White House Conference on the Family to the plural *Families* in 1978. Reading it as a subversion of the monolithic heterosexual nuclear family that validated other social arrangements, including, possibly, queer ones, Christian Right leaders loudly condemned the conference.[11]

More to their liking was Ronald Reagan, whose defeat of Carter in 1980 heralded the political maturation of the New Right. The Reagan administration commenced almost simultaneously with the first recognition of the AIDS epidemic, and the two would remain interwoven throughout the decade. Although Reagan had little personal affinity for evangelical Christianity, and no deep political ties to the movement during his earlier tenure as California governor, his advisers recognized the growing political power of the Christian Right. His administration was far less responsive to gay activists and lobbyists than Carter's had been. Notwithstanding his 1978 public opposition to the homophobic Briggs Amendment, Reagan moved quickly to consolidate the support of the Christian Right, repeatedly endorsing its so-called family values agenda.

"Family values," in this context, entailed a bundled set of sexual politics: opposition to feminism, reproductive rights, and pornography; and support for abstinence-based sex education (which received massive boosts in funding under Reagan). Hostility to homosexuality, too, occupied a dominant position in this constellation. While hosting his popular *Old Time Gospel Hour* show, before establishing the Moral Majority, Falwell sent out mailings in 1978, which began by asking, "Do you approve of known practicing HOMOSEXUALS teaching in public schools?" before moving on to ask about abortion and pornography.[12]

Understanding family values is absolutely central to understanding the New Right. While the substantive concerns of the Reagan administration focused primarily on his economic agenda of deregulation and the upward redistribution of wealth that marked the 1980s, the family values agenda was on abundant display as well. One early New Right congressional effort, the Family Protection Act, would have reasserted parental control over school curricula, in addition to other matters such as promoting husbands as heads of households and opposing federal action against domestic violence, which was seen as an intrusion into family privacy. As first proposed in 1979, the act would have denied federal funding for any educational efforts that deemed homosexuality "an acceptable lifestyle." It also would have explicitly removed homosexuals and those "who proclaim homosexual tendencies" from the antidiscrimination protections of the 1964 Civil Rights Act. Even though the Family Protection Act failed, it reflected the fundamental sexual politics of the New Right. More successful was the Adolescent Family Life Act of 1981, which initiated federal funding for abstinence-based sex education. By restricting proper sex to marriage, of course, queer sex in toto was simply written out of legitimate existence.[13] Integrating such efforts into our memory of the 1980s encourages students to recognize the political importance of—and sheer *work* that goes into—defining and protecting "normalcy" and preserving its dominance.

Meanwhile, Reagan effectively ignored the growing AIDS crisis for the first several years of his presidency, not meaningfully mentioning the epidemic until 1987, by which point well over ten thousand deaths had already occurred in the United States. Yet others with ties to his administration used the crisis as grounds for moralistic and homophobic assertions. Longtime Republican insider Pat Buchanan offered mock pity in a 1983 newspaper column about "the poor homosexuals." "They have declared war on nature," Buchanan wrote, and "now nature is extracting an awful retribution."[14] Buchanan went on to join the Reagan administration as White House communications director in 1985. As Jennifer Brier notes in her essay in this volume, and also in her book *Infectious Ideas*, some Reagan administration members, particularly Surgeon General C. Everett Koop, took sensitive and nuanced positions on AIDS. Reagan, however, was greatly influenced by distinctly antigay advisers such as Secretary of Education William Bennett and his undersecretary, Gary Bauer, who aggressively prioritized "morality" over public health.[15]

With so much antigay work being done within the administration, Reagan could appease Christian Right voters without himself taking a visible stand. Indeed, just as he kept quiet about AIDS, he also said little about LGBT rights. A 1986 interview, however, proved telling; asked about housing and employment antidiscrimination laws, Reagan turned the issue on its head and asked "whether they are demanding an acceptance of their particular lifestyle that others of us don't demand." Taking a direct cue from the Anita Bryant rhetoric, he asked as an example, "[S]hould a teacher in a classroom be invoking their personal habits and advocating them to their students as a way of life?"[16] Once more, it was heterosexuals threatened by homosexual demands, a framework that resonated with Reagan's conservative white voting base, which likewise opposed affirmative action measures to facilitate racial equality as "reverse racism." Again, this is where sexual politics proves instructive on a larger level: we see how sexuality and race both become venues through which a straight white majority whose demographic, political, and financial dominance is unquestionable repositions itself as the aggrieved party and civil rights becomes a zero-sum game in which advances by marginalized groups are rendered legible only as losses by dominant groups.

The sheer volume of Reagan's invocations of family values across the decade can be contrasted with his quite few direct references to gays, lesbians, homosexuality, or AIDS at the website of the American Presidency Project, University of California, Santa Barbara, an excellent teaching resource where students can track presidential discourse through targeted word and subject searches.

## Jesse Helms and the Culture Wars of the 1980s

One of the main architects of the New Right antigay backlash was North Carolina Republican senator Jesse Helms. Like Falwell and many other key southern figures in the movement, he was a long-time opponent of African American civil rights until that stance became untenable in the wake of 1960s advances. Helms had found new political sustenance in the various moral positions of the 1970s and 1980s, even supporting his first-ever civil rights legislation, for the unborn, in 1984. Vocal homophobia became increasingly central to Helms's political position in the 1980s, and he led two of the decade's strongest antigay efforts. Most famously, in his 1989 war against the National Endowment for the Arts (NEA), Helms considered the homoerotic inherently obscene and, in a proposed amendment to the annual NEA funding appropriation, would have barred any federal funding for homoerotic material on those grounds. A slightly weakened version of the Helms Amendment passed into law. Such was the political storm that he created, particularly in his campaign against gay photographer Robert Mapplethorpe, that when the Contemporary Art Center in Cincinnati held a Mapplethorpe exhibition in 1990, criminal obscenity charges ensued for the museum's director, Dennis Barrie.[17]

The Helms/NEA/Mapplethorpe controversy became an iconic moment in the so-called culture wars of the 1980s, and it provides a treasure trove of primary source material for students to excavate and explore. The national press covered the Cincinnati trial and Barrie's ultimate acquittal, which can be fairly easily recovered and reconstructed. As well, the bluntly homophobic comments made by Helms and other

New Right congressional colleagues, particularly California Republicans William Dannemeyer and Robert Dornan, make the transcripts of the *Congressional Record* another rich source for student research.

Less iconic than the NEA wars but of more momentous impact was another Helms amendment, which derailed public health measures related to HIV and AIDS. Two years earlier, in an amendment to the 1988 fiscal year federal appropriations bill for AIDS research and prevention, Helms had initiated a gag order against Center for Disease Control (CDC) funding of any materials that might "promote, condone, or encourage homosexual activities." He thereby brought an immediate end to federal funding for explicit, affirmative, safer-sex materials, which often eroticized condom use, at the precise instant when AIDS fatalities were skyrocketing in the United States. Public health officials were effectively unanimous in agreeing that the graphic, blunt, erotic, and pro-queer pamphlets and videos of such groups as the Gay Men's Health Crisis were effective in expanding safer sex practices. Under this Helms Amendment and its blanket disregard for public-health empiricism, such efforts were defunded and had to seek private funding in order to continue. Placing Helms's interventions in the CDC and NEA alongside one another helps show the ways in which abstract, ideological homophobia can translate from the political arena into very direct, tangible human costs.[18] Notably, ninety-four senators voted in favor of the Helms Amendment for the CDC—a powerful reminder that, while overt political homophobia tended to concentrate in the Republican Party, the Democrats often remained quietly complacent and complicit in this backlash.

State and local iterations of the backlash recurred frequently throughout the 1980s and 1990s, often utilizing the pseudoscientific arguments of family-values-oriented organizations and think tanks, such as Paul Cameron's Family Research Institute. Despite his formal repudiation by leading psychological and sociological groups, Cameron's prolific publications continuously spread harmful misinformation: gays were sexual predators, mentally imbalanced, and prone to perverse sexual practices and child molestation. As well, the language of "no special rights" continued to reverberate, with more local gay rights ordinances repealed in the 1980s. A California state proposition in 1986 that would have opened the door to quarantining people with AIDS received approximately 30 percent of the vote, and a 1992 Oregon ballot measure that defined homosexuality as "abnormal, wrong, unnatural and perverse" drew over 40 percent support; more successful was a Colorado constitutional amendment passed that same year, which repealed all gay rights ordinances in the state and barred any new ones. (See Marc Stein's essay in this volume for a discussion of the Supreme Court case that invalidated this amendment.)

Colorado's Amendment 2, as it was known, passed with 53 percent of the vote, delivering one of the most powerful backlash moments of the New Right era; as a state constitutional amendment, it carried more legal weight than a mere law, and its sweeping nature ensured protection for homophobic discrimination in housing, jobs, and other areas of public and private life. The group that sponsored Amendment 2 reflected its origins in New Right discourse in its name, Coloradans for Family Values. That same year the city of Cincinnati passed a similar measure, Issue 3, by an overwhelming 67 percent.[19] Videos such as *The Gay Agenda* (1992) circulated widely in evangelical communities and continued to link gays and lesbians to child molestation and sexual practices deemed perverse.[20] It is important to convey to students the insular informational structures that helped shape public perceptions within conservative social groups, particularly in the pre-Internet era. Emphasizing the competing definitions of *equality* and *special rights* also helps link antigay politics to the larger rhetorical frameworks of the New Right.

## The Continued Influence of the New Right Agenda

While the presidential administrations of Bill Clinton replaced the overtly antigay policies of the 1980s with far more socially liberal stances, Clinton often offered more rhetoric than substance, as Aaron Belkin's and Shannon Weber's essays in this volume, on gays in the military and the Republican-sponsored but Clinton-signed Defense of Marriage Act (DOMA), show. Although he increased funding for AIDS research, he opposed measures such as clean needle exchanges, uncontroversial among public health experts as lifesaving interventions, for fear of drawing moral objections.

If the antigay backlash seemed to recede somewhat under Clinton, it reappeared vigorously under the presidency of George W. Bush. Deeply beholden to conservative white evangelical voters, Bush seemed eager to avoid LGBT issues as much as possible during his first years in office, instead catering to his voting base through other social issues, such as antichoice measures and an amplification of adult obscenity prosecutions. But as the 2004 election season heated up, Bush endorsed and promoted the Federal Marriage Amendment, an attempt to inscribe DOMA in the U.S. constitution. Although the amendment never passed, it served to invigorate conservative voters, and well over half of the states ultimately passed state-level constitutional amendments barring legal recognition of same-sex marriage. The centrality of antigay politics to conservative mobilization thus persisted well into the early twenty-first century.

Like Reagan and George H. W. Bush, George W. Bush himself strove to avoid overt homophobic discourse, but others in the Republican Party carried backlash rhetoric into the new century. Most famously, Pennsylvania senator Rick Santorum linked "man on child, man on dog, or whatever the case may be" to same-sex marriage in a 2003 interview.[21] The Republican Party continued to take strong stands against LGBT rights throughout the 2012 presidential election campaign. Only in 2013, when Democratic president Barack Obama endorsed marriage equality and polls showed for the first time that a majority of the American public supported it, did some Republicans begin questioning the party's stance.

As radical queer critics observe, even endorsing equality within the profoundly heteronormative institution of marriage did not signify the end of the four-decade-long backlash.[22] And, while the social, cultural, and political drifts of the twenty-first century reflect an undeniable mainstreaming and normalizing of LGBT identity and visibility, acceptance remains tenuous. Whereas Cincinnati, for instance, repealed its homophobic Issue 3 by popular vote in 2004, after it survived a court challenge in the 1990s, the spirit of Anita Bryant remained alive and well in Anchorage, Alaska, where voters in 2012 decisively rejected an antidiscrimination ordinance that would have added sexual orientation and gender identity to the categories protected in housing, employment, and accommodations.[23]

Among the most important aspects of this narrative for contemporary students are, first, the unbroken line of organic antigay continuity that runs from the Cold War through Anita Bryant and on into the Reagan and both Bush administrations—a legacy the current Right has inherited but shows no willingness to embrace or acknowledge. Next, and related, more contemporary efforts to downplay overt homophobia in favor of more subtle heterosexism and heteronormativity merit close scrutiny. As the American public seemingly embraced mainstream

LGBT politics in 2013, longtime enemies of gay equality in the *National Review*, the *Weekly Standard*, and even the *New York Times* worked hard to rearticulate their antiequality positions in language that carefully avoided overt homophobia.[24]

The historian Peggy Pascoe has written brilliantly of how rapidly the American public erased the blatant racism of the recent past from its collective memory after the 1967 *Loving v. Virginia* case that protected interracial marriage rights.[25] It is imperative that we as teachers do not allow a similar whitewash of antigay history to occur now that homophobia is supposedly a thing of the past. Antigay politics has been central to the modern conservative movement and must be included in the history that we pass on to our students.

## NOTES

1. National Public Radio, http://www.npr.org/2012/09/05/160607418/in-1972-davis-blazed-party-trail-on-gay-rights.

2. *Perversion for Profit*, Citizens for Decent Literature, 1963.

3. Phyllis Schlafly, *The Power of the Positive Woman* (New Rochelle, NY: Arlington, 1977), 90.

4. Stephanie Coontz, *Marriage, a History: How Love Conquered Marriage* (New York: Penguin, 2006), 256.

5. Anita Bryant, *The Anita Bryant Story: The Survival of Our Nation's Families and the Threat of Militant Homosexuality* (Old Tappan, NJ: Revell, 1977), 114.

6. On Bryant, see Fred Fejes, *Gay Rights and Moral Panics: The Origins of America's Debate on Homosexuality* (New York: Palgrave Macmillan, 2008); and Gillian Frank, "'The Civil Rights of Parents': Race and Conservative Politics in Anita Bryant's Campaign against Gay Rights in 1970s Florida," *Journal of the History of Sexuality* 22, no. 1 (2013): 126–60.

7. *Anita Bryant Story*, 13, 16.

8. Tim LaHaye, *The Unhappy Gays* (Wheaton, IL: Tyndale, 1978), 74–82.

9. Ibid., 193, 21.

10. Ibid., 22.

11. William Turner, "Mirror Images: Lesbian/Gay Civil Rights in the Carter and Reagan Administrations," in *Creating Change: Sexuality, Public Policy, and Civil Rights*, ed. John D'Emilio, William Turner, and Urvashi Vaid (New York: St. Martin's, 2000), 3–28; Claire Bond Potter, "Paths to Political Citizenship: Gay Rights, Feminism, and the Carter Administration," *Journal of Policy History* 24, no. 1 (2012): 95–113.

12. *Old Time Gospel Hour* advertisement, *La Crosse Tribune* (La Crosse, Wisconsin), July 23, 1978.

13. Rosalind Petchesky discusses the legislative agenda of the New Right in *Abortion and Woman's Choice: The State, Sexuality, and Reproductive Freedom* (Boston: Northeastern University Press, 1990), esp. 264–74.

14. Pat Buchanan, 1983 syndicated newspaper column, quoted in Randy Shilts, *And the Band Played On: Politics, People, and the AIDS Epidemic,* twentieth anniversary ed. (New York: St. Martin's Griffin, 2007), 311.

15. Jennifer Brier, *Infectious Ideas: U.S. Political Responses to the AIDS Crisis* (Chapel Hill: University of North Carolina Press, 2009), 78–121.

16. Ronald Reagan, "Interview with R.W. Apple, Jr., Gerald M. Boyd, and Bernard Weinraub of the *New York Times,*" March 21, 1986, American Presidency Project, http://www.presidency.ucsb.edu/ws/index.php?pid=37035& st=homosexual&st1.

17. Richard Meyer, "The Jesse Helms Theory of Art," *October* 104 (Spring 2003): 131–48.

18. Perhaps the best essay on this, suitable for advanced undergraduates, is Douglas Crimp, "How to Have Promiscuity in an Epidemic" (1987), reprinted in his *Melancholia and Moralism: Essays on AIDS and Queer Politics* (Cambridge, MA: MIT Press, 2002), 43–81.

19. Didi Herman, *The Antigay Agenda: Orthodox Vision and the Christian Right* (Chicago: University of Chicago Press, 1997), 137–69; John Gallagher and Chris Bull, *Perfect Enemies: The Battle between the Religious Right and the Gay Movement,* updated ed. (Lanham, MD: Madison, 2001), 161–79.

20. *The Gay Agenda,* The Report, 1992.

21. "Excerpt from Santorum Interview," *USA Today,* April 23, 2003, http:// usatoday30.usatoday.com/news/washington/2003-04-23-santorum-excerpt _x.htm.

22. A superb compendium of these critiques can be found at the website of Against Equality, http://www.againstequality.org/about/marriage/.

23. Yereth Rosen, "Anchorage Voters Reject Gay Rights Ballot Measure," Reuters, April 4, 2012, http://www.reuters.com/article/2012/04/05/us-usa- gays-alaska-idUSBRE83401Q20120405.

24. For representative examples, see Mona Charen, "Why We're Losing the Gay-Marriage War," *National Review Online,* March 29, 2013, http://www .nationalreview.com/articles/344221/why-were-losing-gay-marriage-debate- mona-charen; and Ross Douthat, "Marriage Looks Different Now," *New York Times,* March 30, 2013, http://www.nytimes.com/2013/03/31/opinion/sunday /douthat-marriage-looks-different-now.html.

25. Peggy Pascoe, *What Comes Naturally: Miscegenation Law and the Making of Race in America* (New York: Oxford University Press, 2009), 291–96.

# How to Teach AIDS in a U.S. History Survey

JENNIFER BRIER

There are few LGBT history topics that are more easily incorporated into the U.S. history survey than the history of AIDS (acquired immune deficiency syndrome). As a disease that has been about more than medicine since its discovery in the summer of 1981, AIDS is best understood and taught through the "standard" frames of postwar political and cultural U.S. history. AIDS highlights the political transformations and realignments of the late twentieth century, particularly as they affected the shape and scope of state action against or on behalf of citizens. AIDS elucidates how and why citizens responded to the state and demanded that state and civil society care for people with AIDS and not patronize them as victims. AIDS exemplifies postwar transformations in big science, whether in terms of the expanding research establishment emerging out of the Cold War, the exploding pharmaceutical industry, or how those institutions interacted with one another to create massive capital. AIDS exposes how the social movements of the 1960s and 1970s evolved to insist that identity politics and attention to political economy could exist side by side. AIDS makes globalization visible in concrete ways by showing the disease's unequal effect on the global South, as well as the ways activists around the world have advocated for political and medical change.

Whether you seek a topic that lets you cover the last two decades of the twentieth century and the beginning of the twenty-first so you do not have to end your course in 1968 or 1972, or you want actively to engage the evolution of political history, including (and potentially troubling) the rise of conservatism and the devolution of liberalism, or you want to find a topic that lets you convey the long arc of LGBT history to your students, the history of AIDS is a perfect place to start. In this essay, I outline three models you might use wholly or in conjunction with one another easily and effectively to incorporate AIDS into the U.S. history survey. The models also suggest new ways to teach recent history and the relationship between the history of medicine and the history of politics.

## Using AIDS to Teach Social Movements and Activism since 1980

When reports of the disease that became known as AIDS first appeared in newspapers in 1981, only a very small group of people, made up almost entirely of public health officials and gay men and lesbians, noticed or cared. With a short report buried in the *New York Times* on page A20, it was possible to ignore a disease that seemed to affect only a tiny subsection of gay men. As the initial refusal to even acknowledge AIDS subsided, fear of the disease, and people affected by it, emerged. This fear fostered a pernicious homophobia that reentrenched the connection between gayness and disease, a linkage that gay activists had been battling for decades.

Initial queer responses to AIDS pushed back against the fear and the societal abandonment it produced. Over the course of the next decade, men and women with same-sex desires, many of whom identified as gay, lesbian, and bisexual, alongside gender nonconformists, many of whom identified as trans, created and sustained responses to these fears by insisting on new forms of sexual practice. Alongside reimagining sex, they also developed new models for caring for people living with and dying from AIDS. In essence these ordinary people—some of whom had AIDS, some of whom did not, some of whom had been activists in the 1970s, some of whom had never been to a protest—filled the gaping void created by a state that ignored the unfolding health crisis.[1] Working together, they exhibited a powerful alternative to the political conservatism of the 1980s. Much as our teaching of 1950s conformity has been transformed by gender history and the history of the civil rights movement, AIDS allows for new ways of teaching the 1980s as an era of the New Right (see the essay by Whitney Strub in this volume).

People with AIDS, Fifth National Lesbian and Gay Health Conference, Denver, June 1983
(© John Schoenwalter, reprinted with permission)

Budding AIDS activists, as early as 1982, made numerous arguments against and demands on the state. First, they refused to allow AIDS to be defined as a "gay disease." By insisting that AIDS prevention strategies focus on certain kinds of behaviors (unprotected sex and sharing needles for intravenous drug use) rather than identities (homosexuals and drug users), the first activists made a case for understanding how the disease actually spread. They acknowledged that racial and economic inequality directly affected the scope of the epidemic in the United States, even though solutions that addressed the underlying racism and classism did not necessarily follow.[2]

The first AIDS activists took the idea that AIDS was spread by certain behaviors and used that to invent "safer sex," a ubiquitous concept in the twenty-first century. Michael Callen and Richard Berkowitz, two gay men with AIDS living in New York City, were among the first people to imagine healthy sexual practices in the age of AIDS. In 1983 they wrote and published *How to Have Sex in an Epidemic* (phrasing that would be copied again and again over the next thirty years), a book that laid out how men could have sex with one another and not spread AIDS.[3] In addition to suggesting that men use condoms when having sex with other men, Callen and Berkowitz made a case for how to have sex without exchanging bodily fluids. The booklet sold out its first print run of five thousand and sparked a transformation in talking about AIDS and healthy sexual practices that had a lasting effect on subsequent AIDS prevention material, including gay-positive public health materials distributed in bars and bathhouses and displayed on public transportation.

Gay men were not the only AIDS activists looking for ways to talk about safer sex. In 1987 the activist, writer, and theorist Cindy Patton collaborated with Janis Kelly to write *Making It: A Woman's Guide to Sex in the Age of AIDS*, a book illustrated by lesbian artist Alison Bechdel.[4] These primary documents provide a stunningly detailed map of how gay men and lesbians created erotic safer sex in response to AIDS. These documents make it clear that gay liberation and the sexual revolution were not the cause of AIDS but rather an answer to it.

The efforts of independent AIDS activists, many of whom were artists and writers, were bolstered in the early 1980s by AIDS service organizations (ASOs), the nongovernmental organizations that became the backbone of a nonprofit industry that cared for people with AIDS in the face of the state's indifference and inaction. Activists organized AIDS projects in major metropolitan areas, and some targeted particular groups, most notably people of color and women. The Minority AIDS Project in Los Angeles, the Third World AIDS Advisory Taskforce in San Francisco, and the Lesbian AIDS Project in New York City's Gay Men's Health Crisis, for example, reveal the diverse names and missions of ASOs, as well as the imperative to address the gendered and racial inequalities inherent in the AIDS epidemic. Much of the early AIDS work focused on "gay men," who were often assumed to be white, as opposed to "men who have sex with men," who were assumed to be African American or Latino. Such assumptions about gender, sexuality, whiteness, and economic affluence were built into AIDS service provision, and activists of color struggled to persuade the public that AIDS prevention and treatment required more than erotic safer sex and access to AZT, the only drug available in the late 1980s to treat AIDS. For communities that experience historical disenfranchisement and structural inequality, AIDS service needed to include health care, housing, and economic empowerment.[5]

It was against this fledgling service model that some of the best-known and best-documented AIDS activism emerged in the form of ACT UP (AIDS Coalition to Unleash Power), an activist organization that staged its first direct action protest in the spring of 1987 by shutting down Wall Street. ACT UP fundamentally changed the way drugs to treat AIDS were produced, tested, and distributed; it also generated a progressive vision of public health that included housing for people with AIDS and needle exchanges for intravenous drug users to reduce the harm they faced while shooting drugs. The history of this activist

ACT UP/Philadelphia mock funeral march, Pennsylvania governor's mansion, August 30, 2012 (photograph by Joe Hermitt of The Patriot-News © 2012, all rights reserved, reprinted with permission)

group has been well archived for use in the classroom. I have used the ACT UP/NY Oral History Project in upper- and lower-division history courses as a model of oral history methods illustrative of how direct action changed the course of the AIDS epidemic and a way to talk about how gender and racial differences manifest themselves in LGBT organizing.[6]

Activists, whether working in AIDS service provision or direct action, made it impossible to ignore the growing inequalities that permeated this era, whether in the form of homophobia or the persistence of structural racism and economic inequality. By the end of the 1980s, activists had fundamentally changed the conversation about AIDS from one about a virus that functioned as a death sentence to one about how inequality spreads disease and how the U.S. government failed to address one of the largest public health crises of the postwar era. They also consistently rejected the argument that AIDS marked the end of gay liberation by imagining how safer sex could make it possible to have healthy sex in the age of HIV.

### Using AIDS to Teach Reagan's America in New and Surprising Ways

Many scholars have argued that AIDS, alongside the fight for gay rights more generally, served to coalesce social and economic conservatives of the 1980s, yet I have found that AIDS produced fissures within conservatism and therefore provides a critical intervention into how you might teach Ronald Reagan's America. We know from the extant political historiography that one of the strongest tenets of U.S. conservative ideology in 1980s was the commitment to heteronormative morality defined as "family values." Whether voiced by New Right activists or senior officials serving in the Reagan administration, this thread of argumentation was a refusal to talk about sex and sexuality, in any form, in public. Clearly, AIDS activism was anathema to this political ideology, and so was the first public report on AIDS published and distributed by the federal government. When President Reagan appointed Dr. C. Everett Koop as surgeon general, he did so because he believed the pediatrician would be willing and able to implement a socially conservative public health agenda. Relying on this vision of Koop, Reagan charged him in 1985 with writing the federal government's first report on AIDS. Koop's document, known as the "Surgeon General's Report on AIDS," defied all conservative expectations. The doctor, who identified himself as a Christian conservative, published a report that not only called for condom use and comprehensive sex education at a very early age but also advocated treating all people with AIDS with respect and acknowledged the racial disparities of the epidemic.[7]

Koop infuriated social conservatives in the Reagan administration, especially Gary Bauer and William Bennett, the senior officials charged with producing the national AIDS strategy. Bauer and Bennett wanted to see a federal position that prevented any and all public discussions of sexual practice, but could not stop the distribution of twenty million copies of Koop's report, many by local Parent Teacher Associations. Koop's argument for condom usage and sex education also found support in the final reports produced by the Presidential Commission on

HIV and parts of the State Department, each of which was run by people appointed because of their conservative bona fides.[8]

Introducing students to the materials Koop consulted while doing his work, as well as the materials he produced, provides not only a way to highlight the political and historical differences within Christian conservatism but also a potentially more palatable form of AIDS work to present in school districts where you cannot talk about queer movements. Koop used bureaucratic language to translate erotic safer sex content into something usable for parents and teachers: he wrote the report, in essence, in such a way that it could be utilized by school districts across the country. Beyond the lesson about how Koop's language functions, the report also suggests that the abstinence-only education that began under the Reagan administration did not truly gain steam and become ascendant until the mid-1990s and then the election of George W. Bush.[9]

## Using AIDS to Teach Late-Twentieth-Century Globalization

In this last model, I make a case for using AIDS to talk about globalization in the late twentieth century. Over the course of the late 1980s, it became clear that AIDS was a global pandemic, as opposed to a national epidemic. In the process of quantifying and qualifying that fact, AIDS became one of the loci of activism to combat global inequality worldwide. This was put in even sharper relief when protease inhibitors, a complex drug treatment regimen for AIDS, were released in 1996. Paradoxically, the discovery of treatment options made the global inequities of AIDS even more apparent: treatments were available, but the mechanisms and will to make them accessible were nowhere to be found. It would take another decade of activism, much of it centered in the global South in such countries as South Africa, Brazil, and Thailand, for the question of access to begin to be answered.

South African AIDS activism after 1996 is one of the best places to lead students for a discussion of the links between AIDS, sexuality, and economic and racial inequality.[10] I begin with a discussion of South Africa's legacy of anti-apartheid activism, offering the history of oppression and struggle against apartheid as a context for talking about the country with one of the highest incidences of AIDS in the twenty-first century: The incidence of AIDS in South Africa is as much about the legacy of apartheid as the reality of sexual practices. I then turn to a discussion about the Treatment Action Campaign (TAC) and its work with the Congress of South African Trade Unions (COSATU), the largest trade union federation in South Africa. Since the early twenty-first century, this collaboration, led by TAC, has produced a vibrant and forceful AIDS activism that pushes for economic and medical solutions to the pandemic at the same time that it refuses claims that homosexuality is a form of western imperialism. South African AIDS activists insist on making drugs affordable and accessible, demanding that the state provide them for all its citizens, a position that explicitly pushes against the infamous denial by President Thabo Mbeki that HIV causes AIDS. But drugs alone would be insufficient for TAC and COSATU, which both seek forms of income redistribution targeting multinational conglomerates, including the pharmaceutical industry and its lobbyists. Lest students conclude that AIDS activism in the United States has been more organized around questions of queerness than it has in South Africa, it is important to note that TAC's membership grew out of decades of gay activism as much as it did out of anti-apartheid activism.

Organizing the class so that students can develop a comparative perspective on the history of LGBT activism—with attention to both the United States and South Africa—allows me to challenge common assumptions about the universal efficacy of U.S. activism. I see this most clearly in activists' demands and their relationship to one another. In the case of ACT UP, major internal battles arose over the order in which demands need to be made: should drugs get into bodies before bodies get into housing? In the case of TAC, this tactical disagreement never came to the fore because the activists recognized that the only effective way to prevent and treat AIDS is to get antiretroviral drugs distributed and ameliorate the conditions of poverty.

## Conclusion

Although there are many more possible ways to bring AIDS into the history classroom, it is perhaps especially timely to teach about AIDS as a topical hinge connecting the extended history of postwar LGBT activism to the more contemporary LGBT struggles for marriage equality. While I have emphasized the tremendous power of activism in this essay, I in no way want to understate the devastating effects of the AIDS epidemic on numerous communities. Giving students a space in which to acknowledge their own (and your own) grief about AIDS is tremendously powerful, and potentially inevitable, in the history classroom. By providing you with models for thinking about how public health crises and responses to them evolve over time, I hope to suggest how AIDS workers, in various sectors and myriad ways, revitalized struggles for social and economic justice by harnessing their despair to effect change in individual and societal practices.

## NOTES

1. The secondary literature on AIDS written in historical perspective is voluminous. Almost every account begins with Randy Shilts, *And the Band Played On: Politics, People, and the AIDS Epidemic* (New York: St. Martin's Press, 1987). As I have written elsewhere (see Jennifer Brier, *Infectious Ideas: U.S. Political Responses to the AIDS Crisis* [Chapel Hill: University of North Carolina Press, 2009]), Shilts cannot be the only place you look. For a powerful first-person account, see Richard Berkowitz, *Stayin' Alive: The Invention of Safe Sex* (Boulder, CO: Westview Press, 2003). Berkowitz provides an important counterpoint to both Shilts and Larry Kramer, the other writer most commonly associated with AIDS. For Kramer's writing, see his *Reports from the Holocaust: The Story of an AIDS Activist* (New York: St. Martin's Press, 1994); and Lawrence Mass, *We Must Love One Another or Die: The Life and Legacy of Larry Kramer* (New York: St. Martin's Press, 1997). For accounts that attend to gender and care, see Amy Hoffman, *Hospital Time* (Durham, NC: Duke University Press, 1997). Students are usually riveted by Hoffman's memoir. For the most detailed account of the evolution of AIDS activism as a reclamation of scientific practice, see Steven Epstein, *Impure Science: AIDS, Activism, and the Politics of Knowledge* (Berkeley: University of California Press, 1996). For a collection of primary sources on AIDS and a series of lesson plans for using them at various levels from middle school to college, see U.S. National Library of Medicine, www.nlm.nih.gov /survivingandthriving, accessed September 25, 2013.

2. Medical geographer Michelle Cochrane's work on the way San Francisco public health officials wrongly characterized the first cases of AIDS as gay related and not connected to poverty suggests how this paradox came to be. See her *When AIDS Began: San Francisco and the Making of an Epidemic* (New York: Routledge, 2004). For the failure to address the intersection of race and sexuality see Cathy J. Cohen, *Boundaries of Blackness: AIDS and the Breakdown of Black Politics* (Chicago: University of Chicago Press, 1999).

3. The booklet is out of print but can be found at Richard Berkowitz.com, http://richardberkowitz.com/category/4-how-to-have-sex-in-an-epidemic/, accessed July 17, 2013. For the homage to Callen and Berkowitz's title, see

Douglas Crimp, "How to Have Promiscuity in an Epidemic," *October* 43 (Winter 1987): 237–71; Paula Treichler, *How to Have Theory in an Epidemic: Cultural Chronicles of AIDS* (Durham, NC: Duke University Press, 1999); and the documentary *How to Survive a Plague* (David France, director/producer, 2012).

4. Cindy Patton and Janise Kelly, *Making It: A Woman's Guide to Sex in the Age of AIDS* (Ithaca, NY: Firebrand, 1987).

5. While many of the sources cited here speak to this point (see, e.g., Brier, *Infectious Ideas*; Cohen, *Boundaries of Blackness*; and Treichler, *How to Have Theory in an Epidemic*), the scholar who has made the most sustained and developed case for this kind of analysis is Paul Farmer. See, for example, his *Infections and Inequalities: The Modern Plagues* (Berkeley: University of California Press, 2001).

6. On ACT UP, see Deborah B. Gould, *Moving Politics: Emotion and ACT UP's Fight against AIDS* (Chicago: University of Chicago Press, 2009); and the ACT UP Oral History Project, http://www.actuporalhistory.org/, accessed July 13, 2013.

7. The National Library of Medicine has put much of Koop's AIDS archive online. See U.S. National Library of Medicine, http://profiles.nlm.nih.gov/ps/retrieve/Narrative/QQ/p-nid/87/, accessed July 15, 2013.

8. See Brier, *Infectious Ideas*, chap. 3, for more details.

9. See Sexuality Information and Education Council of the United States, http://www.siecus.org/index.cfm?fuseaction=Page,ViewPage&PageID=1160, accessed July 20, 2013.

10. See the epilogue in Brier, *Infectious Ideas*; and Mandisa Mbali, *South African AIDS Activism and Global Health Politics* (New York: Palgrave Macmillan, 2013).

# "Don't Ask, Don't Tell"

## The Politics of Military Change

AARON BELKIN

The issue of gays and lesbians in the military, much in the news in the first decades of the twenty-first century, opens up historical questions about changing attitudes toward same-sex sexuality and the process of policy evolution. On September 20, 2011, President Barack Obama, as well as the leaders of the U.S. military, signed a document certifying that the armed forces were ready to allow gay men and lesbians to serve openly. Certification revoked the law that was known as "don't ask, don't tell" (DADT), allowing gay and lesbian troops to utter the words "I am gay" without facing the risk of losing their jobs. The march toward equality had taken a long time—233 years to be exact—since historical records indicate that the first discharge of a presumably homosexual soldier occurred in 1778, when General George Washington drummed a member of the Continental Army out of Valley Forge for having engaged in sodomy with another man.[1]

### Changing Policy on Gay and Lesbian Military Personnel

The ways in which policy on gay and lesbian military personnel has changed over time offer one way that students can see how attitudes toward same-sex sexuality have evolved, sometimes in an inconsistent manner. Historians have not been able to determine, with precision, how many gay and lesbian service members the military fired between 1778 and 2011, but scholars estimate that between the end of the Second World War and the revocation of DADT, the military discharged approximately one hundred thousand service members for being gay.[2] During that time, the rules governing sexual orientation and military service were complex. Some rules punished service members simply for having a gay or lesbian identity. Other rules punished them for engaging in gay sex. And yet other rules punished them for having a gay or lesbian identity and engaging in sexual conduct.[3] This confusing situation provides a useful way to help students see how distinctions between sexual behavior and sexual identity play out in U.S. society.

There were other inconsistencies as well. In some eras, the military enforced its rules rigorously and fired large numbers of gay and lesbian military personnel. In other eras, not only did the military fail to enforce its own rules, but commanders forced gay and lesbian troops to remain in service even if they wanted to be discharged. In some eras, the rules governing sexual orientation and military service were spelled out in Pentagon regulations, meaning that the president (as commander in chief) had the authority to rewrite them without consulting Congress. In other eras, the rules were spelled out in a statute, meaning that only Congress or the federal courts could change them.

When Bill Clinton became president in 1993, the Pentagon's ban was formalized in regulations, not in law, so he had the authority to change the rules. As a candidate for president, Clinton had promised to lift the military's ban if elected, and after he took office he tried to persuade the Pentagon to allow gays and lesbians to serve openly. He was opposed, however, by a powerful coalition of military leaders and a large, veto-proof majority of Democratic and Republican senators, who said that if Clinton changed the rules Congress would pass a law restoring the old order. Clinton, the military, and Congress decided to compromise, and DADT was the result. According to the DADT law that Congress passed and Clinton signed in 1993, gay and lesbian troops would be allowed to remain in the military but only if they never acknowledged their sexual orientation to anyone and never engaged in same-sex sexual conduct. This compromise policy provides an opportunity to teach students about the complex forces that shape legislation in the U.S. political system.

Clinton was ahead of his time in trying to compel the military to allow gay and lesbian troops to serve openly. No president had ever spent political capital trying to improve the lives of gay men and lesbians, and no president had even gone so far as to discuss gay and lesbian people in respectful, matter-of-fact ways. There were no openly gay characters on television and very few in the movies. Only a minority of the public supported gay rights, and even moderate politicians felt free to say viciously homophobic things in public. It was in this context that Clinton tried and failed to lift the military's ban. Even though he had the authority to rewrite the Pentagon's rules, neither the military nor the public seemed ready for the change.

Between 1993 and 2010, advocates waged an intense campaign to repeal DADT, and Congress finally passed a law in December 2010 authorizing the president and Pentagon leaders to lift the ban once they determined that the military was ready to allow gay and lesbian troops to serve openly. That determination, as noted above, occurred on September 20, 2011, and as a result, the Pentagon no longer has the authority to fire service members for being gay. The repeal of DADT is an excellent example of the ways in which the gay and lesbian movement succeeded in bringing about an important change in U.S. policy.

## What Don't Ask, Don't Tell Means for U.S. History

At least four aspects of DADT, as well as the struggle to repeal it, might warrant consideration in high school and undergraduate college courses on U.S. history and politics. First, military discrimination against gays and lesbians has echoed but also differed from discrimination against other minorities. For many years, the military banned racial minorities, as well as women, from serving in the armed forces on an equal basis with white heterosexual men. And the political debates surrounding different types of discrimination have sounded somewhat similar. For example, in the 1940s, opponents of racial integration said that white enlisted personnel would refuse to follow orders issued by African American commanders. In the 1980s, opponents of gender integration insisted that male service members would fail to respect female officers. And during the 1993 debates over President Clinton's attempt to lift the Pentagon's gay ban, opponents said that heterosexual troops would not follow the orders of gay and lesbian officers. Another common feature of conversations about military discrimination is that racial minorities, women, and gays and lesbians (groups that, of course, overlap) all militarized themselves and portrayed the U.S. armed forces as a noble institution as part of their case for why they should be allowed to serve.[4] All that said, racism, sexism, and homophobia are distinct phenomena, and the military experiences of people of color, women, and gays and lesbians have not been the same. Students might consider the similarities and differences among these different struggles, using the story of inclusion in the military as a case study.

Second, the case of gays and lesbians in the military makes clear that law and practice are not always consistent. In one form or another, various rules required the military to discharge gay and lesbian troops for most of the last century. Nevertheless, the military started firing gay service members more than a century before any rules on the subject were written or enacted. Margot Canaday, in her book *The Straight State*, has shown how military policy shifted from targeting only public or violent same-sex sexual behavior before the Second World War to trying to ferret out those with "homosexual tendencies" during and after the war.[5] And, even after rules requiring the discharge of gay troops took effect, the military sometimes allowed or even forced gays and lesbians to serve—hence violating its own rules—during wartime, when troops were in short supply. As Marilyn E. Hegarty's essay in this volume points out, gay and lesbian military personnel during the Second World War often were tolerated, yet they faced discharge after the war.[6] Students might consider what forces came into play in different periods that either tolerated or targeted those participating in same-sex sexual acts or claiming a gay or lesbian identity.

Third, the march toward equality occurred in small steps, not all at once, and not all policy changes were for the better. The compromise of DADT made things worse for gay and lesbian military personnel in some ways. Not only did gay and lesbian troops have to hide their identities, but in fact the annual discharge rate of those troops increased after DADT was enacted. Even the 2011 repeal of DADT was a partial rather than total victory because the military still bans transgender troops from serving and because heterosexual troops received more military benefits, such as housing and health care for their husbands and wives, than their gay and lesbian colleagues. Following the Supreme Court's 2013 ruling invalidating a section of the Defense of Marriage Act, gay and lesbian military spouses began to receive the same benefits as heterosexual spouses.

Finally, DADT repeal is an important case study of the relationship among public opinion, scientific data, and policy. Social scientists had

Sailor reunited with her fiancée, December 21, 2011, following a three-month deployment in the Caribbean (photograph by Joshua Mann, U.S. Navy News Service)

long understood that allowing gays and lesbians to serve openly would not harm the military. And solid majorities of the public supported allowing gay and lesbian troops to serve openly. Nevertheless, there was no real chance of repealing DADT while George W. Bush was president. Even after Barack Obama became president, efforts to repeal DADT almost failed because it was difficult for the White House to convince at least sixty senators to support repeal. The story of the repeal of DADT helps students to see that even when data suggest that a certain policy change would be beneficial, and the public supports that change, rational and popular change might not prevail immediately. Politics, in the broadest sense of the term, can matter as much or more than data and popular support.

Instructors who wish to include discussions of gays and lesbians in the military in their courses are encouraged to consult two helpful sources. The DADT online database maintained by the Stanford University Law School includes numerous primary documents relevant to the topic: http://dont.law.stanford.edu/. And the publications section

293

of the Palm Center think tank's website includes a large number of social science studies about gay and lesbian troops: http://www.palmcenter .org/publications/recent. For a history of DADT, see Nathaniel Frank's definitive book *Unfriendly Fire*, and for a discussion about the campaign to repeal DADT, see my e-book *How We Won*.[7]

### NOTES

1. Randy Shilts, *Conduct Unbecoming: Gays and Lesbians in the U.S. Military* (New York: Ballantine Books, 1994).

2. Allan Bérubé, *Coming Out under Fire: The History of Gay Men and Women in World War II* (Chapel Hill: University of North Carolina Press, 2010).

3. Janet Halley, *Don't: A Guide to the Military's Anti-gay Policy* (Durham, NC: Duke University Press, 1999).

4. Aaron Belkin, *Bring Me Men: Military Masculinity and the Benign Façade of American Empire, 1998–2001* (New York: Columbia University Press, 2012).

5. Margot Canaday, *The Straight State: Sexuality and Citizenship in Twentieth-Century America* (Princeton, NJ: Princeton University Press, 2009).

6. Also see Bérubé, *Coming Out under Fire*; and Leisa D. Meyer, *Creating GI Jane: Sexuality and Power in the Women's Army Corps during World War II* (New York: Columbia University Press, 1998), for a broader discussion of gay and lesbian troops during the Second World War.

7. Nathaniel Frank, *Unfriendly Fire: How the Gay Ban Undermines the Military and Weakens America* (New York: St. Martin's, 2010); Aaron Belkin, *How We Won: Progressive Lessons from the Repeal of "Don't Ask, Don't Tell"* (New York: Huffington Post Media Group, 2011).

# Teaching
# Same-Sex Marriage
# as U.S. History

SHANNON WEBER

Contemporary battles in the United States over the "hot-button" issue of same-sex marriage might lead us to believe that the fight for marriage equality is a fairly recent phenomenon. However, marriage has been a topic of discussion and personal yearning for many gay and lesbian people for at least the past sixty years, and forms of what could be described as same-sex marriage have been occurring for centuries. For example, on June 13, 1821, the English noblewoman and diarist Anne Lister wrote of her lover, Mariana Belcombe, "She is my wife in honor and in love and why not acknowledge her [as] such openly and at once?"[1] The two women even exchanged rings, although Mariana's dutiful marriage to a man brought much heartache and complication to her relationship with Anne.

Incorporating historical documents into the classroom can be a particularly engaging way to show students the day-to-day concerns of ordinary people from history, and so including snippets from Anne Lister's diary would be an instructive way to personalize same-sex marriage history for students. Through the example of Anne's life, we can see that the issue of same-sex marriage is not an ahistorical concern that surfaced in the early twenty-first century. It is an issue that has deeper roots in Anglo-American history, even in historical contexts in which the idea of pursuing same-sex marriage as a matter of equality under the law was scarcely thinkable. The inclusion of the history of same-sex marriage in general discussions about marriage enables students to understand that marriage as an institution has changed over time, from the development of love-based companionate marriage to the removal of antimiscegenation laws in the 1967 Supreme Court case *Loving v. Virginia*. For students to learn that norms governing who can marry whom change across time and space is an important lesson in honing critical thinking skills about the relationship between the social and the historical.

## Historical Overview

It is possible to incorporate same-sex marriage into the earliest known history of what we now consider the United States, as indigenous tribal understandings of gender and sexuality often lent themselves to more permeable marital, familial, and sexual arrangements than did the rigid Christian doctrines related to gender, sex, and sin that European colonists brought to the "New World."[2] As Genny Beemyn's essay in this volume points out, there are documented cases, in both the United States and Europe, of individuals who passed as men, married women, and later were discovered to be female bodied. Although we do not know how all such individuals identified, whether as men, as women passing as men, or as some other configuration of gender entirely, and we also do not know all of these individuals' reasons for taking up a male gender, what we do know is that such marriages existed, as did some instances in which men married one another with one party disguised as a woman. Without mapping contemporary cultural understandings about same-sex marriage as a phenomenon involving self-identified lesbian, gay, bisexual, and/or queer people onto these earlier historical cases, it is possible to see how marriage has been entered into by people whose lives conflicted with prevailing ideologies about normative gender and sexual expression.

Including the above discussion in a classroom lesson about historical understandings of marriage, relationships, and/or gender would fit in perfectly with asking students to think about the ways that dominant ideas about gender and relationships are questioned and change over time. Students are already confronted with this reality in U.S. history textbooks documenting women's fight for suffrage and property-owning rights, the way gender roles for men and women were questioned during the hippie counterculture of the 1960s, and the grievances leading to the second-wave feminist movement. For students to have access to this additional information is to help broaden those understandings of change over time and in various cultural contexts, which is crucial in helping them understand the role that culture and history play in shaping social norms and institutions.

The "romantic friendships" of the late nineteenth and early twentieth centuries in America and Britain are a useful case study for showing students how women found ways to build kinship structures with one another outside the prevailing gendered mandates of their day. Women, including famous women often studied in high school and college contexts, such as Emily Dickinson, entered into romantic friendships that involved several hallmarks of what would now be considered conventional intimate relationships, including kissing, cuddling in bed, and writing passionate love letters, as Dáša Frančíková's essay in this volume explores. In most cases, romantic friendship was looked on favorably by the larger society as long as it ended in heterosexual marriage for the women involved. This is because women's love for one another was seen as nurturing, coming from a place of spiritual purity, and as excellent preparation for doting on a man. What became known as "Boston marriages" enabled a woman of economic means to take up long-term residence with her female companion, thereby avoiding heterosexual marriage.

Internal debates within gay and lesbian communities around issues of marriage, respectability, and governmental legitimation stretch back at least into the mid-twentieth century. You might distribute the debates found in ONE, the first gay American news publication, to your college students and ask them to compare these arguments to current queer debates over same-sex marriage, which I will address. When ONE took up the question of marriage for same-sex couples in August 1953, the daring of even considering such a possibility was evident in the question posed on the cover: "Homosexual Marriage?" In an article featured in the issue, "Reformer's Choice: Marriage License or Just License?," by E. B. Saunders, the author makes the self-described "impertinent" argument that "homosexual marriage" is important in promoting marriage as an institution for everyone rather than "allowing . . . deviates" (gay people) to continue to pursue sex outside marriage while heterosexuals are held to a higher legal standard.

In a surprising twist on what we often hear voiced—that same-sex marriage is a threat to heterosexual marriage—Saunders argues that the *absence* of same-sex marriage is a threat for heterosexual marriage: "The

"Homosexual marriage" in the 1950s, *ONE* magazine, August 1953 (courtesy of the ONE National Gay & Lesbian Archives)

problem of marriage versus promiscuity is an old one . . . fondly dwelt upon by the dissatisfied. Yet for heterosexuals, at least, there yet has not been a better arrangement on which to base the family unit. Heterosexual marriage must be protected. The acceptance of homosexuality without homosexual marriage ties would be an attack upon it." Thus, it seems, if queer people are allowed to be promiscuous because they are unable to enter into marriage, but heterosexual people are expected to marry and remain faithful to their husband or wife, heterosexual marriage will be imperiled. Saunders argues that many gay and lesbian people do not seem to care for the idea of marriage, but "one would think that in a movement demanding acceptance for this group, legalized marriage would be one of its primary issues . . . [and] it must be before such a movement can hope for any success."[3]

Despite Saunders's traditionalist argument, there is an acknowledgment that there may very well be some internal dissent among gay and lesbian people over the issue of entering into marriage. Saunders's musings on the subject seem to have been met with frustration by some writers of letters to the editor. R. H. Karcher wrote in part, in response to the question of whether gay and lesbian people should be allowed to continue their promiscuity in the future, "Well, why the hell not? What is this tendency on the part of some people to seek more and more restrictions? . . . Saunders assumes that homosexuals are fighting for acceptance as 'normals.' I, for one, am not."[4]

The 1967 *Loving v. Virginia* case legalizing interracial marriage across the United States became a significant precedent in federal marriage law that gay rights activists and lawyers have used to argue for the analogous need for equal treatment for same-sex couples. When teaching students about the history of both interracial and same-sex marriage, it is important to make them aware of the complex historical and cultural contexts of both issues. Taboos on interracial marriage, for example, have been and continue to be based in white supremacist, eugenic ideologies about promoting a "pure" white race "untainted" by non-white blood, whereas same-sex couples' presumed inability to reproduce has rendered them "unnatural" and outside the family to those who tie notions of marriage to reproduction. The history of interracial relationships is also fraught with the history of sexual violence by white slave owners and overseers against black women and the "one-drop" rule, in which individuals "qualified" as black and thus subject to racist treatment if they had even one black ancestor ("one drop" of African blood), that in part justified slavery and, later, Jim Crow. On the other hand, violence against black men, particularly in the form of lynchings, has been justified historically through the trope of black men as dangerous sexual aggressors against white women's virtue; thus, interracial sexuality and intimacy have become imbued with various forms of violence throughout American history. Therefore, while both interracial and same-sex marriage involve state policing of "appropriate" family structures, reproduction, and sexuality, and while American jurisprudence rests on a system of legal precedent that of necessity must emphasize that which is analogous between cases, it is important for students to understand the complexities of how systems of racism and homophobia differently impact marginalized groups' access to marriage.

After the Stonewall riots of 1969 in New York City, in which largely economically disenfranchised lesbian, gay, and transgender youth of color and white youth fought back against police brutality during a gay bar raid at the Stonewall Inn, and the subsequent formation of the gay liberation movement, the idea of pursuing same-sex marriage rights became more of a palpable goal for some people. Although many individuals in the gay liberation and the lesbian feminist movements of the

1970s were highly critical of the patriarchal aspects of the institution of (heterosexual) marriage, others remained interested in the possibility of entering into it. In May 1970, Richard Baker and James Michael McConnell sued when they were denied a marriage license in Minnesota. Their lawsuit ultimately led to the 1972 U.S. Supreme Court decision in *Baker v. Nelson*, in which the men's suit was dismissed for "want of a substantial federal question."[5]

The 1980s and 1990s spurred gay men and lesbian women in the United States to focus on marriage rights due in large part to two important historical phenomena: the HIV/AIDS crisis beginning in the 1980s and the lesbian baby boom of the 1990s (see the essays by Jennifer Brier and Daniel Rivers in this volume).[6] During the AIDS crisis, gay men watched their friends and partners get sick and die all around them and then were forced to grapple with the added trauma of not having access to crucial end-of-life decisions for their loved ones as estranged family members of origin, often homophobic parents who had rejected, abused, and/or disowned their sons for being gay, had full control over hospice care and funeral arrangements. For these men, who had no legal rights of inheritance or ability to collect on their partners' Social Security benefits, let alone be offered the dignity of being acknowledged openly as the partner of the deceased or included in the eulogy during funerals, securing marriage rights became a goal of the utmost practicality and urgency.

Lesbian women increasingly turned to advocating for marriage rights during the period of time in the 1990s called the lesbian baby boom, in which same-sex female couples began making use of new assisted reproductive technologies, as well as turning to sperm banks in larger numbers. The parental rights tied to marriage become even more of an issue for same-sex couples, for at least one parent does not have a biological link to the child and thus occupies a more legally tenuous position in the child's life. This tenuousness is only compounded by homophobia in the legal system on the part of judges and juries alike. In this context, having the legal power of marriage behind one's family also becomes a safeguard against certain legal manifestations of anti-gay oppression. As these issues continue to impact LGBT families, you might ask students to research current events having to do with same-sex parents, transgender parents, and/or LGBT children and have them present their findings in class. Students could address some of the following questions. How are families with same-sex parents treated under the law compared to families with different-sex parents? Does the answer to this question hinge at least in part on marital status? How do the wildly fluctuating protections for sexual orientation and gender identity from state to state impact LGBT families? How are LGBT parents, LGBT children, and their allies fighting back against discrimination?

The 2010 federal case against Proposition 8, the California same-sex marriage ban that passed via a popular referendum in 2008, was the next federal lawsuit after *Baker v. Nelson* to address same-sex marriage. A classroom analysis of Proposition 8 enables educators to engage students around a number of issues such as civil rights, the politics of the referendum process, media representations of gay and lesbian people as threats to children, the influence of fund-raising on campaign messaging and public opinion, and issues of states' rights versus federal protections for marginalized groups. The U.S. Supreme Court ruled in *Hollingsworth v. Perry* in June 2013 that the opponents of same-sex marriage lacked standing to file a federal appeal after Judge Vaughn Walker struck down Proposition 8. This ruling allowed same-sex marriages to resume in California, and couples began marrying within a few days after the Ninth Circuit Federal Court of Appeals lifted its stay on the resumption of same-sex marriages. (See Marc Stein's essay in this volume on the U.S. Supreme Court's marriage decisions.)

An illuminating exercise educators might give their students would be to compare the legal arguments proposed by the lawyers for the same-sex couples in *Baker v. Nelson* to those put forward in *Hollingsworth v. Perry* and analyze what the similarities and differences tell us about societal changes from the 1970s to the 2000s. How does the evidence presented in *Hollingsworth*, the two lower court decisions striking down Proposition 8 as unconstitutional, and the eventual Supreme Court decision against the defenders of Proposition 8 compare to the arguments and ruling in *Baker* in 1972? What are the similarities and differences between the arguments used in these cases, including the arguments used by those seeking to prevent same-sex couples from marrying? How have social attitudes toward same-sex couples shifted in American society, and how might this shift have affected the way these cases were received by the courts and the public? What has stayed the same?

## Queer Critiques of Same-Sex Marriage

Conservative opponents of same-sex marriage commonly rely on a notion of marriage that enforces rigid gender roles, prioritizes heterosexual reproduction, and centers on religious condemnations of same-sex sexuality. However, as we have seen, there have also been, and continue to be, critiques of queer people entering into the institution of marriage from people within LGBT communities. While perhaps too advanced for a high school class, these arguments are important when teaching a college-level course and speak to the diversity of LGBT people's philosophical and lived relationship with the institution of marriage.

Even while many members of LGBT communities fight passionately for the right to marry, others question the way marriage as an institution is premised on granting key legal rights, such as hospital visitation, immigration, and in many cases health care and citizenship, to those recognized as married while disenfranchising people whose relationships fall outside the realm of legal marriage. According to these arguments, marriage as a system is premised in hierarchy and exclusion and does not promote a radical politics of sexual liberation, which many queer people argue was originally at the center of the gay liberationist struggles that began in the late 1960s. Many individuals would prefer to disengage from and/or dismantle marriage as an institution rather than fight for inclusion within it, echoing a common tension in social movements between incrementalism and reform versus separatism and radical anti-institutional politics. Some critics argue that marriage is an antiquated and harmful way to structure familial relationships premised on a flawed idea of the heterosexual nuclear family and that queer people should reject conforming to an institution that is so exclusive and "heteronormative." Further, many individuals question the tendency for marriage equality to be seen as a stand-in for "gay rights" such that other issues, including employment discrimination, bullying and street violence, HIV/AIDS, queer youth homelessness, and incarceration, are not given the proper attention and funding that they so crucially deserve.

Nonetheless, some American LGBT groups are engaged in the fight for marriage equality while also attending to other important issues of social justice. The group GetEQUAL continues to embrace marriage equality activism while also engaging in coalitional campaigns to pass the Employment Non-discrimination Act (ENDA), which would federally protect individuals from being fired from their places of employment based on sexual orientation, gender identity, or gender expression, and promote LGBT-inclusive immigration reform. Educators might explore this debate with students at the college level by assigning readings on this issue written from various queer perspectives, such as selections from Michael Warner's *The Trouble with Normal* (1999), Adam Isaiah Green's "Queer Unions" (2010), and Katrina Kimport's *Queering Marriage* (2013).[7] They might pair these readings with a discussion about how students conceptualize marriage, what meanings they assign to it, whether they desire marriage in their own lives and why, what the benefits and drawbacks of entering into marriage might be for various groups of people (e.g., marrying for citizenship as an undocumented person), and what types of alternatives to marriage some students might like to see.

## The Present and Future of the Marriage Equality Fight

In the twenty-first century, the fight for marriage equality has embodied and expanded on the longer historical trajectory of the marriage-related concerns and struggles detailed in this essay. As marriage morphed into a modern institution providing 1,183 state- and federal-based rights over the course of the twentieth century, legally separate from the religious sphere, it has become an increasingly important locus for the attainment of equality under the law. It has also become a cultural battleground for warring ideas about whose relationships are seen as legitimate in American society and whose relationships are recognized as families. This debate has increasingly taken on the shape of a popular referendum on the acceptability of same-sex love and desire in the public sphere.

After the Hawai'ian Supreme Court ruled in 1993 in *Baehr v. Miike* that there must be a compelling state interest in prohibiting same-sex marriage, many groups opposed to gay rights feared a domino effect on legal same-sex civil unions and even marriages in other states. One result of this panic was President Bill Clinton's 1996 signature on the federal Defense of Marriage Act (DOMA), an act he would eventually come to repudiate and which was partially struck down in the landmark 2013 Supreme Court decision *United States v. Windsor*. After Massachusetts became the first state to legalize same-sex marriage in 2004, many states again feared a domino effect and passed their own "mini-DOMAs" during the 2004 election campaign.

A discussion of DOMA, as well as the states' mini-DOMAs, would enhance both high-school- and college-level discussions about U.S. government and history, as federal passage of DOMA resulted in the U.S. government denying same-sex couples federal marriage rights even when they lived in a state recognizing their right to marry. This denial of federal benefits contained in Section III of DOMA was successfully challenged by a New York widow, Edith Windsor, after her wife, Thea Spyer, died and Windsor was forced to pay over $360,000 in estate taxes. Section II of DOMA, which allows states to refuse to recognize same-sex marriages performed in other states, awaits legal remedy. The importance of the *Windsor* case cannot be overstated, however, and the momentum of both the *Windsor* and *Perry* cases, as well as more favorable wins at the ballot box, has led to numerous lawsuits and referenda against existing mini-DOMAs in states as diverse as Pennsylvania, Florida, and Arkansas. As a result of the *Windsor* case, the federal government also began processing green cards for married U.S. citizens and their transnational spouses as well as extended federal tax benefits for married same-sex couples regardless of their state of residence.

The question of the balance of power between the federal government and states' rights is a classic one in the study of American legal and political thought. Married same-sex couples often find themselves subjected to what has been termed a "crazy quilt of laws" under which they may reside in a state with marriage equality but find themselves legal strangers on crossing the border to another state lacking such protections.[8] While the *Windsor* case paved the way for the federal government to extend federal benefits to same-sex couples that married in a state with legal recognition of same-sex marriage, regardless of whether the couple's home state recognizes their marriage, state-based benefits are still denied to married same-sex couples in states that do not recognize same-sex marriage. Adding to the confusion is the fact that some states allow domestic partnerships or civil unions for same-sex couples, sometimes without all the same rights that married couples enjoy. Further, a same-sex couple that marries in one state and then moves to a state with domestic partnership or civil union recognition must opt into one of those other legal arrangements; their marriage does not transfer. There is also the legal mess around divorce for same-sex couples who marry in a state with marriage equality and then seek a legal end to their relationship in a state where their marriage was never legal to begin with. The question of federal power to define marriage versus states' autonomy is crucially bound up in all these situations as same-sex couples continue to be subject to the whims of state law and the punishing scope of Section II of DOMA.

Since the backlash against state mini-DOMAs began in 2004, multiple states and the District of Columbia have legalized same-sex marriage through their legislatures, the courts, or popular referendums. At the end of 2013, this list included Massachusetts (2004), Connecticut (2008), Iowa (2009), Vermont (2009), New Hampshire (2010), New York (2011), Maine (legalized by the state legislature in 2009, prevented from becoming law via popular referendum, then legalized via popular referendum in 2012), Maryland (2012), Washington (2012), Rhode Island (2013), Delaware (2013), Minnesota (2013), California (June through early November 2008 and once again in 2013 due to the *Perry* victory), New Jersey (2013), Hawai'i (2013), Illinois (2013), and New Mexico (2013). Eight tribal jurisdictions also recognized equal marriage.

As we see with the passage of marriage equality via popular vote in Maine, Maryland, and Washington, the 2012 election represented a stark contrast from the infamous 2008 passage of Proposition 8 in California and the similar 2009 people's veto of same-sex marriage in Maine. Countering these popular displays of antigay sentiment, 2012 proved to be the year that demolished the argument that when given the chance voters will without fail vote against same-sex marriage at the ballot box. The elections in Maine, Maryland, and Washington thus signaled an important turning point in the fight for marriage equality, suggesting that voters are increasingly drawn to the side of marriage equality advocates and that the antimarriage equality battle cry of giving "the people" a voice is beginning to backfire. Even Maggie Gallagher, head of the anti-gay National Organization for Marriage that helped pass the anti-gay marriage referenda in California and Maine, stated in March 2014, "We are now in the 'gay marriage in all fifty states' phase whether we like it or not."[9]

For any classes incorporating discussions about civil rights, the voter initiative process, the three branches of government and separation of powers, and/or the interplay between law and public opinion, same-sex marriage would serve as a fruitful case study through which to deepen students' understanding of how these issues play out in a contemporary context to affect real people's lives. For classes analyzing elections and media, you might want to have students watch commercials from both sides of the 2008 Proposition 8 campaigns in California and 2012 Question 1 campaigns in Maine. You might ask the following questions. What strategies were used by both sides during these campaigns to persuade the public to adopt their points of view? What do you think helped the "vote yes on Proposition 8" campaign to succeed in California? How do the pro-marriage-equality ads of Question 1 compare to those that opposed Proposition 8? What about the ads do you think helped win marriage equality in Maine?

Marriage equality as a global movement provides an important way for students to consider the relevance of the marriage equality question for populations outside the United States, and it also allows educators to engage with possible assumptions on the part of students about American exceptionalism, the idea that the United States is necessarily more progressive on LGBT rights compared to other parts of the world. As Americans anxiously awaited the Supreme Court's rulings in the *Perry* and *Windsor* cases, Uruguay, New Zealand, France, Brazil, and the countries comprising the United Kingdom (England, Wales, and Scotland) became the latest countries to legalize same-sex marriage. As of May 2014, eighteen countries had fully legalized same-sex marriage, demonstrating that the drive for marriage equality is certainly not limited to the United States or even Western Europe, and that in the case of marriage, the United States is not leading the way on LGBT rights.

### The Importance of Discussing Same-Sex Marriage in the Classroom

Inclusion of LGBT issues in such topics as marriage in the U.S. history curriculum validates the lived realities of many students, whether they identify as lesbian, gay, bisexual, transgender, or queer; have same-sex parents, a gay sibling, or queer friends; or simply come into contact with LGBT people in their daily lives. This point cannot be overstated. Of course the inclusion of LGBT topics in the classroom is not without risks. The state legislature of Tennessee, for example, has continued to debate the Classroom Protection Act, more informally known as the "Don't Say Gay Bill," which not only would prevent teachers from addressing topics related to sexual orientation in the classroom but would also require them to notify students' parents if their children are suspected to be queer. A new provision in the 2013 version of the bill would also require teachers to give queer children a referral for counseling to "treat" their sexual orientation. While a similar bill failed in Missouri in 2012, Steve Cookson, the state legislator who

306

sponsored the bill, became the chairman of the Missouri House Elementary and Secondary Education Committee.[10]

Although the Tennessee bill died in a House committee later the same year, these types of sanctioned, adult-driven anti-LGBT bullying continue to surface in educational spaces, including at least one documented case of a Tennessee teacher attempting to silence a gay seventh grader in 2014 by falsely claiming that the anti-gay bill had become law.[11] Cultural anxieties about children being tainted by knowledge about queer people and becoming queer themselves were particularly instrumental in the advertisements used by the successful campaign to pass Proposition 8 in California in 2008. Key to these arguments was the fear of children learning about same-sex marriage in school, which was seen as a threat to religious liberty and heterosexual marriage and, in the most extreme variations of this argument, as jeopardizing the future of western civilization at large.

Yet public opinion has changed. On the issue of marriage equality in particular, a 2013 Washington Post–ABC News poll placed support for marriage equality at a record-breaking 58 percent, with 81 percent of young voters between the ages of eighteen and twenty-nine favoring the legalization of same-sex marriage.[12] According to another 2013 poll, conducted by a firm with ties to the conservative, evangelical Southern Baptist Convention, 64 percent of Americans thought that the legalization of same-sex marriage across the nation was "inevitable" regardless of their personal views on the issue.[13] A 2014 poll conducted by the Pew Research Center found that 61 percent of Republicans under thirty support same-sex marriage.[14] Knowing that this issue has a history can help put the struggle in context and will undoubtedly enrich students' understandings of histories as diverse as western kinship formations, social justice movements, and American legal thought. Incorporating same-sex marriage into existing curricula, on a basic level, advances the project of underscoring the fact that queer people's lives matter and queer people are a part of U.S. history.

### NOTES

1. Helena Whitbread, *The Secret Diaries of Miss Anne Lister* (London: Little Brown Book Group, 2011), 170.

2. See Leila J. Rupp, *A Desired Past: A Short History of Same-Sex Love in America* (Chicago: University of Chicago Press, 1999), 12–36.

3. E. B. Saunders, "Reformer's Choice: Marriage License or Just License?"

*ONE*, August 1953, 11, 14, available at http://www.queermusicheritage.us
/jun2008one.html.

4. Letter to the editor, *ONE*, August 1953, 14.

5. *Baker v. Nelson*, 409 U.S. 810 (1972).

6. See George Chauncey, *Why Marriage? The History Shaping Today's Debate over Gay Equality* (New York: Basic Books, 2004), 95–111.

7. Michael Warner, *The Trouble with Normal: Sex, Politics, and the Ethics of Queer Life* (Cambridge: Harvard University Press, 2000); Adam Isaiah Greene, "Queer Unions: Same-Sex Spouses Marrying Tradition and Innovation," *Canadian Journal of Sociology* 35, no. 3 (2010): 399–436; Katrina Kimport, *Queering Marriage: Challenging Family Formation in the United States* (New Brunswick: Rutgers University Press, 2013).

8. For one discussion of the crazy quilt of laws, see Bob Witeck and Gary Gates, "Same-Sex Marriage: What's at Stake for Business?," Urban Institute, 2004, www.urban.org/publications/900722.html, accessed May 1, 2014.

9. Lila Shapiro, "Leading Gay Marriage Opponent on Losing the Battle: 'I Have a Lot More Freedom Now,'" *Huffington Post*, March 21, 2014, www.huffing tonpost.com/2014/03/20/maggie-gallagher_n_5001848.html.

10. See Meredith Bennett-Smith, "Tennessee 'Don't Say Gay' Bill Is Back, Now Requires Teachers to Tell Parents if Child Is Gay," *Huffington Post*, January 30, 2013, http://www.huffingtonpost.com/2013/01/30/tennessee-dont-say-gay-bill_n_2582390.html.

11. See Tom Humphrey, "Tennessee GOP 'Supermajority' Eases Up on Silly Bills," *Knoxville News Sentinel*, April 7, 2013, www.knoxnews.com/news/2013/apr/07/tennessee-gop-supermajority-eases-up-on-silly/; and David Badash, "Gay Tennessee Seventh Grader Attacked With 'Don't Say Gay' Law He Defeated," *The New Civil Rights Movement*, March 11, 2014, thenewcivilrights movement.com/gay-tennessee-seventh-grader-attacked-with-dont-say-gay-law-he-defeated/discrimination/2014/03/11/84236.

12. See Jon Cohen, "Gay Marriage Support Hits New High in Post-ABC Poll," *Washington Post*, March 18, 2013, http://www.washingtonpost.com/blogs/the-fix/wp/2013/03/18/gay-marriage-support-hits-new-high-in-post-abc-poll/?wpisrc=al_comboNP_p.

13. Caleb K. Bell, "Gay Marriage Seen as Inevitable by Americans: Poll," *Huffington Post*, March 14, 2013, http://www.huffingtonpost.com/2013/03/14/gay-marriage-inevitable-americans_n_2876601.html.

14. See Jocelyn Kiley, "Young Republicans Favor Same-Sex Marriage," *Pew Research Center*, March 10, 2014, www.pewresearch.org/fact-tank/2014/03/10/61-of-young-republicans-favor-same-sex-marriage/.

# PART THREE

# Discovery and Interpretation of Lesbian, Gay, Bisexual, and Transgender History

# History as Social Change

*Queer Archives and Oral History Projects*

NAN ALAMILLA BOYD

U ntil the twenty-first century, most archives in the
United States, both public and private, failed to col-
lect materials related to lesbian, gay, bisexual, and transgender lives.
The existing collections that contained materials expressing same-sex
attractions or documenting queer relationships and communities were
often restricted, usually by the families of the deceased, and as a result
were inaccessible to researchers. This essay tells the story of how a hand-
ful of activists built community-based archives and oral history projects in the 1970s and 1980s. Their efforts to construct and safeguard a
collection of materials that reflect a multiplicity of queer lives had the
surprising effect of supporting a coterie of scholars whose academic
publications would frame the fledgling field of LGBT history. At the
same time, queer oral history projects developed methods that became
central to the field of LGBT history and suggested new ways for historians in other fields to use oral testimonies. Archival resources and oral
histories have also become useful in the classroom. As history surveys
become more inclusive of queer histories—or the ways queer lives have
shaped mainstream historical narratives—oral histories documenting
queer lives enable students to connect on a personal level with queer
historical actors. Online archives of queer oral histories are now widely
available, and teachers have experimented with a variety of ways to
engage students in oral history work. This essay provides a context for
using queer oral histories in the classroom by describing the way these
histories were collected and the activist impulses behind their creation.

## Queer Lives in the Archives

Queer historians working in the 1970s and 1980s had to work hard to locate information in existing archives that shed light on queer lives. Many of us swap stories about negative encounters with archival gatekeepers, and researchers sometimes found themselves bending the truth about their topic in order to gain access to certain collections. I, myself, lied about my topic while doing research in the California State Archives in the mid-1990s. For many years, historical materials documenting queer lives were not simply ignored by archivists but were purposefully uncollected—sometimes even thrown in the trash.

The suppression of queer histories made LGBT lives seem insignificant or invisible, so these modes of subjugation led queer historians and community activists to find new ways to tell their stories. In the 1970s, activists and historians—sometimes legitimized by the academy with degrees and teaching positions, but more often not—organized to create community-based archives to preserve the history of LGBT lives.

The Lesbian Herstory Archives (LHA) of New York City was one of the first groups to begin collecting materials about queer lives and activities, hoping that future generations would have more access to materials relevant to their lives. The LHA grew out of another liberation era organization in New York City, the Gay Academic Union (GAU), which saw education as a path to social change and tried to encourage the production of queer scholarship within academia. In 1973 lesbian feminists in the GAU formed a consciousness-raising group and split off from the union in order to focus their energies on "women who loved women." As founder Joan Nestle explains, "We wanted our story to be told by us, shared by us and preserved by us. We were tired of being the medical, legal, and religious other."[1]

In 1974 the LHA took up residence in the midtown apartment of Joan Nestle and Deborah Edel, and a steady group of volunteers began to collect and preserve any materials "relevant to the lives and experiences of lesbians: books, magazines, journals, news clippings (from establishment, feminist, or lesbian media), bibliographies, photos, herstorical information, tapes, films, diaries, oral herstories, poetry and prose, biographies, autobiographies, notices of events, posters, graphics, and other memorabilia and obscure references to our lives." Using a slide show as an organizational tool, LHA volunteers brought lesbian stories back to the community; they wanted lesbians everywhere to have access to their own living past: "[It] helped us make the point that one of our battles was to change secrecy into disclosure, shame into memory."[2] Forgoing government support, LHA raised funds from community members, and in 1993 the group purchased a three-story building in Brooklyn to house its expanding collections, establishing a permanent home for the archives.

In San Francisco, a similar movement was afoot. In 1979 a constellation of activists interested in gay and lesbian history joined forces to found the San Francisco Lesbian and Gay History Project. They met regularly to discuss books, share ideas, and encourage each other's research interests. Soon the group began planning community events, again using a slide show format to bring images and historical analysis back to the community. Like the founders of the LHA, the scholars and activists who participated in the History Project believed that uncovering and sharing the history of queer people was part of the process of liberation and would have deep political significance. Estelle Freedman and John D'Emilio, early participants in the History Project, remember that they "believed that understanding history endowed individuals and communities with the power to act more effectively in the world."[3]

Soon some members of the History Project began to preserve gay culture by building an archive of existing gay and lesbian periodicals, and it was this archival collection that, in 1985, became the heart of the San Francisco Bay Area Gay and Lesbian Historical Society (now the GLBT Historical Society). Willie Walker, a trained archivist and early member of the Historical Society, worked (for pay) as a nurse on the so-called AIDS ward at San Francisco's General Hospital. He, like others who witnessed the AIDS epidemic firsthand, was convinced that if no one collected and preserved the records of gay people, a whole generation of information about the past would soon be lost. Walker and a cohort of like-minded volunteers helped build the San Francisco GLBT Historical Society into one of the largest collections of queer historical materials in the world. Today, the Historical Society's archives contain an unmatched periodicals collection—over four thousand titles—and also personal papers, organizational records, rare books, historical photographs, printed ephemera, sound recordings, original artwork, and textiles, including almost three thousand t-shirts. In 2011 the GLBT

Historical Society opened a separate museum space in San Francisco's Castro district, where revolving exhibits showcase the Historical Society's many-faceted collections.[4]

## Oral History as a Tool for Gay Liberation

Alongside community-based archives, queer oral history projects have played a central role in the production of LGBT history. In fact, the development of oral history methods among queer historians and of LGBT history as a field go hand in hand. Again, because mainstream academic and public archives failed to collect materials related to LGBT lives, decades of living history were fading from memory with the passing of each generation. Without the preservation of materials to guide historical analysis, late-nineteenth and early-twentieth-century queer histories threatened to become the stuff of hearsay and innuendo. In the 1970s, however, community-based historians quickly recognized the importance of oral history as a method for recuperating lost histories. Talking to people who had lived queer lives was one way to recapture or reclaim the material culture that had been cast aside or burned. Not coincidentally, oral history as a method was gaining traction in the academy just as liberation movements, including the gay and lesbian liberation movement of the 1970s, were demanding new historical sources and analysis.

Oral history, as a field, came of age in the 1960s when a few universities, such as Columbia University and the University of North Carolina at Chapel Hill, built oral history programs and expanded the utility of oral history within the historical profession. In 1966 oral historians in the United States founded the Oral History Association, which was anchored to the Columbia University's Oral History Research Office for many years and has subsequently worked to develop professional standards for the collection, preservation, and distribution of oral testimony.

Oral history methods eventually became established practices with thoughtful guidelines ("best practices") in place, but in the 1970s, as the method was evolving and being embraced by liberation-seeking activists and community-based historians, the practice was more freewheeling. In the spirit of the age, queer activists and community-based historians saw oral history as a method that could build community and connect cross-generationally, and they embraced the do-it-yourself method of simply getting together and talking about the past. With an emphasis on empowerment and disclosure, oral history methods also resonated with the era's powerful rhetoric of pride and the politics of coming out. Oral history seemed a potent antidote to the legacy of silence, secrecy, and shame that many queer people seemed to carry on their shoulders. For all these reasons, queer oral history projects proliferated, and, as with archive building, they took on a political momentum of their own.

In the 1980s, a number of local-, activist-, and graduate-student-initiated queer oral history projects inspired the development of local archives and historical societies, and they also laid the foundation for the slow development of academic research and, later, the appearance of publications that would frame the fledgling field of LGBT history. Elizabeth Lapovsky Kennedy and Madeline D. Davis's Buffalo Women's Oral History Project, founded in 1978, evolved into a decades-long research project in which dozens of informants patiently shared their stories of butch-fem life in Buffalo's working-class bars and taverns. Kennedy and Davis's oral history methods set a high standard for work in the field, and their research led to the 1993 publication of a remarkable text, *Boots of Leather, Slippers of Gold: The Story of a Lesbian Community.*[5]

Likewise, in Chicago in the 1980s, Gregory Sprague's graduate student research on Chicago's gay history evolved into an oral history project that helped seed what would become Chicago's Gerber/Hart Library, a vast archive of LGBT historical materials. And in San Francisco, community historian Allan Bérubé's discovery, in the late-1970s, of a cache of letters written between gay men during the Second World War inspired him to develop an oral history project documenting the lives of lesbians and gay men in the military.

As with Kennedy, Davis, and Sprague, Bérubé's project was a labor of love, unpaid and decades in the making. It started as a popular slide show, "Marching to a Different Drummer," and audience members who had served in the military would sometimes approach Bérubé after a show, offering to contribute their stories to his evolving narrative. In this way, Bérubé's oral history project, like so many others, became a communal project wherein many hearts and minds added to the archives of materials that framed what would become, in 1991, Bérubé's prize-winning book, *Coming Out under Fire: The History of Gay Men and Women in World War II.*[6] The book was a recuperative story, inspired by liberation era politics, upending dominant and national narratives of the war, challenging the historical profession to restructure its thinking, and earning Bérubé a MacArthur Foundation "genius grant" for his innovations.

## Publishing and Queering Oral Histories

With Bérubé's success, academic presses began to take notice of the work of queer historians, and (again, because of the absence of print materials) oral history remained a crucial method undergirding their research. Indeed, in 1997 graduate student Brett (now Genny) Beemyn edited an anthology of new work in queer history, fittingly entitled *Creating a Place for Ourselves*, in which each of the eleven chapters focused on a community-based history and almost all based their research on oral history projects conducted by the authors.[7] This little-known Routledge anthology is now out of print, but it captured a moment in the development of the field, foretelling its maturation with chapters by such luminaries as George Chauncey, Esther Newton, Elizabeth Lapovsky Kennedy, David K. Johnson, Marc Stein, and Joan Nestle.

It is in *Creating a Place for Ourselves* that I scored my first publication as a newly minted tenure-track professor. Following in the footsteps of Kennedy and Bérubé, my research on San Francisco's queer history was structured around a community-based oral history project. Luckily for me, a decade of work had grown the collections of the GLBT Historical Society into a usable archive chock full of print materials and ephemera. So carefully, between 1989 and 1992, I read just about all the periodicals and manuscript collections and, in addition, conducted forty-five oral history interviews. The resulting work, a doctoral dissertation that morphed into a book entitled *Wide Open Town: A Queer History of San Francisco to 1965*, published in 2003, was certainly my creation, but it reflected a conglomeration of voices: the oral history narrators who shared their stories with me (and whose stories I painstakingly transcribed), but also the archival instincts of people such as Willie Walker, whose contributions to the archives framed new intellectual perspectives and encouraged new histories to be told.[8]

Later, noticing the striking dependence U.S. queer historiography has had on oral history methods, I conspired with a colleague, the historian Horacio N. Roque Ramírez, to edit a volume of essays written by queer oral historians.[9] The idea was to ask each historian to write a methodological essay on queer oral history and to pair that essay with an oral history he or she had conducted and transcribed. The resulting book, *Bodies of Evidence: The Practice of Queer Oral History*, published in 2012, includes fourteen chapters by historians working on a stunning array of topics, including social life after the Cuban revolution, the organization of transvestite social clubs in the U.S. Midwest in the 1960s, Australian gay liberation activism in the 1970s, San Francisco electoral politics and the career of Harvey Milk, Asian American community organizing in pre-AIDS Los Angeles, lesbian feminist "sex war" cultural politics, 1980s Latino/Latina transgender community memory and activism, and the United States' "don't ask, don't tell" policy in the context of the wars in Iraq and Afghanistan.[10]

The book's central conceit is the question "what's queer about queer oral history?," and each of the book's essays answers this question in a different way. In our introduction, Horacio and I discuss body-based knowing, and we speculate that the intimacy of the oral history interview—what Horacio calls "the physical presence of sexual or gendered bodies"—has a material impact on the historical narratives produced, the "data" culled for the public record. Although we did not mention it in our introduction, I now wonder if the lack of print documents combined with feminist deconstructions of power (the free-wheeling methods described above) made the materiality of the body in early queer oral history projects all the more significant. Clearly, a politics of recognition—seeing and being seen—undergirded much of what felt real and powerful and hopeful about the era. And, while this dynamic encouraged queer people, regular people as well as community leaders, to participate eagerly in grassroots oral history projects, it also raised questions about who was able to recognize whom: who came out of the closet to be recognized, and who was empowered to do the recognizing?[11]

## Oral History in the Twenty-First-Century Classroom

Since those days, oral history has become an accepted and well-disciplined historical method. A wealth of print documents and manuscript collections now exist in queer community archives, and universities and public libraries have become great collectors of LGBT materials. Still, there are many ways in which LGBT histories are "hidden from history" in mainstream classrooms. Without access, students unfamiliar with queer histories tend to shy away from these heretofore taboo topics, maintaining the invisibility of queer lives and reiterating a heterocentric classroom. However, as queer histories are inserted into standardized curricula, oral history can be a valuable tool for teachers. It is also a simple tool, made even simpler with the advent of digital technology. Anyone with a smart phone can conduct a good-quality oral history interview, and new technologies are well on their way to making the onerous task of transcribing interviews a thing of the past.[12]

Teachers in classrooms across the United States are engaging students in activities that involve oral history methods, often having students donate their transcriptions to local archives and repositories. Teachers find that oral history can be a way for students to go "narrow and deep," to investigate something deeply and gain personal experience with a thin slice of history. With a research question in one hand and a digital recorder in the other, a student who spends an hour listening to someone (even a family member) recount their memories of historical events or situations will gain vital insight into both history and the process of making history. Students will discover the pleasure of getting closer to the subject they are studying. They will also find that histories are subjective, and while the politics of recognition are still at play, a truth can be found in the everyday voices that make stories about the past come alive.

NOTES

1. Joan Nestle, "The Will to Remember: The Lesbian Herstory Archives of New York," *Journal of Homosexuality* 34, nos. 3–4 (1998): 225–35, quotation on 227.

2. Ibid., 227, 229.

3. John D'Emilio and Estelle B. Freedman, "Introduction: Allan Bérubé and the Power of Community," in Allan Bérubé, *My Desire for History* (Chapel Hill: University of North Carolina Press, 2011), 11.

4. San Francisco and New York City are not the only places where queer activists collect and preserve the histories of LGBT people. Archives can be found in many cities, including Chicago, Fort Lauderdale, Los Angeles, and Minneapolis. See "Archives 'R' Us," *The Advocate*, November 22, 2005, 44.

5. Elizabeth Lapovsky Kennedy and Madeline D. Davis, *Boots of Leather, Slippers of Gold: The History of a Lesbian Community* (New York: Routledge, 1993).

6. Allan Bérubé, *Coming Out under Fire: The History of Gay Men and Women in World War II* (New York: Free Press, 1990).

7. Brett Beemyn, ed., *Creating a Place for Ourselves: Lesbian, Gay, and Bisexual Community Histories* (New York: Routledge, 1997).

8. Nan Alamilla Boyd, *Wide Open Town: A Queer History of San Francisco to 1965* (Berkeley: University of California Press, 2003).

9. On the history of oral history methods in LGBT histories, see Nan Alamilla Boyd, "Who Is the Subject? Queer Theory Meets Oral History," *Journal of the History of Sexuality* 17, no. 2 (May 2008): 177–89.

10. Nan Alamilla Boyd and Horacio N. Roque Ramírez, eds., *Bodies of Evidence: The Practice of Queer Oral History* (New York: Oxford University Press, 2012).

11. Another text that combines queer oral history and methods is Twin Cities GLBT Oral History Project, *Queer Twin Cities* (Minneapolis: University of Minnesota Press, 2010).

12. Recommended online oral history resources include the Regional Oral History Office at the University of California Berkeley campus's Bancroft Library, http://bancroft.berkeley.edu/ROHO/resources/ohlinks.html, especially the "Interviewing Tips," http://bancroft.berkeley.edu/ROHO/resources/roho tips.html; Carole Hicks's "One Minute Guide to Oral History," http://www .id.uscourts.gov/history/9thOralHistoryGuide.pdf; and the Baylor University Institute for Oral History's "Oral History Workshop on the Web," http:// www.baylor.edu/oralhistory/index.php?id=23560. Print resources include Valerie Yow, *Recording Oral History: A Guide for the Humanities and Social Sciences*, 2nd ed. (Lanham, MD: AltaMira Press, 2005); Donald A. Ritchie, *Doing Oral History: A Practical Guide*, 2nd ed. (New York: Oxford University Press, 2003); and Robert Perks and Alistair Thomson, eds., *The Oral History Reader*, 2nd ed. (New York: Routledge, 2006). See also H-Oralhist, www.h-net.org/~oralhist, especially the discussion logs, for further guidance from teachers. My thanks go to Ian Lekus for these suggestions.

# Teaching LGBT History through Fiction

*A Story-Logic Approach to the Problems of Naming and Evidence*

NORMAN W. JONES

Why teach fiction in a history class? Teachers typically feel there is already too much material to cover in most of our classes, so why would we risk obscuring the facts by adding fictional readings? The easiest answer derives from the fact that some people tend to be transported by stories: when reading, they "see" the story unfold and experience emotional responses to it. Psychologists describe such people as "highly transportable," and fictional texts help them engage more deeply with the subject and remember more about it. Yet this is not a sure thing: some students are not easily transported by stories; even for those who are, not all stories are equally engaging. Moreover, one can often find vivid nonfiction primary and secondary narratives for students to read. So why use fiction? Arguably the best reason in the case of LGBT history is that fiction offers unique ways to help students explore two problems that especially trouble the study of this field: naming and evidence. After elaborating on these two problems, this essay provides concrete examples of literary texts that can help students develop more productive ways of thinking about LGBT history.

## Problems of Naming and Evidence

The variety of terms packed into the LGBT acronym and its expanded versions, such as LGBTQIA (which adds *queer, intersex,* and *allies* to the list), provides a useful point of entry for helping students think more carefully about the complexities entailed in trying to categorize sex and gender behaviors and self-concepts. This is one of the first topics I address when teaching the subject; not only does it introduce students to larger issues, but also it begins to develop a common vocabulary for us to use in the classroom.

I start by asking the students to define the various terms, which usually helps me clarify the confusing connotative baggage such terms carry. Take the term *lesbian*, for example. Can one be a lesbian and be sexually attracted to men as well as women, or should one identify as bisexual in that case? Can someone be "more" of a lesbian than someone else? Can one be a lesbian for a time and then be straight or bisexual later in one's life, or does such a change mean one was never "really" a lesbian in the first place? Does the term *lesbian* connote some degree of nonconformity with conventional gender norms? (The existence of the term *lipstick lesbian* suggests that some people believe the answer is yes, as it implies that conventionally feminine lesbians constitute a special subcategory of lesbians.) I explain to students that such connotative baggage, as well as more general negative associations with these terms (not only social stigmas but also their association with white, middle-class cultural perspectives), leads some people to not use them. This is why social scientists and health care professionals often use alternative labels such as *WSW* (women who have sex with women) and *MSM* (men who have sex with men). All this becomes even more complex when one moves beyond English-language terms commonly used in the United States to consider terms used in other languages and cultures around the world.

When we study texts and artifacts from various cultures that existed in earlier historical periods, the complexities multiply. Historians sometimes use *same-sex desire* as a term that might be considered "neutral" insofar as it seems stripped of inappropriate connotations. Yet this decontextualizing term does not entirely solve the problem: it, too, potentially harbors distortions because it presents itself as an "objective," ahistorical category whereas it actually reflects the particular historical perspectives of contemporary scholars. This is not a term people have ever used to describe their own experiences; instead, it is imposed by outsiders. Using *same-sex desire* to describe a historical figure such as the nineteenth-century poet Walt Whitman, for example, could attribute to him an emphasis on genital sex to which he might have objected, and it could attribute to him a sexual desire for males in general rather than for the specific type of young, masculine, working-class men Whitman sought out for what he called "comradeship."

Students are often eager to jettison all such terms: they reject the "labels" as false generalizations that erase particular differences by imputing a uniformity that does not exist. This argument has some merit. Yet there are also good reasons for not getting rid of such terminology. After all, making generalizations—dividing things into categories by similarity and dissimilarity—is the foundation of analysis. We can certainly test our conceptual categories, find fault with them, and try to make them more accurate and useful, but to eschew them entirely could seem tantamount to avoiding analysis itself. As discussed by Kevin Mumford in this volume, some of the most exciting scholarly analyses of marginalization today focus on intersectionality—the ways in which variously stigmatized markers of sociocultural difference (including nationality, citizenship status, class, race, religion, dis/ability, gender, sex, and sexual orientation) intersect and shape each other in critical ways. Naming such stigmatized markers helps us critique various forms of marginalization. At the same time, if we take these names as an unexamined given, we can insidiously and unwittingly reinforce the marginalizing stigmas. Not to name them, however, also risks reinforcing oppressive cultural norms, especially the long history of shaming and silencing in the case of same-sex desire and romance—the "love that dare not speak its name." Teaching LGBT history can help illuminate this broader set of issues in U.S. history.

In the classroom, I find it productive to use the terms *gay, lesbian, bisexual,* and *transgender* according to their common dictionary definitions, which usually offer minimal denotative qualifications for admission to their respective categories. After all, the connotative baggage that often comes with these terms can vary widely depending on the context of their use. At the same time, however, I encourage students to view our class as an extended invitation to consider that categorical terms for sex and gender, while useful to some extent, might merely constitute a kind of shorthand: what if such terms work best not as tightly defined categories but rather as loose, provisional shorthand for a variety of different but related stories about particular experiences? In this sense, such terms constitute just one point of entry for exploring questions they help describe but cannot fully define.

To elaborate I ask students to consider that, although creating generalized categories is a foundational tool for reasoning, "story logic" constitutes another such tool—one that is arguably more foundational, although it is probably most productive to think of categorical analysis and story logic as being so interrelated as to name different ends of a single spectrum. Drawing on research in narrative theory, psychology, and cognitive science, I explain that stories and storytelling constitute a mode of reasoning that does not merely offer illustrative examples for analysis but actually organizes, reflects on, and tests understandings of time, change, and processes.[1] Below I offer a few specific examples of the kinds of reasoning stories can facilitate. For now let's begin with the simple proposition that stories by or about people who might fit somewhere in the LGBT or LGBTQIA acronyms do not necessarily need to use such labels at all: instead of worrying about what defines *lesbian* as a category that pertains to lots of different people, stories can focus on the details of one person's experience, regardless of whether or not that experience fits what someone else might define as *lesbian*. That said, stories do entail generalizations of their own: they inevitably use words that generalize; they almost always follow some storytelling conventions, even clichés, both formally and thematically; and they can falsify lived experience by trying too hard to fit experience into such conventions. Even so, they have the capacity to emphasize particularity to a far greater extent than a label ever could.

This still leaves the question of why we would use fiction rather than nonfiction stories in a history course. There are several reasons. For starters their heightened artifice can help students recognize and think more carefully about the art that goes into creating even nonfiction stories—which is to say that they can help us think about how narrative works as a medium of communication, be it in a history textbook or a short story. Storytellers choose where to begin, where to end, and what events to include, all of which implicitly conveys what the storyteller interprets as being causational, climactic, and generally important or interesting. Yet a story can imply these things without having to argue for them, which can make a nonfiction narrative seem objectively factual when it is actually the product of interpretation. This is why analysis is necessary for studying even nonfiction historical narratives; yet sometimes the most effective rebuttal to a story comes not just from analysis but also from an alternative story.

Another reason why fiction can be useful in a history class is that it raises the issue of audience reception, as I elaborate shortly: how have audiences at different historical times read a given story? This, too, can help students understand that our interpretations (of fiction and nonfiction alike) are shaped by our historical context. Finally, fiction tends (far more than nonfiction) to work indirectly, using symbols, metaphors, allusions, and the like to suggest larger and more complex meanings than are conveyed literally. Such indirect suggestion can be especially productive for studying LGBT histories because it can help us think through key problems of evidence, reminding us that these histories remain something other than what we can literally represent in words.

Affairs of the heart, including those that might more accurately be described as affairs of the hormones, are notoriously subjective. In studying LGBT history, we are interested in large-scale movements, subcultures, legislative and judicial records, and the "scientific" literature of medical and psychological researchers—but we are also interested in what individual people felt and experienced and how they thought about themselves. This is notoriously difficult to determine even in the present, let alone in the past. Throughout history, sexual desire and sexual activity have rarely been viewed as something to be documented for posterity. In addition LGBT history focuses on nonnormative expressions of sexual desire and gender that have a long history of being suppressed. Indeed, most of the relevant historical evidence attests primarily to oppression. When it comes to people who have also been marginalized and suppressed in other ways, such as women, slaves, and laborers, historical records give us almost nothing of their voices. This does not mean we should replace the lack of facts with made-up facts that we pretend are true, but it does mean we need to think creatively about what we do not know and probably will never know—a kind of thinking that typical historical analysis does not do very well, since it tends to try to make strong, positive claims based on whatever evidence is available. Stories are potentially better suited to acknowledging the gaps in our knowledge by helping us conceptualize and explore the mysteries we cannot solve.

Historians such as Carolyn Dinshaw and Leila J. Rupp recognize this potential in fiction. Rupp argues that fiction can help us imagine how our accounts of history might change if we had access to voices that are not available in the historical record, such as those of certain ancient Greek women "who commissioned erotic spells."[2] We know that such women existed, but we do not have their own words. Furthermore, "literary texts, as imaginative interpretations, remind us that historical scholarship, too, although based on evidence, is also an act of interpretation" (5). Rupp shows, for example, how Jackie Kay's 1998 novel *Trumpet* can teach us to think more critically about how we interpret historical evidence. Inspired by Billy Tipton (1914–89), a white American jazz pianist who was born female and lived his adult life as a man, *Trumpet* suggests that newspaper accounts of Tipton from his own time might have got his story wrong: a journalist in the novel interprets one character's tears as indicating that she must feel betrayed by the musician's gender self-presentation, yet the character actually feels no such betrayal but simply mourns the loss of the person she loved (104). She does not reveal this to the journalist, presumably because doing so might stigmatize her. How might nonfiction historical evidence pertaining to LGBT histories be similarly misleading or completely wrong for the same kinds of reasons? *Trumpet* also gives us a sense of what LGBT histories might look like if we prioritized story logic rather than categorical terms to conceptualize these histories: Rupp contends, "[W]hat lingers is the image of two people in love, without concepts or identities and without the need for them: two people who desire each other" (104).

## Using Fiction to Teach LGBT History

The remainder of this essay outlines additional ways in which four different kinds of fiction narratives can be useful in teaching LGBT history. Social studies or history teachers might find it helpful to collaborate with their English colleagues in preparing to use such narratives in the classroom.

The first category, coded stories, comprises stories published in a given historical era—which therefore constitute primary sources about that era—that could potentially be read as coded expressions of the kinds of nonnormative gender and sexual experiences relevant to LGBT history. Elizabeth Stuart Phelps's "Since I Died" (1873), for example, imaginatively relates the experience of a woman who has recently died and is struggling to communicate with a woman she loves who remains alive: "Lips that my mortal lips have pressed, can you not quiver when I cry? Soul that my eternal soul has loved, can you stand enveloped in my presence, and not spring like a fountain to me?"[3] I use the following kinds of questions as discussion starters, often asking students to brainstorm reflective notes about each question before they answer. Is this an account of romantic love between women?[4] If so, then why was it not recognized as such by many readers of its day? Might it instead be describing what scholars call "romantic friendship"—a nonsexual friendship of such passionate intensity that it might appear sexual to a present-day reader but was not imagined to involve sex in its own day? Is there a way to read this story without subjecting it to what might be a reductive and possibly anachronistic either-or dichotomy of "romantic friendship" versus "romantic love"? If those labels represent the wrong kinds of questions to be asking, then what other kinds of things might the story be about? These kinds of questions could be asked about many stories that fall into this "coded" category.[5]

*Scribner's Monthly* magazine originally published "Since I Died," but its founding editor, Josiah Gilbert Holland, refused to print Walt Whitman's work because he deemed it morally questionable. The following excerpt from a poem published in Whitman's 1860 version of *Leaves of Grass* (poem 11 of the *Calamus* section, "When I Heard at the Close of the Day"), seems today to suggest what might have worried Holland.

. . . when I thought how my dear friend, my lover, was on his way coming, O then I was happy,
O then each breath tasted sweeter—and all that day my food nourish'd me more—and the beautiful day pass'd well,
And the next came with equal joy—and with the next, at evening, came my friend;
And that night, while all was still, I heard the waters roll slowly continually up the shores,
I heard the hissing rustle of the liquid and sands, as directed to me, whispering to congratulate me,
For the one I love most lay sleeping by me under the same cover in the cool night,

In the stillness, his face was inclined toward me,
And his arm lay lightly around my breast—and that night I was happy.

One could ask students why they think Holland might have objected to this poem but not to Phelps's story. While Whitman's poems aroused concern for some, not all readers at the time thought they described erotic love between men.[6] That fact might help students explore the following questions as they pertain to our own time. What is the difference between being "just friends" and being something more? Is there always a clear, precise line between the two? Is it possible for two friends to share a more intimate and profound love than two people who are engaged in a sexual relationship? How can one tell the degree of intimacy involved in a particular sexual activity? What exactly constitutes "having sex"? Wrestling with such questions in the context of the reception history of coded stories can help students understand not only how murky the answers can be today but also that the answers— and even what kinds of questions seem most interesting and relevant— can change in different cultural contexts and historical eras.

Willa Cather's "Paul's Case: A Study in Temperament" (1905) likewise raises a useful range of questions. It describes an effeminate young man who is passionate about the arts and who perplexes and offends his high school teachers and peers; at the end of the story, Paul takes his own life. Is this a coded story about a gay teenager? It might be read as depicting an Oscar Wilde model of male homosexuality associated with the arts and effeminacy (as opposed to Walt Whitman's depiction of love between conventionally masculine men). Or could it instead have much less to do with sexuality than with gender nonconformity? As with most stories, these questions do not exhaust its possibilities: it might be less about gender or sexuality than about the arts enabling a space (possibly a dangerously naive space) for critiquing broader economic and social issues related to class and early-twentieth-century capitalism. Such a reading might help remind us that focusing exclusively on questions about sexual desire and gender presentation can lead us to minimize or ignore other kinds of important historical issues.

The second category concerns a rarer type of story: those that are also primary sources but are explicit, noncoded stories published before the 1960s. One of the most famous examples is the English author Radclyffe Hall's *The Well of Loneliness* (1928). For a fascinating slice of

U.S. history, however, *Strange Brother* (1931), by Blair Niles (the pen name of Mary Blair Rice), is a treasure trove. Even the first three or four chapters (it is a quick read) paint a vividly detailed portrait of various New York City subcultures of the Jazz Age, including not only white and black gay characters but also upper-class white society and its love affair with African American culture (as sold to it in specially crafted Harlem venues).[7] While some of the gay characters accord with early-twentieth-century stereotypes of gender "inversion," the gay protagonist is not effeminate and passes for straight rather easily. Interestingly, *Strange Brother* was reviewed more or less favorably when it was published in 1931 despite its taboo subject. Critics did not praise its artistry, but they did commend its "interesting and informative" portrayal of what "a homosexual suffers in a modern civilization."

The third category comprises the explicitly LGBT literature published since the 1960s in the context of a growing public recognition of LGBT political movements and subcultures. These works can also be considered primary sources. For a U.S. history survey, two of the most important contributions offered by this large body of literature are, first, a sense of the successes of LGBT political movements in the 1960s and 1970s and their indebtedness to feminism, the sexual revolution, and the civil rights movement; and, second, a sense of the changes wrought by the onset of AIDS in the early 1980s. Rita Mae Brown's *Rubyfruit Jungle* (1973) is a lesbian *Huckleberry Finn*; if I had to choose an excerpt, section 3 (chapters 11 through 13) provides a gritty and gripping view of the time. The 1988 film version of Harvey Fierstein's 1982 play *Torch Song Trilogy* presents its own 120-minute perspective on the pre-AIDS years of gay liberation, especially giving a sense of the importance of drag and its complex camp humor. Larry Kramer's play *The Normal Heart* (1985) is an appropriately angry look at the early years of the pandemic; most of its characters are based on actual historical figures. (A film adaptation, also titled *The Normal Heart*, debuted on HBO in 2014.) There are many such stories that can bring these decades to life.

The fourth category is historical fiction. Historical novels with LGBT themes began appearing in the first half of the twentieth century, but most have been published since the 1960s; in just a few decades, the genre has grown considerably. Critics of the genre typically assume that most readers of historical fiction are improbably naive people who believe that fictional stories are perfectly true. Research shows that this assumption is inaccurate. Fans of historical fiction tend to approach these stories as starting points for further historical exploration, feeling quite free to question the stories' historical accuracy. Indeed, while non-fiction histories tend to present themselves as authoritative and objective accounts even though they entail subjective interpretation, historical fictions openly present themselves as "what if?" interpretations based on the author's imagination as well as historical evidence. These fictions can therefore help us recognize and think more carefully about what we do not know.

Given that historical novels are too long to fit in most history classes, I will focus on a ninety-minute film by Cheryl Dunye, *The Watermelon Woman* (1996), which rapidly and effectively explores the challenges of researching LGBT history and how such research means very different things to different people. For some characters, the (fictional) early-twentieth-century film actress who is the subject of the film is a hero of African American history or women's history but not LGBT history. For others she is a celebrity, a Hollywood legend, and the idol of old-school "butch" lesbians. For the contemporary young filmmaker telling the story, the legendary actress is a black, lesbian film star who serves as a personal and professional forerunner. The film depicts history as a story that is created and re-created in the context of specific relationships between the past and the present, such that as the present changes—which it is always doing—history changes, too, in order to reflect newly emerging concerns and issues. Successive generations of different characters interpret the film actress's importance quite differently. The film also depicts the study of LGBT history as frustratingly stymied by a lack of evidence, as well as barriers related to race, class, and gender; it portrays such barriers in both the present and the past. All this provides a helpful illustration of how history is the product of specific cultural and historical contexts, as well as individual historians' interpretations of the available evidence.

For those with an appetite for longer works, there are many noteworthy examples of LGBT historical novels.[8] While Mary Renault's *The Persian Boy* (1972) is not about U.S. history, students often enjoy it and find its portrayal of Alexander the Great thought provoking. Walter L. Williams and Toby Johnson's *Two Spirits: A Story of Life with the Navajo* (2006), set in the nineteenth century, productively explores the complexities of the American Indian two-spirit figure.

As a practical teaching matter, it is important to recognize that analyzing fiction requires an overlapping but also significantly different skill set than that used in analyzing nonfiction primary and secondary historical texts. There are insightful queer historical novels I teach only to students who have advanced skills in literary analysis, such as William Faulkner's *Absalom, Absalom!* (1936) or Monique Truong's *The Book of Salt* (2003). For a U.S. history survey, I would instead use one or more of the other stories mentioned in this essay because they are more accessible. These stories offer a special kind of lens through which students can discover illuminating complexities in LGBT history—complexities that will also illuminate and enrich their study of history more broadly.

## NOTES

1. The relevant research is vast and growing. For an overview related to the topic at hand, see Norman W. Jones, *Gay and Lesbian Historical Fiction: Sexual Mystery and Post-Secular Narrative* (New York: Palgrave Macmillan, 2007), 15–20.

2. Leila J. Rupp, *Sapphistries: A Global History of Love between Women* (New York: New York University Press, 2009), 40. Hereafter page numbers from this work are cited parenthetically.

3. Full-text versions of this story, as well as the Willa Cather story referenced below, are available free of charge on the Internet; search for them by author and title.

4. See also Dáša Frančíková's essay in this volume.

5. Of the many stories that have been read as coded, some of the more teachable include Brett Harte's "Tennessee's Partner" (1869), Constance Fenimore Woolson's "Miss Grief" (1880), Sarah Orne Jewett's "Martha's Lady" (1897), and James Baldwin's *Go Tell It on the Mountain* (1953). With the latter, part 1 by itself could be used to excellent effect in the classroom.

6. See also David D. Doyle Jr.'s essay in this volume.

7. See also Red Vaughan Tremmel's essay on early-twentieth-century sexual cultures in this volume.

8. For further reading, see my *Gay and Lesbian Historical Fiction*, which includes an annotated bibliography of historical novels published before early 2006. For those published since, an Internet search for LGBT historical fiction will turn up several helpful fan sites. In addition to *Trumpet*, discussed above, other noteworthy transgender historical novels include Leslie Feinberg's *Stone Butch Blues* (1993), set in the 1950s, 1960s, and early 1970s, and David Ebershoff's *The Danish Girl: A Novel* (2001), which reimagines the story of Einar Weigener (Lili Elbe), who in 1931 became the first man to undergo sex-change surgery.

# Screening the Queer Past

*Teaching LGBT History
with Documentary Films*

NICHOLAS L. SYRETT

In teaching both halves of the U.S. history survey, I have found that using film makes the material more visceral to students, and usually more relatable. I often look to documentary films when I want to humanize those who are different from my twenty-first-century, largely white, middle-class college students, many of whom seem to have had little experience with people who do not look like themselves. Instead of simply lecturing about the struggles of the civil rights movement, for instance, showing students an episode of the PBS television series *Eyes on the Prize* not only brings to life what actually happened to protesters who dared to defy white southern segregationists but also makes clear that many protesters were young people who were in many ways not unlike the students in my class.

The same is true of films about LGBT experiences. While my students have heard lots about queer people, many of them seem to have had little experience with those who are openly gay, lesbian, bisexual, or transgender. Interviews with queer people in documentary films humanize them and in some ways demonstrate just how ordinary queer people can be, how reasonable their desires for acceptance and equal rights. At the same time, historical footage documenting antiqueer prejudice and bigotry also makes real to viewers the struggles that queer people experienced in the past (and continue to face in some circumstances). The activist history many of these films portray thus also comes to seem like a reasonable response to queer people's treatment in the United States.

Like the majority of documentary films available for use in history classrooms, most that focus on queer history cover the more recent past, precisely because the medium relies on the use of contemporaneous footage, photographs, and interviews with those who have witnessed or participated in history. Thus, with one exception, the films I discuss in this essay document the twentieth century, when queer identities were emerging, undergoing redefinition, and finally coming to resemble those with which we are now familiar. They are mostly films document-ing the actions of gay, lesbian, and transgender people (there are almost no representations of self-identified bisexual people), not films that document how people came to think of themselves as being those kinds of identities in the first place. They disproportionately highlight a heroic narrative, moving from closetedness and persecution to activism and acceptance. While the history of queer activism in the United States is certainly rich and storied, the lives of everyday queer people, and indeed the emergence of LGBT identities themselves, deserve far more treat-ment than they have received.

The majority of films focus on San Francisco and, to a lesser extent, New York City. While there are good historical reasons to document queer culture in these cities, which were central to the emergence of queer life in the United States, the major drawback of this focus is that it makes it seem as though queer people have largely lived in urban spaces on the coasts, which is clearly not the case. Some films documenting twenty-first-century queer life help to fill this void, but I have yet to find one that focuses on the nonmetropolitan queer past.[1] Although the largest number of available documentaries focus on contemporary LGBT politics and lives, I have limited my discussion to those with a historical focus.[2] Most of the films I include here are available on DVD, and I found them either at my local library or through Netflix, which currently has the majority of them, many available for streaming.

## The Films

*She Drank, She Swore, She Courted Girls . . . She Even Chewed Tobacco: Passing Women in 19th Century America* (1983), a film by the San Francisco Lesbian and Gay History Project, is the one film (to my knowl-edge) made exclusively by historians, not professional filmmakers.[3] Perhaps for that reason it is also the only film that takes on the messier period before lesbian, gay, or transgender identities took their current forms. Developed out of a slide show, the film is the least glossy in terms of its production values, and it relies primarily on newspaper accounts, some of which are dramatized through the use of different women's voices. It spans the nineteenth to early twentieth centuries and runs about thirty-five minutes, so is easily shown during one class while still allowing time for discussion. It begins with ideals of nineteenth-century womanhood, which were primarily achievable by white middle-class women in the Northeast, and then contrasts those with life for men and women in the West (especially California), the primary focus of the film. Because of this it might add interest to lectures about westward expansion and women's lives on the frontier.

The film asks viewers to consider the different reasons why a woman might have desired to pass as a man: for safety, for money, for love and sex with other women, or perhaps because "she" felt more like a "he" (see Genny Beemyn's essay in this volume). Never claiming to know the answer with any certainty, the film nevertheless makes clear that many passing women did marry other women, so same-sex desire was clearly part of their lives. But at the same time, the film prompts questions about the fuzzy line between what we now recognize as the different categories of lesbian and transgender. Concentrating on two figures in Northern California, one white (Jeanne Bonnet) and one of mixed-race heritage who passed for white (Babe Bean), the film is also particularly useful for talking about women's roles, as one of its main points is that living as a (white) man offered opportunities that would never have been available to women. It concludes with early-twentieth-century lesbians, who inherited the traditions of passing women from their nineteenth-century forebears at the same time that lesbianism was increasingly being pathologized in medical discourse.

The 1969 riots at the Stonewall Inn in New York's Greenwich Village are perhaps the best known of any event in gay American history. Even as scholars have questioned Stonewall's centrality to queer history, the riots are implicitly (and in most cases explicitly) the point of reference for almost all these films. As such, even a film that takes the first half of the twentieth century as its focus is called *Before Stonewall* (1985) and ends, not surprisingly, in 1969.[4] It includes interviews with about twenty-five people, including pioneers of gay liberation and culture such as Harry Hay, Audre Lorde, Allen Ginsberg, Craig Rodwell, and Ann Bannon.

*Before Stonewall* is organized around specific decades. Beginning with the 1920s (bohemian life, slumming, Harlem), 1930s (harassment during the Depression), and 1940s (Second World War era opportunities), the film provides more in-depth coverage of the 1950s (Kinsey, Cold War domesticity, butch-fem culture, the homophile movement) and 1960s (lesbian pulp novels, the growth of gay bars in cities, more militant organizing in line with civil rights and the feminist movement). *Before Stonewall* is also particularly easy to use in a classroom because one can show just one or two chapters to align with a lecture on that particular decade, thus allowing for incorporation of queer material into a lecture on the 1920s, say, or the massive disruptions and opportunities of the Second World War. Despite the film's title emphasizing the centrality of Stonewall, it demonstrates that the Stonewall rebellion did not appear out of nowhere—in terms of both the raid as a form of continued persecution and earlier organizing that laid the groundwork for post-Stonewall militancy—as some other films implicitly suggest.

Reflecting later historiography that rejects the singularity of Stonewall, *Screaming Queens: The Riot at Compton's Cafeteria* (2005) concentrates on the first recorded instance of violent resistance by queer people in the United States.[5] The film is useful not just in documenting this particular riot but also as a case study in the development of resistance to police harassment, injustice, and poverty, all themes pertinent to teaching about the 1960s. Depicting the antipolice rebellion by transgender people at Gene Compton's Cafeteria, a twenty-four-hour diner at the corner of Turk and Taylor Streets in San Francisco's Tenderloin district, at just under an hour the film also works well for showing in classes. Perhaps most significant, the riot occurred in 1966, three years before the famed Stonewall riots, which are usually credited as being the United States' first instance of queer revolution.

Narrated and codirected by the historian Susan Stryker, and using interviews with racially diverse transwomen who participated in the riot, as well as a minister and police officer who worked in the Tenderloin, *Screaming Queens* does an excellent job of connecting the riot to a myriad of other forces at work in both San Francisco and the United States more broadly. These include the increasing militancy of the antiwar and civil rights movements; the gentrification of nearby neighborhoods; the inability of transwomen to find employment outside the dangerous field of sex work; local activists who benefited from funding by President Lyndon Johnson's Great Society programs; and, perhaps most significant, the popularization of the category of transsexuality as a medical diagnosis that could be addressed through sex reassignment surgery.

One of the newer films available, the television documentary *Stonewall Uprising* (2011), is based on David Carter's book *Stonewall*.[6] Using still footage and interviews with historians and participants (including one of the police officers who conducted the raid), the film gives an in-depth recounting of the riots themselves and then situates them in their times. For those who want a film that concentrates on this momentous uprising, this is the best option. The film emphasizes, in interesting detail (including helpful maps), what actually happened, the location of the Stonewall Inn on Christopher Street, and the coercive relationship among gay bars, the mafia, and the police. It is also particularly good in demonstrating who the participants in the riot were: street kids, drag queens, and others who were already poor enough that they had very little to lose.

Class discussion of the significance of Stonewall will be aided by the viewing of *Stonewall Uprising*, as the film documents the first commemorative march in 1970 and demonstrates how the incident invigorated and changed the gay movement during the 1970s. That said, the film reifies Stonewall as the dividing and defining moment of gay history in the United States. It makes it seem as if there was very little gay life pre-Stonewall and that what did exist was by definition sad and terrifying. As the films I have discussed and countless books on queer history make clear, this was not the case. Students may want to discuss the historical significance of Stonewall, the degree to which its early commemoration has caused it to be remembered as so singularly momentous, and the general public's seeming need to be able to pinpoint precise moments of social change. Also interesting, perhaps as a provocation for class discussion, are the pictures of contemporary gay pride parades with which the film concludes. The contrast between the interview with the police officer who participated in the raid and the presence of gay cops in a pride parade is particularly striking. So, too, are the posters for Google seen among the rainbow balloons, demonstrating the company's support for gay rights. Students might consider how social movement strategies have changed over time and the impact of the mainstreaming of gay and lesbian identities within consumer culture. Has acceptance been achieved? Or is recognition by corporations and other mainstream institutions a form of co-optation?

*Word Is Out: Stories of Some of Our Lives* (1977) premiered as the first feature-length gay documentary made by gay filmmakers.[7] It was restored and rereleased in 2009, yet it retains the quality of a primary source from the gay liberation era. It is made up almost exclusively of interviews with about twenty-five gay men and lesbians, many of them living in San Francisco, who talk about their childhoods in a variety of eras and their lives in the late 1970s. Among them are Harry Hay and Sally Gearhart, as well as other political activists, but also a number who were not active in the movement. They represent a range of ages, races, and gendered self-presentations and discuss a wide variety of subjects: childhood same-sex experiences, prior marriages, their children, realizations of queer feelings, the coming out process, life in the military, moves to cities, and being closeted in rural America. The final section is about politics in the late 1970s, and the interviewees offer up a variety of interesting and nuanced perspectives on gay liberation, being single, sex without emotional intimacy, butch-fem roles, the pleasures of being in an "in-group" even if it is reviled, lesbian feminism and separatism, and queer families.

In contrast to most historical documentaries, *Word Is Out* is not organized by period. Instead, it explores themes as experienced by narrators of different ages. Because of this and the fact that the film is long (133 minutes), it is best shown in clips. But the interviewees are eloquent, and, unlike documentaries made long after the fact, these people are describing what they felt at the time about their lives as gay people in the 1970s. It is particularly good on complicating the unity of gay identity and revealing its messiness. While most of the narrators are resolutely gay or lesbian in their identification, some allow for a much greater degree of flexibility in their sexual identity, although they stop short of detailed explorations of bisexuality. *Word Is Out* is also particularly insightful on the intersection of gender and sexual identity: for men, the theme of effeminacy and proving masculinity; for women, the constant need to show deference to men in order to demonstrate their femininity. It also shows how during the 1970s many of the movement's goals were decidedly not normative; many of these people really wanted to shake up the system and the status quo.

Documenting a period concurrent with *Word Is Out*, *The Times of Harvey Milk* (1984) is the Oscar-winning documentary on the life and assassination of San Francisco's first openly gay city supervisor, Harvey Milk.[8] It also focuses attention on the growth of gay liberation in the 1970s, as well as the national backlash against that very visibility, especially in the form of antigay ordinances across the country. One particular arc in the film follows the efforts of Milk, Sally Gearhart, and other gay activists in defeating the 1978 Briggs initiative, which would have banned openly gay teachers from California schools. While many students may be familiar with the dramatic feature film *Milk* (2008), which also won an Oscar, true to its title, *The Times of Harvey Milk* concentrates less on the drama of Milk's personal life and more on the changing life of the city of San Francisco and the development of the Castro district as a gay neighborhood.

*The Times of Harvey Milk* ends after the conviction of Milk's assassin, Dan White, on the lesser charge of manslaughter and the violent reaction by San Francisco queers to his sentence. The final moments emphasize the strategy of Milk's politics, which was the union of all those who had previously been disenfranchised: queers, people of color, the poor, the elderly, women, and the disabled. It is thus a useful tool for talking about the political history of the later twentieth century, especially as the rise of the New Right in the next decade took aim at those very coalitions.

Also documenting activist work during the same period (and beyond), *No Secret Anymore: The Times of Del Martin and Phyllis Lyon* (2003) takes us on a journey through the second half of the twentieth century with the longtime activist couple named in the title.[9] Martin and Lyon were instrumental in the founding of the Daughters of Bilitis in 1955 in San Francisco, the first lesbian rights organization in the country, but they were also active in the broader women's rights movement, founding or cofounding more than fifteen organizations. *No Secret Anymore* begins with the repression of the 1950s and does an excellent job of focusing on the different issues facing lesbians, particularly during the periods when gay men and lesbians were most divided in their politics prior to AIDS. Also documenting the shared concerns of, and conflicts between, lesbian activists and other women's liberationists, the film would be useful for showing while discussing the second wave of the women's movement.

A number of similarly biographical films bring more racial and gendered diversity to the depiction of twentieth-century queer history, and also take us away from San Francisco. *Brother Outsider: The Life of Bayard Rustin* (2003) tells the story of civil rights activist Bayard Rustin, from his childhood in early-twentieth-century West Chester, Pennsylvania, to his efforts to desegregate the South and his organizing of the 1963 March on Washington.[10] Rustin's homosexuality, the film argues, particularly a 1953 arrest for lewd conduct, kept him from more high-profile leadership positions in the civil rights movement (see the essay by Ian Lekus in this volume). *Brother Outsider* is primarily a movie about civil rights for African Americans, the cause to which Rustin devoted his life, but it would be useful in a survey class for demonstrating the intersectional identity of black gay men.

*Living with Pride: Ruth Ellis @ 100* (1999) documents the life of African American centenarian Ruth Ellis, who was born in 1899 in segregated Springfield, Illinois, and spent most of her life in Detroit, where she and her partner offered their home as a center for black gay life from the 1940s through 1971.[11] The film takes a deservedly celebratory approach to Ellis's life and is most useful for depicting the lives of black lesbians and gay men through the 1960s. While it also documents the impact of civil rights, feminism, and gay rights on Ellis's life, the latter part of the film is largely an exploration of her day-to-day life and circle of friends.

Two films document both the devastation of AIDS and the extraordinary reaction by queers to the epidemic when the government largely left them to fend for themselves. *We Were Here: The AIDS Years in San Francisco* (2011) uses interviews with activists and footage from the late 1970s through the early 1990s to document the AIDS epidemic as it was lived in San Francisco.[12] It traces the development of the gay community in the 1970s, the first infections, and, perhaps most poignantly, the community response to AIDS, documenting an unprecedented unity between lesbians and gay men, especially in the face of government apathy. It also includes minor segments on the AIDS Coalition to Unleash Power (ACT UP), the NAMES Project's AIDS quilt, and the eventual decline in deaths by the 1990s. *We Were Here* is truly wrenching at times, but it provides a ninety-minute overview of what AIDS did to San Francisco's community and what members of that community did in response.

Taking us to the East Coast and New York City, *How to Survive a Plague* (2012) is a chronicle of ACT UP from 1987 to 1996.[13] The emphasis in this film is on the way people with AIDS and their allies, faced with an inactive government that seemed to care little about their fate, took medicine and activism into their own hands to fight for their lives. The film follows the work of about ten key figures, including Peter Staley, Bob Rafsky, Mark Harrington, Larry Kramer, and Garance Franke-Ruta. It gives major attention to particular protests and the inaction of the Reagan and Bush administrations during the late 1980s and early 1990s. It is more technical than *We Were Here*, however; the filmmakers discuss the science of various drugs, and there are informative but complex interviews with officials from public health agencies and drug companies. It ends in 1996 with the development of dual drug treatments and protease inhibitors, heralded by most as lifesavers. Like *We Were Here*, the film is also very moving, particularly in the moments toward the end as the activists remember those who died. Both films do much to humanize people with AIDS, a population that many of our students either do not know or believe they do not know.

Two final films take a long and sweeping view of queer history in the United States. *After Stonewall* (1999), the sequel to *Before Stonewall*, follows the same format as its prequel but is less successful, only because it attempts to describe with unity what is ultimately thirty complicated years of diversity and an ever-growing queer presence in the country.[14] Narrated by Melissa Etheridge and including interviews with a wide variety of queer public figures (Barney Frank, Dorothy Allison, Barbara Smith, Karla Jay, Harry Hay, Larry Kramer, Armistead Maupin, Rita Mae Brown, Jewelle Gomez, Barbara Gittings, and many more), the film is a bit like a greatest (and worst) hits of LGBT post-Stonewall politics and culture. It is largely a triumphant narrative march from 1969 to increased visibility at century's end, though tempered by the grief of AIDS and the anxiety of continued violence and discrimination. It ends on a hopeful note with the globalization of a gay identity, which the film casts uncritically as a good thing, instead of also seeing it as the westernizing of much more complicated sexual identities that might have predated "gayness" in other places. With easily accessed chapters, segments of *After Stonewall* could easily accompany a lecture related to particular late-twentieth-century topics.

The Oscar-winning *The Celluloid Closet* (1996), based on Vito Russo's book of the same name, documents the portrayal of gay and lesbian characters in the movies from 1914 to the mid-1990s.[15] Arguing for the role of film in the construction of all people's identities, *The Celluloid Closet* uses compelling film clips alongside interviews with directors, actors, and screenwriters, including Shirley MacLaine, Tony Curtis, Tom Hanks, Gore Vidal, and a particularly eloquent Susan Sarandon. Demonstrating that queer figures have been present in film since the movies were born, if not always in positive or open portrayals, the film challenges the belief that media depictions of same-sex sexuality are new. Because it covers the whole twentieth century it would be difficult to use it in its entirety in a class; chapters on the DVD facilitate the use of clips when discussing the popular culture of an era. Its representations of gay people during the Cold War are especially powerful.

These films have their limits. The most obvious for anyone teaching a survey class is that there is almost nothing available for the first half. In part this is a limitation of the genre itself, but it is also the case that most of the available films have sought to document triumphant, uplifting narratives that focus on gay, lesbian, and transgender activism. This means focusing on people who identify as lesbian, gay, bisexual, or transgender, categories only available relatively recently. It should also go without saying that even by the twentieth century, when more and more people actually did come to identify with these categories, the vast majority of them were not the activists depicted in these films. This means that the films available to us document a minority of queer people. They do this in one other obvious way, by primarily focusing on white men and women. While almost all the films make a real effort to introduce the perspectives of people of color, their voices remain underrepresented. So, too, are bisexual people, who are virtually absent from the genre, and transgender people, who make only limited appearances.

That said, and particularly given the political and social movement focus of most teaching about LGBT people in survey history classes, many of these films are excellent. It is always a struggle when teaching the survey to achieve the ever-elusive coverage of a vast array of themes, issues, and events. Using documentary films is one particularly effective way to include LGBT history. Some of them—*Brother Outsider*, *Screaming Queens*, *No Secret Anymore*—also do double duty by exploring multiple movements and issues that belong in any class on twentieth-century U.S. history. Exposure to these documentaries also brings an added benefit: humanizing queer people for students who may have little experience with the LGBT community.

NOTES

1. For takes on early 2000s gay life in rural America, see *Small Town Gay Bar*, dir. Malcolm Ingram, Genius Entertainment, Santa Monica, CA, 2007, DVD; *Out in the Silence*, dir. Joe Wilson and Dean Hamer, Garden Thieves Pictures, Washington, DC, 2009, DVD; and *Out in the Heartland*, dir. Gretchen Hildebran, Frameline, San Francisco, 2008, DVD.

2. For further examples of films that date from the twenty-first century and focus variously on politics, family, youth, religion, the workplace, violence, and queer culture in specific places and among particular racial or ethnic groups, see *8: The Mormon Proposition*, dir. Reed Cowan, Wolfe Video, New Almaden, CA, 2010, DVD; *Dear Jesse*, dir. Tim Kirkman, New Yorker Video, New York, 1999, DVD; *Outrage*, dir. Kirby Dick, Magnolia Home Entertainment, New York, 2010, DVD; *Tying the Knot*, dir. Jim de Sève, Docurama/New Video, New York, 2005, DVD; *In My Shoes: Stories of Youth with LGBT Parents*, dir. Jen Gilomen and COLAGE, Frameline, San Francisco, 2005, DVD; *A Jihad for Love*, dir. Parvez Sharma, First Run Features, New York, 2009, DVD; *Trembling before G-d*, dir. Sandi Simcha Dubowski, New Yorker Video, New York, 2003, DVD; *This Is What Love in Action Looks Like*, dir. Jon Fox, TLA, Philadelphia, 2012, DVD; *Freeheld*, dir. Cynthia Wade, Brooklyn, NY, 2007, DVD; *Out at Work*, dir. Kelly Anderson and Tami Gold, New Day Films, Harriman, NY, 2009, DVD; *The Brandon Teena Story*, dir. Susan Muska and Greta Olafsdottir, Docurama/New Video, New York, 1998, DVD; *Ke Kulana He Mahu: Remembering a Sense of Place*, dir. Brent Anbe and Kathryn Xian, Zang Pictures, Honolulu, 2001, DVD; *Paris Is Burning*, dir. Jennie Livingston, Miramax, Burbank, CA, [1990] 2005, DVD; and *Tongues Untied: Black Men Loving Black Men*, dir. Marlon Riggs, Frameline, San Francisco, [1989] 2006, DVD.

3. *She Drank, She Swore, She Courted Girls . . . She Even Chewed Tobacco: Passing Women in 19th Century America*, dir. San Francisco Lesbian and Gay History Project, Women Make Movies, New York, 1983, DVD.

4. *Before Stonewall*, dir. Greta Schiller, First Run Features, New York, 2004, DVD.

5. *Screaming Queens: The Riot at Compton's Cafeteria*, dir. Victor Silverman and Susan Stryker, Frameline, San Francisco, 2005, DVD.

6. *Stonewall Uprising*, dir. Kate Davis and David Heilbroner, PBS, New York, 2011, DVD; David Carter, *Stonewall: The Riots That Sparked the Gay Revolution* (New York: St. Martin's Press, 2004).

7. *Word Is Out: Stories of Some of Our Lives*, dir. Nancy Adair, Andrew Brown, and Rob Epstein, Millarium Zero, Huntington Park, NJ, [1977] 2009, DVD.

8. *The Times of Harvey Milk*, dir. Rob Epstein, New Yorker Video, New York, [1984] 2004, DVD.

9. *No Secret Anymore: The Times of Del Martin and Phyllis Lyon*, dir. Joan E. Biren, Frameline, San Francisco, 2003, DVD. Also of interest in documenting some similar themes and conflicts and a number of the same activists is *Last Call at Maud's*, dir. Paris Poirier, Waterbearer Films, New York, 2001, DVD.

10. *Brother Outsider: The Life of Bayard Rustin*, dir. Nancy Kates and Bennett Singer, California Newsreel, San Francisco, 2002, DVD.

11. *Living with Pride: Ruth Ellis @ 100*, dir. Yvonne Welbon, Our Film Works, Chicago, 1999, DVD.

12. *We Were Here: The AIDS Years in San Francisco*, dir. David Weissman and Bill Weber, New Video, New York, 2011, DVD.

13. *How to Survive a Plague*, dir. David France, MPI Home Video, Orland Park, IL, 2012, DVD.

14. *After Stonewall: From the Riots to the Millennium*, dir. John Scagliotti, First Run, New York, 1999, DVD.

15. *The Celluloid Closet*, dir. Rob Epstein and Jeffrey Friedman, TriStar, Culver City, CA, 1996, DVD; Vito Russo, *The Celluloid Closet: Homosexuality in the Movies* (New York: Harper, 1981).

# Popular Culture

## Using Television, Film, and the Media to Explore LGBT History

SHARON ULLMAN

Some might wonder if using popular culture is the most appropriate vehicle for bringing the history of same-sex sexuality to life for students. After all, what kinds of images has the popular culture so many of our students consume actually presented of queer life in America? It seems self-evident that popular culture, until very recently, could be considered the best example of mainstream "invisibility" for this history. Besides . . . pop culture? Seriously? What can pop culture actually tell us that more substantial, archival-based research cannot present more effectively?

In the battle over who in U.S. history gets to speak, about what, and where, popular culture actually provides the most direct avenue for successfully incorporating LGBT history into an emerging technologically mediated collective past and reaching across differences in our students' backgrounds as we do so. What does that mean in practice? It means that when I show the 2008 movie *Milk*, about the life and murder of the 1970s San Francisco gay politician Harvey Milk, to students in my modern U.S. history lecture survey, everyone cries. Milk's story becomes my students' American history. Their grief is for themselves and this terrible loss in their "shared" past.

Our students often complain that history is boring or dry. But this kind of emotional connection helps animate their desire to learn more. While there is a risk that students might overinvest in the simplified, sentimental narratives that Hollywood usually provides and thereby ignore important complexities, nevertheless we risk even more if we dismiss the power these images have on them. Popular culture is an essential tool in helping teachers construct a wider narrative of U.S. history, not only one that includes "others" but one in which all students collectively see themselves as connected, both factually and emotionally, to a common, usable past.

In May 2012 Vice President Joe Biden told *Meet the Press* host David Gregory that the TV program "*Will & Grace* probably did more to educate the American public than almost anybody's ever done so far. People fear that which is different. Now they're beginning to understand."[1] Biden's well-meaning affection for this NBC situation comedy (1998–2006) about a gay man and his best friend, a straight woman, may have unintentionally wronged two generations of queer political activism, but his comment reflected a widespread social perception. Many heterosexuals of a particular age claim that they had never met a gay man or lesbian until quite recently. This implies a history of cultural silence around same-sex sexuality that the historical record simply does not bear out. Americans have been discussing homosexuality and gender-variant behavior for well over a hundred years, and references to both homosexuality and gender challenges have been staples of popular culture for a very long time.

There are a variety of ways to use popular culture to make this point to students. We can use recent films, television programs, YouTube content, and so on that have LGBT history content.[2] We can also use past examples of popular culture that included characters intended to be understood by audiences as gender variant and/or someone exhibiting same-sex desire. The first option offers the safety of narrative closure; we know what will happen, and we can often feel confident of the tone. Unfortunately, these kinds of sources are few and far between. I try to work with a combination of both current popular culture that tells the history in its own way and films and other earlier forms of pop culture that presented LGBT characters in their own time.

In some ways, this second set surprises students more. They come to realize that gender-variant activity and same-sex desire have been elements of popular culture for much longer than they had imagined. It also helps them understand why the prejudices against homosexuals and transgender individuals have lasted so long. After all, if no one ever met anyone "like that" and there was no discussion, how did stereotypes and bigotry flourish through the generations? One answer is, in fact, in a very vigorous popular culture.

In order to bring this point home, I use the famous 1914 silent comedy *A Florida Enchantment*. This film tells the story of magic seeds that turn the central characters into members of the "opposite" gender. Incorporating contemporary images of blackface comedy as well, *A Florida Enchantment* provides an excellent visual text through which to discuss the circulation of gendered, racial, and sexual assumptions in the early-twentieth-century United States. Both the film—and my students when they watch it—find the man becoming a woman much more amusing than the woman becoming a man. The ridicule heaped on this character gives students the chance to discuss the ways in which our culture finds male effeminacy much more disturbing than female masculinity. This conversation is helpful in exploring not only transgender history and the history of same-sex sexuality but also the history of sexism as a backdrop to thinking about changes in women's lives over time.[3]

*A Florida Enchantment* is covered in Vito Russo's 1981 book *The Celluloid Closet*,[4] which studies images of homosexuality in Hollywood through the mid–twentieth century and is a good general introductory resource for students. Additionally, the book was made into a fine documentary of the same name in 1995 and is excellent for classroom use, as Nicholas L. Syrett's essay in this volume notes. The documentary provides examples of numerous movie scenes through the 1950s and 1960s in which a character's homosexuality is highlighted. These images are very stereotyped, and students may find them offensive, so they need to be discussed with care. But they provide the opportunity for students to study the widespread availability of queer images prior to the 1990s. How the audiences watching films with these images in their own time understood what they were seeing can reveal a great deal about the social values that governed gender, race, and often class in the periods in question. This helps students realize that there is a deep history in the value structures they live with today.

Like all histories, the narrative that works best is one in which the conflicts emerge visibly in the society at large. As David K. Johnson's and Claire Bond Potter's essays in this volume make clear, the Cold War era, which lasted from the end of the Second World War to the early 1960s, tells our students a great deal about the ways governments overreach, become hysterical, and persecute minorities in times of fear. Homosexuals and gender-variant citizens were but some of many groups that faced intense persecution in this era. Additionally, the era is usually presented as one characterized by suffocating conformity and sharply policed social norms for sexual behavior. But when I teach the Cold War, I take a different approach, one similar to that suggested in Craig M. Loftin's and Ian Lekus's essays in this volume. I look for cracks in the system that reveal the history to come—the 1960s and beyond.

One approach I use is to have students investigate the popular culture frenzy surrounding Christine Jorgensen, one of the first genuinely famous male-to-female transsexuals. This obsession with Jorgensen helps us recognize that there were deep undercurrents of dissatisfaction with the government crackdown on individuality and the beginnings of resistance to accepted norms. Here was someone who chose her own gender and stood up to the public scrutiny with wit and dignity. Her 1952 surgery in Denmark made international news, and Jorgensen did her best to help manage the overwhelming fascination with her transition. Students can research and find online copies of almost everything Jorgensen wrote and/or produced. *The American Mercury*, a significant mid-twentieth-century national magazine, printed her self-penned account as a five-part series beginning on February 15, 1953. She also published a memoir in 1967. She made recordings, had a nightclub act, and became, herself, part of popular culture. The Jorgensen story is embedded in the 1950s public culture, if not always recalled by later generations. It is an important lesson about both the power and the limits of popular culture to sustain histories that challenge gender and sexual hierarchies.[5]

Another way to explore the limits of the closeted culture of the 1950s is through more recent cinematic depictions. A particularly useful film in this regard is director Todd Haynes's 2002 *Far from Heaven*. Haynes, probably the most significant figure in what came to be called the New Queer Cinema of the 1990s, has created numerous films with queer content. *Far from Heaven* rewrites 1950s melodrama conventions explicitly to incorporate closeted homosexuality as one of the famously repressed behaviors of the era. One assignment could be to ask students to watch *Far from Heaven* alongside *All That Heaven Allows*, Douglas Sirk's 1955 melodrama with Rock Hudson and Jane Wyman, which Haynes draws on for his 2007 update. The presence of Rock Hudson, a 1950s and 1960s superstar and a closeted gay man throughout his career, calls forth the fifties sensibility for students as well.

Joe Biden came of age during the Jorgensen publicity frenzy and no doubt watched many of the films addressed in *The Celluloid Closet*. What his comment about *Will & Grace* tells us is that he did not identify with those marginal, often ridiculed, popular culture characters. Like most audience members in the 1990s, however, he could identify with Will. How does a historically marginalized, criminalized, and supposedly silenced population move into the mainstream of society? A strong and vibrant activist movement for social justice propelled this particular transformation, but popular culture played a distinct role in the expansion of a vision of citizenship that now includes LGBT individuals.

In 1969 the famed Stonewall riots shone a new public light on those engaged in same-sex sexual practices and gender-variant self-presentations. The timing of Stonewall was no accident. The years preceding it marked one of the great moments in civil rights activism in American history. We often associate this era with Martin Luther King Jr. and the civil rights movement to end apartheid in the U.S. South, but we should not forget Cesar Chavez building the United Farm Workers Union and leading migrant farm worker strikes in the West throughout the late 1960s and early 1970s, members of the American Indian Movement occupying Alcatraz in 1969, or the Third World student strike at San Francisco State University in 1968. This was a period of significant activism when many who felt left out of the dominant society aggressively demanded to be heard. Why not the drag queens, queers, and transgender customers of the Stonewall Inn too? In a period famous for sexual liberation, driven initially by heterosexuals excited by advances in contraceptive technology, such as "the pill" (introduced in 1960), and the growing second-wave feminist movement, which critiqued sexual double standards and limits on women's freedom, why should it not have been "good to be gay"—the rallying cry of groups such as the Gay Liberation Front, Gay Activist Alliance, and radical lesbian groups that flourished in Stonewall's aftermath and forced a new consciousness on the public at large?

Unsurprisingly, then, the 1970s marked a watershed in popular representations of LGBT individuals. While many of these representations were limited to individual TV episodes and remained deeply problematic, a clear shift occurred over the decade. Students can find episodes of popular television series such as *Police Woman*, *Marcus Welby MD*, *The Streets of San Francisco*, *All in the Family*, and *The Bob Newhart Show* with which to chronicle the TV transformation from tormented gay malcontents (or even psychopaths) to the personal friend who challenges the homophobia of the central character.[6] As early as 1972, *That Certain Summer*, a TV movie starring Hal Holbrook as a father who tells his son he is gay, won a Golden Globe for Best Drama. By the mid- to late 1970s, the change was well under way. In 1978 Gena Rowlands and Jane Alexander could sympathetically portray a lesbian couple about to lose their son in *A Question of Love*. Students can also find and study *Soap*, an ABC comedy that ran from 1977 to 1981. One of the first television programs with a central, positive gay character (played by Billy Crystal), *Soap* was the *Will & Grace* of its day, making audiences like and care about a gay male protagonist.

Movies in the immediate post-Stonewall era followed a less clear trajectory. Popular films from the 1970s include the filmed version of the Broadway play *Boys in the Band* (1970), which excoriated gay male life while still focusing on it openly to the thrill of many gay men in the audience. The original French version of *La Cage aux Folles* appeared on American screens in 1978 and became a massive hit. Yet in 1980 director William Friedkin created the despised thriller *Cruising*, starring Al Pacino as a policeman going undercover in the New York gay S/M leather subculture to catch a murderer. This film prompted large protests as LGBT activists haunted the production and forced periodic set shutdowns. One excellent assignment for exploring the expanding queer popular culture of the 1970s is to focus on the (still popular) cult classic *The Rocky Horror Picture Show* (1975), which celebrated its sense of perversity in all arenas. Students can research the film, its social context, and the lengthy cult status it attained with the performance culture that accompanied it.[7] Not until the 1980s and movies such as *Personal Best* (1982), *Lianna* (1983), *The Hunger* (1983), and *Desert Hearts* (1985) did lesbians became part of pop culture iconography.

As students survey this explosion of imagery in the 1970s and 1980s, they might discuss the impact of Stonewall and increasing LGBT activism on television and movie portrayals of LGBT individuals and communities. They should also contrast the two media. Television is more intimate, entering the home and potentially available to a much wider and more diverse audience. The simultaneity of television, in this era before technology made it possible to record and watch videos at home, means that everyone watched the same program at the same broadcast moment. Television had the capacity to be much more influential than cinema in disseminating new imagery. Working with both kinds of visual popular culture is essential, however, for revealing not only the emerging change but also the conflicted and halting steps it took to get there. This, too, mirrors the society at large. The decade of the 1970s is a fascinating period of expanding opportunity for many women and minorities but also an era of political retrenchment, national economic decline, and reaction as the country moved to the right with the election of Ronald Reagan in 1980.

It is, of course, at that exact moment—the linked and conflicting trends represented by the push for women's rights, acknowledgment of LGBT citizenship, and sexual freedom broadly defined, along with the election of Reagan and the rise of the Religious Right—that the United States and the world came to grips with a new deadly illness. Most students know very little about the history of the AIDS epidemic, and popular culture is an inadequate vehicle through which to educate them. Still, it can be a useful element when combined with other sources, as Nicholas Syrett's essay in this volume discusses. There are several films commonly used when exploring this history. *An Early Frost*, a 1985 TV movie, and *Philadelphia* (1992) give students a window into the national conversation of the period. The film that I regularly assign when teaching this history is 1989's *Longtime Companion*. Released at the height of the epidemic, this melodrama traces its impact on a small group of friends. Students often find the film sentimental and insufficiently conscious of race and class, but *Longtime Companion* accomplishes real work in engaging students' interest and provoking questions for further study. I usually pair the film with David Román's 2006 essay "Remembering AIDS: A Reconsideration of the Film *Longtime Companion*."[8]

Both the AIDS epidemic and the subsequent early-twenty-first-century civil rights successes for the LGBT movement have created a much richer popular culture canvas. The modern LGBT era is suffused with popular culture references. From Madonna to Lady Gaga to the ABC hit comedy *Modern Family* to the *It Gets Better* YouTube series, students can turn in any direction to see entertaining images that celebrate queer life and community. To students popular culture is *the* place to see LGBT full citizenship enacted. One of the great advantages of pulling students into the past universe of pop culture is that it allows them to reflect on the dramatic changes that took place in a single generation of cultural imagery. Additionally, however, they can be called on to identify what remains the same. Despite the boomlet of cable television offerings such as *Queer as Folk* (2000–5) and *The L Word* (2004–9), gay men remain trapped in specific cultural stereotypes. Lesbians are seen rarely and are still often framed as cultural gifts to heterosexual sexual fantasy. Bisexuals are missing, too. Transgender individuals remain relatively invisible in mainstream popular culture, although they are increasingly sought out for reality TV.[9] None of this feels particularly revolutionary.

The future of popular culture lies, however, in the fragmented digital universe. As popular entertainment migrates entirely to the virtual, the effects of popular culture on the LGBT future remain unclear. Individuals will gain greater access to presenting their own stories, and millions of others will find themselves more willing to listen; the potential is extraordinary. As a final exercise on the use of popular culture, we might all ask our students what they see today and ask them to imagine what their children will see "tomorrow."[10]

### NOTES

1. Adam B. Vary, "Joe Biden Credits 'Will and Grace' in His (Sorta) Endorsement of Gay Marriage: The Stars Respond," *Entertainment Weekly*, May 6, 2012, http://insidetv.ew.com/2012/05/06/joe-biden-will-and-grace-gay-marriage/, accessed May 7, 2013.

2. See, for example, the films *A Single Man*, set in the isolation of the early 1960s; *Milk*, on the life and death of Harvey Milk; *Brokeback Mountain*, which interrogates the frustrated longtime relationship of two men starting in the 1960s; *The Laramie Project*, on the 1998 murder of Matthew Shepard in Wyoming; *Hedwig and the Angry Inch*, a rock musical with a transgender heroine set at the end of the Cold War; *Boys Don't Cry*, about the murder of Brandon Teena, a young transgender man, in 1993; and *The Wedding Banquet*, which addresses immigration issues and culture conflict. The *It Gets Better* video series on YouTube calls forth numerous individual personal histories, http://www.itgetsbetter.org/, accessed July 13, 2013.

3. Texts that might accompany the film include Bruce R. Brasell, "A Seed for Change: The Engenderment of *A Florida Enchantment*," *Cinema Journal* 36, no. 4 (1997): 3–21; and Siobhan B. Somerville, "The Queer Career of Jim Crow: Racial and Sexual Transformation in *A Florida Enchantment*," in *A Feminist Reader in Early Cinema*, ed. Diane Negra (Durham, NC: Duke University Press, 2002), 251–69.

4. Vito Russo, *The Celluloid Closet: Homosexuality in the Movies*, rev. ed. (New York: HarperCollins, 1987).

5. Sources on Jorgensen are wide ranging. The website http://www.christine jorgensen.org/ (accessed May 7, 2013) provides links to her publications and

recordings. There is a fine chapter on Jorgensen in Joanne Meyerowitz, *How Sex Changed: A History of Transsexuality in the United States* (Cambridge, MA: Harvard University Press, 2004).

6. See Ron Becker, *Gay TV and Straight America* (New Brunswick, NJ: Rutgers University Press, 2006); Stephen Tropiano, *The Prime Time Closet: A History of Gays and Lesbians on TV* (New York: Applause Books, 2002); "Archive Study Guide: Lesbian, Gay, Bisexual, and Transgender Television: Sitcoms and Episodic Dramas," UCLA Film and Television Archive, http://www.cinema.ucla.edu/sites/default/files/LGBT_TV.pdf, accessed May 7, 2013; and "Archive Study Guide: Lesbian, Gay, Bisexual, and Transgender Television, Made for TV Movies," UCLA Film and Television Archive, http://www.cinema.ucla.edu/sites/default/files/LGBT_TV_MOVIES.pdf, accessed May 7, 2013.

7. There are many sources to consult on *The Rocky Horror Picture Show*. A representative sample includes Jeffrey Andrew Weinstock, ed., *Reading Rocky Horror: The Rocky Horror Picture Show and Popular Culture* (New York: Palgrave Macmillan, 2008); and Larry Gross, "Out of the Mainstream: Sexual Minorities and the Mass Media," *Journal of Homosexuality* 21, nos. 1–2 (1991): 19–46.

8. David Román, "Remembering AIDS: A Reconsideration of the Film *Longtime Companion*," *GLQ: A Journal of Lesbian and Gay Studies* 12, no. 2 (2006): 281–301. Other well-known "AIDS films" from the period are *Parting Glances* and *And the Band Played On*.

9. Jacob Bernstein, "In Their Own Terms: The Growing Transgender Presence in Popular Culture," *New York Times*, March 12, 2014.

10. For further information, see Guillermo Avila-Saavedra, "Nothing Queer about Queer Television: Televised Construction of Gay Masculinities," *Media, Culture, and Society* 31, no. 1 (2009): 5–21; Amber B. Raley and Jennifer L. Lucas, "Stereotype or Success? Prime-Time Television's Portrayals of Gay Male, Lesbian, and Bisexual Characters," *Journal of Homosexuality* 51, no. 2 (2006): 19–38; C. Lee Harrington, "Homosexuality on *All My Children*: Transforming the Daytime Landscape," *Journal of Broadcasting and Electronic Media* 47, no. 2 (2003): 216–35; Kathleen Battles and Wendy Hilton-Morrow, "Gay Characters in Conventional Spaces: Will and Grace and the Situation Comedy Genre," *Critical Studies in Media Communication* 19, no. 1 (2002): 87–105; Larry Gross, "Out of the Mainstream: Sexual Minorities and the Mass Media," *Journal of Homosexuality* 21, nos. 1–2 (1991): 19–46; Rodger Streitmatter, *From Perverts to Fab Five: The Media's Changing Depiction of Gay Men and Lesbians* (New York: Routledge, 2008).

# Queer History Goes Digital

*Using Outhistory.org in the Classroom*

CATHERINE O. JACQUET

Since its inception in the early 1990s, digital history has evolved into an exciting and dynamic field.[1] Historical websites provide unparalleled access to resources and materials to help scholars, teachers, and students engage with and understand the past. Online resources are particularly useful when studying emerging subfields, such as LGBT history, that lack the stature or presence of long-standing traditional disciplines. As a relatively young field, LGBT history is still developing and not embedded in most history and social studies curricula. As such, scholarship and sources on the queer past are generally not easily or widely accessible. The Web has helped to change that. Indeed, LGBT history has joined the digital age, and an incredible range of resources are now available online, providing unique opportunities for teachers and students to access and learn about the queer past.[2]

This essay focuses on Outhistory.org, the premier site for LGBT history on the Web.[3] Founded in 2003 by gay historian Jonathan Ned Katz, Outhistory.org boasts rich collections on the LGBT past that are particularly well suited for classroom use.[4] Focused on the United States, the website features an array of community histories, biographies, digitized archival material, oral histories, and primary sources from the precolonial era to the present, providing essential resources for classroom teachers. With a simple click, teachers and students can investigate, conceptualize, and contribute to the making of the LGBT past.

This essay focuses on some highlights from the site selected specifically with college and high school teachers in mind. Many of the suggestions outlined here are ones that I have used in college classrooms, and most can easily be adapted for high school classrooms. The possibilities of Outhistory are numerous and ever changing, as the community-based site is always expanding with new material created and added by site visitors. This unique user participation feature is another exciting way to incorporate Outhistory into the classroom. Students can contribute material to the site and thus engage in the production of historical knowledge, becoming not just consumers but also makers of history.

To guide teachers in their use of Outhistory, I begin by focusing on two major types of sources that the site offers: primary sources and community histories. I then highlight several examples of user-created content, demonstrating how students have effectively participated in history making. It is my hope that this brief survey of the website will orient and inspire teachers and scholars to take advantage of its distinctive features and myriad possibilities for creatively engaging students with queer history.

## Primary Sources

With Outhistory, students are able to easily access primary sources, as well as read additional commentary by collectors and historians about the sources. These editorial notes are useful for classroom conversations about the making, collecting, and writing of LGBT history. Three of the primary source collections are especially well suited for use in history survey courses, and below I provide an overview and suggest classroom exercises for each.

The collection titled "Native Americans/Gay Americans 1528–1976" (http://outhistory.org/exhibits/show/native-americans-gay-americans) is adapted from Jonathan Ned Katz's 1976 primary source reader, *Gay American History*.[5] This collection is instructive for students of U.S. and LGBT history in multiple ways. First, it provides essential primary sources on European and indigenous contact in the Americas. Using these sources, students in standard U.S. history courses can see how concerns around sexuality and sexual customs prominently figured in European discourses and actions in response to indigenous peoples. Europeans justified their conquest of indigenous peoples partially by pointing to what they deemed the natives' sinful and perverse sexual customs. In my classes, I've had students pick five primary sources and consider the following questions.

1. Who wrote the document? Whose perspective are we getting?
2. How did newcomers respond to the gender and sexual customs of indigenous peoples?
3. What words does the author use to describe indigenous peoples and practices?
4. What can we learn from these documents? How do the biases of the authors inform what we can know?

These questions are useful when compiled as a worksheet to be used as either an in-class activity or a take-home assignment that students complete in advance of group discussion.

"Native Americans/Gay Americans" is also productive for thinking about the development of the scholarship on LGBT history. When Katz compiled *Gay American History*, gay and lesbian scholars were in the very early stages of creating and recording a cohesive and viable gay past. This was also a time when very little historical scholarship existed on indigenous peoples from their own perspectives. In his 1976 introduction to the sources, reproduced on Outhistory, Katz attributed an identity of "gay" or "lesbian" to his subjects. What might have seemed appropriate in his historical context is less so today. In the decades since, Native American scholars and activists have developed a prolific scholarship on traditional indigenous gender and sexual systems.[6] The newer scholarship departs significantly from both early European accounts of the indigenous "berdache" and 1970s accounts of native homosexuality or cross-dressing. Since then we have come to recognize that the majority of the people described in Katz's documents were not "homosexual" but are better understood as Two-Spirit, occupying an identity category not based on sexuality but on gender, occupation, or spirituality.[7] Katz's introduction, then, is itself a historical document and provides a unique way for students to see the evolution of the field of LGBT history. Questions students might consider are:

1. How does Katz define the sexual and gendered identities of the people who are described in the primary sources?
2. Considering Katz's historical context, what assumptions does he

make and why? How would you rewrite Katz's introduction today?

While Katz's collection offers critical perspectives on the contact period, a significant portion of the content available on Outhistory focuses on the late nineteenth and twentieth centuries. Earl Lind's partial memoir *The Riddle of the Underworld* (http://outhistory.org/exhibits /show/earl-lind), for example, offers students a rare firsthand account of the gender-nonconforming experience in the early twentieth century. *Riddle* is the last of a trilogy of memoirs written between 1919 and 1922 by Earl Lind, aka Ralph Werther, aka Jennie June, a self-described "androgyne." While Lind's first two memoirs are available in print, *Riddle* is only available on Outhistory. The three works of the trilogy stand as one of the earliest accounts of what we might today identify as "transgender" experience in the United States.

*Riddle* is a useful text for considering the construction of sexual and gendered identities and how identity categories and terminology change over time. Lind understood themselves[8] to be bisexual; in their context, this meant a person who was both male and female. In their words, "I was foreordained to live part of my life as a man and part as woman." Students will recognize the very different use of the term *bisexual* during Lind's time compared to our own. In addition, Lind identified as an *androgyne*, a term never encountered today, while terms such as *gay* and *transgender* are absent from the memoir. Using *Riddle*, students can see how terms appear and disappear, and that no identity category is inevitable. The narrative challenges students to think critically about constructions of sex and gender, both historically and currently, and to consider the problems of attributing modern labels to historical actors. Questions to consider include:

1. How does Lind self-identify? What evidence (physical, psychic, etc.) do they use to base that identity?
2. How is Lind's gendered identity connected to their understanding of their sexual identity?
3. Based on the memoir, what can we learn about the dominant understandings of sex, sexuality, and sexual behavior at this time?
4. How does Lind name and describe different kinds of sexual and gendered identities?

5. What do we learn about urban life and the sexual subcultures in large American cities at this time period?
6. What kind of lives had so-called sexual deviants made for themselves by the early twentieth century?

Linked to the manuscript is Drexel University professor Randall Sell's account of finding *Riddle of the Underworld* in 2010 (http://out history.org/exhibits/show/earl-lind/related). Sell describes the process of searching for and collecting LGBT-related materials as a graduate student in the 1990s. He haphazardly discovered a portion of Lind's third memoir tucked in an unrelated manuscript collection at the National Library of Medicine. With Sell's account, students get a firsthand look at the often unexpected and surprising turns of historical research. Students will also recognize that the history of LGBT experience is still very much in the making.

For the gay liberation era, Outhistory features all but one of the nine-issue run of one of the first gay liberation movement periodicals in the United States, *Come Out!* (http://outhistory.org/exhibits/show /come-out-magazine-1969-1972/the-come-out-archive).[9] Originally published by the Gay Liberation Front in New York City between 1969 and 1972, the digitized collection gives students direct access to gay liberation in its formative years.[10] In a standard U.S. history course, teachers can assign *Come Out!* as part of a unit on the social movements of the 1950s–70s. The content of the magazine not only gives students an in-depth look at gay liberation, but it also clearly demonstrates the connections between progressive movements of the time. Students will be able to recognize the antiracist, socialist, and feminist perspectives found in many of the articles throughout the nine-issue run of *Come Out!*

The availability of multiple issues makes *Come Out!* an ideal source for group work. As either a classroom activity or a homework assignment, split students into small groups. Each group member should pick one issue of the magazine to read. Have students answer questions about their issues and then reconvene as a group to discuss their findings. Questions for students to consider as they are reading the magazine include:

1. What were some of the political issues that the authors of *Come Out!* tackled?

2. What does *gay liberation* mean? Who does it include?
3. What other movements are discussed or represented in the magazine? What does this tell you?
4. What did you learn about the Gay Liberation Front by reading this magazine?
5. What did you learn about the early days of the gay liberation movement in New York City?

Questions for students to consider as a group include:

1. How did gay liberation change over time? What stayed the same and what did not?
2. Did any contested topics or new topics emerge in the magazine during this three-year time period?

Linked to the collection is Gay Liberation Front member and *Come Out!* contributor Perry Brass's recollections about his own experiences coming out as a gay teen in the 1960s and later helping to create one of the seminal publications of the early gay liberation movement (http://outhistory.org/exhibits/show/coming-out-into-come-out/perrys-story). Reading Brass's firsthand account gives students a view into gay life in the 1960s and 1970s, an insider's look at an early gay liberation organization, and the process by which *Come Out!* was created. With Brass's account, the magazine and the movement come to life in a unique way, helping students to understand how movements happen.

Outhistory features additional collections on Stonewall and the early gay liberation movement, including digitized copies of the Stonewall police reports (http://outhistory.org/exhibits/show/stonewall-riot-police-reports) and a community history of gay liberation in New York City (http://outhistory.org/exhibits/show/gay-liberation-in-new-york-city).

### Community Histories

One of the many strengths of Outhistory is the wide range of community histories available on the site. These local histories introduce students to queer community formation and bring historical figures, activists, groups, and movements to life. Spanning the country from coast to coast, the community histories include both well-known urban gay meccas, such as San Francisco, New York City, and Chicago, and areas less often recognized as significant in queer history, such as Las Vegas, Nevada; Bloomington, Indiana; and Richmond, Virginia. With these community histories students can examine queer life in local contexts and get a much more nuanced understanding of LGBT history and struggles for justice.

Much of the literature on trans history centers on male-to-female (MTF) experience. The collection "Man-i-fest: FTM Mentorship in San Francisco, 1976–2009," provides a much-needed corrective to this (http://outhistory.org/exhibits/show/man-i-fest). It focuses on the life and work of Lou Sullivan, a gay-identified transman who founded FTM International, the first female-to-male (FTM) organization in the country.[11] Sullivan became a mentor and leader in the FTM community, corresponding with FTM-identified individuals globally throughout the 1980s. Showcasing letters and selections from the organization's *Gateway* newsletter, this collection gives students a firsthand look at how Sullivan mentored and advocated for the community. Sullivan is thought to be the first FTM to die of AIDS. His story thus provides an important alternative lens through which to view the AIDS crisis. The collection includes links to obscure interviews with Sullivan, now available as YouTube videos, where he discusses his transition and his struggle with AIDS. Questions for students to consider include:

1. What issues does Sullivan talk about in his letters to a correspondent named David?
2. Based on your reading of the *Gateway* newsletter, what were some key issues for FTMs at the time? What kinds of experiences and medical advice are transmen sharing with one another?
3. Why do you think newsletters such as *Gateway* were so important to the FTM community?

The collection "Queer Bronzeville: The History of African American Gays and Lesbians on Chicago's South Side (1885–1985)" (http://outhistory.org/exhibits/show/queer-bronzeville) looks at the development of queer culture over the course of the twentieth century in Chicago's Bronzeville neighborhood. Its coverage extends from the lives of masculine women blues singers of the 1920s to the emergence of gay liberation in the 1970s. I have used the "Queer Bronzeville" collection in my classes to introduce students to the early history of drag balls, a particularly queer form of performance art.[12] The drag balls were wildly popular events, and by the 1950s they attracted thousands of straight and gay patrons in such cities as Chicago, New York, and Atlanta. The "Queer Bronzeville" collection includes substantial sections on early- to mid-twentieth-century drag and features transcripts of interviews with two female impersonators who performed at the time, Nancy Kelly and Jacques Cristion.

Students will be surprised to learn that beginning in the 1930s African American newspapers included fairly extensive coverage of drag balls. I have used the "Bronzeville Collection" as a prompt for students to do their own primary source research on drag balls in the black press, pointing them in particular to the *Chicago Defender*. First, I had students read the "Queer Bronzeville" collection and pick out search terms that they could use to find newspaper articles. They then conducted searches using the *Chicago Defender* online (available through ProQuest). This is a particularly useful exercise for helping students learn how to do historical research. As they conduct their research, they quickly realize that a search for "drag ball(s)" turns up almost no results. It is here that the search terms they identified while reading "Queer Bronzeville" (such as the names of people, places, or events) come into play. Once they enter terms such as "Valda Gray" or "Cabin Inn" or "Finnie's Balls," students find numerous articles. They are also challenged to consider the language used at the time. A search for "female impersonator," for example, turns up dozens of articles, whereas a search for a more modern term such as "drag queen" turns up almost nothing. With this exercise, students get a sense of how to do research in historical newspapers; they are challenged to grapple with the issues that historians face as we delve into the past and to engage with the language of the era we are studying. As a prompt for primary source research and on its own, the "Queer Bronzeville" collection provides a rich community history that gives students a look at queer life and culture in its local context.

Many teachers will find on Outhistory a collection close to home; if not from their actual city or state, at least there is something with regional relevance to their students. From Las Vegas to Lincoln and Minneapolis to New York, the community histories on Outhistory give students an opportunity to understand the LGBT past on a local level, enriching their understanding of a national story that is far less unified than is often assumed.

## History of the Community, for the Community, by the Community

One of the most exciting features of Outhistory is the opportunity for community members to contribute content to the website. When he proposed the site in 2003, Jonathan Ned Katz imagined a "democratic history-making project" that would engage the public in the production of historical knowledge.[13] The result was an interactive website that allows users "to write history themselves or to upload materials from their personal collections."[14] Since Outhistory launched, the website has solicited contributions from scholars, activists, history aficionados, and students of LGBT history nationwide. The result is a website that reflects shared knowledge, rich in diversity and historical depth and breadth. Originally conceived using Wikimedia software, the Outhistory site is now built on Omeka, a user-friendly open-source web-publishing platform that makes uploading content easy. Students do not need to have any web design knowledge to contribute to the site, and the staff members at Outhistory, who vet all the material, are eager to assist.[15]

By encouraging community participation, the website provides a rare and unique opportunity for students to share in the production of knowledge and to publish their work online. There are dozens of ways in which students can participate in content creation. In one of my advanced history courses, for example, the students wrote biographies on historical trans, gender-nonconforming, or intersex individuals (they can be viewed at http://outhistory.org/exhibits/show/tgi-bios/exhibit). From the third-century Roman emperor Elagalabus to twentieth-century radical trans activist Sylvia Rivera, the collection covers a wide range of times and places, and it includes people both well known and mostly unknown in the historical record. My students did their own investigating to select a historical figure, pursued several months of research, and finally wrote and uploaded their biographies. They were encouraged to include images and links to other websites or videos on their final webpages.

Other college teachers have facilitated student contributions, providing new content for Outhistory while demonstrating how class projects might be structured. One such student project is the collection titled "LGBT Identities, Communities, and Resistance in North Carolina, 1945–2012" (http://outhistory.org/exhibits/show/nc-lgbt). Produced by students of David Palmer at the University of North Carolina at Chapel Hill, the collection covers community histories from across this southern state. University of Michigan professor Esther Newton had the students in her Lesbian History course create a collection titled "Lesbians in the Twentieth Century" (http://outhistory.org/exhibits /show/lesbians-20th-century). Newton's students wrote entries on lesbian life from the 1920s to the beginning of the twenty-first century. These are a few of many ways in which students can get hands-on experience creating and publishing history. The staff at Outhistory welcomes your suggestions and ideas for student projects.

## Conclusion

Since its inception in 2003, Outhistory has sought to bring the queer past to a national audience and to engage that audience in the practice of historical inquiry. The possibilities of Outhistory are far more than what can be contained in a short essay. It is my hope that this essay can serve as a reference guide and provide some groundwork on which teachers can build as they present the history of LGBT people and movements to their students. It is also my hope that the materials presented on Outhistory will encourage and inspire teachers and their students to think deeply and critically about historical evidence and the diversity of LGBT life across space and time.[16]

### NOTES

1. For an excellent resource and guide to history online, see Daniel J. Cohen and Roy Rosenzweig, *Digital History: A Guide to Gathering, Preserving, and Presenting the Past on the Web* (Philadelphia: University of Pennsylvania Press, 2006). The premier resource for digital history is the Roy Rosenzweig Center for History and New Media at George Mason University, www.chnm.gmu.edu.

2. While there are thousands of LGBT websites—covering everything from dating to travel to retail to social support networks—I am referencing those sites, typically produced by historians or historical societies, that focus specifically on LGBT history.

3. Outhistory is certainly not the only queer history website available. In my research on queer history online, I have found many excellent sites with rich materials and resources for classroom use. For the purposes of this essay, I have chosen to focus on Outhistory for several reasons. First, the site is national in scope and thus allows teachers and students to get a sense of the broad range

of experiences that make up queer American history. Second, the site is not limited to any particular topic or interest and encompasses the broadest range of LGBT history from politics to popular culture, art to activism, and science to social life. Finally, I worked for one year as project coordinator for Outhistory, managing content and working on the site redesign. As such, I became very well acquainted with the resources available on Outhistory and, having used many of them in my classrooms, can speak to their utility firsthand.

In addition to Outhistory, educators, researchers, and students can access an incredible array of LGBT history resources online. Examples of excellent local history sites include www.chicagogayhistory.com (Chicago), www.glbt historymuseum.com/joomla15/ (central Florida), www.historyproject.org (Boston), http://www.centralpalgbtcenter.org/lgbt-history-project (central Pennsylvania), and www.mkelgbthist.org (Milwaukee). Many LGBT archives, museums, and historical societies maintain websites featuring rich resources such as digitized exhibits and collections. These include the National Archive of Gay and Lesbian History (New York), www.gaycenter.org/community /archive; ONE Archives (Los Angeles), http://www.onearchives.org; GLBT Historical Society (San Francisco), www.glbthistory.org; Lesbian Herstory Archives (New York), www.lesbianherstoryarchives.org; Leather Archives and Museum (Chicago), http://www.leatherarchives.org/home.htm (see also its tumblr page at http://leatherarchives.tumblr.com); Latino GLBT History Project (Washington, DC), http://www.latinoglbthistory.org/home; National LGBT Museum (Washington, DC), http://nationallgbtmuseum.org/#/home/; Tucson Gay Historical Society (Tucson), www.tucsongayhistoricalsociety.org; and Pop-Up Museum of Queer History, http://www.queermuseum.com (see also its tumblr page at http://queermuseum.tumblr.com, which features a rich collection of queer history, mostly focused on people and events in New York City). Websites dealing with specific LGBT interests include the LGBT Religious Archives Network, http://www.lgbtran.org/index.aspx; and Queer Music Heritage, http://queermusicheritage.us. Also of interest is http://www .glbtq.com, an online encyclopedia of gay, lesbian, bisexual, transgender, and queer culture, which includes both contemporary and historical coverage.

4. For an excellent article on the creation and evolution of Outhistory, see Lauren Jae Gutterman, "Outhistory.org: An Experiment in LGBTQ Community History-Making," *Public Historian* 32, no. 4 (November 2010): 96–109.

5. Jonathan Ned Katz, *Gay American History: Lesbians and Gay Men in the U.S.A.* (New York: Thomas Y. Crowell, 1976).

6. I have found selected essays in Sue Ellen Jacobs, Wesley Thomas, and Sabine Lang, eds., *Two-Spirit People: Native American Gender Identity, Sexuality, and Spirituality* (Urbana: University of Illinois Press, 1997), to be incredibly useful in the classroom.

7. See Sabine Lang, "Various Kinds of Two-Spirit People: Gender Variance and Homosexuality in Native American Communities," in *Two-Spirit People: Native American Gender Identity, Sexuality, and Spirituality*, ed. Sue Ellen Jacobs, Wesley Thomas, and Sabine Lang (Urbana: University of Illinois Press, 1997).

8. I use the gender-neutral plural in place of a gendered singular pronoun since Lind/Werther/June occupied different genders at various points in their life.

9. This digitized collection is exclusive to Outhistory. The magazine is otherwise only available via microfiche or in archival collections.

10. The Gay Liberation Front was formed within a month of the Stonewall riots and is self-described as "a coalition of radical and revolutionary homosexual men and women committed to fight the oppression of the homosexual as a minority group."

11. The organization exists to this day and is now the largest and longest-running FTM organization in the world.

12. In conjunction with the "Queer Bronzeville" collection, I have had students read Allen Drexel, "Before Paris Burned: Race, Class, and Male Homosexuality on the Chicago South Side, 1935–1960," in *Creating a Place for Ourselves: Lesbian, Gay, and Bisexual Community Histories*, ed. Brett Beemyn (New York: Routledge, 1997). "Queer Bronzeville" is an essential companion to this article; the newspaper photos, interviews, and other primary sources in the collection allow students to truly capture the era.

13. Gutterman, "Outhistory.org," 104.

14. Ibid., 102.

15. For information on Omeka, see www.omeka.org. The Outhistory team is happy to answer any questions and can be reached at outhistory@gmail.com.

16. "About Outhistory," http://outhistory.org/about-outhistory.

# Contributors

**Genny Beemyn** is director of the Stonewall Center at the University of Massachusetts, Amherst, and the author, with Sue Rankin, of *The Lives of Transgender People* (Columbia University Press, 2011). Hir most recent book is *A Queer Capital: A History of Gay Life in Washington, D.C.* (Routledge, 2014).

**Aaron Belkin** is a professor of political science at San Francisco State University and director of the Palm Center. He is the author of *Bring Me Men: Military Masculinity and the Benign Façade of American Empire, 1998–2001* (Oxford University Press, 2012) and *How We Won: Progressive Lessons from the Repeal of "Don't Ask, Don't Tell"* (Huffington Post Media Group, 2011).

**Nan Alamilla Boyd** is a professor of women and gender studies at San Francisco State University, where she teaches courses in the history of sexuality, queer theory, historical methodology, and urban tourism. A longtime volunteer at the GLBT Historical Society and founder of the society's oral history project, she is the author of *Wide Open Town: A History of Queer San Francisco to 1965* (University of California Press, 2003) and coeditor with Horacio N. Roque Ramírez of *Bodies of Evidence: The Practice of Queer Oral History* (Oxford University Press, 2012).

**Jennifer Brier** is director of gender and women's studies and associate professor of gender and women's studies and history at the University of Illinois at Chicago. She is the author of *Infectious Ideas: U.S. Political Response to the AIDS Crisis* (University of North Carolina Press, 2009). She is also a public historian. Brier curated *Out in Chicago*, the Chicago History Museum's prize-winning exhibition on LGBT history in Chicago, and *Surviving and Thriving: AIDS, Politics and Culture*, a traveling and digital exhibition for the National Library of Medicine. She is currently at work on a major public history project called History Moves, a community-curated mobile gallery that will provide a space where Chicago-based community organizers and activists can share their histories with a wide audience.

**John D'Emilio** is a professor of gender and women's studies and history at the University of Illinois at Chicago. A pioneer in the field of LGBT studies and the history of sexuality, he is the author or editor of *Sexual Politics, Sexual Communities: The Making of a Homosexual Minority in the United States, 1940–1970* (University of Chicago Press, 1983); *Lost Prophet: The Life and Times of Bayard Rustin* (University of Chicago Press, 2004); *In a New Century: Essays on Queer History, Politics, and Community Life* (University of Wisconsin Press, 2014); and *Intimate Matters: A History of Sexuality in America* (University of Chicago Press, 1988), coauthored with Estelle B. Freedman and now in its third edition. His awards include the Brudner Prize from Yale University for lifetime contributions to gay and lesbian studies, the Lifetime Achievement Award of the Publishing Triangle, and the Roy Rosenzweig Distinguished Service Award of the Organization of American Historians.

**David D. Doyle Jr.** is the director of the University Honors Program, assistant dean of Dedman College, and adjunct assistant professor in the Clements Department of History at Southern Methodist University in Dallas. He is currently at work on a book examining male sexuality in late-nineteenth-century New York and New England and has published reviews and articles in *Reviews in American History* and the *Journal of the History of Sexuality*.

**Thomas A. Foster** is an associate professor of history at DePaul University. He is the author of *Sex and the Eighteenth-Century Man: Massachusetts and the History of Sexuality in America* (Beacon Press, 2007) and the editor of three volumes, including *Long before Stonewall: Histories of Same-Sex Sexuality in Early America* (New York University Press, 2007).

**Dáša Frančíková** received her PhD in history and women's studies from the University of Michigan. She is a lecturer in the Department of Feminist Studies at the University of California, Santa Barbara, and has published in the *Journal of Women's History* and *Gender & History*. Her new project is entitled "Going Global, Getting Personal: Transnational Lesbian Organizing and Relationships in the Late Twentieth and the Early Twenty-First Centuries."

**Susan K. Freeman** is an associate professor and chair of gender and women's studies at Western Michigan University. She is the author of *Sex Goes to School: Girls and Sex Education before the 1960s* (University of Illinois Press, 2008). Her current research examines the development of gay and lesbian studies classes beginning in 1969.

**Marilyn E. Hegarty** received her PhD from Ohio State University, where she also taught for several years, including courses in U.S. history, women's history, and sexuality studies. She is the author of *Victory Girls, Khaki-Wackies, and Patriotutes: The Regulation of Female Sexuality during World War II* (New York University Press, 2008).

**Emily K. Hobson** is an assistant professor of history and gender, race, and identity at the University of Nevada, Reno, where she teaches twentieth-century U.S. history, LGBT history, race and ethnicity, and gender and queer studies. From 2000 through 2004, she worked with Californians for Justice, a nonprofit organization that organizes low-income high school students of color to achieve racial justice, immigrant rights, and LGBTQ rights in public schools. She is currently completing her first book, *Lavender and Red: Race, Empire, and Solidarity in the Gay and Lesbian Left*.

**Daniel Hurewitz** teaches U.S. history at Hunter College in New York, where his classes include the second half of the U.S. survey as well as courses on the history of gender and sexuality, postwar America, and LGBT American history. He is the author of *Bohemian Los Angeles and the Making of Modern Politics* (University of California Press, 2007) and *Stepping Out: Nine Walks through New York City's Gay and Lesbian Past* (Holt, 1997) and is currently working on a project about homophobic policing.

**Catherine O. Jacquet** is an assistant professor of history at Louisiana State University where she teaches courses in the history of women, gender, and sexuality. She graduated with a PhD in U.S. history from the University of Illinois at Chicago in 2012. While at UIC, she spent one year as project coordinator for Outhistory.org, managing content and working on the site redesign.

**Colin R. Johnson** is an associate professor of gender studies and an adjunct associate professor of American studies, history, and human biology at Indiana University, Bloomington. He is the author of *Just Queer Folks: Gender and Sexuality in Rural America* (Temple University Press, 2013).

**David K. Johnson** is an associate professor of history at the University of South Florida, where he teaches courses on post-1945 U.S. history, the history of gender and sexuality, and gay and lesbian American history. His first book, *The Lavender Scare: The Cold War Persecution of Gays and Lesbians in the Federal Government* (University of Chicago Press, 2004), won the Herbert Hoover Book Award for the best book in U.S. history covering the period 1914 to 1964, the Randy Shilts Award for gay nonfiction, and an Outstanding Book Award from the Gustavus Myers Center for the Study of Bigotry and Human Rights. He coedited *The U.S. since 1945: A Documentary Reader*

(Wiley-Blackwell, 2009), an anthology of primary source documents for students studying modern American politics and culture.

**Norman W. Jones** is an associate professor of English at Ohio State University. He is the author of *Gay and Lesbian Historical Fiction: Sexual Mystery and Post-Secular Narrative* (Palgrave Macmillan, 2007), as well as articles and reviews about queer literature and history published in *American Literature, Modern Fiction Studies,* and *Studies in American Fiction.*

**Ian Lekus** is a lecturer in LGBT studies at the University of Maryland and an LGBT thematic specialist for Amnesty International USA. He has taught U.S. and world history, LGBT, sexuality, and gender studies, U.S. foreign policy, social movements, and American studies at Harvard, Tufts, Duke, and other universities. He has served as chair of the Committee on LGBT History, the main professional association for LGBT historians, and on the board of the Sexuality, Gender, and Human Rights Program at the Harvard Kennedy School. He is currently working on *Queer and Present Dangers: Sexuality, Masculinity, and the Sixties,* forthcoming from the University of North Carolina Press.

**Craig M. Loftin** is the author of *Masked Voices: Gay Men and Lesbians in Cold War America* (State University of New York Press, 2012) and the editor of *Letters to ONE: Gay and Lesbian Voices from the 1950s and 1960s* (State University of New York Press, 2012). He teaches in the American Studies Department at California State University, Fullerton.

**Kevin Mumford** is a professor of history at the University of Illinois at Urbana-Champaign, where he teaches African American history, civil rights, and the history of sexuality. He is the author of *Interzones: Black/White Sex Districts in Chicago and New York in the Early Twentieth Century* (Columbia University Press, 1997) and *Newark: A History of Race, Rights, and Riots in America* (New York University Press, 2007) and is at work on a study of black gay history from the 1960s to the 1990s.

**Felicia T. Perez** graduated with a bachelor's degree from the University of California, Santa Barbara, and holds a master's in curriculum and instruction. She taught middle and high school social studies from 1999 to 2012 at Los Angeles Senior High School and the New Open World (NOW) Academy in the Los Angeles Unified School District. She develops innovative social studies curricula and participatory museum exhibits and publishes the curriculum series History's Mysteries: Solve the Crime of the Time.

**Claire Bond Potter** is a professor of history at the New School for Public Engagement. She is the author of *War on Crime: Bandits, G-Men, and the Politics of Mass Culture* (Rutgers University Press, 1998) and coeditor, with Renee Romano, of *Doing Recent History: On Privacy, Copyright, Video Games, Institutional Review Boards, Activist Scholarship, and History That Talks Back* (University of Georgia Press, 2012).

**Daniel Rivers** is an assistant professor of history at Ohio State University. The author of *Radical Relations: Lesbian Mothers, Gay Fathers, and Their Children in the United States since World War II* (University of North Carolina Press, 2013), he specializes in LGBT postwar history, the history of women and gender, Native American history, and social movement history.

**Leila J. Rupp** is a professor of feminist studies and associate dean of the Division of Social Sciences at the University of California, Santa Barbara. She is the author of several books, including *Sapphistries: A Global History of Love between Women* (New York University Press, 2009); *Drag Queens at the 801 Cabaret* (University of Chicago Press, 2003), with Verta Taylor; and *A Desired Past: A Short History of Same-Sex Love in America* (University of Chicago Press, 1999).

**Marc Stein** is the Jamie and Phyllis Pasker Professor of History at San Francisco State University. He is the author of *City of Sisterly and Brotherly Loves: Lesbian and Gay Philadelphia* (University of Chicago Press, 2000), *Sexual Injustice: Supreme Court Decisions from "Griswold" to "Roe"* (University of North Carolina Press, 2010), and *Rethinking the Gay and Lesbian Movement* (Routledge, 2012).

**Whitney Strub** is an associate professor of history, American studies, and women's and gender studies at Rutgers University, Newark. He is the author of *Perversion for Profit: The Politics of Pornography and the Rise of the New Right* (Columbia University Press, 2011) and *Obscenity Rules: "Roth v. United States" and the Long Struggle over Sexual Expression* (University Press of Kansas, 2013).

**Nicholas L. Syrett** is an associate professor of history at the University of Northern Colorado and the author of *The Company He Keeps: A History of White College Fraternities* (University of North Carolina Press, 2009). His articles on queer history have appeared in *American Studies, Genders, GLQ, Journal of the History of Sexuality*, and *Pacific Historical Review*, and he is a former governing board member of the Committee on LGBT History.

**Red Vaughan Tremmel** is an administrative assistant professor of history and gender and sexuality studies at Tulane University. His research focuses on spaces of play and pleasure as historically significant sites of social struggle. His documentary film *Exotic World and the Burlesque Revival* (2013) follows elderly striptease dancers who turned a goat ranch in the middle of the Mojave Desert into a history museum and retirement home for fellow burlesque dancers. As an installation artist, Tremmel also recently exhibited work on sexuality, knowledge production, and memory for dOCUMENTA(13).

**Sharon Ullman** is a professor of history at Bryn Mawr College. She has published two books on the history of sexuality: *Sex Seen: The Emergence of Modern Sexuality in America* (University of California Press, 1997) and *Sexual Borderlands: Constructing an American Sexual Past* (Ohio State University Press, 2003), co-edited with Kathleen Kennedy.

**Shannon Weber** is a visiting lecturer in the Women's, Gender, and Sexuality Studies and Sociology Departments at Tufts University. She is also a PhD candidate in feminist studies at the University of California, Santa Barbara. In addition to Tufts and UCSB, she has taught courses about gender and sexuality at Northeastern University and Brandeis University. Her research has been published in *Sexualities* and is forthcoming in *Journal of Homosexuality*. She is currently completing her dissertation on the experiences of LGBTQ students at Massachusetts women's colleges.

# Index

The Harvey Goldberg Series
for Understanding and Teaching History